THE
WOODWORKER'S
BIBLE

•••

THE WOODWORKER'S BIBLE

PERCY W. BLANDFORD

GREENWICH HOUSE
Distributed by Crown Publishers, Inc.
New York

Copyright © MCMLXXVI by TAB BOOKS Inc.
All rights reserved.

This 1984 edition is published by Greenwich House, a division
of Arlington House, Inc., distributed by Crown Publishers, Inc.,
by arrangement with Tab Books Inc.

Manufactured in the United States of America

Library of Congress Cataloging in Publication Data

Blandford, Percy W.
    The woodworker's bible.

    Reprint. Originally published: Blue Ridge Summit,
Pa. : Tab Books, c1976.
    Includes index.
    1. Woodwork. I. Title.
TT185.B62 1984   684'.08   84-5988
ISBN: 0-517-448629

h g f e d c b a

Contents

Preface

Man has used wood longer than he has any other natural material. Its many qualities make it suitable for a large range of uses. Different trees yield different woods, each with its own characteristics but all uniquely attractive. In recent years plastics and other synthetic materials have replaced wood and other natural materials to a certain extent; but it is still wood that is used when a quality product is desired.

This makes the man who can work with wood an important craftsman. He may produce things purely utilitarian or those that rank among the highest forms of art. Whatever branch of woodworking his may be, it is part of an honored trade with a history that goes back far beyond Biblical days. The present-day woodworker is carrying on a noble tradition in a craft that is not only important today but will always be needed, even if some of its aspects change and new developments are contributed by other fields.

Fortunately, wood is an adaptable material. It is as amenable to the efforts of the beginner with little skill as it is to those with considerable ability. The novice woodworker, without skill and a minimum of tools, can produce simple yet satisfactory work in a very short time—in doing so, maybe appreciating job satisfaction for the first time in his life. From this he can go on to greater things, for woodworking is not only an absorbing hobby, it can become a part- or full-time profession.

Power tools have their place in taking some of the drudgery out of woodworking, but anyone who wants to become skilled in the craft should master hand methods before trying to use power tools extensively. Only in this way can the worker appreciate the characteristics of wood and learn to make the most of the material. An important part of woodworking craftsmanship is a *feel* for wood, not as easily acquired when an electric motor is substituted for muscle power.

An examination of the contents of this book will show that it is an accumulation of information on all aspects of woodworking. I believe it to be one of the most comprehensive guides to woodworking available in a single volume. Most woodworkers who start by doing a few simple things, like making shelves or boxes, eventually want to move on to more ambitious projects. Woodwork construction has evolved over centuries, producing joints, methods, techniques, and processes that have stood the test of time, even though some have been adapted to suit present-day needs and improved facilities; this book details all of these.

If you want to go on to make furniture, alter your home, or make things for your garden, you will be guided through enough steps to put you well on your way. If you are attracted by the more specialized activities of turning, carving, marquetry, or picture framing, there is enough information here for you to acquire all the basic techniques, bringing you to the point where only your skill will limit what you can do.

Woodworking has in it enough variety to satisfy the widest range of tastes and inclinations. I hope this book will be your guide for whatever direction you want to take.

Percy W. Blandford

THE WOODWORKER'S BIBLE

1
Wood

Investigators looking for a synthetic material to use in aircraft construction during World War II found, after a considerable amount of research, that anything they produced with the desired qualities would be remarkably like wood. Wood has been the main constructional material throughout history. Despite the many developments in materials, particularly in plastics, it is still likely to continue to be the favorite, both for things that are strictly utilitarian and for those in which the beauty of the material is important. No other material has the same appeal for such a wide variety of constructional needs.

It takes a tree a long time to grow to the point where it can be felled and converted to useful wood. A man who plants trees is unlikely to see any return in his lifetime on his investment, other than the pleasure of watching them grow. Many species must produce several generations before they can be converted into commercially valuable material. Despite this, trees continue to be felled at a fast rate, both for lumber and for such things as pulp to make paper. Although trees are felled at a much higher rate than they are being replaced, there still seems to be plenty of wood.

Nearly all wood of interest to the woodworker is *exogenous* or outward-growing. These trees increase in girth each year by growing rings of new timber around the outside of the old. A small number of trees, like bamboo and palm, do not grow outward; but they are of little use to woodworkers.

Exogenous trees are generally divided into *broad-leaf* and *needle-leaf* types. Most broad-leaf trees lose their leaves during the winter, while most needle-leaf trees retain theirs.

As far as their users are concerned, the broad-leaf (anglospermic) trees produce "hardwoods"; the needle-leaf (gymnospermic) trees produce "softwoods." Unfortunately, *hard* and *soft* are not strictly correct descriptions for the physical properties of woods, although they are correct for the vast majority. (A few "hardwoods" are softer than some "softwoods.") In general, pines, firs, spruces, and others of that type are what the average worker handles as softwoods, while all the better woods used for furniture and quality work are hardwoods. Altogether there are over 3000 tree species with commercial value.

The classifications *hardwood* and *softwood* refer to differences in structure that can only be seen with the aid of a microscope. Wood is made up of long cells that give it its fibrous nature. In softwoods there are large numbers of long spindle-shaped cells called tracheids. In hardwoods they are wider and arranged end to end, forming slender tubes.

Colder climates encourage the growth of *coniferous* or cone-bearing needle-leaf trees; the forests containing both large trees and large numbers of trees producing softwoods are mostly in the northern temperate zones.

The warmer conditions of countries nearer the equator encourage the growth of deciduous (leaf-shedding) trees, which produce hardwoods. Hot, wet, tropical forests produce the largest trees and the finest specimens of hardwoods.

When trees grow together in forests they compete with each other to reach sunlight; forest-grown trees are taller and straighter than trees grown in more open places. They also have fewer branches of any great size. This may be an advantage where straight grain is important, but for some things the wood of a tree that has not grown straight may give a more attractive finished product.

Fibers within a tree run in the direction of its axis. A crosswise cut will show their approximately circular pattern; a lengthwise cut, the lines of fibers. There is much more strength with the grain than *across* it, because cross-grain cuts sever the fibers.

The original center of the sapling from which a tree grows is called the *pith* (Fig. 1-1). It has no strength and, in many trees, is so compressed as to be invisible. In others it may be removed as a thin, loose cylinder.

Surrounding the pith are the *annual* or growth rings. The effect of growth, the passage of sap up and down the tree, adds one ring each year. Consequently, the age of a tree can be

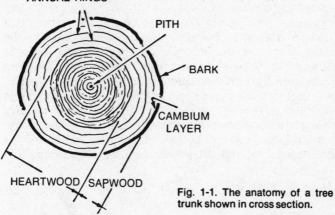

ANNUAL RINGS

PITH

BARK

CAMBIUM
LAYER

HEARTWOOD / SAPWOOD

Fig. 1-1. The anatomy of a tree
trunk shown in cross section.

found by counting the annual rings in its cross section. How prominent the annual rings are depends on several factors, mainly the species of tree. Most coniferous trees have prominent rings, but in some of the hardwoods, such as mahogany, the rings are very difficult to distinguish. Other hardwoods, such as oak, may not have very prominent rings, but they can be counted. Seldom are the rings anywhere near true circles; nor are they defined along the grain as straight cylinders. But it is these meanderings and indefinite shapes of grain markings that give beauty to cut wood.

Newly produced rings are soft and wet with sap; but as the tree grows, the inner rings are compressed, becoming more solid and often darker. This is the heartwood, the part of the tree that yields the most valuable lumber. In some softwoods, such as spruce, there is no visible distinction between heartwood and sapwood, while in many hardwoods there is a marked difference in color.

The newer rings make up the sapwood, the young living wood; although it is very important to the growth of the tree, it is of little use as lumber. After the heartwood has served its purpose in helping growth, it continues to provide support for the tree as it gets taller and larger.

Outside the sapwood is a very thin *cambium* layer, the source of growth. The life-giving sap causes it to form new rings on the inside and new bark on the outside.

The bark or *outer cortex* surrounds and protects the cambium layer; it is the barrier between the wood and the weather. The bark of most trees has no value after the tree is felled, although some bark has been used for tanning leather and smoking bacon.

Besides the rings in the trunk of the tree, there are *medullary rays* that radiate from the center toward the outside. They bind the annual rings together and serve to distribute sap. Although present in all trees, in many they can only be seen through a magnifying glass or microscope. In other trees they are more obvious. Oak is a good example in which to observe them; a radial cut through the medullary rays would show them as the markings peculiar to that wood. When cut this way (Fig. 1-2), it may be described as quarter-sawed, figured oak, wainscot oak, or *silver grain*.

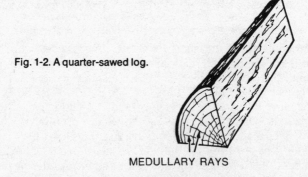

Fig. 1-2. A quarter-sawed log.

MEDULLARY RAYS

The outer part of a board, called a *waney edge*, is cut off together with much of the sapwood when a log is converted to useful lumber. The sapwood of softwoods is more useful than that of hardwoods. Useful wood comes mostly from the trunk of a tree, but some branches are used; the joint between the branch and trunk may be cut to take advantage of the curved grain. These *natural crooks* were highly prized for ship- and boat-building before the days of laminated "knees" and other manufactured brackets.

There are some defects in trees that may not be apparent until they are felled. These include *shakes* or splits in the length of the trunk (Fig. 1-3). Those that follow the annual rings are *cup* or *ring* shakes, depending on whether they go part of the way or all the way around. A single crack in a radial direction is a *heart* shake; if more than one is involved, it is a *star* shake. They affect the usefulness of at least part of the trunk.

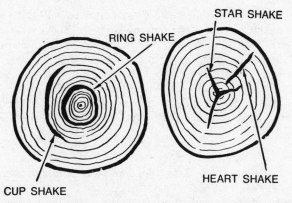

Fig. 1-3. A shake is a defect in a tree that may not be seen until it is felled.

Knots are the places where branches join the main trunk. The upset in grain they cause may be objectionable in that they weaken wood and spoil its appearance. In other trees and other circumstances, however, the difference in grain caused by a knot may be used for improved appearance. When cut across, a knot is round; but when a radial cut is made in the trunk, the knot is seen as a pointed deflection of grain. In a softwood board a loose, dead knot may actually fall out and leave a hole. The knot from a branch that was alive when the tree was felled is intimately fused with the rest of the wood.

Like any other living thing, a tree grows to its prime, declines past maturity, and deteriorates. Even though a tree will continue to grow after part or all of it has begun to rot, it will be useless as lumber. This state is sometimes described as *doaty*, *foxy*, or *druxy*. Another defect, more likely in an overmature tree, is *thunder shake*, a cracking or severing of the grain, not as a wide opening (as in lengthwise shakes), but as a ragged, hairline crack across the grain. This weakens the wood, usually sufficiently to make it useless at that point.

Some features of grain are actually defects, but they can be used to gain an attractive appearance. A tree that has grown in an exposed place may be so twisted and bent that any straight cut will show a very tortuous grain; but it can be used to give beauty to a piece of furniture, or if the part is designed to allow the grain to follow the outline, to make it stronger. Wood selected for this quality was used for the shafts of horse-drawn vehicles.

Some trees, such as walnut, oak, and elm, often display abnormal outgrowths in the form of lumps. These *burls* are cut

15

into slices to make fancy veneers that have a confused pattern. A ripple effect occurs when many adjacent fibers end together in tiers, instead of overlapping normally. This is sometimes called "fiddle-back," from its use on violins. Another form, sometimes seen in maple, gives a "bird's-eye" effect: large numbers of tiny knots all over the finished surface. These special decorative grains are usually only obtainable as veneers. They would be too expensive and too wasteful used as solid wood.

CONVERSION

There are many ways a log can be cut into boards. There are several considerations besides getting the maximum number of pieces out of a log. How a board is cut affects its grain marking, which may be important for appearance; it also affects how the board may shrink or warp. The wood near the center of a tree contains less sap than that nearer the outside. As the sap dries, the outer wood will shrink more than that near the center. This means that a dry board cut across the center will be thinner at its sides than at its center (Fig. 1-4). This effect will only be slight, and could be easily corrected by planing or other methods.

Fig. 1-4. Because there is more sap near the center of a log than near the bark, cut boards will tend to warp as shown in this cross section.

A board cut near the outside of a log will tend to warp hollow—convex on one side, concave on the other—as its extremities shrink. (The outer surface shrinks more than the inner one.) A trunk cut for many boards is described as cut "through and through." An examination of the end of a board will show if it has been cut this way and how far from the center of the tree it was. Only the center board will be free from warpage as it dries.

To get the greatest number of boards with an attractive grain from a log known to have this characteristic, the bulk of the wood is cut square (Fig. 1-5). Boards then are cut from each side in turn, working toward the center. Of course, such boards may warp or twist, but this risk has to be accepted for the sake of preserving the grain marking.

Fig. 1-5. The pattern of cuts made to derive the most boards with a desirable grain, from a log that still has more sap in the center than near the outside.

The only way to cut boards that will show the figuration of oak (and certain ohter woods) is to quarter-saw them radially, parallel with the medullary rays. In through-and-through conversion only the center board will show any characteristic grain pattern; but sometimes it may also be visible on those on either side of it. To get the medullary rays to show the best pattern, each board has to be cut radially (Fig. 1-6A); because this is wasteful, such boards are expensive. A less wasteful method is to cut the boards into pieces that become progressively narrower as they get further from the center (Fig. 1-6B); this method produces a fair proportion of wider boards with a good chance of having choice grain. Of course, not all wood cut from a log known to offer good grain need be cut for that quality. Legs and rails for furniture, for example, need not have exemplary grain markings. Consequently, it may be possible to cut some boards radially to get the desired figuration, and cut the remainder more economically for less decorative parts.

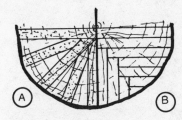

Fig. 1-6. Each board has to be cut radially to take best advantage of the appearance of the medullary rays (A); the method shown at B is less wasteful and nearly as successful.

SEASONING

Freshly felled lumber contains a large amount of water, which holds substances of value to the tree. The amount of water can be large, often half the dry weight of most lumber and up to 200% in swamp cypress, an exceptional case. Before the wood can be made workable (brought to a stable condition), the water content has to be reduced to an acceptable amount. It would be unsatisfactory to remove all the water, but for normal use the content has to be reduced considerably. Fortunately, the figure is not critical; a water content between about 6% and 18% is usual.

Seasoning, the reduction of the water content, is done for a number of reasons. Unseasoned wood is difficult to work: ordinary saws will bind and not cut; planes and other surfacing tools will not work, making a good surface unobtainable. Unseasoned wood is unstable, it will warp, shrink, and twist. And not only will it be heavier and weaker than seasoned wood, it will be more apt to decay.

Wood, being a natural material, may still suffer from some of these defects (to a lesser extent) after seasoning, but proper seasoning will bring it to the stage where the qualities wanted will be as close to the exceptable standard as possible.

Traditionally, wood was subjected to natural seasoning, leaving it to dry slowly under normal atmospheric conditions. The log was cut into broad boards and stacked with spacers so air could circulate (Fig. 1-7). A requirement of seasoning is that the outside should not dry much quicker than the inside, otherwise cracking and distortion may occur. A damp atmosphere is an advantage in the early stages, as it prevents too rapid drying of the outer wood. Sometimes wood was placed in an open-sided shed to protect it from extreme weather. Natural seasoning is still practiced and, where time allows, it is a very good method; but because wood is usually wanted much quicker than this method permits, methods of speeding the process are used today.

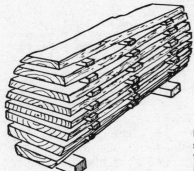

Fig. 1-7. Freshly cut logs are stacked with spacers to allow for the natural seasoning of circulating air.

One way of speeding seasoning is to soak the wood for a few weeks in fresh, running water. This is particularly suitable for softwoods, as the water washing through the grain removes the sap and the many things suspended and dissolved in it. Floating logs downriver to a sawmill actually aids the eventual seasoning of the wood. (Leaving the wood in water also protects it from fungi and insects.) After soaking, the wood is stacked in an area with good air circulation to dry out the unwanted fresh water—in a much shorter time than the sap would dry out naturally. This, like methods of artificial seasoning, may remove some of the strength and elasticity of the wood, but this has to be accepted for expediency.

Many methods of artificial seasoning have been used, providing a controlled method of drying wood in a short time. The most commonly used is kiln-drying. A modern kiln allows very careful control of temperature, humidity, and air circulation. But care has to be taken to prevent the wood from twisting and warping. Excessively fast drying may get the outside too dry, while trapping moisture in the center. The wood is stacked with spacers, and battens are nailed across the ends to reduce the risk of *shakes* or *splits*.

Lumber bought from a commercial yard will almost certainly be kiln-dried. Although it should have a reasonably reduced water content, it is good policy to buy wood well in advance, so it can be kept to season further. Professional woodworkers who specialize in fine furniture buy stocks of wood a year or more ahead of their needs. It is laid flat with spacers, so no matter what seasoning the wood has had, it will continue to season naturally. An amateur woodworker may not have the space nor the time to do this, but he would be unwise to buy wood and use it immediately, particularly for any item to be made from one of the better, more expensive hardwoods.

Another risk is the wood altering its shape slightly after being planed. This can be taken care of by only partially shaping a piece, then leaving it for a few days before going on with the woodwork. If it warps, there will still be enough wood left to allow corrections as the job is finished to size. This is often done by turning the parts on a lathe.

Even when wood has been properly seasoned, it is still liable to expand and contract as it takes in or gives up moisture. This is taken care of by using one of many expedients in construction methods. But because the main cause is a change in humidity, trouble can be reduced by making the part in an atmosphere similar to that in which it is likely to be kept and used. If something is made in a cold, damp workshop and used constantly in a dry, centrally heated room, it is liable to shrink as its moisture dries out to a lower level. At one time this was a common problem with broad panels, but today these parts are more likely to be plywood, which is stable.

Shrinkage in the direction of the grain is negligible. If problems develop due to changes in atmospheric conditions, movement will be greatest in the direction of the annual rings. If the end of a piece of wood is examined, shrinkage or swelling will be seen around the rings (Fig.1-8A); if they curve on the end of a narrow piece, they will try to straighten during shrinkage (Fig. 1-8B). Construction can often be planned to minimize these effects. For instance, any movement of the boards making up a table top will be less apparent if the side likely to become rounded faces upward. With proper seasoning and care in construction, these risks will be very slight; but it is well to be aware of what could happen.

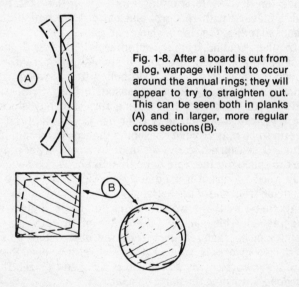

Fig. 1-8. After a board is cut from a log, warpage will tend to occur around the annual rings; they will appear to try to straighten out. This can be seen both in planks (A) and in larger, more regular cross sections (B).

Of course, the best known use of wood, and certainly the one of interest to you, is as a material for making furniture, buildings, and other structures. But wood also yields a vast array of other products. The skeletal, or cell wall, substances of all wood is 50% to 60% cellulose; the balance is mainly lignin and hemicellulose in proportions varying according to the species. Some minor organic components in the cell cavities and cell walls can be extracted. The amounts vary among different species, but in some they are present in sufficiently large quantities to be of commercial worth; some are tannins, dyestuffs, gums, resins, and oils.

Wood is used extensively as a fuel. The ashes left contain minerals valuable for soil fertilization. The mechanical pulping of wood produces newsprint, but pulp is also used for making insulation boards and fiberboard. The cellulose content goes into such diversified things as explosives, plastics, and adhesives. Sugars and yeast can be obtained from wood.

Wood is of great value to man in more ways than are immediately obvious. Fortunately, it is self-regenerating in its natural state—seeds are scattered, new trees start growing—but man has to play his part by systematically planting trees of all kinds, so succeeding generations can benefit from wood, a resource not likely to be completely replaced by synthetic materials.

WOOD'S ATTACKERS

Besides shakes and other defects that may affect the successful conversion of wood to useful lumber, wood may be attacked by fungi or wood-boring insects—affecting unfelled trees, wood being seasoned, or wood after it has been used to build a structure.

Fungal growth in the form of decay and rot can cause irreversible damage. Fungi, being parasitic, live on other materials. They feed on the organic matter in the tree. Fungus spores may settle on wood at any time. Moist conditions must prevail for it to attack wood; if the moisture content of the wood is less than 20%, it will not be attacked. Fairly temperate conditions are favorable—not below freezing and not very hot. Nondurable woods are most likely to be attacked. This means some woods could be attacked in their entirety, while only the sapwood of others may be affected.

When a fungus spore germinates it sends out roots or hypae (Fig. 1-9), that spread throughout the natural cavities in wood. The roots extract food from the wood for its flower. This depletes the cellulose, causing a complete breakdown of the

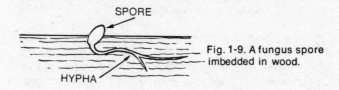

Fig. 1-9. A fungus spore imbedded in wood.

character of the wood. In an advanced attack the breakdown is so complete that the wood becomes powder. As it feeds, the fungus produces many more spores that may attack adjoining wood and be carried by the wind, animals, tools, or man, causing further destruction elsewhere.

There are two main types of rot, commonly called *dry* and *wet*. The first is not aptly named because it only occurs in the presence of dampness. However, it is the more common type and the one needing the most drastic treatment. Wood attacked by dry rot will be found in areas where the air is stagnant. The affected wood will change color. There may be a certain amount of staining, varying according to the species of wood involved; it may be yellow, red, blue, or black. In general, the change in color is likely to be a lightening of the overall tint. Rotten wood will soften, lose weight, and will probably have a musty smell. In an advanced stage of growth, the rot will be obvious—but its recognition in the early stages is important. The fungus looks like a soft, white spongy cushion.

Because there is no cure for dry rot, all of the affected wood must be removed and burned. To be certain that the fungus and its spores have been eradicated, it is necessary to cut into apparently healthy wood at least 18 inches along the grain and 4 inches across the grain, outside the obviously affected area (Fig. 1-10). Since spores may be present in the vicinity, it is important to remove the conditions conducive to their germination by removing the cause—damp

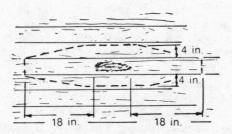

Fig. 1-10. The size of the piece of wood that must be cut out to insure the complete eradication of a fungus-affected area.

conditions—and by providing good ventilation. Replacement wood should be a durable type, and healthy wood in the vicinity should be treated with a preservative. This is particularly important if *any* of the wood is not durable. Stone, bricks, and metalwork should also be brushed with a preservative or something that will sterilize the areas concerned. Alternately, go over them with a blowtorch to kill any spores remaining. A suitable sterilizing solution is a 4% solution of sodium fluoride in water. Clean tools, clothing, and footwear before leaving the site.

An example showing conditions which will and, at the same time, will not encourage rot, is a fence post. The part exposed to the air is generally too dry to be attacked; the part underground will usually be exposed to too little air for decay's action. The part just above and below ground level (Fig. 1-11) may be wet and have ample oxygen, making it susceptible to attack.

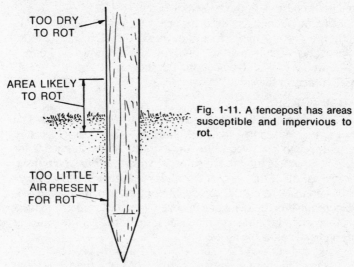

TOO DRY TO ROT

AREA LIKELY TO ROT

TOO LITTLE AIR PRESENT FOR ROT

Fig. 1-11. A fencepost has areas susceptible and impervious to rot.

Preventing dry rot is much easier than attempting to eradicate it after it has taken hold. The precautions are:

- Use wood with a moisture content below 20%; fungus cannot live in wood dryer than that.
- Make sure that moisture cannot build up in the wood after it is used, by providing adequate ventilation.
- While the wood is dry, treat it with a preservative or provide a barrier against moisture on the surface with paint, varnish, or some other surface treatment.
- Remember that certain woods are immune to fungus because of their chemical constituents; use one of these types where fungus threatens to be problematic.

Wet rot is not easy to identify by casual examination. A specimen would have to be identified by an expert; but as a precaution, it should be treated as if it had dry rot.

There are less serious types of fungi, but they are more likely to be encountered during seasoning than after the wood is bought by the user. A moss-like mold may appear on the surface of wood while it is being seasoned. It does not affect the wood, but it should be removed so moisture can dry out. Other fungi, as they feed on starches and sugar in wood, cause stains without destroying the wood, but do not affect the cellulose. Both of these attacks are avoidable by quick conversion after felling and by providing good air circulation between seasoning boards. The sapwood should be removed and the wood kept dry after seasoning.

Chemical stains sometimes occur that have nothing to do with rot and do not affect the wood, but they do mar its appearance. The iron or steel in nails, for example, will cause some woods to blacken. Soot and dirt may penetrate the grain, particularly at the ends of a board.

WOOD BORERS

Insects can cause as much damage to wood as fungi. The damage is caused by the insects' larvae (worm stage) as they bore through the wood. In an extreme case the maze of complex tunnels may leave so little wood that the whole thing collapses. Al' of this may occur under the surface and become only apparent when the top surface of the wood is removed. Except for this the evidence is boreholes scattered around the surface and, during certain seasons, the dust from the boring around and below the holes.

The insects that feast on wood are mainly beetles. There are many, but their life cycles (Fig. 1-12) are the same. The beetle lays its eggs in the cracks and crevices of wood; the larvae appear and feed on the wood as they bore into it. How long they do this depends on the species, but it may be for a year or longer. Eventually the larvae become pupae that live near the surface. The pupae, through metamorphosis, become beetles and emerge from the wood to mate and start the cycle again.

Wood borers are not necessarily native to the country they operate in, as they may be in imported wood; because a large variety may have to be dealt with, the activities of some should be understood

A common type is the powder post beetle (*Lyctus brunneus*), which is about ⅛ inch long and can fly. It attacks

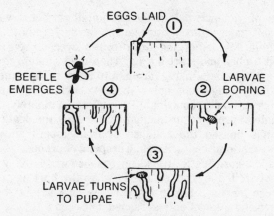

Fig. 1-12. The life cycle of the beetle, wood's insect enemy.

the sapwood of hardwoods, rather than their heartwoods or softwoods. The bore dust is flour-fine when rubbed between the fingers. The female lays upward of 30 eggs in the sapwood of open-grained wood. The larva, about ⅛ inch long, is yellowish-white and has brown jaws. Not much dust is expelled because it gets packed tightly behind the larva as it bores.

The exit hole is only about $1/16$ inches wide. If these holes are seen in stacked boards, the affected sapwood and any wood nearby should be cut off and burned. There are worm-killing solutions that can be injected into the holes in furniture, but thorough saturation is necessary for them to be effective. The best "treatment" is to avoid using sapwood in making furniture.

The furniture beetle (*Anobium punctatum*) will attack the sapwood in hardwoods and softwoods first. It also attacks plywood. The bore dust is left in cigar-shaped pellets and feels grittier than that of the powder post beetle. Attack by this beetle can be severe, its large numbers of burrows eventually causing complete collapse of the wood structure. For slight damage the wood can be treated in the same way as for the powder post beetle. Severe damage has to be treated by expert fumigation. (The gas used is toxic.) Both kinds of beetles have been treated by X-ray to make the emerging larvae sterile (unable to produce young), thus ending their life cycle.

The deathwatch beetle (*Xestobium rufovillosum*), picturesquely named, is about a ¼ inch long and chocolate-brown with yellow hairs on its wing covers. Associated with dampness and decay, it attacks old structural timbers, particularly oak in ancient buildings; but it will also attack softwoods. The eggs are laid on the surface of the wood and the larvae, emerging after a few weeks, search for decayed timber and start boring. Then they make a maze of borrows, maybe continuing for up to 10 years before emerging as beetles through exit holes about ⅛ inches in diameter. Control is difficult, requiring a specialist; fortunately, this is not usually a problem for the homeowner, but the deathwatch beetle has caused the collapse of many roofs and other structures in some centuries-old European churches.

The longhorn beetle attacks unseasoned wood, dying trees, and newly felled logs, particularly when the bark is present. The house longhorn beetle (*Hylotrupes bajulus*) is about ¾ inch long and attacks only seasoned softwoods. Its exit holes are oval and the dust, in the form of fine chips, is very coarse.

Other insects that devour wood are forest pests. Any wood they have attacked should be discarded during conversion, but an occasional hole in a board will not affect the wood because the worm will be inactive. However, suspect wood should be discarded; it is not always easy to identify the form of attack, and it could be still in progress.

The wood wasp may be up to 2 inches long and usually only attacks living trees. The bark sap beetle (*Ernobius mollis*) only attacks softwoods when the bark is present, so waney edges (ones with bark) should be cleaned before seasoning. Pinhole borers (*Scolytidaea* and *Platypodidae*) may leave evidence of their activity in freshly sawed wood. They differ from the majority of other borers in that they make their burrows perpendicular to the grain. They are black and leave no bore dust, and their activity does not involve seasoned wood.

To eradicate these borers the wood needs a thorough application of an insecticide. Although kerosene, benzene, and turpentine have some effect, prepared insecticides, some of which are provided with a syringe, are preferable. This is the only method recommended for amateur woodworkers; among professional methods are fumigation and kiln sterilization of new wood. The bark should certainly be removed from affected wood as soon as possible.

PRESERVATIVES

The prevention of decay and insect attack is always more successful than attempts at their eradication and cure. This can be done by choosing appropriate woods with the correct moisture content and treating them with a preservative. The best methods of preservation are only suitable for industrial application, but it may be possible to buy wood so treated.

Tar-oil products that thoroughly impregnate the wood give good protection; but they darken wood and retain their characteristic smell for some time, and so are best suited to outdoor use. There are organic-solvent types, such as napthalenes, copper and zinc napthenates, and pentachlorophenol. There is a large range of water-soluble preservatives, such as copper or chrome arsenate, fluoride dinitrophenol, and sodium fluoride.

The best method of application is to force the preservative into the wood. The wood may be soaked in a hot or cold preservative, then stacked closely so the preservative diffuses through the stack. It is sometimes possible for the amateur woodworker to soak wood in a preservative. A fence post can be placed in something long enough for it and soaked. Usually, the nonprofessional has to apply preservatives by brushing or spraying. Because preservatives interfere with the grip of glues, it is usually better to delay the preserving treatment until the construction is finished.

Preservatives often interfere with surface finishes, but some of the organic-solvent types can be painted over. Water-soluble preservatives should be allowed to dry and the excess salts brushed from the surface; then stain, paint, or varnish may be applied. Many preservatives are inflammable while wet, requiring that suitable precautions be taken. Some give off vapors that may be unpleasant, if not dangerous; they should be used outdoors or at least in a well-ventilated place.

MARINE BORERS

Wood for the underwater parts of a boat needs special consideration. The internal parts of any enclosed craft can produce conditions that will lead to rot and decay if proper care is not given to ventilation. Fresh water is really the enemy in this case. Rainwater running into the bilges can create the sort of atmosphere in which fungus spores thrive. (Salt water is actually a preservative.)

Exposed surfaces under water and at the waterline are vunerable to attack. The type of sea animals that will attack wood vary according to geographical location. In most temperate areas the risk of serious attack is slight, while in some tropical waters an unprotected wooden hull might be reduced to a wreck in a matter of weeks.

A crustacean commonly called the *gribble* will attack a wooden ship's bottom. But the real danger comes from the teredo worm. Technically it is not a worm—its long white body explains the choice of name. A mature teredo releases vast numbers of microscopic larvae that settle on wood and penetrate through almost invisible holes. The larva grows inside the wood, and so does the hole it bores by grinding together two shells in its head.

The gribble (*limnoria*) is something like a wood louse in appearance and is about ⅛ inch long. It does not penetrate wood for more than a half-inch, but a multiple attack can so weaken the surface that it erodes away. Wood on the bottom of a ship afloat continuously and wooden piles may suffer from a surface wet rot that is not serious in itself, but does encourage the attack of gribbles.

Some durable hardwoods that have a resistance to attack may be expected to give long service in fresh water. Elsewhere these and other woods need protection.

Preservatives used on wood that will be under water will give a certain amount of protection. Among these are the antifouling paints for yacht bottoms. The most effective of these, which are quite thick when applied, are used immediately before the boat is launched; they give off chemicals that discourage marine borers and weeds that could foul the bottom. The period during which the chemicals are effective can be months, but the craft has to be brought ashore periodically for further treatment. Other antifouling paints are allowed to dry before launch. They give a smooth bottom that may be desirable for a racing yacht, but the protection is much less.

Usually, wooden hulls to be used in waters known to harbor teredos and other borers are sheathed in copper from the keel to above the waterline. This gives good protection, providing there are no breaks in the sheathing. Plastic sheathing is also used. Layers of fiberglass and resin can protect wood from borers; but because they have to be bonded to a dry hull, the method is only suitable during construction. Plastic sheathing prevents oxygen from getting to the hull, thereby suffocating any animals already in the wood. However, pockets of moisture could be trapped behind the sheathing, possibly encouraging fungal decay.

SOFTWOODS

Most softwoods for woodwork grow in the forests of the northern temperate zones of North America, Europe, and

Asia. Vast quantities are grown and felled in those regions. Some trees of this type are found elsewhere, but not in any great quantity. Unfortunately, supplies of the same wood from different sources may not be recognized by the same name. This makes the range of softwoods available seem larger than it really is. The Latin name, when available, is a more positive identification. Some softwoods are listed below, with a range of alternate names. (The first name given is not necessarily preferred.)

Cedar, Western red (*Thuya plicata*). A soft, reddish-brown straight-grained durable wood, mostly of Canadian origin, and available in long lengths.

Cypress (*Taxodium distichum*). A swamp-grown tree that yields a straight-grained light-brown wood that has a greasy feel and a sour smell. It does not take glue well, but it is very durable in situations where it has to withstand heat and moisture.

Fir, Douglas; also Columbian pine, Douglas pine, Oregon pine (*Pseudotsuga taxiflora*). A medium-hard straight-grained reddish-brown moderately durable wood that is fairly easy to work, but its raised grain and resin may be troublesome. (Used for plywood.)

Hemlock. Not a wood for a fine finish, but it has uses in boatbuilding and exterior carpentery.

Larch (*Larix decidua*). A mainly European durable medium-textured, easily worked wood, light orange-brown in color. Some is grown in the Eastern United States.

Pine, parana (*Araucaria augustifolia*). A Brazilian wood that is mostly a pale straw color; there may be darker streaks. It has a smooth texture and is available in wide boards, so it is suitable for interior work; but it lacks the durability required for outside work.

Pine, pitch (*Pinus*). A very resinous wood with a pronounced straight, medium-textured grain. Because of its resin, it is one of the heaviest softwoods; it is very durable, but difficult to bring to a good finish.

Pine, yellow; also Quebec pine, Ottawa pine, Weymouth pine, white pine (*Pinus strobus*). A wood that is soft and even in texture (straw to deeper color). Shrinkage and warpage in this wood is minimal, making it favorable for making patterns for metal castings. Southern yellow pine grown south of New Jersey has a very tough heartwood.

Pines (other types). Eastern white pine, found mostly in the Northeastern states, is light and has little strength; Ponderosa pine has similar properties. The sugar pine grows in the central states and is the largest pine; like the others, its durability is poor. A similar pine found in Idaho, Washington, and Montana, is the western white pine.

Redwood; also yellow or red deal, red pine, red fir, Scots pine, northern pine (*Pinus sylvestris*). Moderately durable reddish-brown straight-grained and sometimes resinous wood, which works and finishes well.

Sequoia; also California redwood (*Sequoia Sempbervirens.*) A wood obtainable in long pieces and considerable widths because of the size of the tree. It is reddish-brown and straight-grained, with a rather open and porous texture; its strength is not very great.

Spruce, Sitka; also silver spruce (*Picea sitchensis*). A nondurable wood that combines light weight with relatively high strength, as required in aircraft construction and the making of yacht spars. It is moderately soft, light in color, and has straight grain.

Spruce; also whitewood, white deal (*Picea Excelsa*). Sometimes regarded as an inferior form of redwood, this wood is almost white, and may have large knots as well as occasional resin pockets. Eastern spruce, a general-purpose wood for rough carpentery, grows in the Great Lake States and New England.

HARDWOODS

Of the considerable variety of hardwoods, some are imported because of their special qualities; but many are native to America. Their distribution varies according to topography and climate, but most of those that yield wood of commercial value are listed according to region.

Northern region. Ash, aspen, basswood (*Tilia Americana*), yellow birch (Betula lutea), butternut, cherry, elm, hickory, locust, hard maple (*Acer saccharum*), oak, walnut.

Central region. White ash (*Fraxinus Americana*), basswood, beech, buckeye, chestnut, cottonwood, American elm (*Ulmus Americana*), hackberry, shagbark hickory (*Quercus Alba*), sycamore, yellow poplar (*Liriodendron tulipifera*), American walnut (*Juglans nigra*).

Appalachian region. Ash, beech, red oak (*Quercus rubra*), hard maple, white oak.

Southern region. Ash, basswood, beech, birch, cottonwood (*Populos dildoides*), elm, hackberry, hickory, locust, maple, red oak and cherry-bark oak, pecan, sweet and red gum (*Liquidambar styraciflua*), sycamore, tupelo gum (*Nyassa aquatica*), black willow (*Salix nigra*).

Several extremely hard woods, including lignum vitae and greenheart, will sink in water. Believed the hardest of the hardwoods, black ironwood (*Krugiodendron ferrum*) grows in Southern Florida and Central America. The softest and lightest of the (technically) hardwoods is balsa (*Ochroma*), which comes from Central America. It is actually softer and lighter than most softwoods.

Details on some hardwoods are given below, but the list possible is almost limitless. The examples given will provide comparisons when other woods are selected for particular qualities.

Ash (*Fraximus exelsior*). Straight, rather coarse-grained, and not durable, but valued for its springiness and bending ability. Ash is used in hammer handles and cart shafts because it is flexible and resists shock.

Basswood; lime (*Tilia Americana*). Near-white and close-grained, this lightweight wood is easy to work and is particularly suitable for carving.

Beech. A red or white wood with a tough, close grain, it turns well and was the traditional wood for planes, tool handles, and bench tops. Beech and birch are both used for making doweling.

Chestnut (*Castanea sativa*). This wood looks and works like oak, but has no figuring when quarter-sawed. It cleaves well for fencing and similar applications.

Elm (*Ulmus*). A durable wood resistant to splitting. Its confused grain may make working difficult, but it was the wood used for wheel hubs and coffins. Rock elm (*Ulmus thomasi*) and Wych elm (*Ulmus glabra*) are straighter-grained, hard, strong, and elastic, which made them valued in boatbuilding.

Gaboon; Okoume (*Aucoumea klaineana*). A nondurable African wood, often classed as a mahogany, it is used for plywood where lightness is required along with a mahogany color.

Gum, red; also sweet gum, satin walnut (*Liquidambar styraciflua*). Even brown in color with little sign of grain, this wood tends to warp and twist, but is easy to work; because it takes stain and polish well, it may be made to match other woods.

Maple. This wood varies in color from light yellow to yellow-brown. The bird's-eye effect in some of the grain is used for decorative purposes.

Mahogany, African. Many African woods are sold as mahogany, some useful alternatives to the original mahoganies.

Mahogany, Honduras; also baywood (*Swietenia macrophyela*). This wood is light, both in weight and color (brown), and is usually easy to work; it is suitable for cabinetwork.

Mahogany, Spanish; **Cuban mahogany** (*Swietenia Mahogani*). A rich brown with close, straight grain, this is really the original mahogany. There are now many more, some of which are not true mahoganies.

Oak english (*Quercus*). This oak, used for medieval ships and furniture, is light to dark brown, open-grained, and has prominent figuring in quarter-sawed boards; it is very strong and durable.

Oak japanese; Austrian oak. These are easier to work and are favored for interior work, when available.

Oak red, (*Quercus rubra*). An open-grained wood of the usual brown oak color but with a pink tint. Figuring shows in quarter-sawed boards. It is obtainable as large boards without flaws, but it tends to be coarse and heavy to work.

Poplar yellow; also canary wood, American whitewood (*Liriodendron tulipfera*). Even, close-grained yellow wood, and obtainable in many sizes. Its quality varies from very workable to coarse and stringy (sometimes confused with basswood).

Sapele (*Entandrophragma cylindricum*. This mahogany-like wood, often with an attractive grain, may be difficult to work. It is used for making plywood.

Sycamore (*Acer pseudoplatanus*). A whitish-yellow close-grained wood with figuring or ripples often apparent in the grain. Its quality varies, but good specimens are used for turnery; its white color makes it suitable for use with food or dairy work.

Teak. This wood comes mostly from India and Burma; it is dark brown but bleaches to near-white in the sun. Its peculiar property is that it secretes a resin which hardens, making it difficult to work, but prized for use on boats where it has a good resistance to marine conditions with little or no surface treatment.

Walnut; also American black walnut (*Juglans nigra*). There is a shade of purple mixed with the brown color of this durable wood; it will take a good finish.

BUYING WOOD

Wood is converted into suitable sections for use in certain stock sizes; it is worthwhile checking into what is available and arranging your work accordingly for economy. Stock sizes come as sawed. If the wood ordered is machine-planed, it is likely to finish about ⅛ inch undersize. A 1 inch planed board will actually be about ⅞ inch thick. Work should be arranged to allow for this. If a finished thickness of 1 inch is absolutely necessary, the board may have to be planed down from a piece 1¼ inches thick, which will be correspondingly more expensive.

The size of stock wood is obviously governed by the size of the tree it came from. Some wood may be obtainable in very long and wide pieces. Other woods can only be bought in much smaller sizes; the only way to obtain a greater width is to make it up with several narrow pieces. Wood has to be cut from a log in a way that will give the largest quantity of commercially usable pieces. Wide boards are cut across the log, while smaller sections are taken from wherever they can be cut, from sapwood or branches. There is always a good chance that better wood will be found in the wider boards. Assuming the price is not vastly different, there may be some advantage in getting the best parts of the tree, wide pieces, and cutting them down to make narrower parts. Wood with sufficiently prominent annual ring markings on the end can give a clue as to how close to the heart it was cut: by the curvature of the rings.

It is usually helpful to show the wood supplier a complete list of the finished sizes you need, so he can sort out short lengths for you. Some longer pieces of wood, because of their comparative scarcity, cost proportionately more; so if you let the supplier know you want, say four pieces 3 feet long, rather than one a foot long, you may get better service—and pay less. Lumberyards accumulate short ends; if you take these off their hands, you may get odd pieces with extra length at no extra cost. Pieces like this make useful stock.

VENEERS

A veneer is a thin piece of wood that needs some sort of backing to be usable. Veneers for furniture are usually chosen for decorative grain, which in woods unsuitable for construction could not be shown in any other way. Veneers are also used constructionally, the best known example being plywood. Some plywoods are faced with a decorative veneer, but usually the wood chosen for making plywood has to have strength and an even grain to make it structurally sound, rather than having to be particularly beautiful in itself.

Veneers range from paper-thin to about ⅛ inch thick; above that, it is too thick to be a veneer. Most of the older veneers were sawed, the only method that will yield some grain effects. Sawing thin pieces from a large block of wood removes as much in sawdust as it produces in veneer, a wasteful method that makes veneers expensive. Some veneers are cut with a *machine knife* that works with a slicing action (Fig. 1-13A).

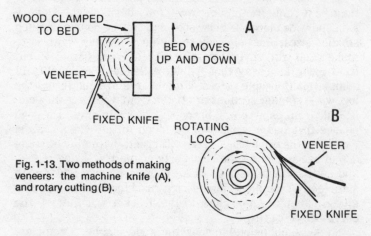

Fig. 1-13. Two methods of making veneers: the machine knife (A), and rotary cutting (B).

Both of these methods can only produce veneers the width of the solid block. For getting the desired grain effect in a particular wood, they may be the only acceptable methods.

Other veneers, in particular those for making plywood, are rotary cut. The log is turned in a machine like a lathe, and a knife takes off a continuous slice (Fig. 1-13B). The plugs glued in place of knots that were cut out can be seen on the surface of plywood. The wood is soaked in hot water or steamed to make it easier for rotary cutting to take off a continuous veneer. This method produces a grain marking different from that of any solid wood because the cut follows approximately the lines of the annual rings.

For veneers with quarter-sawed markings the less common method of half-rotary cutting is used. The wood swings through an arc against a knife that progressively takes off slices of veneers on lines that approximate the lines of the medullary rays (Fig. 1-14).

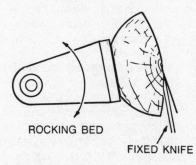

Fig. 1-14. Half-rotary cutting is used to produce veneers with quarter-sawed medullary-ray markings.

ROCKING BED

FIXED KNIFE

MANUFACTURED BOARDS

Plywood is built up from many layers of veneer laid perpendicular to each other; the result: a stable panel of reasonable size without joints that is stronger for its thickness than comparable solid wood. Plywood used to be commonly known as three-ply, but now plywood may have any number of veneers. However, it nearly always has an odd number of layers, so the outside veneers have grain aligned the same way on both sides.

At one time plywood was bonded with natural animal or vegetable glues that were far from waterproof—much of it delaminated in damp conditions, giving the material a bad name. The synthetic resin glues used in nearly all plywood today is either fully waterproof or has at least a very high resistance to dampness.

Most plywood has plies of the same thickness. The thickness of the plies varies according to the wood used; some cannot be cut as thin as others. In general, a greater number of plies in a given thickness produces a stiffer and better board than a lesser number; thus 5-ply quarter-inch plywood is better than 3-ply stock of the same thickness—however, other factors may have to be considered.

Plywood may be manufactured for a particular quality, such as extra flexibility, or the core in a veneer may be thicker in one direction to give stiffness in that direction, as that used in the lifting keel of a small sailing boat. Because of the naturally variable characteristics of wood, veneers for plywood are likewise variable in quality. This means there are different qualities of plywood; poorer quality may be good enough for rough, external work, while more expensive material would be needed in furniture.

Besides the general quality of veneers, there are other factors that affect plywood. Some cheaper plywoods may have core veneers inferior in quality, and the joints between their edges may not mate perfectly. Some veneers contain knots or a large number of patches.

Marine-grade plywood is usually the most expensive, but it has good faces on both sides. The internal plies are of a good quality, without gaps, and with a bonding glue that can withstand conditions afloat. Exterior-grade plywood is comparable in many ways. It will withstand wet conditions, but although it may have good surfaces on one or both sides, the core veneers may not be very good and there could be gaps. For most purposes, plywood is supplied with both surfaces sanded; the cheapest plywood, for rough work, is unsanded.

A lot of plywood is made from the reddish woods, but a considerable quantity used in the United States and Canada is made from Douglas fir. Many other woods have been used, but those cited are common for general woodwork. A great range of sizes is available. Although you can buy pieces cut to size, they can be much more expensive per total area than one sheet; it is advisable to plan a job so stock sizes are used, or buy whole sheets for several projects. Sheets are usually 48 inches wide and 96 inches long (4 by 8 feet); however, longer sheets are available.

An average-sized sheet is the largest that can be comfortably handled by one man. The width can be spanned with the arms, but there are devices that allow more convenient carrying to one side (Fig. 1-16). Plywood comes in thicknesses from a quarter-inch (or thinner) up to about ¾ inch; some manufacturers use metric measure, the range being 6 mm to 18 mm.

Thicker plywood made from thin plies involves a large number of layers of veneer, thus involving greater expense in manufacture. One alternative is lumber-core birch, or pine plywood, that has surface veneers like plywood, but the center is made up of solid strips; the pieces are glued to each other and the veneers. The external veneers are usually thicker than those in plywood, and their grain goes across the width of the sheet. In some construction the surface veneers are double thickness, with their grain going the same way to minimize any risk of warping.

Another constructional board, made up from wood particles embedded in synthetic resin, is particle board. In itself it may have adequate strength for some purposes, but it is unattractive. The material is veneered when used in manufacturing, either with a wood veneer or plastic having a wood-grain appearance. Such boards may be veneered around the edges as well as on the main surfaces. Providing they can be used without having to be cut, they are adequate; if they are cut, the sawed edges have to be hidden. Veneering particle board by hand is not easy, and the material presents problems in taking screws and other fasteners.

Several kinds of boards are manufactured from wood pulp. Insulating boards are very loosely bonded. Many boards are more like cardboard than wood, but when pulp is sufficiently compressed with a suitable bonding agent, a hard material is produced that has uses as an alternative to plywood for some purposes. Such hardboards, Masonite for example, are commonly available in the same sheet sizes as plywood; but ⅛ inch is the usual thickness available. One surface is hard and smooth; the other, rough and patterned. (The normal method of manufacture does not allow a smooth surface on both sides.) There are several grades, depending mainly on the degree of compression and the resulting hardness. Some boards treated with oil, or by other means to give them tougher water-resistant qualities, are described as *oil-tempered* (or some similar term). Tough hardboards have uses in many woodworking projects, but the poorer quality materials are not intended for permanent or important ones.

2
Hand Tools

The skill that makes a craftsman comes easier if hand tools are mastered first. For most beginners, working with hand tools gives an appreciation of the problems involved and a feel for wood. There are, of course, many things that can only be done by hand. Whatever power tools are eventually added to your tool kit, there will always be times when you will have to turn to hand tools. If you wish to reproduce specimens of earlier craftsmanship, power tools can make your work easier than it was for the original craftsman; but when it comes to the actual cutting of joints and other finer techniques, there is no substitute for hand tools—and the skill needed to use them.

The large number of power tools available to the woodworker today makes it possible to do many jobs that formerly required hand tools. Some are large immovable machines, others are lighter self-powered portable tools; and many are attachments to electric drills or other small power-driven tools.

Having a large range of power tools may seem attractive, but their considerable expense often is not. The ambitious amateur woodworker who plans to do a large amount of work might feel the cost is justified, but the beginner may not have the money to spare. In any case, the amount of equipment available can be bewildering, making the novice uncertain as to what power tools may eventually suit his needs.

While the initial investment is obviously an important consideration, there are other factors probably more important to the woodworker who hopes to progress to a real craftsman. No machine will do the job for you; whether you are using hand tools or power tools, it is your skill in handling them that determines the result. Power tools enable you to get the desired result quicker with less labor and sometimes more accurately. There is no virtue in laboriously sawing a large piece of lumber by hand when a power saw could do it for you. Without certain power tools you may have to buy wood already cut to the sizes you want.

The ability to use hand tools will make you better able to employ power tools when you want to. An understanding of what happens to wood fibers when a particular cutting action is used on them will be better acquired from using hand tools. And if the result is not all that was expected, the reason behind the trouble is more likely to be understood from the experience of using hand tools. Because power tools are electrically powered, you could be wholly dependent on hand tools for work, say, on your boat away from shore or for a project out in the boondocks.

There may not be the need today for the large range of hand tools needed by the woodworker of only a couple of generations ago; but there are certain basic items that must be obtained, items that are likely to become your favorite tools, the ones on which you rely most often. Good hand tools are not only very pleasant to have, they are an important investment for anyone who wants to call himself a craftman.

CHOOSING HAND TOOLS

As it is with many other things, you get what you pay for—nearly always, the higher the price, the higher the quality. The only time a higher price may not be justified is when it is for something unduly complicated. Usually, a simple tool that does one job properly is better than one that has been adapted in some way to do the work of another tool as well. Sometimes a combination tool is justified; but for basic woodworking operations, tools that have stood the test of time and have been made in a form that experience has shown to be best are preferred.

Boxed sets of hand tools are obtainable, but if you buy one it means that someone else has done the selecting for you. You may find that some of the tools are not quite what you would have selected yourself. You may even find yourself with some tools you will never have any use for. Although the total price of a boxed set might be lower than you would pay for the tools individually, if one or more of the tools is of no use to you, any cost advantage will be canceled. And although the fitted box for the tools may seem attractive, usually there is no room for storing other tools you will certainly buy later.

Another disadvantage of assembled sets is that some may be inferior in quality. A poor tool is a bad buy—at any price—particularly if it is a cutting tool. Poor quality steel, incorrectly hardened and tempered, will never take a good cutting edge; it can never do good work. A poor quality saw will blunt quickly no matter how carefully it is resharpened and set. A screwdriver that bends or has an end that twists when a load is put on a stubborn screw has no place in a craftsman's tool kit.

About the only acceptable kind of preassembled tool kit is one offered as a gift. Otherwise, it is better to select tools individually and buy the best you can afford. One way to obtain good tools at a low price is to watch for sales of equipment once owned by a deceased or retired craftsman. Providing the tools have not been allowed to rust, and things like chisels have not been worn away until they are useless, the fact that a craftsman used them may be regarded as almost a guarantee of good quality.

A BASIC TOOL KIT

Few homes are without basic maintenance tools such as a hammer, pliers, a saw, and a few wrenches; but because these things are generally misused and in poor condition, most woodworking craftsmen prefer to have tools specifically suited to their trade. (Greater detail on individual tools is given later in this chapter, but these notes may help in your first selection.)

Among the first items needed will be at least one saw. If you buy wood already cut to length, most of your sawing will be done with a fine-toothed backsaw. A tenon saw 10 or 12 inches long with 14 or 16 teeth to the inch is a good first choice. If your woodwork is more likely to be making rustic furniture or general carpentry, a hand saw 18 to 24 inches long with 8 or 10 teeth to the inch will be more useful.

For most woodworking the best first choice of planes is a steel smoothing plane, such as the Stanley No. 4. Although this tool will not easily bring a roughly sawed board to a good finish by itself, it will do all the finishing to size, and can also be used across end grain with reasonable success. When parts have to be finished to size or a few shavings have to be taken off to make parts fit, this is the tool to have. It is normally used with both hands, but it is light enough to use occasionally with one hand when you have to use the other to hold the work.

If you progress very far in woodworking, you will eventually feel that you can never have too many chisels. For a start, a half-inch bevel-edged chisel is a good general-purpose tool. Bevel-edged chisels cost a little more than square-edged ones, but they do the same things with the additional advantage of being able to get close in to angles. Another, much wider chisel, say, 1¼ inches wide, is useful for paring; a quarter-inch chisel is the next logical choice.

Almost any hammer can be used, but a 12 ounce one is the most utilitarian. It may have a narrow peen (the end opposite the hitting face) for getting into confined places or a claw for extracting nails (especially if outdoor carpentry is more likely to be your work).

Screwdrivers in several sizes will be needed. Long ones give better leverage but will not go into confined spaces. Start with one that has a 6 inch blade and is no wider than $^3/_{16}$ inch. Later, bigger and smaller ones can be added, but first rely on good, plain screwdrivers rather than ratchet or other special types. If you use Phillips-head screws, you will need two or three sizes to fit them.

You will have to have a means of making holes. Small hand-operated wheel braces have chucks to take drills in sizes up to about a quarter-inch. For screw holes and similar careful work, this is a safer choice than an electric drill, even if you already have one; it is too easy for a power drill to go too deep.

For larger holes the traditional carpenter's brace can't be beat; the choice of bits now available is much greater than earlier craftsmen had. There are several types with screwlike twists in the shaft that will do all a simple center bit will; the parallel twists keep the hole straight when drilling deep, and are worth the slight extra cost. As with chisels, you may eventually accumulate a large range of bits, but a half-inch bit is the best first choice, followed by those in ⅛ inch steps above and below for as many sizes as you need.

Because cutting tools have to be sharpened, a sharpening stone will have to be included in the basic tool kit. A double-sided stone with fine and coarse surfaces, about 8 inches long, will give the proper sharpening action. And an oilcan will be needed to wet the stone.

A list of the miscellaneous tools that could be accumulated would be almost endless, but some basic things worth including are: a good knife, possibly the type with replaceable blades; a pair of pincers for removing nails; pliers— preferably vise-type locking pliers; a spike (such as an ice pick); a rule; and a square.

The dividing line between a basic tool kit and a more comprehensive one is open to individual interpretation, but the tools mentioned so far will get you started. You can add other tools later as you feel the need for them.

Hammers and Mallets

The hammer is the general tool for nailing and many other woodworking jobs, but because of its small face and hard nature, it is unsuitable for striking the end of wooden chisel handles. Although some plastic chisel handles are unaffected by steel hammers, the small area of a hammer's face may make hitting the end of the handle difficult, especially when your attention is concentrated more on what is happening at the cutting end of the chisel.

Most hammerheads made today are cast in steel, but some of the better, larger ones are forged. A cast head is made by pouring liquid steel into a mold. A forged head is made by hammering a red-hot steel bar into a die. A forged head is claimed to be stronger, but a properly heat-treated cast head is adequate for normal purposes. Usually, the ends of the head are tempered, the center being softer.

Hammer handles are usually made of ash or hickory, because of these woods' springiness and ability to absorb shock. Hammers are also made with the head and handle as one piece of steel, but although attempts are made to cushion the jarring of their hammering, their use for a long period will produce tired and sore arm muscles.

Hammer handles are usually oval in cross section to aid in directing the blows, and big enough to give a good grip; they are thinner toward the head end to increase springiness, thereby helping to shock. In the majority of hammers, there is an oversize hole in the head through which the handle is

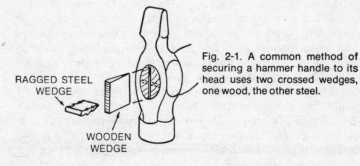

RAGGED STEEL
WEDGE

WOODEN
WEDGE

Fig. 2-1. A common method of securing a hammer handle to its head uses two crossed wedges, one wood, the other steel.

inserted and spread with wedges to secure it. Commonly, a wooden wedge is forced in the long way and a steel wedge, often with a ragged edge to aid its grip, is put in perpendicular to the first (Fig. 2-1).

Some hammers have their heads secured with straps or cheeks that extend down the side of the handle from the head and are riveted in place (Fig. 2-2); but this is more common in certain axes and other hitting tools.

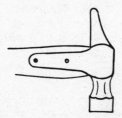

Fig. 2-2. Used more often for axes, this method of head attachment uses rivets to secure head to handle.

Nearly all hammering is done with the face of the hammer, the other end providing balance. Although the face may be described as flat, it is usually slightly domed and may be called bell-faced. The edges are beveled to avoid damaging the wood. On most hammers the surface is polished smooth, but some hammers for heavy constructional exterior work may have a pattern of grooves across the surface to prevent slipping on large nails.

The general-purpose hammer has a cross peen, which may be symmetrical around the axis of the flat face, or it may be flat toward the handle and slope toward the head. The cross peen is rounded and is useful for getting into awkward places, for riveting, and for starting a nail held between finger and thumb. Another common type is the claw hammer; it has a cleft, curved end for removing nails and prying woodwork apart.

Hammer sizes may be described in a series of arbitrary numbers, but they are also graded by the weight of the head. Cross-peen hammers have heads weighing between 6 and 25 ounces in approximately 2 ounce steps. For general bench use something between 10 and 14 ounces should be satisfactory, depending on the work being undertaken. If heavy constructional work is not involved, a lighter hammer will do. For driving fine nails and pins, there are slender 4 ounce hammers. Claw hammers tend to be heavy, ranging from about 13 to 28 ounces in 3- or 4-ounce steps.

A mallet of sufficient size and weight (and of almost any shape) should be satisfactory. The traditional carpenter's mallet has a rectangular head and a square tapered handle. The handle and head may be made of beech or some other close-grained hardwood. Much of the shock of a blow is actually absorbed better by a wooden head than a steel head; less is transferred, via the handle, to the worker's arm. The faces of the head are given a slight taper that projects to the user's wrist (Fig. 2-3). The mortise (hole) for the handle is tapered so the head cannot fly off. Centrifugal force would tend to throw the head outward during a blow, thus tightening it. Mallets are graded by the length of the head, usually between 4 and 7 inches.

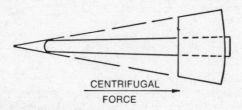

CENTRIFUGAL
FORCE

Fig. 2-3. Mallets are designed so the centrifugal force of a blow tightens the head on the handle.

Most wood-carvers use a carpenter's mallet, but some prefer the round-headed mallets used by stone masons. The head, made from a close-grained hardwood, has a hole through which the handle is wedged. The size is the greatest diameter of the head, which may be from 2 to 7 inches; a carver may have several that he selects according to the weight of the blow required.

There are a number of mallets or hammers with special faces not intended for woodworking, but one with screw-in plastic faces would be a good alternative to the traditional carpenter's mallet for hitting chisels or driving parts of a wooden structure together.

Many craftsmen have their own specialized hammers. Leatherworkers and upholsterers use a slender, light hammer (for driving tacks), which could have a similar use in woodworking. There are several axes with hammer faces that can be used for fixing slate or shingle roofs. Some of them have a nick in the side of the blade for removing nails—especially handy when a worker has to remain in an awkward position and can't easily change over to other tools when he wants to chop, hammer, or remove a nail.

A veneering hammer (Fig. 2-4) is not a percussive tool, despite its name. It has a thick strip of brass (or other metal) with a rounded edge, which is held in a slot in a piece of wood about 4 inches long, with a projecting rod as a handle. It is used in rubbing down veneer to squeeze out air and spread the glue underneath (as will be described later).

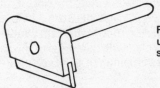

Fig. 2-4. A veneering hammer, used to squeeze out air and spread the glue beneath veneers.

For some constructional work—particularly in the quantity production of light furniture and fittings—a staple gun or tacker is useful. It drives two-pronged staples by spring action, one staple driven each time the handle is squeezed. There are several sizes; the lightest drive staples as small as those used in office work, and the largest drive staples with the grip of large nails.

Punches, used with hammers to drive nails below the surface, have a knurled or shaped grip and a beveled top to minimize the risk of the end spreading under repeated hammer blows. The end may be flat or slightly hollowed. Several sizes are needed, but they are not difficult to improvise from pieces of iron or large nails.

While a claw hammer will extract a partially driven nail or one that has a large head under which the claw can be fitted, pincers will be needed for a better job. They are graded by overall length—between 6 and 12 inches. To get under a nail head that is flush with a surface, they have to have edges beveled almost to a cutting edge at the outside (Fig 2-5). Some pincers have almost semicircular ends; others are wider. This

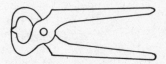

Fig. 2-5. Pincers are specially designed to remove nails that have been hammered flush with a surface, and do a much better job of it than a claw hammer.

affects the amount of leverage available to withdraw a nail, but in practice the difference is not enough to matter. (The end of the handle may have a claw for removing upholstery tacks.)

Saws

In the history of tools the appreciation of scientific saw-tooth design came rather late. Many early saws relied on a row of jagged teeth; if the user was lucky *some* of the teeth had a form approaching the best shape for the saw to cut, but mostly it just wore away the wood. Early craftsmen depended on axes and burning their way through wood, because they simply did not have saws capable of doing the job. Some medieval saws were reasonably efficient, because saw-tooth design began to be understood during that period: the value of cutting a notch (*kerf*) that would clear the thickness of the saw was realized. Modern saws are refinements of developments of those days.

The fibrous nature of wood makes it take a cut differently *across* the grain than *with* it. Saw teeth used across the grain have to sever the fibers; teeth cutting along the grain have to act like little chisels or planes, cutting grooves by removing tiny shavings. A *crosscut* saw has teeth intended for cutting across the grain; *ripsaws* have special teeth for work along the grain. Because most large cuts along the grain are usually made (today) with power saws, a ripsaw can probably be omitted from the average tool kit.

A saw intended for cutting across the grain has teeth alternately bent in opposite directions. The teeth are sharpened so they are pointed on the outside. The effect is to sever the fibers in two lines a short distance apart, making a cut wider than the thickness of the steel plate of the saw. This gives clearance for the blade as it cuts through the wood, reducing friction.

The teeth have an inclusive angle of 60° (convenient for sharpening with a triangular file) and are tilted so the forward edge is more upright than the back of the tooth (Fig. 2-6A). The cutting angle is about 70° to the edge of the saw. In cross

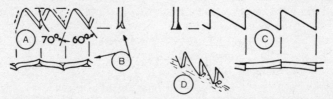

Fig. 2-6. The teeth of a saw intended for cutting across the grain (A) have an inclusive angle of 60°, and in cross section can be seen to slope outward toward both sides (B); the leading edge of ripsaw teeth (C) is at right angles to the edge of the saw, and cut a series of shavings that curl away in front of them (D).

section the teeth can be seen to slope outward toward both sides (Fig. 2-6B). A test for a newly sharpened and set crosscut saw is to slide a sewing needle down the edge; if it goes the whole length without falling off the side, the job can be considered satisfactory.

Ripsaw teeth also have an inclusive angle of 60°, but they are sharpened straight across. The leading edge is perpendicular to the edge of the saw (Fig. 2-6C). This, along with straight-across sharpening, makes the saw cut a series of little shavings that curl away in front of the teeth (Fig. 2-6D).

Ripsaws, are between 16 and 30 inches long, but most are nearer the longer end of this range. Modern handles and the method of affixing them to blades, vary from traditional types, but the important thing is that the grip for the hand makes a right angle to a line projected about halfway along the cutting edge (Fig. 2-7).

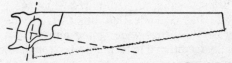

Fig. 2-7. It is important that the grip of the hand is perpendicular to a line extended about halfway along the cutting edge of a saw.

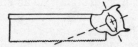

Ripsaw teeth, usually much larger than crosscut teeth, may be four points to an inch for hardwoods, and close to three to an inch for softwoods, although some saws for both purposes may have five teeth to an inch. Much depends on the amount of sap in the wood; drier wood can be cut with smaller teeth.

General-purpose handsaws with crosscut teeth are made in the same sizes as ripsaws, with between 8 and 12 teeth to the inch; for general purposes, a saw 24 inches long with 10 teeth to the inch is a good selection. Half-ripsaws, with a compromise tooth, give a reasonable cut across the grain as well as with it. If it is likely that heavy cuts along the grain will be made with a power saw, it is probably better to select a handsaw with crosscut teeth.

The saw for the accurate cutting of joints, or cutting pieces of wood to shape on the bench, is a backsaw, often called a tenon saw (see bottom of Fig. 2-7). The stiff back may be iron or brass, but the latter is considered superior because of its appearance and extra weight. Tenon saws range from 10 inches to 24 inches long along the edge, but for most purposes, 10-, 12-, or 14-inch models are suitable. Their teeth, crosscut in form and finer than those of hand- or panel-saws, are 14 or 16 teeth to an inch. The handles may be traditional in form with a family likeness to the handsaw—or of a more streamlined, modern form—but the grip should be almost perpendicular to a line extending to the center of the cutting edge.

The dovetail saw, a smaller version of the backsaw, has a blade 8 to 10 inches long with 16 or 17 teeth to the inch. It is used for fine work, particularly for cutting joints. Despite their names, both saws have much wider applications than cutting tenon and dovetail joints; they are the general-purpose bench saws for making furniture and similar work.

Tenon and dovetail saws only make straight cuts. For sawing curves there are several saws with narrow blades. A compass saw (Fig. 2-8) has a blade that tapers from the handle, where it may be 1½ inches wide, going almost to a point. The handle, usually traditional in form, is often rounded, without "horns" to get in the way when working in an awkward situation. For greater stiffness, the blade is thicker than that of other saws; but to reduce the risk of breaking, it is softer than most saws. If it bends, it can be straightened again. A variation of this is a set of several saw blades that can be fixed with bolts into one handle. The blades may come in different sizes, and some handles are adjustable to different angles and positions to allow working in difficult situations.

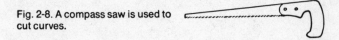

Fig. 2-8. A compass saw is used to cut curves.

Even smaller is the keyhole saw (Fig. 2-9). The blade fits through a handle with no more than needed projecting from it, so there is a lessened risk of buckling. The same handle will also take a metalworking hacksaw blade. Both blades can be reversed in the handle, reducing the risk of buckling, but they make a ragged edge on the front of the wood.

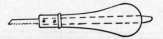

Fig. 2-9. The keyhole saw will take blades that fit through its handle and can be exposed as needed.

For even finer and sharper curves a saw blade has to be held under tension. The traditional type was the bow saw (Fig. 2-10A). Some quite large were used for straight cuts in the days when the steel for saws was more easily obtained in pieces narrower than those needed for what we now regard as normal saws. The steel was often of a quality that would only hold its shape under tension. Traditionally, tension was applied by twisting a cord in a manner sometimes called "Spanish windlass." Later versions were screw-adjustable. Although this tool is regarded as a relic of the past, it is an interesting thing to handle, and is still quite efficient for cutting curves.

A more modern saw for fine curves is the very narrow-bladed coping saw (Fig. 2-10B), which depends on the springiness of the frame and the adjustment of a screw in the handle for tension. The end of the blade is held by a loop or by a pin going through it (Fig. 2-10C). The finest of the woodworking saws is the fretsaw. The teeth of its blade can be so fine as to be difficult to see. The blades are held by clamps in a deep spring frame (Fig. 2-10D). Both saws are sometimes called jigsaws. Their blades, even though used carefully, may not last very long; they have to be bought in quantity to allow for wear.

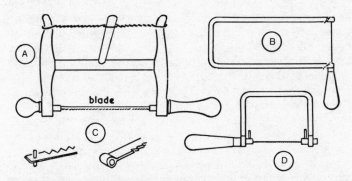

Fig. 2-10. The bow saw (A) is the predecessor of the modern coping saw (B), whose blade has a loop or pin in its end for attachment to the frame (C); the fretsaw (D), a member of the same family, is the finest of the woodworking saws.

A saw is only satisfactory when it is sharp. Some saws have teeth treated to retain their sharpness longer than plain steel teeth. However, care is always needed in using and storing them. A woodworking saw will blunt quickly if it meets a nail or other piece of metal as it passes through wood. When not is use, saws should be hung or put up in a cabinet with their teeth covered. A saw should not be stored loosely with other tools. The teeth may be protected with a grooved piece of wood; some saws are supplied with a clip-on plastic cover.

Chisels and Gouges

A chisel is a tool with a straight cutting end. A gouge is similar, but has a curved cutting edge. Because the word *chisel* is used for a metal-cutting tool as well, when there is a need to differentiate the two, the metal-working chisel is called a *cold chisel* (the blacksmith uses a *hot chisel*) and the woodworking tool, a *wood chisel*.

A chisel cuts with a combination of a fine cutting edge and a wedge-shaped cross section, the actual angle varying according to the material being worked. Although a very fine edge is desirable for best cutting properties, it would not last long on very hard wood. With too obtuse an angle it would fail to cut; although it might then serve as a wedge to split wood along the grain, it would be useless for its intended job of accurate paring and shaping.

The cutting angle has to be a compromise. A very thin chisel may be angled only to one side, but the majority of chisel blades have sides that slope to meet in a 25° cutting edge, which is usually made and renewed with a grinding wheel; the angle is often referred to as the grinding angle or *bevel*. The actual cutting edge is sharpened on an oilstone by holding it at an angle slightly more obtuse than the grinding angle by 5° or more (Fig. 2-11A). This is called the *sharpening* angle. The other side of a chisel is always kept absolutely flat. Even a small amount of "backing off" (Fig. 2-11B) will affect control of the cutting. The only exceptions are some carving tools. Because the edge is repeatedly renewed by rubbing it on an oilstone, the sharpening angle gradually becomes longer. When it becomes excessively long, the end is ground again; but in normal use, grinding will only have to be done at quite long intervals.

The basic chisel, often called a *firmer* chisel (Fig. 2-11C), has square edges and is made entirely of hardened and tempered steel; even when it has been ground back several inches, the quality of the edge that can be obtained will always be the same.

Chisel-widths start at ³/₁₆ inch (sometimes ⅛ inch), and go in ⅛ inch steps up to 2 inches. Lengths are proportional, but are not usually stated. A new chisel will have a blade at least 4 inches long. All the widths up to 1 inch are used in woodworking; wider ones are often used for paring. The thickness of a chisel depends on its width; a narrow chisel needs to be proportionately thicker to provide strength and stiffness.

Some chisels are socketed (Fig. 2-11D), but the majority have tangs that fit into a handle and a shoulder to resist pressure (Fig. 2-11E). The socket puts a compressive load on the wood of the handle so it can withstand heavy hitting. Chisels are made with wood or plastic handles. The plastic now used has considerable strength and holds the tang securely, but some craftsmen prefer wood.

Handles are made of a number hardwoods and come in several shapes. A barrel form (Fig. 2-11F) is common. Another form has grip consisting of parallel grooves in the handle. A variation of this is an octagonal-shaped handle (Fig. 2-11G), that helps to prevent the chisel from rolling. Wood handles, and some plastic ones, have a metal collar or *ferrule* (Fig. 2-11H) around the tang end to prevent it from splitting.

Firmer chisels are available with beveled edges (Fig. 2-11I). They will cut into corners and do most of the work of a square-edged chisel, but are not quite as strong. Firmer chisels can be used alone or they may be hit with a mallet. For regular work with a mallet, there are stronger chisels, often called mortise chisels (Fig. 2-11J) from their traditional use in chopping out mortises; but today this job is commonly done by less laborious means. Thinner and longer paring chisels, with both square and beveled edges (Fig. 2-11K) in all the normal widths, are used only for careful paring, never for hitting.

Firmer gouges are made in the same widths as chisels and have similar handles. The amount of curve in the blade is standard; there is usually no choice. It is usual for the end of a gouge to be sharpened straight across its cutting edge; it may be ground on the outside (Fig. 2-12A) or inside (Fig. 2-12B).

A gouge sharpened on the inside is used for handwork only. It is long and thin, comparable to a paring chisel. It may be described as a paring or scribing gouge.

Gouges are made in the same widths as firmer chisels for turning wood on a lathe, but they are much longer and usually have very long handles. Standard turning gouges adequate for most work are available, as well as range of "long, strong" ones for very heavy work. A turning gouge (Fig. 2-12C) is ground on the outside, but its end is rounded. Turning chisels,

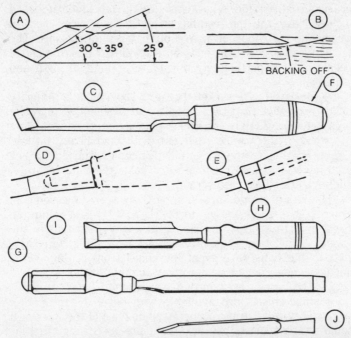

Fig. 2-11. Chisels are sharpened by holding them against the oilstone at an angle greater than the cutting angle (A); anything less than an absolutely straight back will impair their cutting ability (B). The basic firmer chisel (C) may have a socketed handle (D) or one that simply accepts a blade tang with a shoulder (E). Handles can be barrel-shaped (F) with, possibly, parallel grooves as a grip, or they can have octagonal sides (G), which will prevent rolling on a bench. All wood handles have a metal furrule (H) to prevent them from splitting, and can accommodate blades with beveled edges (I); for regular use with a mallet, a mortise chisel (J) is recommended.

available in the same widths and lengths as gouges, are ground on both sides of their sloping cutting edge (Fig. 2-12D). Because turning tools are not struck like a chisel, there is usually no shoulder where the tang enters the handle. Handles take many forms; because a wood turner can make his own, he can use his own ideas concerning their shape and size. (A turner uses several adaptions of the chisel and gouge; more information on this is given in the chapter on wood turning.)

A wood-carver uses a very large range of chisels and gouges, a real enthusiast possibly having well over a hundred, all different in shape. Obviously, such a large range is unnecessary for the beginner, about twenty is desirable for a start; others can be added as your skill and versatility increase. Most carver's tools are gouge-types, each available in many widths and a choice of eight or more curves (Fig. 2-12E). The carver sharpens his tools to suit his work. They are usually lighter and thinner than firmer gouges and have the main bevel on the outside. (There may be a slight bevel inside.)

Straight carving chisels may be sharp on one or both sides; the end may be square across, or beveled as in a *corner* chisel (Fig. 2-12F). The range is complicated by all the widths and curves available: bent, either front (Fig. 2-12G) or back (Fig. 2-12H); curved in various amounts (Fig. 2-12I); or specially shaped in many other ways. There are also V-shaped gouge-like tools (Fig. 2-12J). Called *parting* tools in general, and small ones, *veiners*, they are usually only straight—the effect is like two chisels joined together. Sharpening adjoining bevels to match can be difficult.

There are other chisel-like tools suited to other crafts, but anyone assembling his first tool kit will find that a few firmer chisels, preferably bevel-edged and in the popular widths, will do most of the work. Others can be added as the need for them arises. Because chisels play a big part in most woodworking projects, good chisels—kept in good condition—will form an important part of your tool kit. Gouges will be needed often,

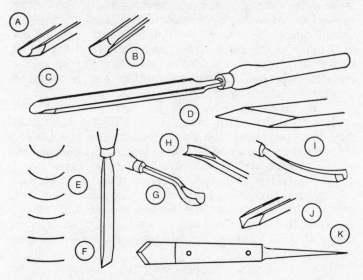

Fig. 2-12. The family of gouges and chisels, and their particular characteristics. (See text for descriptions.)

but one or two, particularly those sharpened on the inside, are useful for paring the inside of holes and shaping outlines.

Knives may be considered to be in the chisel family. Occasionally, a general-purpose knife might be needed; but for most woodworking, a knife with a sharp point, especially useful for marking lines across the grain, should be the first to get. The traditional woodworking knife is shown in Fig. 2-12K. The cutting blade is at the broad end of the handle and may be diagonal from one or both sides; the spike at the other end is used for marking wood, particularly in places difficult for a knife blade or pencil to reach, as when one part of a joint has to be marked against another. A separate slender marking awl (like a small ice pick) may also be used for this purpose. A point at the opposite end of a knife could be dangerous, unless it is covered with some sort of sheath.

The traditional marking knife has been largely replaced by the trimming knife, made by Stanley and other manufacturers, which has a similar form but has a handle that will accept replaceable blades and, often, many other knife or sawblades.

Planes

A plane applies control to the chisel action, usually to make a fine cut that produces a smooth surface. The control comes from allowing only a small portion of the chisel (now usually called a *plane* or *cutting* iron) to project through a slot in the sole of the plane. Traditional planes had cutters of wrought-iron with steel welded to their cutting edges—hence the name *plane iron*. Although most modern cutters are made entirely of steel, the name persists.

Some early planes had a single cutter, but nearly all modern planes have a *cap iron* to break off wood shavings as they come up through the plane's mouth. This reduces the tendency of the surface being worked to tear, as would happen with many woods if there was only a single plane iron.

The plane iron is sharpened somewhat like a chisel, with grinding and sharpening bevels if it is thick; but many with very thin irons have one bevel, because the effort of rubbing the whole thickness on an oilstone is not great. The cap iron (Fig. 2-13A) is attached to the plane iron with a screw that goes through a slot.

In use, the cutting edge projects through the mouth of the plane by the amount equal to the thickness of the wood being removed. The cap iron is set only just above the level of the plane's sole. The other factor affecting the result is the width of the mouth. If it is wide, the wedging, splitting approach of the blade to the wood will lift and tear away the shaving (Fig. 2-13B), resulting in a rough surface. If the mouth is narrow, the shaving will be held down, reducing the splitting action; the cap iron can break off the shaving (Fig. 2-13C) without a splitting action developing.

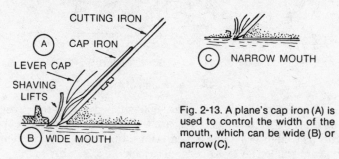

Fig. 2-13. A plane's cap iron (A) is used to control the width of the mouth, which can be wide (B) or narrow (C).

Obviously, there has to be a compromise. If you are removing a very fine shaving from a surface that is already reasonably flat, the cap iron can be close to the edge, projecting only very slightly, while the mouth can be very narrow. The first planing of a roughly sawed piece of wood requires that the cutting edge project more; the mouth must be wide enough to take a thick shaving, and the cap iron must be back far enough so the shaving will clear it. The resulting surface may not be very good, but it is the first step, followed by a more finely set plane.

In practice, the width of the mouth will not have to be altered frequently. One width will suit many conditions; the adjustment of edge protection and the position of the cap iron will take care of most needs. However, metal planes are given a mouth adjustment. It may the movement of that part of the sole ahead of the mouth, but in others the actual mounting and assembly that holds the cutter and its adjsutments, called a *frog*, can be moved back and forth slightly by turning a screw (Fig. 2-14); the cutting edge moves toward, or away from, the forward edge of the mouth.

The cap iron/cutting iron assembly is held in place with a lever cap, sometimes called a wedge from the earlier use of simple wedges. The cap tapers to a point above the mouth where it presses against the cap iron, helping to deflect shavings upward.

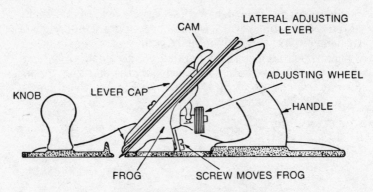

Fig. 2-14. The anatomy of a plane.

A screw going through a keyhole-shaped slot in the lever cap makes it removable to release the cutting iron and its cap iron, as well as providing a means for adjusting pressure when the cam-shaped lever is operated to lock the assembly.

In most planes a knurled adjusting wheel provides up and down movement for the blade. A lateral adjusting lever is moved sideways to tilt the cutting edge for an even cut or a deeper cut to one side.

There are three basic groups of plane sizes: an average-sized, general-purpose plane with a sole 14 inches long, called a *jack* plane, from the phrase "Jack-of-all trades"; a shorter, *smoothing* plane, from 8 to 10 inches long; and the very long soled *jointer*, *shuting*, or *try* (trying) planes (18 to 22 inches long).

The jack plane is normally set fairly coarsely with a mouth opened more than the other two types. If a piece of wood has to be planed close to size quickly, if a rough surface has to be removed in one cut—this is the tool to use. In skilled hands it can do many jobs with an acceptable degree of accuracy. A longer plane is more accurate for making a straight edge because the long, straight base spans broad, uneven areas, while taking off raised spots. If a surface is already flat enough but its texture is poor, a smoothing plane would be more convenient to use. Today, with heavy planing often being done by machine, a smoothing plane will get the most use, particularly for removing machine-plane marks.

Traditional planes (comparable in size to those used today) can still be found. Although mechanically more crude than modern types, some older craftsmen claim they produce superior work. The only way to adjust them is to tap the cutting iron with a hammer and lock it by driving in a wedge. To retract or withdraw the cutting iron, the plane is hit in the front (Fig. 2-15), where there may be a hardwood striking button. The effect is to momentarily stretch the fibers of the wood, releasing pressure on the wedge.

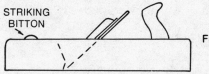

STRIKING BITTON

Fig. 2-15. A wooden plane.

Planes are used with both hands. American and British planes are designed to be held by a shaped handle (behind the cutting iron) with one hand, the other resting on a knob or over the body of the plane in front. The technique of operation is not universal. Many craftsmen around the world use a plane that is pulled. They are characterized by a horn-shaped handle in front (Fig. 2-16) to provide a good grip for pulling.

Fig. 2-16. This plane, with a horn-shaped handle in front, is pulled rather than pushed.

General-purpose planes are available with cutting edges in several widths. For getting a broad surface true, there is some advantage in having a broad cut (2⅜ inches). Most of the things that can be done with a narrow plane can be done with a wide one; but a wide plane may be too heavy. A smoothing plane with a 1¾ inch cutting iron is light enough for many people to use with one hand, if necessary.

There is an advantage in having a heavy try plane; its weight prevents if from chattering and holds it close to the wood—even without great hand pressure.

The alternative to having one of the planes described thus far is to have a single iron, turned over and set at a low angle. Of course, if the angle is not very low, the actual angle of cut (Fig. 2-17) will be no different. Single-iron planes are rarely used today for general planing, but a low-angle *block* plane is useful for working across the grain. There are several varieties, but basically the single iron is set in a body 5 to 8 inches long. The cap is shaped to fit the palm of the hand, with

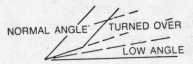

NORMAL ANGLE / TURNED OVER
LOW ANGLE

Fig. 2-17. A single iron, turned over, can produce the same cut as one normally situated and used with a cap iron.

a hollow spot on the knob (a finger rest) for single-handed use. Larger, low-angle planes have been made for two-hand use, but the single-hand block plane is a more useful tool, both for work across the grain and for many other light jobs, such as taking off sharp or ragged edges.

By nature of their construction, ordinary planes do not cut a path the same width as the sole; they cannot plane a surface close into angles. To do this a plane has to have a cutting edge as wide as its sole. The general name for such planes is *rebate* (or rabbett) plane; there are several versions, all with shoulders on their cutting irons (Fig. 2-18A) so that just the broader part does the cutting. There are planes with bodies similar to those already described, with the sides cut away to take wider blades (Fig. 1-18B); but most rebate planes are narrower—and many are low-angled—because they are used more often across the grain.

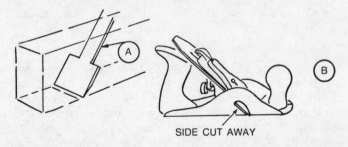

SIDE CUT AWAY

Fig. 2-18. The general configuration of a rebate plane's cutting iron (A); in B, a plane with its side cut away to accept wider cutting irons.

Rebate plane widths vary from as little as ⅜ inch to 2 inches or more. While it may be easy to make a surface true with a broad-soled plane, the narrow versions will get into awkward places and narrow recesses. One low-angle type, often having a screw adjustment for the blade and a sliding part for adjusting the mouth, is the *shoulder* plane (Fig. 2-19A), a name taken from its use in planing the shoulders of wide tenons. One variation has a bull nose, a front that allows getting close into a stopped recess (Fig. 2-19B), which is either

Fig. 2-19. Two planes for getting into awkward places: the shoulder plane (A), and one with a bull nose (B).

a permanent feature or an attachment. For normal use a greater length in front of the mouth is better for getting an accurate result, but the bull nose leaves little in a corner to be finished with a chisel.

Most rebate planes have a cutting edge that is perpendicular to the length of the plane, but some have been made with slanted (skewed) cutters that give more of a slicing cut. This produces a better surface on some grains. It is also an advantage in helping to clear shavings from the plane; they curl sideways instead of piling up inside the confined space above the mouth. A skew cut also helps to keep the plane close into an angle when cutting in one direction; but when the cut is reversed, it needs extra pressure because the plane is forced away from the angle. For most purposes, the normal square-cut rebate plane is adequate.

No ordinary plane will work the bottom of a recess. When working joints, there is often a need to get the bottom of a space level, but not necessarily finished to a very smooth surface. The tool for doing this is called a *router*. In its simplest form, it is a chisel or narrow plane iron put through a piece of wood and held by a wedge (Fig. 2-20A). The projecting edge is set at a depth suitable to scratch the previously chiseled surface, giving a reasonably uniform depth. Better routers are made of metal and may have two knobs (Fig. 2-20B). The cutter is bent to cut with more of a slicing action. The depth of the cut may be controlled with a knurled nut or

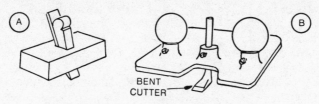

Fig. 2-20. A simple router (A); a better router. (B)

set by hand; the stem of the cutter is locked with a screw. In some tools the knobs are on stems the same size; if the tool has to be used in a recess close to a rebate (or other obstruction), the cutter can be moved to the side and into one of the handle stem holes.

There are two special planes that were once essential in any tool kit, but much of their work can now be done with power tools. However, they are still obtainable and have their uses. A *fillister*, a development of the rebate plane, is in effect a rebate plane fitted with stops to control the width and depth of the cut; a rebate, such as would be needed in a picture frame, can be cut by adjusting the steps or fences without having to mark the wood beforehand.

When the tool cuts a rebate on the side nearest the side fence, it is called a side fillister (Fig. 2-21A). The sole of a metal plane may be 1½ inches wide, the side fence on one or two rods, and the depth gage held by a wing screw going through a slot at the side of the body. Sometimes there is a second forward position for the blade (a single iron) close to the front of the body, giving it a bull-nose effect. There may be a spur (Fig. 2-21B) on the side of the tool in front of the cutter to sever fibers, and to produce a clean edge when the tool is used across the grain.

Another version, known as a sash fillister (Fig. 2-21C)—from its original use in rebating sash windows—cuts a rebate on the side furthest from the side fence. The tool is uncommon today; a careful worker can do all of the same

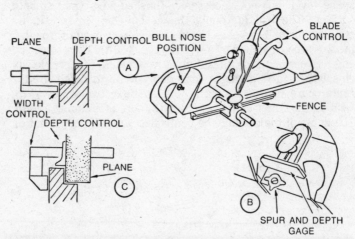

Fig. 2-21. A side fillister (A) may have a spur (B) to sever wood fibers; sash fillister detail is shown in C.

work with the simpler side fillister. But if you find one in good condition, it would be worth having.

A plow plane (Fig. 2-22) is generally similar to a fillister. Used to make grooves with the grain, it has a side fence and depth gage similar to those on a fillister; but its sole is as narrow as the narrowest groove to be cut; it is used with a set of single plane irons in various widths, ⅛ to ½ inch in $1/16$ inch steps, to cover most needs.

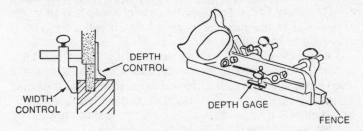

Fig. 2-22. A plow plane.

A development of the plow and fillister planes is the combination plane. In its most advanced form it uses the basic concept of the plane body and fences to control width and depth, with a great many attachments and a considerable range of cutters that can be used for rebating and grooving; but its forte is making moldings, each requiring a specially shaped cutting edge and, usually, a special sole. This sort of plane has been largely superseded by power tools, and might not be worth buying new; but an old, reasonably priced one might be worth having. At one time craftsmen used many wooden planes to make moldings, but they are really only of historic interest. The plane principle has been used in several special tools. Planes similar to wooden molding planes were made in many sizes, with bottoms and cutters either hollowed or rounded. They were known as *hollows* and *rounds*, from the shape they produced—not from the shape of their bottoms. Although a small round (with a hollow bottom) is useful for rounding edges, much of the work of these planes can now be done better with power tools. Planes, usually wooden, were also made curved, but a metal compass plane with a flexible bottom can be adjusted for a wide range of convex and concave curves.

A normal cutting iron, one that usually has a cap iron, is the most suitable type for the amateur woodworker's tool kit.

But some with disposable cutters can be used; others allow the lower end of the cap iron to be removed, so the cutting iron can be sharpened on an oilstone without having to loosen and readjust the cap iron.

It is often helpful to scratch fine grooves in broad surfaces to be glued to give the glue a better grip. This was more important in the days when natural glues were used, but it may still be worthwhile when using some of the stronger, modern synthetics. The plane employed for this task has a finely serrated edge to its cutter, set at quite a high angle (about 70°) to the surface, so as to scratch instead of cut. It was called a *toothing* plane.

A spokeshave (Fig. 2-23) differs from a plane in that it has a narrow sole and handles at the sides, but it cuts like a single-iron plane. Details differ between makes, but the blade is usually held by a lever cap with one or two screws for adjustment. The advantage of two screws is that they can be used to regulate the tilt of the blade.

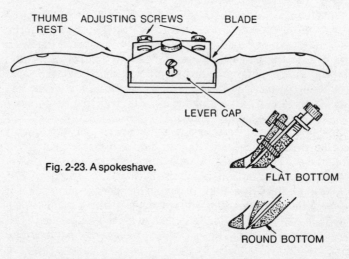

Fig. 2-23. A spokeshave.

A spokeshave is used for planing long curves. A flat bottom is suitable for anything between a flat surface and one with sharp, convex curves, while a round bottom will work into concave curves and is only limited by the amount of the bottom's curvature. Spokeshaves are usually straight across their width, but some have been curved in both dimensions for getting into compound-curved hollows, such as the insides of wooden barrel staves. The name *spokeshave* is not particularly appropriate, because the tool originally was infrequently used to shave wooden wheel spokes. (Most of this work was done with a two-handled drawknife.)

Traditional craftsmen argued that a better surface was obtained on wood by a proper cutting action rather than by any sort of abrasion—whether by sanding or filing. There is some truth in this, as abrasion can press down tiny wood fibers, which may rise later to spoil the surface. A sharp cutting tool severs them. However, modern thinking accepts various forms of power sanding; several newer tools use independent cutting points for a filing action on wood.

A file intended for metal will clog quickly on wood, unless it is fairly coarse. Files and rasps are made specially for woodworking, but their place has been taken, for most purposes, by power sanders. A file has teeth cut into, and across, the surface of the tool. A rasp has individual raised teeth and usually makes a coarser cut than a file. Files and rasps are made in several lengths. Half-round is the best shape for a general-purpose tool.

Similar tools are obtainable with disposable blades. Some have thin steel blades held under tension to allow the wood shavings to pass through, removing the risk of clogging. Besides those with flat blades, there are others with blades that are curved in their width or length; and there are tools whose lengthwise curve can be adjusted. Such tools are valuable, but the traditional craftsman's argument about a better surface resulting from the pure cut of a plane or chisel should be kept in mind; these tools should be regarded as complementary rather than alternatives.

A scraper is used for finishing prior to planing. The grain of some hardwoods—in particular those decorative ones with a confused grain pattern—will not finish smoothly under a plane, no matter how it is used or how sharp and finely set it is. A scraper will succeed where a plane will fail, and produce a much better surface (particularly under polish) than will a power sander.

Many scrapers have handles, but the basic *cabinet scraper* is a plain rectangle of steel, usually as thick as a saw blade and up to 6 inches long. It is thin enough to bend slightly under hand pressure, but is not otherwise very flexible. Its ancestor was a piece of broken glass; if a newly broken piece of glass is pulled over a wood surface, an angle can be found where it will take off thin shavings (Fig. 2-24).

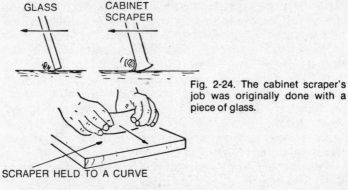

GLASS CABINET SCRAPER

Fig. 2-24. The cabinet scraper's job was originally done with a piece of glass.

SCRAPER HELD TO A CURVE

A cabinet scraper will produce the same effect, but as it is held, it is forced to curve slightly to maintain contact over a flat surface. Shaped scrapers made for curved work may be needed for reproductions of old furniture that have curved parts or elaborate moldings.

Scraper-planes, in which a cabinet scraper was held at the correct angle and forced to a slight curve (the sole of the plane providing control of the cut), have been made in smoothing-plane form, or as two-handled types like a spokeshave.

The cabinet scraper is probably still the best tool for a fine finish on a difficult grain. But much of the work it did in less exacting situations, like removing paint or glue, or correcting unevenness on the otherwise good surface of a plain piece of wood, can be done with a handled scraper with a disposable, hook-like blade. It has a handle (for one or both hands) used with a pulling action. (Several versions are available.)

Screwdrivers

Wood screws of many sizes and types are used in all branches of woodworking. The number of screwdrivers required has to very nearly match the variety of screws used, it is important that the screwdriver closely matches the screw head—if the screw is to be driven properly with a minimum of slipping that would damage the screw or the surrounding wood.

The end of a screwdriver should have a long bevel and match the screw's slot. If a screwdriver is too narrow, it will not exert enough leverage to turn the screw, and there is the risk of having it jump out of the slot; the edges of the blade may also chew up the slot. If the screwdriver blade is too wide, it will either not drive the screw in fully, or it will damage the surrounding wood. Several sizes (end widths) between ⅛ and ⅜ inch are needed for general woodworking.

The end of a screwdriver blade should be square. After much use the end and the corners may become rounded, causing it to jump out of the screw slot, which is comparatively small for the amount of torque it is often required to take.

To reduce the risk of power screwdrivers jumping out of screws during quantity-production assembly, some screws have star-shaped recesses instead of slots. The best-known of these is the *Phillips head*, but there are others. They require screwdrivers with special ends to match the heads; three sizes should make a range big enough for most woodworking needs.

Screwdriver blades are made of tool steel, but their heat treatment is a compromise. If they were tempered to the hardness of a cutting tool, their corners would crumble away or their ends would break. Instead, they are just soft enough to be filed or hammered straight if they bend. Screwdrivers intended for Phillips head screws are usually harder than those for slotted-head screws, because there is less strain (torque) to damage corners.

Most screwdrivers have blades with round shanks, the end being the same width as the diameter in small sizes or broader for larger screws. Some blades are flat in cross section, while others are square. An advantage of these, particularly in the larger sizes, is that pliers or a wrench can be used to help turn the tool.

Besides the several blade widths, screwdrivers are made in various lengths. It is easier to exert power with a long screwdriver than with a short one, so where there are no restrictions in space, there is an advantage to having a long screwdriver. However, there are often awkward places to be reached on constructional woodwork, making several shorter screwdrivers necessary, including a few with an overall handle-and-blade length of only 3 inches.

A screwdriver handle must be secured firmly to the blade, and must be able to take a grip that can apply torque without slipping. Many screwdrivers have plastic grips, often more secure than older wooden handles, but their surface does not offer such a good grip. A good handle has a bulbous end, to fit the palm of the hand, and an elliptical cross section (Fig. 2-25A). This effect is obtained on a round handle that has two parallel flat surfaces (Fig. 2-25B), or one that has a fluted grip (Fig. 2-25C). The end of the blade usually has a tang; a broader

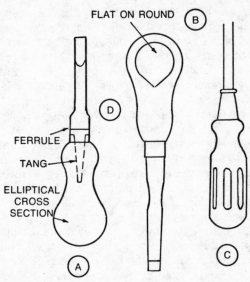

FLAT ON ROUND

FERRULE

TANG

ELLIPTICAL
CROSS
SECTION

Fig. 2-25. A good screwdriver handle has a bulbous end with an elliptical cross section (A), possibly with two parallel flat surfaces (B), or flues (C); usually, it is slotted to take a tang secured within a ferrule (D).

flat part of the tang fits into a slot in the ferrule (Fig. 2-25D) to resist torque.

Some screwdrivers have a ratchet action. They are useful for the quick and accurate driving of screws, because your hand does not have to be released and moved after each half-turn. Because a ratchet screwdriver is unsuitable for high torque, it is more appropriate for small-diameter screws. There is a control for the ratchet (Fig. 2-26A) that allows the blade to drive or withdraw a screw, or it can be locked solid with the handle.

A step further from the ratchet screwdriver is the automatic "Yankee" type (Fig. 2-26B); a pumping action applied to the handle causes the ratchet assembly to move in a hellical groove, turning the screw. It has a three-way ratchet control. These screwdrivers have a chuck at the end to take several sizes and bit types; some are provided with drill and countersink bits, making them more versatile. There are several sizes of automatic screwdrivers that provide a speedy method of driving screws. They can save time when many easily driven screws have to be installed, but they are unsuitable for tougher jobs, like driving large screws into hard wood.

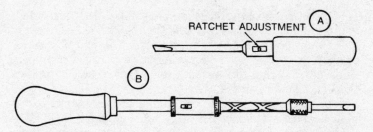

Fig. 2-26. Some screwdrivers with ratchet adjustments (A) are automatic pump types (B).

Screwdriver bits (Fig. 2-27A) can be used in an ordinary brace. They are good for large screws when it might be difficult to apply sufficient torque with an ordinary handle. But these bits are inadvisable for small screws, because the great amount of torque applied could be enough to shear the screw head.

A magnetized screwdriver helps hold steel screws that have to be put into difficult places; some screwdrivers have springlike fingers for gripping screws. For turning screws in very restricted places, there are offset screwdrivers (Fig. 2-27B), usually with two blades at a right angle to each other at opposite ends of a single shaft. In a very cramped space, the two ends have to be turned alternately by a quarter-turn.

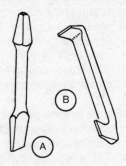

Fig. 2-27. A screwdriver bit (A); an offset screwdriver (B).

Hole-Making Tools

Holes are usually made in wood with bits that fit into a brace or other hand tool. Basically, similar bits have been developed for power drilling, but only in the smaller sizes are the bits interchangeable between power and hand tools.

Very small holes for starting screws may be made with a simple *awl*; but slightly larger holes are made with a *bradawl*

(Fig. 2-28A), a steel rod sharpened to a chisel point and fitted with a handle. It is pushed in with the edge placed across the line of the grain to sever wood fibers. The hole it makes provides a good grip for screws because no wood has been removed; the joint that results (for a thin screw) is tighter than if a hole were drilled.

Another tool with a purpose similar to the bradawl is the gimlet, which may be a twist (Fig. 2-28B) or shell (Fig. 2-28C) configuration. Both work with a bursting action: they penetrate and may split wood. But the cutting action of the shell gimlet's edge reduces this risk. However, today it is probably better to rely on Morse-pattern twist drills for screw holes larger than those made with a bradawl.

For holes up to about a quarter-inch wide, metalworking Morse-pattern twist drills (Fig. 2-28D) are also suitable. The hole produced may be rough, but as it most likely will be intended for a nail or screw, it doesn't matter. For more precisely cut small holes, there are bits (similar to larger ones) that cut holes cleanly down to about $^3/_{16}$ inch; but they are rare.

A hand drill or wheel brace (Fig. 2-28E) is usually used for driving small Morse-pattern drill bits by hand. The bit has a parallel shank that fits into a three-jawed chuck. In its simplest form, the jaws are held apart by springs. Turning the chuck causes the jaws' tapered outsides to be pressed in by the matching taper of the casing; the jaws move evenly to the center and grip the parallel shank of the bit (whatever its size). There are many variations on the hand drill. Most have a handle at the end, which may house a supply of bits, and a second removable handle at the side. Larger drills (*breast* drills) have a shaped top to lean against for applying pressure when drilling horizontally.

Because the Morse-pattern drill bit does not have a long center spur to locate it when starting, it is usually pushed into a dent made by an awl or a center punch (Fig. 2-28F) sharpened to a point more acute than would be used on metal.

A brace (Fig. 2-28G) is used to drive a bit for larger holes. It is possible to get different sizes, each with its crank moving through different amounts of sweep (Fig. 2-29). A long sweep provides greater leverage, but a short sweep has a quicker action. The knob at the head takes hand pressure and should be fitted with ball bearings, or at least a single ball, to take the thrust. Friction in turning the handle is not great, so it can have a plain bearing, but it should have a provision for oiling.

There are several variations on the design details of the chuck, but nearly all brace chucks have two jaws grooved to take the tapered, square end of a bit. There is not much tolerance; bits intended for all hole sizes have very similar (square) ends. The chuck is made to grip a bit by turning it by hand. Many chucks have flat surfaces (*flats*) on the outside so a wrench or vise can be used to further tighten them; but because a square-ended bit resists turning, it does not require the great tightening sometimes needed with round metalworking drill shanks.

A simple brace has a chuck fixed rigidly to it, but some are made with a simple ratchet mechanism, usually with two pawls and a ratchet wheel above the chuck. A collar is turned to lift one pawl or allow both to engage, giving a ratchet action in either direction, as well as position.

The basic woodworking drill bit, on which most of the others are based, is the center bit. It has been largely superseded by others, but an understanding of its operation may help in appreciating the action of the modern bit. The center bit (Fig. 2-28H) has a central point that extends further than its other parts. It enters the wood first and the bit revolves on it. Next in length is the spur, sharpened on the inside to cut an outline of the hole as it rotates (clockwise). The distance from the outside of the spur to the central point controls the size of the hole. The cutter, which doesn't work as deeply as the spur, has an outside radius very slightly less than that of the spur. Its purpose is to remove waste from the core of the hole after the spur cuts the outline.

The plain center bit, made in sizes from about a quarter-inch to 2 inches in ⅛-inch steps, penetrates to a depth dependent on the pressure provided by the brace operator. Larger bits used on hard woods could require some strenuous work. An improved version of the center bit has a center screw (Fig. 2-28I), as well as an improved shape, to follow the outline of the hole. Like the basic center bit, it is suitable for shallow holes; but when great depth is needed, the bit is liable to wander if the operator fails to maintain a straight push, or when there are inequalities in the grain structure.

Auger bits are for deeper holes. They are equally suitable for shallow holes; so except for their greater cost, they are preferred. Some have an eye to take a wooden handle; most are very long, and are used for the deep drilling needed in boatbuilding and other specialized work. Normal woodworking auger bits have square ends to fit brace chucks.

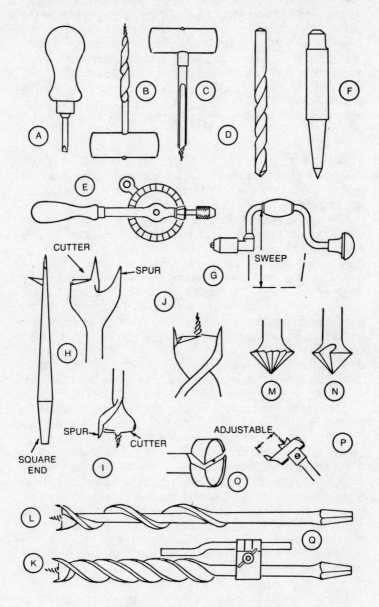

Fig. 2-28. The family of hole-making tools.

An auger bit has a twisted, parallel body to serve as a guide in keeping it straight as it penetrates deeply into wood. The twist also clears waste wood as it cuts. Some auger bits have a single spur and cutter, but usually there are two spurs, with the cutter built in behind them (Fig. 2-28J).

All auger bits have a center screw. They have been made with various thread steepness to give different entry speeds, but only an average steepness is available today. There are several types of *twist* available. A single twist is unlikely to be found, although augers were at one time made this way to clear waste wood very cleanly; but the bit lacked stiffness. The more usual auger bit with a double twist is called a *Jennings* bit (Fig. 2-28K). Another type, which is stiffer and clears waste via broad grooves, is the solid-center or *Irwin* bit (Fig. 2-28L). It comes in sizes from $3/16$ inch to 1½ inches. Normally, only a standard length is available; the length increases with the diameter, a half-inch bit being able to drill about 6 inches deep. Sometimes extra long bits are obtainable. Shorter bits may be described as *dowel* bits—from their use in making holes for dowels. Extensions are made that fit into a brace chuck, the bit fitting into a small chuck on the end of the extension, allowing greater reach; but deep drilling is only possible when the hole is larger in diameter than the extension chuck.

At one time *shell* or *spoon* bits were used extensively. They were like pieces of a gouge made to fit a brace, but some had ends like gimlets. In small sizes, they were a less successful means of doing the same job as a Morse-pattern drill, which has taken their place.

Many small holes have to be countersunk for screw heads or to take the sharpness off the edge of the hole. Countersinking bits are made to fit wheel and sweep braces. Because countersinking is done best at a low speed, a bit turned by hand can produce a better result than one used in a power drill. The usual countersink bit has a *rosehead* (Fig. 2-28M), consisting of many cutters meeting at a point. It scrapes, but is usually satisfactory.

The snailhorn type (Fig. 2-28N), with a single cutting edge, makes a cleaner cut in some woods. A rosehead bit will also countersink brass, if it is necessary to deal with screw holes in hinges or other metal fittings; but there are flat countersinking bits for metal that are made to fit braces. The angle is usually set to match the head of a screw, but alternatives are available. Combination drills that tap and clear a hole for a screw of a particular size, and countersink it in one action, are only suitable for power drills.

Nearly all woodworking drills have a long point. If a hole is to be only partially drilled through wood, and its bottom is to remain visible, the mark left by the center point may be undesirable. The bit for drilling a flat-bottomed hole without a mark in the center is the *Forstner* bit. It ranges in size from ⅜ inch to 2 inches in $1/16$ inch steps, and differs from other bits by being controlled by an outer rim that follows almost completely the circumference of the hole (Fig. 2-28O). A Forstner bit works well in end grain, a place where a screw center bit may be difficult to control; it can't be deflected by knots and will drill a larger hole over a smaller one. It can also be used at the edge of a piece of wood to drill only part of a hole.

There are expanding bits that allow one bit to be used for many hole sizes. Variations of the center screw bit are not suitable for deep drilling. The center screw is followed by a spur and cutter that make a small hole of a fixed size; but above it is an adjustable, combined spur-and-cutter that can be moved across the bit and locked with a screw. The cutter (Fig. 2-28P) allows a limited range of hole sizes to be drilled, but there is a range of cutters available. One bit size, along with the standard cutters provided, will make holes between ½ inch and 1½ inches wide, while a larger bit will make holes between ⅞ inch and 3 inches. (Extra cutters allow up to 6 inch holes to be made in thin material.)

A depth gage may be clamped onto a bit with a parallel shank; some have a plain end (Fig. 2-28Q), while others have a ball. A simple depth gage is a piece of wood with a hole that slips over the bit; or it may be two pieces screwed to each other at the depth limit on opposite sides of the bit.

Holding Devices

The first requirement for woodwork, other than the roughest, crudest outdoor carpentery, is a bench. It should be rigid enough to withstand stress in any direction, and its parts should all be strong enough to resist hammering and heavy knocks. The top should be flat and long enough to accommodate most work. The height should be convenient to the individual worker, about 2½ feet is about right. If there is any variation, slightly too low is generally better than too high—the legs can be put up on blocks if necessary. If the top is too high, it may put more strain on your arms when sawing or planing.

The bench will be stronger and more convenient to use if there is a wide board in the front, forming an *apron* (Fig. 2-29A). The whole top does not have to be thick; the rear part can be made of thinner boards to form a recess for tools. Ideally, the front of the top, and the apron, should be made of a close-grained hardwood, parts glued and screwed together at a right angle. All screw heads should be sunk below the surface and plugged, so that no metal is near the surface to damage the cutting edges of tools. The top should be stiff enough to take blows without bending or rebounding. A thickness of 2 inches is reasonable; supporting cross pieces below could be placed at about 2 foot intervals.

There will often be a need for a sawhorse (Fig. 2-29B), at a height where work can be sawed while being held with a knee. Two are convenient for supporting parts being assembled, as

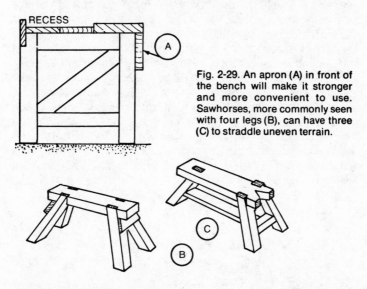

Fig. 2-29. An apron (A) in front of the bench will make it stronger and more convenient to use. Sawhorses, more commonly seen with four legs (B), can have three (C) to straddle uneven terrain.

when building a door. A height of 1½ feet is about right. As well as the traditional form, there are special types for several other purposes, such as for clamping or drilling support. Some will fold flat for transport or storage. Another idea to consider is having one with only three legs (Fig. 2-29C), particularly for work to be done on an uneven surface. A tripod will stand without wobbling on any surface.

A vise is an important piece of bench equipment. It is normally mounted toward the left-hand side of the front, because most workers use tools toward that side. (Even left-handed people usually work a plane to the left, the same way right-handed workers do.) At one time all woodworking vises were made entirely of wood. Commonly, they had a massive hardwood screw and a board in front that was movable and locked in incremental positions with pegs. Although such vises may be considered obsolete, there are still high-quality benches with built-in wood-screw vises made in Scandinavia.

Parallel-action metal vises are more common. Some have a quick-release lever so they can be adjusted quickly; it is usually a trigger located next to the handle, which allows the front jaw to be moved in or out without turning the handle. In any case, the screw has a strong coarsely pitched thread. Most vises are turned with a sliding drop-handle.

A vise should be mounted so the top edges of its jaws are well below the top of the bench (Fig. 2-30). The rear jaw should be set far enough into the apron for the jaw to be covered by wood. Hardwood inner jaws will prevent the metal jaws from coming into contact with the work or the edges of cutting tools. The fixing bolts going through the bench top should have countersunk heads covered by wood plugs. The wood jaws should be attached with screws, so they can be removed and renewed as necessary. After a lot of use, the top of the bench may need planing to remove cuts and dents to present a true surface on which accurate work can be done. The metal jaws should be low enough so that ample wood remains above them after planing.

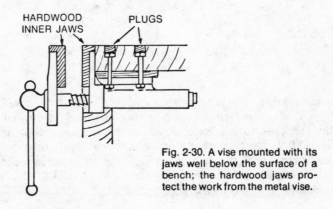

HARDWOOD INNER JAWS   PLUGS

Fig. 2-30. A vise mounted with its jaws well below the surface of a bench; the hardwood jaws protect the work from the metal vise.

For temporary use there are clamp-on vises that allow a work surface to be set up on any convenient board; but they are always less satisfactory than permanently mounted types. Some vises are mounted with their jaws at least partially above the bench surface, but this limits their use; a flushing-fitting vise is always better for woodworking. An engineer's vise, which mounts atop a bench, may be adapted to woodworking by covering its steel jaws with wood, but this is best regarded as only a temporary expedient. In woodworking there are occasions when a small amount of metalwork has to be done—altering hinges, enlarging holes, sawing and filing metal fittings. A metalworking vise is better than a woodworking one when it is mounted higher on a strong T-shaped assembly (Fig. 2-31), gripped in the woodworking vise; if there is no permanent metalworking bench in the home workshop, this is a good way to go.

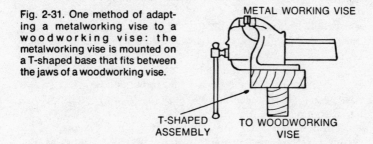

Fig. 2-31. One method of adapting a metalworking vise to a woodworking vise: the metalworking vise is mounted on a T-shaped base that fits between the jaws of a woodworking vise.

METAL WORKING VISE

T-SHAPED ASSEMBLY

TO WOODWORKING VISE

After the vise, the next holding device for the bench is some sort of *stop*, usually placed to the left side of the bench, against which work can be pressed when being planed. The simplest is just a piece of wood screwed down across the bench top (Fig. 2-32A). However, because a completely flat bench top is occasionally required, a retracting stop (Fig. 2-32B) is better. One can be made from a block of hardwood put through a hole in the bench top, preferably against a leg. It may be raised and lowered by sliding it, like the action found on similar, under-bench devices. A wing nut and washer, working in a slot (Fig. 2-33A), is a simple version of the control. Surface-mounted bench stops take the form of a metal jaw with teeth (Fig. 2-33B) that can be raised or lowered over a spring by turning a screw. They have the disadvantage of presenting exposed metal on the bench top, but they are commonly used and are generally satisfactory.

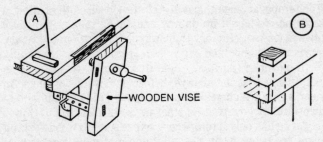

Fig. 2-32. A bench stop can be permanently exposed (A) or retractable (B).

Another useful tool often called a *holdfast*, holds wood on the surface of the bench, either with its end against the stop or independent of it. In its simplest form it is a fairly strong rod with a screw-operated lever at the top (Fig. 2-33C). In use, the rod goes through a hole in the bench top; then, as the screw is tightened and the jaw presses on the work, the sideways thrust on the rod makes it grip. The holdfast puts considerable strain on the hole in the bench; the grip is much better if the wood is thick. Using a holdfast too often can wear the edge of the hole away, marring the accuracy of the bench top.

There are improved holdfasts with notched rods that engage special metal collars set into the bench top. They have a surer grip, but the collars leave metal exposed on the bench top. Two holdfasts are convenient, if they are provided with several positions. The plain rod holdfast can be improved by setting a strong metal tube into the bench as a lining for the hole, with its top edge kept below the surface (Fig. 2-33D). Because the swivel shoe on the end of the arm usually has a

Fig. 2-33. A wing nut and washer, working in a slot (A), is a simple control to raise and lower a bench stop; (B) a bench stop consisting of a retractable, hinged jaw. The rod part of a **holdfast** (C) can't wear out its hole in the bench top if the hole is lined with a metal tube (D).

rough surface to grip, a piece of scrap wood should be put below it to avoid marring a finished surface.

Bench hooks get their share of use in the shop. Although they may also be described as sawing boards, they are used for many things besides holding work to be cut with a backsaw. A bench hook will fit in a vise, but for most work it is merely pressed against the side of the bench. Some workers favor using two narrow hooks cut from solid wood (Fig. 2-34A) and spaced apart to suit the length of wood being cut. It is more usual to have a general-purpose bench hook about 5 inches wide, but a second one would be valuable for longer work. The solitary bench hook has two crossbars screwed or doweled in place. Because there is a risk of a saw or chisel slipping over the bars, glued dowels are better than exposed screw heads.

The crossbars may be flush with the sides of the bench hook, but this could cause a saw to drop through a cut and damage the bench top. It is better to indent the crossbar slightly from the body of the bench hook (Fig. 2-34B); that way, the saw will only damage the bench hook itself—which is easier to replace than the bench top. If one crossbar is indented to allow for sawing on the right or left, the other may be flush; this is sometimes useful for using a block plane on edge to make the end of a piece of wood true. It is best to regard bench hooks as expendable. Let them take cuts and knocks, then make new ones.

Besides the simple bench stops described thus far, it is sometimes useful to have a device to hold thin pieces of wood on edge: a thick block of wood with a *V*-shaped notch (Fig.

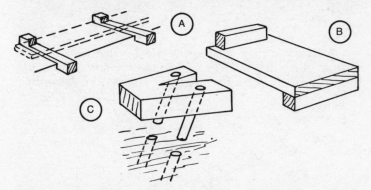

Fig. 2-35. Simple bench hooks may be used in pairs (A), or a single benchhook may be used (B); one version is a thick V-shaped piece of wood (C) supported on dowels that are inserted in holes in the bench.

2-34C). Supported on two dowels, preferably sloping, it can be lifted out of its holes when not required. Another version is two interlocking jaws (Fig. 2-35) that press on the sides of the wood, as well as holding it in the V where their teeth meet.

WORK ENTERS
HERE

Fig. 2-35. This bench stop, consisting of two interlocking jaws, holds a piece of wood against the V of the enmeshed jaw teeth.

Something providing a simple wedge action (Fig. 2-36A) can be used on the side of the bench to support wood on edge. An improvement on this is two wedges, one attached to the bench to form a *V*-shaped slot for the other to fit into (Fig. 2-36B).

Fig. 2-36. Work can be wedged into the simple affair shown at A; the addition of a movable wedge (B) is an improvement.

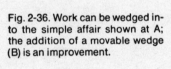

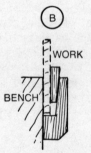

A trough can be made with two beveled pieces and a built-in stop (Fig. 2-37) to hold square or round pieces for planing. If it is made deeper than it is wide, it can be gripped in

PIECES TO PROVIDE
ADDITIONAL LENGTH

Fig. 2-37. A trough for holding square or round pieces of wood to be planed.

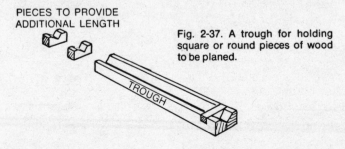

TROUGH

a vise. If it is to be used atop the bench against a stop, it should be shallow. To support pieces of wood longer than the trough, small additional matching blocks can be made to make up for the overhang.

A bench hook can have a 45° cut in the crossbar to serve as a saw guide when cutting miters (edges to be fitted together to form a joint) by hand; but a separate *miter block* (Fig. 2-38A) has a longer supporting surface. A miter box (Fig. 2-38B) is even better, as it gives more support to a saw. Some have metal saw guides, and there are elaborate miter-sawing devices in which the saw is held with more precision; but they are more appropriate for the craftsman who makes picture frames regularly than for the amateur who only occasionally cuts miters.

Fig. 2-38. A bench stop can have cuts (A) to guide a saw in making miters, but a miter box (B) will support a greater length.

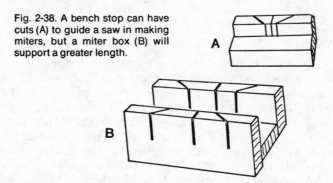

Getting a truly square edge on a piece of wood by planing calls for skill and experience. A *shooting* (i.e., planing) board (Fig. 2-39A) is a device on which a square-edged plane is used on its side, while the work is held against a stop. Normally, the rebate (the rise in the step formed by the parts) in the shooting board is placed so the work is cut by the middle of the blade. There is some advantage in making a slight slicing cut, so the board may be made with the bed (on which the work rests) raised at one end (Fig. 2-39B).

A shooting board that guides a slicing cut across the grain is particularly effective if the plane has a low angle and is precisely set. There is an advantage in having a fence (Fig. 2-39C) on the shooting board for very narrow pieces of wood. It takes the pressure of the plane, while preventing the wood from buckling as it is held with one hand (possibly with another piece of wood held over a thin piece to be cut).

Fig. 2-39. **A shooting** (planing) board (A) can have its bed raised at one end (B) to make the plane give a slicing cut; a movable fence (C) allows the planing of very narrow pieces of wood.

Miters can be planed using an appropriately shaped block attached to its own shooting board, or one with dowels to fit a plain shooting board. Because wood has to be planed with the grain, there has to be a provision for working in both directions (Fig. 2-40A). Another shooting board, intended for wide miters, is often called a *donkey's ear* (Fig. 2-40B). It is used for such things as corner joints in mitered boxes. It works like other shooting boards, but is supported at an angle of 45°.

A large shooting board may be used flat on the bench top; a smaller one can have a block underneath to be held in a vise, allowing work to be done along the length of the bench as well as across it.

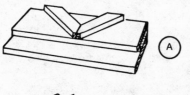

Fig. 2-40. A shooting board (A) that allows the planing of wood with its grain at an angle; a **donkey's ear** (B) is used to plane a mitered edge. A notched sawing board (C) clamped to, and extending over, the edge of the bench is useful as a support for wood to be cut with a fretsaw.

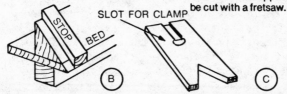

When using a fretsaw or any very fine piercing saw, it is best to have guide marks on the work, facing up, so the accuracy of the cut can be observed. In this case, the work can be placed on a sawing board with a V-shaped notch (Fig. 2-40C) projecting over the side of the bench. It may have a slot to take a flat clamp, or it may have a block under the back to be held in a vise.

Some of the devices for holding wood being worked can also be used for holding parts being glued, or to hold them together while screws or other fasteners are being installed. There are many other clamping devices, some improvisations to suit particular circumstances.

The basic C clamp (Fig. 2-41A) has a strong frame to resist force. Its screw is often topped by a shoe that swivels on a ball to accommodate parts that are not parallel. Force is applied by turning a handle at the end, which is usually a rod or a paddle-like thumb piece. These clamps are made in many sizes, beginning with a 2 inch capacity; having as big a variety as possible is always useful.

There are other clamps that work on the same principle. One has a head that slides along a bar (Fig. 2-41B). This tool can take the place of many C clamp sizes. Some are rather light in construction and are excellent within their limits; but C clamps are generally more suitable for heavy work. Some lighter clamps with plain round handles, although adequate for their intended scope, are difficult to tighten for greatest pressure.

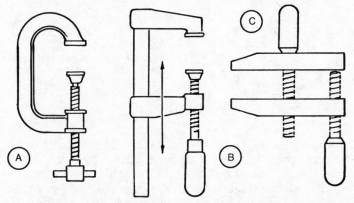

Fig. 2-41. The C clamp (A) is better suited to heavy work than one with a sliding bar (B); another type, with two opposing screws (C), provides pressure over a greater area.

Another type of clamp—which may be wood, metal, or plastic—uses two opposing screws, one to draw the jaws together, the other to push their ends apart (Fig. 2-41C). Their jaws may be quite long, having a reach greater than that of *C* clamps of comparable size. Their design permits their jaws to provide pressure over a greater area than a *C* clamp can.

For reaching further than a *C* clamp, there are several forms of *bar clamps* (Fig. 2-42A), sometimes called *sash clamps*, from their original use for pulling the parts of sash windows together. The important thing is the stiffness of the bar. The moveable jaw can be located in many ways, but a simple form uses a tapered steel peg that can be put through any of a series of holes. The other jaw has a range of movement similar to that of a comparable *C* clamp.

Jaws, generally similar in form to those of the clamps described, can be obtained as separate items to be attached to the edge of a board (Fig. 2-42B), giving almost any capacity you could want. Within their capacity, bar clamps are the best tools for pulling together such things as a number of boards being glued. For this sort of work they are normally used in pairs.

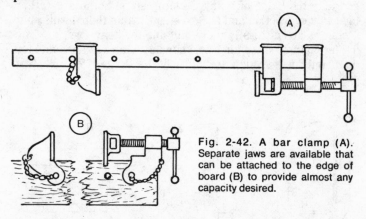

Fig. 2-42. A bar clamp (A). Separate jaws are available that can be attached to the edge of board (B) to provide almost any capacity desired.

Clamps can take several special forms. Miter clamps have two screws used to bring together two parts of a picture frame being glued and nailed. *C* clamps made with an extra screw through the center of the back give extra sideways pressure.

Wedges are especially useful for applying pressure. A wedge can be driven against a peg or temporary block, screwed onto the bench, to press a lamination around a form

(Fig. 2-43A), or to force parts together. Folding wedges (Fig. 2-43B) are two similar wedges driven against each other. Their movement may be slight, but the pressure they can exert is considerable.

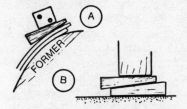

Fig. 2-43. A single wedge can be used to hold laminations against a former (A); used in pairs, they are **folding** wedges (B).

Wedges can be used to act as a bar clamp. Blocks secured to the bench, or a strong strip of wood, can act to take the pressure (Fig. 2-44A). Another clamping device for this sort of work has two bars that pivot on screws, the assembly being only slightly wider than the work; tapping from the side applies pressure (Fig. 2-44B).

Two strong boards loosely bolted together, with a wedge driven between them (Fig. 2-44C), can be used when pressure has to be applied to work from a distance.

The *joiner's dog* is a simple tool that is not as widely used as it should be. It is made of steel and has legs tapered on the insides (Fig. 2-44D). The device, when driven into two adjoining pieces of wood, draws them together, making a very effective gluing clamp.

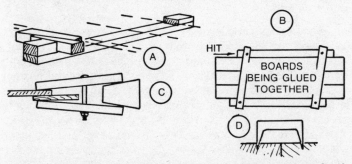

Fig. 2-44. The function of the bar clamp can be taken by wedges. A collapsible framework is good for applying a wedge action to boards being glued together (B). For a longer reach, two boards loosely bolted together and forced apart at one end with a wedge (C) will do the trick. The **joiner's dog** is a simple yet effective device for clamping together boards being glued.

Rope can also be used for clamping. A wedge may be driven under a loop to apply pressure (Fig. 2-45A), or the loop can be twisted into a Spanish windlass (Fig. 2-45B) for the same effect. A four-sided assembly can be held together with a rope tied around it. (Use wood blocks at the corners.) With the rope tied as tightly as possible, wedges are driven under it (around the sides) to apply pressure (Fig. 2-45C).

Occasionally, parts to be brought together do not have external surfaces that will take a clamp. However, it may be possible to make pieces shaped to fit the work, having outside surfaces that *can* be clamped (Fig. 2-45D). If there is a taper (as in a miter), it may be necessary to glue on blocks (Fig. 2-45E) which can be cut off after the joint is completed.

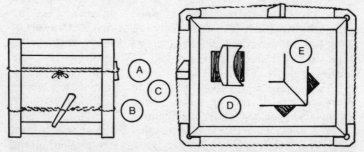

Fig. 2-45. A wedge can be forced under a loop (A) to provide clamping pressure, as well as one used to twist a loop (B). A mitered framework (C) being held together with a rope and wedges while the glue sets. Parts whose shape won't permit the direct application of a clamp can be held between blocks (D). For some situations, clamping blocks have to be glued on (E) and cut off later.

Fortunately, modern glues do not require the tight clamping for long periods that was necessary with older, natural glues; now it is sufficient to bring the surfaces into contact without great pressure. However, because there is not much tolerance in the degree of contact, accurate clamping is essential. Holding devices, for keeping a job rigid while freeing hands to do the work, and for drawing the parts of an assembly together, are valuable in the workshop; a large variety will be assembled by a really enthusiastic woodworker.

MEASURING AND MARKING

Measuring means comparing one thing to another. For convenience in transferring measurements, we use rules marked in feet and inches, or meters and centimeters. The most accurate way of comparing parts is to put one against the other, thus eliminating the intermediate use of a rule, and removing one possible source of error. In practice, many parts can be tested in this way. For example, a gage may be set to the width of a chisel, rather than using some arbitrary measurement to find the size of the cut.

When a number of parts of an assembly have to conform to certain standards of length, or when the positions of joints and the size of shelves or other things must match, it is safer to use the edge of a piece of wood marked with the key positions to mark out the parts of the job, rather than measuring each separately with a rule.

Because wood cannot be worked to the tolerances metal can, measuring devices that work to fine limits are unnecessary for woodworking. Parts must fit, of course, but the natural expansion and contraction of wood will cancel any attempt at engineering exactness. For most woodworking purposes, there is no need for a rule (or other measuring device) with divisions any smaller than $1/16$ inch or 1 millimeter.

Woodworkers in the past used wooden rules, most of which folded for convenience in carrying; but joints complicated accurate marking in their vicinity. Steel rules are better.

A 1 foot steel rule without joints, and with clear markings, will handle most measuring done on the bench, and will serve as a straightedge for drawing lines and testing surfaces. A 2 foot rule without joints is similarly useful on the bench, but is too long to carry around. For greater measurements, the most useful tool is a steel tape, specifically the type with a hooked end, that springs into a case. Its curved cross section keeps it straight over a reasonable length. A 10 foot tape will cover most needs. A folding rule could be used for outside work, but a steel rule will handle most things.

Besides having a steel rule as a straightedge, it is worthwhile making a longer one from a well-seasoned piece of straight-grained hardwood; given a beveled edge and clearly marked, it won't be confused with any ordinary lumber lying around.

Marking and testing right angles is important; the basic tool for it is a try square (Fig. 2-46A), they ranging in size from 4 to 12 inches (blade length). The traditional square had a wooden (rosewood or ebony) stock, a brass face, and a steel blade; but the less attractive all steel square is likely to remain more accurate. Measurements taken along the edge of the blade may be useful. Some squares have the end of their stock cut at a 45° angle, making them useful for marking miters (Fig. 2-46B), but it is better to have a separate miter square (Fig. 2-46C) for the specific task.

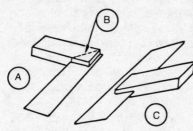

Fig. 2-46. The try square (A) may have the end of its stock cut at a 45° angle (B) for work on miters, but a miter square (C) is better for the job.

A combination square (Fig. 2-47A), in which a square and miter head slides to any position on a rule, can take the place of a try square. Some have a spirit level and a small, pointed scriber (or awl). It is also possible to get a *center head* to fit a rule for drawing lines at a right angle to a curved edge (Fig. 2-47B), or for finding the center of a circular part by placing it at two positions around the circumference and drawing two intersection lines; the center of the circle is where they cross (Fig. 2-47C).

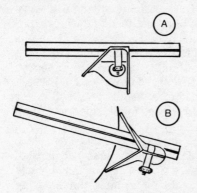
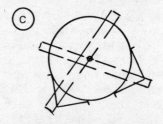

Fig. 2-47. A combination square (A); a sliding head (B) attached to a rule will prove useful in locating the center of a circular part (C).

It is sometimes necessary to mark or transfer other angles, or miters, with a *sliding bevel* (Fig. 2-48) that can be locked in position in several ways. The simplest is with a screw, which requires a screwdriver, or there may be a thumb nut (to turn by hand). Blade sizes range from 6 to 12 inches. A

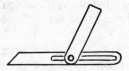

Fig. 2-48. A sliding bevel is used to mark or transfer other than right angles.

slot allows adjustment for getting into restricted places, and for folding the blade into the stock when it is not in use.

There will be occasions when a larger try square or adjustable bevel is needed; some craftsmen make their own from wood. Small triangles or set squares are rarely needed; but for marking out right angles on large panels, it is useful to have a plywood set square with a long edge (about 4 feet). A right angle can be derived by the *3:4:5 method*. A triangle with sides in these proportions must have, by virtue of the Pythagorean theorem, a right angle between the sides 3 and 4 *units* long; the units could be feet, meters, whatever—it doesn't really matter. To use this method, first mark a baseline with a straightedge. From one end use a steel tape with a pencil held against the 3 foot mark to draw a short arc (Fig. 2-49). From the other end of the line, measure 5 feet to a point on the arc. A line drawn from the first end through the 5 foot mark will be at a right angle to the baseline.

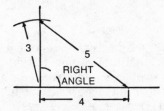

Fig. 2-49. The 3:4:5 method of deriving a right angle.

A *T*-square is really a drafting tool not normally used in woodworking. One version of the *T*-square is used by glaziers. Either version may have woodworking applications, but need not be bought. The *L*-shaped squares used for roofing or framing are commonly 1½ by 2 feet. Its corner, an accurate right angle, may be used for marking and testing angles; but the original purpose of the square was to use it with scales and tables to obtain angles when setting out rafters in roofing.

Although most marking on wood is done with a pencil, the point will wear away quickly unless it is sharpened to a chisel-like end and used on edge. Special woodworking pencils with broad leads have been made, but they are difficult to find. Accurate marking, particularly where there are to be cuts, can be done better with a knife or an awl.

A large pair of steel dividers can be used for scratching circles and transferring measurements. But engineer's dividers are not stiff and strong enough. The dividers for woodworking are called wing compasses (Fig. 2-50A). The wing provides a firm lock; some have a fine-adjustment screw. The size range is from 6 to 18 inches, 10 inches being the most useful size to have.

A pair of trammel heads (Fig. 2-50B) will span the length of a piece wood, forming a beam compass adjustable to any reasonable length; but they may be difficult to obtain new. Some have a provision for fitting a pencil to one head.

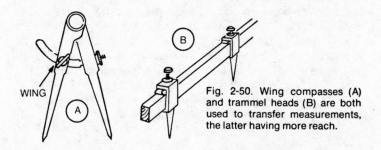

WING

Fig. 2-50. Wing compasses (A) and trammel heads (B) are both used to transfer measurements, the latter having more reach.

In some constructional work it is necessary to get parts absolutely horizontal or vertical. The tool for testing a horizontal surface is the spirit level. When the bubble in its liquid-filled tube comes to rest between the marks on the tube (Fig. 2-51A), the base of the level is horizontal. A long level will be more accurate than a short one in testing a surface for unevenness.

For testing a vertical surface, many levels have another tube going the short way (Fig. 2-51B). A spirit level can be incorporated into a combination square. A plumb line, a weight cord, is a simpler tool for the same purpose. For some things it is more useful. For example, the *plumb bob* (Fig. 2-51C) at the end will locate one point below another.

There are many occasions when a line has to be marked parallel to an edge. The usual tool for scratching such a line is a *marking gage*, made either of metal or wood. Basically, it has a stock with a spur to scratch a line, which slides on a stem

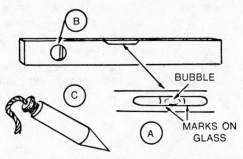

Fig. 2-51. Some levels have two glass tubes (A), one going the short way across the level (B) to see if vertical parts are perpendicular to the horizontal. A plumb line, a line weighted with a **plumb bob** (C), has the same basic function as a level, but is more versatile.

(Fig. 2-52A). The stock can be locked in any position on the stem, usually with a thumbscrew. In use the gage is held with one hand over the stock and tilted as it is pushed forward (Fig. 2-52B). A variation has a rotating cutting wheel on the end (Fig. 2-52C); another has a knife instead of a point (Fig. 2-52D). The cutting gage is used instead of a marking gage for gaging across the grain. It can also be used for cutting veneer into strips, for making a more positive cut than a marking gage would along a difficult grain, or for starting a rebate.

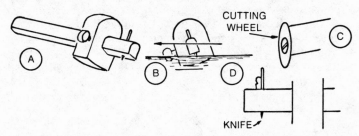

Fig. 2-52. A marking gage (A) is pushed forward at an angle (B) to transfer measurements. Some marking gages have a cutting wheel (C); others, a knife (D) instead of a point.

A mortise gage differs from a marking gage in that it has two spurs (Fig. 2-53A). The second one is on a slide that may be set by hand or with a screw to vary the distance between the spurs for marking the widths of mortises and tenons—or anywhere else parallel lines have to be marked. The screw in the stock is tightened to lock the stock and slide.

The panel gage (Fig. 2-53B) cannot be bought; it has to be made. It is used on plywood panels. The long rebate under the stock (Fig. 2-53C) keeps the tool straight as it is used along an edge. There can be a screw in the stock, but a wedge is satisfactory to lock the parts in place. At one time a wedge with a retaining knob at the end was used to lock many tools, when precision screws were difficult to produce.

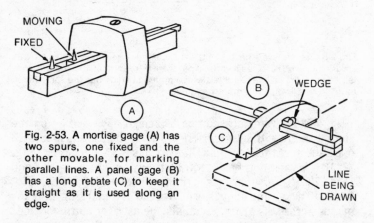

Fig. 2-53. A mortise gage (A) has two spurs, one fixed and the other movable, for marking parallel lines. A panel gage (B) has a long rebate (C) to keep it straight as it is used along an edge.

There are simple ways of marking a line parallel to an edge. Lines up to about an inch from an edge can be made with a pencil held between finger and thumb, while other fingers slide along the side of the wood, maintaining the distance; the accuracy of this method is adequate for many purposes. A thumb gage, a piece of wood with a rebate (Fig. 2-54A), does the same sort of thing. A notched piece (Fig. 2-54B) will mark a line for nails neatly where the overlap of a plywood top will later be planed level. Lines can also be drawn a set distance

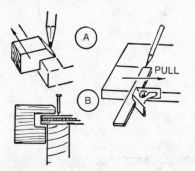

Fig. 2-54. One of the simplest tools for making lines parallel to an edge is the thumb gage (A); a similar device, often used to mark a line for nails, has a notch (B) to accommodate the overlap of the piece being nailed. Similarly, a pencil can be held against the end of a combination square (C) to draw lines parallel to an edge.

from an edge with a pencil held against a combination square adjusted for that distance (Fig. 2-54C).

Templates are used when curves or special shapes have to be repeated in several places. They are useful in turning (on a lathe) for such places as where a matching pattern has to be repeated on a set of stool legs, or when a decorative pattern on half a piece of wood has to be repeated on the other half. A template can be cut from cardboard or from thin plywood cut with a fretsaw. If it has to be used for a great many articles, it is better to cut it from sheet metal. Not only will a template give an outline, it will also carry over details (of diameters at various points) when used in turning (Fig. 2-55). Adjustable

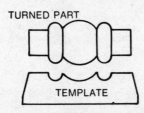

Fig. 2-55. A template is useful for transferring dimensions to a part being turned on a lathe.

templates, consisting of a large number of thin pieces of metal held together in a frame, can be locked after they have been pressed against the thing they have to match; but many are only suitable for patterns a few inches long.

3

Power Tools

For most of the time that man has practiced craftsmanship, he has had to depend almost entirely on the strength of his arms and legs to operate his tools. The power of horses and other animals has been harnessed to drive machinery, as well as that of water and wind. But the application of such power to woodwork has been mainly restricted to the conversion of logs to boards and other heavy preparatory work, rather than in the final working of wood to make furniture or other finished pieces. Even much of this heavy work was done by hand; two men and a pitsaw might have spent days cutting boards from a log.

Early machines were often hand-operated. The wheelwright had a crude lathe turned by a hand wheel. Craftsmen in India still provide power by using a bow the way the American Indian did to make fire (by friction). Treadle lathes may not be quite obsolete, but where they have not been abandoned completely, they have been converted to electric drive.

During the 19th century, the coming of steam power, followed by oil engines, made machine tools possible for many more things. But it was not until the coming of reliable, compact electric motors that craftsman-like woodworking really became mechanized. Today, the term *power tools* is nearly always applied to those that use electric power. Oil or steam power might still do the job, but their application to tools is unlikely to be found in the professional or amateur workshop.

Power tools are just that: tools with a motor to drive them. But machines of this sort cannot think for you. Although there are machines that can be set up to do a repetitive job, the power tools usually used by the woodworking craftsman require just as much skill in their control as do hand tools. The advantage of a power tool is mostly its ability to take over hard work and effort, letting the operator concentrate on skill and control. Some hand processes tire muscles, making the woodworker produce unsatisfactory work. But a power tool doesn't tire; it maintains the quality of its work as long it is properly controlled, until it is switched off.

Electricity can power woodworking machinery in several ways. One motor of sufficient power may drive a shaft, from which belts and pulleys transmit the power to various tools; by moving the belt from fast to slow pulleys, a machine can be brought into, or out of, use without switching the motor on or off. This means of transmission dates from the days of steam and oil engines, when one power source had to be used in this way to drive many machines. In many installations an electric motor could replace an other power source without the attendant equipment having to be altered. It is unlikely that a new installation of this type would be justified, unless circumstances dictated it—the unavailability of a suitable motor or shafting and other transmission equipment, for instance.

It is more usual for machines to be individually motorized. These are more convenient: the motor can be controlled by a switch, allowing cut-off to provide a guard against overloading; there are no belts or shafts to be protected; nothing has to be kept running except the machine being used. This means having a motor for each machine, but a motor that will take less power than the single one needed for multiple transmission.

There is an intermediate means of using electric power. Several machine tools are mounted stands, either built by the manufacturer or the user, which take their drive from a single motor included in the assembly. Such a unit has the advantage of compactness, a valuable attribute in a small shop. For instance, a table saw and planer may be attached to either a drill chuck or sanding disc. These could be driven by a motor through gears or belts, or they may be interconnected by shafts and clutches.

Sometimes difficulty with such an assembly is the way the size of the work, the room to move around in, or the convenience in handling is limited, usually by something for one process being too near another. However, many combination tools available for home workshops provide a greater number of power tool operations than might be impossible any other way.

The next step, the most popular and most sensible if the space is available and the cost is affordable, is to have each power tool driven by its own small electric motor, either built-in for direct-drive, or mounted close by, driving a short belt. In the days of flat belts it was necessary to have pulleys far apart to provide optimum grip, but now V-belts can be quite close.

Built-in motors make possibile two distinct types of tools: the tool may be mounted on a stand and the work brought to it; or it may be portable—taken to the work. An immovable machine is more suitable for heavy work; some, such as a lathe for turning, offer no advantage over portable tools. A compact electric motor is light; its weight and that of the tool it operates can easily be handled.

ELECTRIC DRILLS

The first power tool to get is an electric drill. Electric drilling is quicker and less laborious than using hand methods. In some cases the higher speed of the electric drill produces cleaner holes than a slow turning brace.

The size and weight of an electric drill is related to the capacity of its chuck. Although a large capacity chuck will take smaller drills, it is a clumsy tool for making small holes, often leading to broken drills and inaccurate work. For your first drill it is advisable to have a capacity no greater than ¼ inch. Most of these drills are easily handled and can be operated by one hand. Some cheap drills have hand-turned chucks. They do not provide a tight enough grip; a drill with a key-operated chuck is much better.

A key-operated chuck has a parallel action that will grip the cylindrical end of any drill from $1/16$ inch up to the capacity of the chuck. Without the key it is useless; the key should always be returned to the clip or other storage place provided on the drill. It may be kept on a string attached to the power cord.

The simplest electric drill has only one speed. Electric drills with variable speeds are related to metal-drilling rather than woodworking. Morse-pattern drills, up to the capacity of the chuck, are usually driven at the highest speed.

Woodworking bits up to about an inch in diameter may be obtained with ¼ inch shanks to fit electric drills. A high speed may be used with any bit size on any softwood, but it would be better for the life of the drill motor to reduce the speed for the larger bits.

Morse-pattern drills may be used to drill holes up to a quarter-inch. but will produce cleaner holes when power-driven than they do when used with a hand drill. Above this size. bits differ from similar ones used for hand drilling. For shallow holes or for drilling through thin wood such as plywood. there are spade bits (Fig. 3-1A). There are variations between makes. but none have spurs like those on brace bits; and the high speed gives a clean hole with a bit that would not work at low speeds. The variation shown in Fig. 3-1B, which is more like an auger bit. is better for deeper holes. There are versions of the spade bit in which different-sized ends fit one shaft.

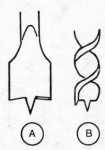

Fig. 3-1. Spade bits (A) are used to drill shallow holes; another bit, something like an auger bit (B), is better for deeper holes.

A hole saw is another means of making larger holes in thin material. It has a central bit held in a chuck and carries a circular block that will take several sizes of curved saws. The saws are like sections of metalworking hacksaw blades. Such a saw will make a clean hole through plywood up to ⅜ inch thick, or even twice that by carefully working from both sides.

Most smaller electric drills have a pistol-grip handle and trigger switch. usually with a catch to lock it *on.* Slightly larger drills may also be used with one hand, but one with a ½ inch capacity should have a provision for the second hand to support the weight. A larger multispeed drill should follow the purchase of your first ¼ inch drill, but there will probably be other power tools needed before this.

The life of the electric motor controls the real value of a drill. In this respect. you get what you pay for. A drill intended for industrial production work can cost three times as much as one sold to the home woodworker. Why? A cheap drill will do satisfactory work within its capacity, but only when used intermittently; however, everyone is tempted occasionally to overload a power tool—this is when a cheap tool suffers. Damage to a motor is permanent: usually nothing can be done economically to fix it. A drill that has suffered motor damage will have to be scrapped. A more expensive drill will have a motor that can withstand occasional misuse, even prolonged running.

A useful (and usually inexpensive) accessory is a stand that converts an electric drill into a *drill press* (Fig. 3-2). Most consist of a base with a pillar, and an assembly that can be locked anywhere on the pillar, to hold the drill while it is worked up and down with a lever. Using a drill mounted in this way helps in precision work. The assembly insures that holes

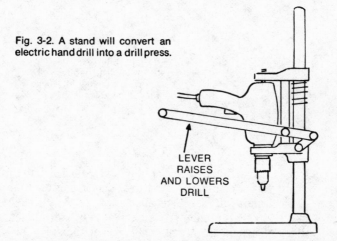

Fig. 3-2. A stand will convert an electric hand drill into a drill press.

LEVER
RAISES
AND LOWERS
DRILL

being drilled are perpendicular to the base, and therefore straight into the work. There are some things that can only be done in a drill press. A plug cutter (Fig. 3-3A) can be used to make plugs to go over screw heads; the plugs should be made from a scrap of the same wood to insure matching grain. Combination drills that will make the tapping and clearance holes for a screw, as well as its countersink (Fig. 3-3B), are only effective in a power drill; and they give a better result used in a drill press, rather than used freehand.

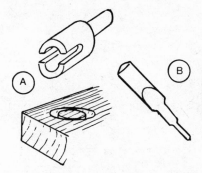

Fig. 3-3. A plug cutter (A) is used to cut the plugs that cover screw heads countersunk below the surface in holes made by a countersink bit (B).

One reason an electric drill is a good first power tool to have is that it can be used as a power source for doing other operations. The chuck will take the shafts of other things the same way it takes a drill bit. Tool makers have produced a very large range of things that can be powered by an electric drill. The idea of using one power source for a whole range of different tools seems attractive. In some ways it is—but only when the adaptation is simple and quick.

Some attachments for drills take a long time to set up. Others only perform with moderate success. Some will actually only do slowly what a hand tool could do faster. For example, a small planer driven by an electric drill may be a novelty, but the results do not compare in speed or finish with hand planing, or with the results of a more powerful electric planer. An attachment that performs satisfactorily in itself loses much of its value if it takes a long time to set up and, conversely, takes an equally long time to dismantle so the drill can be used normally again.

Attachments to electric drills have some value, but in the long run an enthusiastic woodworker would do better to have each of his electric tools self-powered. That way each does what it was designed to do, without the compromise of secondary functions for inadequate power. Most important, it is there, ready for use at any time, needing no lengthy setting up or the altering of something else.

Despite this, there are a few things used with an electric drill that are worth having. A sanding disk is one of them. It can take many forms, but basically it is a rubber disk mounted on a mandrel that fits in the chuck. An abrasive disk (Fig. 3-4A) goes over the rubber one and is usually held by a screw in the center. More rigid disks have a flexible joint drive, allowing them to remain flat on the work. A drum sander (Fig.

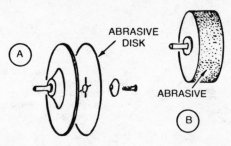

ABRASIVE
DISK

ABRASIVE

Fig. 3-4. A sanding disk (A) and drum sander (B).

3-4B) is a cylinder of abrasive paper or cloth wrapped around a sponge-rubber base. For some work the drill is hand-held; but a bench stand (Fig. 3-5A) will let you hold and manipulate small parts against the abrasive surface.

A polishing cover, made of a buffing material, may be fitted over a sanding disk. Metal cutters and hard mineral-coated disks can be used, instead of abrasive disks mounted on rubber. A mandrel with a threaded end can be used for holding other things. A grinding wheel (Fig. 3-5B) can be clamped between washers and used for tool sharpening, with the electric drill in its bench stand. A wire brush will fit the same mandrel. Several other rotary tools can be mounted, but they are mostly for working metal or plastics. A flexible driveshaft with a chuck on the end may be used on a drill for taking tools into spaces too small for the electric drill itself.

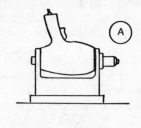

Fig. 3-5. Putting a drill in a bench stand (A) leaves both hands free to hold work against a grinding wheel (B).

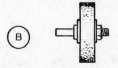

SAWING

Next to drilling, the job where power is valuable is sawing. A power saw (of reasonable size) allows you to use wood that

98

might otherwise be scrapped. It will accurately cut large pieces to the sizes required with little waste. Having the right sawing equipment makes it possible to buy wood in large sections and cut it as required, making you less dependent on the supplier. Instead of paying him to cut wood to the sizes you want, you can do it yourself. The right equipment lets you use the wood from dismantled and discarded furniture or other abandoned wooden articles.

A power saw may cut with a circular blade, as in a table saw (Fig. 3-6A); with a continuous band, as in a band saw (Fig. 3-6B); or with a short, stiff blade, as in a jig- or saber-saw. The circular saw is the one for making straight cuts. The others will make straight cuts, but they are more suited to curves. Where a band saw can be used, it will usually be more accurate than a saber saw; but it is restricted by the size of the area between the blade and its support: its *throat*. Circular saws and saber saws may be mounted permanently in one spot and the work brought to them, or they can be light and portable tools taken to the job.

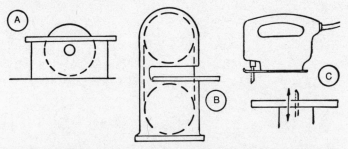

Fig. 3-6. The table saw (A) has a circular blade; the band saw (B), a continuous blade; the saber saw (C), a short, stiff blade.

A circular table saw mounts on a shaft, and is held by sturdy washers and a nut. Many circular saw blades, with teeth for various purposes, may be kept for use on one machine. However, general-purpose teeth for cutting both across and with the grain will be suitable for most jobs in the shop. Finer saws have teeth comparable to those of hand saws; except for power sawing, they have a slightly coarser pitch. (A high saw speed makes a smoother cut, despite the apparent coarseness of pitch.) Fine teeth tend to clog on some woods, particularly if the cut is deep. To aid in clearing sawdust, many saws have *gullets* (Fig. 3-7A) at intervals spaced around the blade to carry it away. Power saw teeth are arranged on the blade like those of handsaws, and are sharpened with a file like those of hand saws. Wear can be quite fast, so sharpening may have to be frequent. There have been experiments with various treatments of the teeth, including tipping them with hard substances to keep them sharp for a very long time. In some cases, sharpening could not be done by the user; the saw had to be returned to the manufacturer, or sent to a place with the special equipment needed. Although the prices of these special saws may be considerably higher than ordinary saws, they may be the only worthwhile way to get efficient cutting and long tooth life. Normally, any saw works best if it is the largest diameter that can be fitted to the power source. For some work, such as rebating, there may be an advantage in having a smaller diameter. Check the holes at the center of an old saw blade before buying a new one; they are not all a standard size.

A table saw may be used freehand, but often a guide is needed. Width is controlled by a fence (guide) on a bar going across the end of the table (Fig. 3-7B), which can be locked or

Fig. 3-7. The gullet (A) in a circular saw blade helps to clear away sawdust. The fence (B) on a table saw is a guide for controlling width. A saw cuts most efficiently when the blade projects as much as possible (C); on stationary machines, blade projection is increased by raising the table (D). With reduced projection, the saw will cut rebates (E). A guide for cutting angles (F).

swung out of the way when not required. Sometimes there is an extension on the side of the table for a fence mounted far enough away to control the cutting of panels.

A saw cuts most efficiently when it is given maximum projection through the table (Fig. 3-7C), cutting nearer vertically. Less projection is given in most stationary machines by raising the table (Fig. 3-7D); but in some machines the table is fixed and the saw assembly is lowered. With reduced projection the saw will cut rebates, tenons, or grooves (Fig 3-7E). Many machines tilt so table cuts can be made to give a beveled edge, but this is limited by the width of the gap in the table through which the saw passes.

Another type of guide is used for cutting angles. A slide, moving in a groove in the table, carries a guide (Fig. 3-7F) that can be set to any angle. The wood is held against it and slid against the saw. Various stops and guides can be made to fit temporarily to the table or to the main guides for cutting a quantity of identical pieces without having to measure each piece.

Because a rotating circular saw can be dangerous, it is important to provide ample protection. Usually, the part under the table is enclosed so the saw cannot accidentally be touched and to prevent clothing from catching in it. A riving knife (Fig. 3-8A) normally follows the saw through the wood above the table. The riving knife keeps the cut open when grain tends to close in the kerf (cut), causing friction on the sides of the saw. Because there are some cuts where it would be an obstruction, the riving knife is removable; but it is normally in position, its top possibly carrying a guard for the saw (Fig. 3-8B). When the saw is out of use, the guard drops down and completely covers it; then, when wood is pushed against the fence, the guard lifts

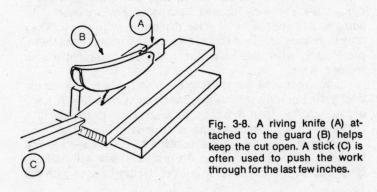

Fig. 3-8. A riving knife (A) attached to the guard (B) helps keep the cut open. A stick (C) is often used to push the work through for the last few inches.

and runs along it, without exposing teeth. The last part of the cut may be made by pulling instead of pushing, but most workers keep a push stick (Fig. 3-8C) to use instead of their hand for the last few inches.

A portable saw, in effect, is a table saw turned upside-down. It is possible to get a unit that will mount on an electric drill. But in the type with an integral motor (Fig. 3-9A), the motor is closer to the saw; because of this, balance is better and control is more positive. This type of saw is useful for cutting across boards that would be too large and awkward to take to a table saw. It can also be used for cutting pieces from a large sheet of plywood.

The depth of cut is adjustable by moving the small table the saw projects through; it may also be tilted. It is usually marked at the front so the line for the cut can be seen ahead of the saw. There is also a removable fence. By using these adjustments, cuts can be made at a controlled depth and distance from the edge. Making rebates and dadoes is possible, but when the wood can be taken to the table saw, greater precision will result. Cutting long lengths down to size is also done better by moving the wood over the saw. Some portable saws have a table that allows the tool to be inverted and mounted as a table saw.

The saw can also be mounted on a *radial* or *swing* arm. In effect, it gives a portable saw mechanical control. Instead of the saw's position being fixed, as in a table saw, the wood is fixed (for most processes), and the saw moves in a controlled manner. In its simplest form (Fig. 3-9B), the saw will cut the end of a board squarely to length. The saw and its motor slide on an arm that can be adjusted in height or angle, allowing the cut to be beveled across the board.

Machines that use circular blades are made in a great many sizes. For some industrial purposes they are enormous. Some saws powered by electric drills are quite small. They may have their uses, but there is a tendency to overwork them, particularly when they are blunt; this can wear out a drill motor quickly.

Saw size may be governed by the power supply in the home workshop. For most serious woodworking, it is best not to have a saw smaller than 8 inches in diameter; 10 inches is a reasonable size, the motor required to drive it, about 1 hp.

There are several ways a bench saw can be used to cut trenches, grooves, or dadoes. An ordinary saw will make a groove about $1/16$ inch wide in one cut. It may be used with the fence moved progressively to make several cuts until the required width is obtained. Dado heads can be used in place of a standard saw. In one type there are two thin saw blades for the sides, but they have deep gullets. Cutters of various thicknesses can be put between the side blades (Fig. 3-9C) to adjust the groove to the desired width. Such a set may make cuts from ⅛ to ¾ inch in width or more. Thick saws made for grooving are mostly used in industry, and can be any size up to 1½ inches.

Another way of making a ⅛ inch saw cut a dado (any size between the blade's thickness and 1½ inches) is to mount it as a wobble, eccentric, or drunk saw with variable wedge-sectioned washers at the center. In one type, the saw clamps between two central washers that rotate on a sleeve between two other beveled washers. The washers (Fig. 3-9D) are calibrated on their edges and can be turned to tilt the saw; as the saw turns eccentrically, it will cut a groove of any preset width.

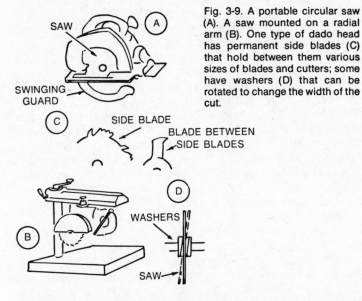

Fig. 3-9. A portable circular saw (A). A saw mounted on a radial arm (B). One type of dado head has permanent side blades (C) that hold between them various sizes of blades and cutters; some have washers (D) that can be rotated to change the width of the cut.

A band saw uses a continuous band of flexible steel with teeth on one edge. A common construction uses two wheels with rubber on the rims, the lower wheel driven by the motor. The capacity of the machine is usually described as the width of wood that can be accommodated (Fig. 3-10A). Some machines have three smaller wheels (Fig. 3-10B). The only way to get a much greater width without very large wheels is to use four wheels (Fig. 3-10C). A band saw blade may wear out, due to the teeth blunting, or it may break. In either case, it is usually better to discard the blade and replace it with a new one. (The risk of breakage is less with larger wheels.)

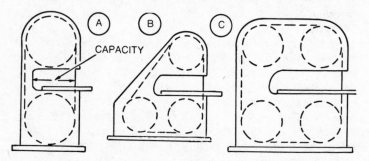

Fig. 3-10. A band saw can have two (A), three (B), or four (C) wheels.

Because a band saw is primarily intended for cutting curves, rather than for crosscutting or ripping along the grain, it is given general-purpose teeth. But there is a choice of blade pitch and width. A coarse tooth is better on thicker, softer woods. A fine tooth gives a cleaner edge. A narrow blade will follow tighter curves than will a wide one; however, it is more likely to break and more difficult to keep on the line when cutting a shallow, sweeping curve. A broader blade is also more suitable for the straightforward crosscutting that might be done with a backsaw. A 12 inch machine blade may range from about $^1/_{16}$ inch to a little more than ½ inch; there is a choice of tooth pitch and, sometimes, of the thickness of steel for each width. It is usual to keep a stock of blades that can be changed to suit the work.

Blades are described by their circumference and are usually bought welded to a size to suit the machine. With suitable welding or brazing equipment, it may be possible to buy saws in long lengths and cut and join them as needed; but care is needed to align the teeth accurately. (Making saw bands this way is rare.)

One or more of the wheels are used to adjust the saw's tension and to adjust for slight differences in circumference. There is also an adjustment to keep the wheels running in line and to keep the saw band running on its crown. The saw is supported by rollers and guides (above and below at the cutting point) that are adjustable; the upper set can be moved up and down, so they can always be kept fairly close to the surface of the work. Using the upper guide (Fig. 3-11) unnecessarily high above the work causes the saw to bend, with a consequent risk of breakage. Providing the wood is moved slowly, it is possible to cut thick wood (up to 3 inches) with a comparatively small band saw.

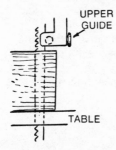

UPPER GUIDE

TABLE

Fig. 3-11. The upper guide on a band saw can be moved up and down to adjust the distance between the saw and the work.

The band saw has guards everywhere—except where it cuts. It is obviously important to keep the guards in place, because if the band flew off, broken or not, it could be dangerous. The saw table is slotted to take new blades, and may be grooved to take a guide similar to the angle guide on a table saw, although this sort of work is done better with a circular saw. It can also be tilted for beveled cuts.

The direction in which a band saw rotates makes it cut downward. This eliminates any risk of the wood rising, and insures a clean edge to the cut on the top surface. Any rough edges are on the lower side. There is one drawback to a band saw: it cannot cut an internal shape completely. For some jobs it is possible to cut across an unimportant part of solid wood to gain entry to the inside shape, but usually some other way of cutting an inside curve has to be used.

The alternative is a saber saw (Fig. 3-12A). It uses a stiff blade that works with a reciprocating motion (Fig. 3-12B), which has one end free. It can project straight out from the end of the motor or it can be at a right angle to it. Because the end of its blade is free, a saber saw can be used on enclosed curves as well as external ones. The reciprocating motion comes from a connection rod and crank, working a slide that holds the blade with screws. Some of the thrust from cutting is taken by a guide and roller. In most saws there is a simple up and down motion, but there can be an arrangement that moves the saw back slightly for a return stroke.

A saber saw blade has to be stiff and not very long. The length depends on the particular tool, but a projection of about 2 inches is common. The saw cuts on the pull stroke. If made to cut the other way, the blade would be in compression: more likely to buckle. This means that the cut is toward the operating mechanism; in a portable saber saw the cut is toward the face surface (Fig. 3-12C). With a fixed saber saw bench, the cut is downward, away from the face surface (Fig. 3-12D).

A saber saw is most effective when cutting thin material. It is particularly suitable for cutting shapes out of plywood. If used on thick material, particularly any that is close to the length of the saw, it may tend to wander with the grain and not cut perpendicularly to the surface.

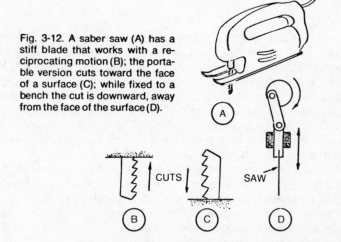

Fig. 3-12. A saber saw (A) has a stiff blade that works with a reciprocating motion (B); the portable version cuts toward the face of a surface (C); while fixed to a bench the cut is downward, away from the face of the surface (D).

It is possible to get saber saw teeth to cut metal or plastics, as well as wood. A finer tooth pitch will leave a cleaner edge than a coarse pitch and does not break out of the grain as much. However, with the comparatively limited movement of the saw, fine teeth do not clear sawdust very well; they may clog and cease to cut. For thicker wood—particularly for softwoods—fairly coarse teeth are needed.

There is no depth control with a saber saw, but the slotted foot through which the blade works may be tilted for cutting angles. Some saws have a blower to clear dust from the surface ahead of the blade. Because of the upward cut, dust deposited by the saw can obscure the line.

At one time a treadle-operated version of the fret- or jig-saw was used for cutting curved and pierced shapes in thin wood. With its treadle mechanism, like that of an old sewing machine, the tool could work intricate shapes accurately as long as the wood was not very thick. There have been powered versions, either with two arms (Fig. 3-13A), or with upward pull provided by a spring or bow (Fig. 3-13B). Both have been largely superseded by newer saws, but these simple tools may have possibilities in some circumstances. The latter has the advantage of accepting almost any size of sheet that can be cut. The short blades are held by clamps at the end, either of which can be released to allow the saw to be threaded through a hole for an internal cut.

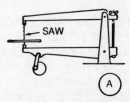

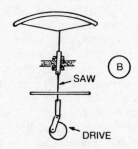

Fig. 3-13. Large saber saws, some with arms holding a blade under tension (A), and others with a bow (B) to supply upward pull, have been generally replaced by newer types.

PLANERS

The electrical counterparts of hand planes use rotary cutters: broad chisel-edged blades mounted on a strong cylinder strike the wood with a slicing action (Fig. 3-14A). The number of blades on the cylinder may vary, but two or three are usually seen in small machines. The table through which the cutter block projects is in two parts. Controlling the adjustment on one (Fig. 3-14B) regulates the amount of cut.

A planer (sometimes called a jointer) makes a series of curved cuts. If wood is forced quickly over the cutters, the hollows may be so large that the surface will be unsatisfactory (except for rough work). A better finish is obtained by much slower progress. A planer is designed to rotate the cutter block at a very high speed. This, coupled with a reasonably slow

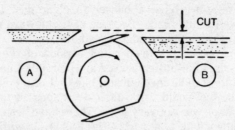

Fig. 3-14. The rotary cutters of an electric planer (A) strike with a slicing action. One part of the table adjusts the cut (B).

feed, can result in a surface with cutter marks so small as to not matter (for many purposes).

To a certain extent the width of its cut governs the usefulness of a planer. For the home workshop, a planing machine with a 4 inch cut is the smallest that should be considered; 6 inches would be better.

A guard is usually provided to shield dangerous rotating cutters. It should be in position whenever possible, but for some work it has to be moved aside. The planer may be fitted with a *thickness* attachment, a broad guard with a flat bottom surface that can be adjusted in height above the cutter block to control if the thickness of wood passing over it. A further adjustment on many machines allows the two parts of the table to be set at sufficiently different levels for cutting rebates. A fence (Fig. 3-15A) can be brought into position as a guide for the wood in planing a rebate at the edge of the planer. The fence can usually be canted to a range of angles (Fig. 3-15B), allowing the accurate planing of beveled edges.

Fig. 3-15. The fence on a planer (A) is useful for cutting rebates at the planer's edge; usually it can be adjusted to various angles (B).

When planing long boards, it is nice to have a planer with extension tables or rollers for extra support; but this can be arranged with workshop benches at the necessary height.

There are combination machines in which a planer is mounted alongside a circular saw and driven by the same motor. If the parts of the planer are all at a level lower than the saw table, there will be no interference between the two functions; thus there will be no need to dismantle one tool to use the other.

The alternative to having a fixed planer (over which wood is moved), is to incorporate the planing machine in a hand-held tool. But because such a tool has to be light enough to handle, it has to be limited in capacity; the width of its cut is little more than that of a hand plane. It reduces labor, to be sure, but a fixed planer has a more useful capacity and can do nearly all a portable planer can. The portable planer scores with work that cannot be brought to the planing machine, work that is awkward to deal with using a hand plane.

A portable electric plane may have a cut of 2⅜ inches (the same as many hand planes) or in other widths up to about 5 inches—near the limit of weight that can be handled. Most planers have their motor mounted across the tool above the cutter block fitted with handles similar to those of hand planes (Fig. 3-16). Some parts may be aluminum alloy for lightness. The sole is made like the table of a planing machine: in two parts that can be varied in relation to each other, usually by a knob to control the depth of the cut.

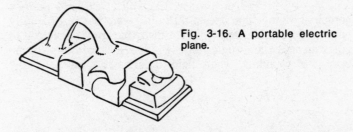

Fig. 3-16. A portable electric plane.

Wide blades pounding against wood need adequate power to drive them. A typical 4 inch planer, with three blades in the cutter block turning at 5000 rpm, gives 15000 cuts per minute and needs a ¾ hp motor.

Cutters have to be kept sharp. To reduce the frequency of sharpening, some are made of a special steel alloy. Their accurate setting, so they share the work equally, is also important. Blunt or badly set blades produce a poor surface. Very blunt blades will *case harden* a wood surface, making it resist the penetration of glue. This can be overcome by power sanding. A blade with a notch in it, caused by hitting metal or stone, will produce ridges in wood. The only cure is sharpening the blade until the notch disappears. The benefit of the speed in power planing compared with hand planing is only outweighed by the time needed to keep the machine in good working condition.

POWER SANDING

Power sanding is mostly for finishing after the wood has been worked by other means. But the application of power to abrasives makes other functions possible. Some power sanders can remove wood that would otherwise have to be planed or sawed. There are places where a sander is the most appropriate tool. For instance, if several parts meet with their grain going in several directions, a sander will level the surface without the risk of grain breaking out that there could be with a cutting tool.

Disk sanders have been mentioned so far only as accessories to electric drills, their most convenient form for the home shop; but some industrial sanders work the same way, usually with a head at an angle to the body containing the motor. Because there is more power, larger and coarser disks may be used. But such tools are more suited to heavier work and quite often, for materials other than wood.

One type of disk sander that may be built into a combination machine uses a disk on a rigid backing, usually with an adjustable table in front of it that may be slotted to carry an adjustable angle guide (Fig. 3-17). This sander can be used for rounding wood held against the disk, or the

ANGLE GUIDE

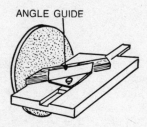

Fig. 3-17. One type of disk sander that might be built into a combination machine.

combination table/guide can be used to work the ends of pieces to bevels more accurate than what could be obtained with hand tools. The abrasive disk has to be fixed with adhesive that will hold tightly during use, but which can be released when the disk has to be replaced. Only the side of the disk that turns toward the surface of the table is used; the other side would lift the work. Consequently, the coverage is only about half the disk diameter. An 8 inch disk is a useful size to have.

A disk sander leaves curved marks on a surface that would have to be removed by hand sanding to produce a surface suitable for varnish or polish. A belt sander is the tool for sanding in a straight line (usually in the direction of the grain). It may be mounted on a bench, over which the wood is moved, or it may be mounted in a body that can be handled like a plane.

Abrasive belts are made in many sizes and types, with various grades of grit on cloth backing joined to form a continuous loop of the right size; sometimes there is an arrow to indicate the direction in which it runs. A common width suitable for most home shop needs is 4 inches; many machines take a belt about 3 feet in circumference.

A basic machine has two rollers, one of which is driven to draw the belt over the flat sanding surface. The sanding surface may be faced with metal, rubber, or fiber padding, depending on the type of sanding being done and the backing hardness required. A fine angular adjustment for one roller makes it align accurately with the other, or allows adjustment for any slight variations between belts. A spring, or some other tensioning arrangement between the rollers, can be released when the belts have to be changed. A bench machine may have an adjustable stop (Fig. 3-18A) that can be used to hold or guide the wood being sanded.

A hand-controlled belt sander (Fig. 3-18B) may take the same size belt as a bench machine. It has two handles and is used like a plane. Adjustments similar to the bench machine are included. Sanding produces a considerable amount of dust. Many belt sanders are provided with a dust bag into which most of the dust is drawn. Some belt sanders are two-speed types to allow for quick stock removal, or for finishing with grits that work best at high speeds; lower speeds are better for paint removal and some surface finishing. A belt speed of about 1000 feet per minute is usual.

The orbital sander is another type of finishing sander. Some are designed to use an electric drill (without its chuck) as the power source; others have an integral motor. But the effect is the same. The sanding surface is rectangular, and the abrasive paper or cloth, which is held over a pad by a grip at the end, moves with an orbital (eliptical) motion at a high

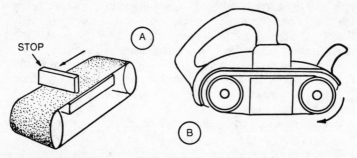

Fig. 3-18. A bench-type sander may have an adjustable stop (A) to hold or guide the wood being worked. Hand-controlled belt sanders (B) are used like a plane.

speed. The rapid action, which is really more of a vibration over a small path, leaves no obvious marks on the surface; thus the tool can be used in any direction. A typical tool has a sanding area about 4 by 8 inches that moves through an orbit of $^3/_{16}$ inch at 5000 orbits (revolutions) per minute.

For a home shop, the disk sander as an attachment for an electric drill costs little and is worth having. An orbital sander is next in cost, and is a good finishing tool for cabinetwork. A belt sander, whether portable or fixed, is much more costly, and may be desirable for a shop comprehensively equipped or when production justifies its purchase.

SPINDLE TOOLS

A cutter rotating at a high speed can cut wood passed over it to a shape that is the reverse of the cutter's profile. Alternatively, the shaped cutter can enter the wood and make a recess that matches its profile. When the cutter's spindle projects through a table and the wood is passed over it, the tool is called a *spindle molder*. When the tool is moved to cut into wood, it is called a router; but it does much more than the hand tool of the same name.

Because the spindle is comparatively small in diameter, many revolutions per minute are needed to get a good peripheral speed for a smooth cut. The spindle may turn at about 20,000 rpm when there is no load; this is reduced to about 10,000 rpm when the tool is cutting. Commonly, the cutter's quarter-inch shaft is held in a collet chuck. A large variety of cutters is available (Fig.3-19A). Straight cutters work profiles and cut grooves or dadoes. A beveled or conical shape will make a chamfer on an edge or slot; a hollowed edge will round off corners. More elaborate cutters will make moldings on shaped or straight edges. A simple cutter has a cutting edge with a single flute (Fig. 3-19B); others have two flutes (Fig. 3-19C).

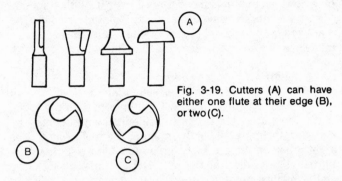

Fig. 3-19. Cutters (A) can have either one flute at their edge (B), or two (C).

A spindle molder has a motor under it and a spindle that projects through a hole in a table. There is a height adjustment. For freehand work along an edge, the small parallel projection, which does not cut, prevents the tool from cutting deeper than intended. For rounding or chamfering, it allows a wavy outline to be followed (Fig. 3-20A). For work on straight edges, there is an adjustable fence (Fig. 3-20B).

A router has a motor on top; the chuck and cutter face downward. A flat base rests on the work. The router is controlled with handles located at each side; some makes have an additional plane-type handle at the back. The base is cut away (Fig. 3-20C) so the action of the cutter can be watched. It

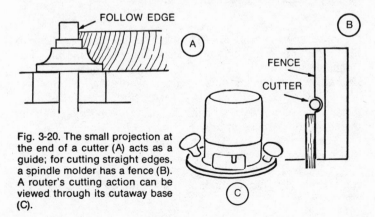

Fig. 3-20. The small projection at the end of a cutter (A) acts as a guide; for cutting straight edges, a spindle molder has a fence (B). A router's cutting action can be viewed through its cutaway base (C).

is possible to obtain an attachment that allows some routers to be mounted upside-down, so they can function as spindle molders.

Both hands are needed to work a router, so the wood has to be held down as the machine is guided over it. With a spindle molder, both hands can be used to manipulate the wood. The type of work governs the choice of method. A molded edge can be made better with a spindle molder; an intricate recess, with a router.

A straight router cutter will make a recess in wood (Fig. 3-21A). The depth of cut can be adjusted, and the bottom will be left smooth. A simple pass will make a groove the same width as the cutter, but it can be widened or made into any shape with another pass, or by moving the tool around. For straight grooving there may be an adjustable fence that runs along the edge of the wood (Fig. 3-21B). It may be set close enough to allow a suitable cutter to run along an edge, or it can be set for a groove several inches from the edge.

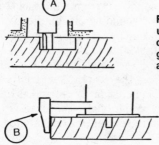

Fig. 3-21. A straight router can be used to make a recess in a piece of wood (A); for cutting straight grooves, there may be a fence (B) as a guide for the work.

Another base attachment allows the tool to be controlled by a template. A bushing on the base follows the outline of a template, and the tool cuts a groove matching the shape. This permits such things as making a recessed case for a tool or other item of a particular shape. A stand can be used to support the router when doing this; but this is more applicable to industrial production work.

There may be a dovetail attachment in the form of a guide that clamps to the work and router; with a suitable cutter it will make both of the mating parts of a dovetail joint at the same time. A similar attachment will make comb joints for box corners.

OTHER POWER TOOLS

The machine tools described in this chapter will handle most of the work in a home shop. Most of the others are more specialized, generally only appropriate to industrial production work. (Lathes are described in Chapter 8.)

Mortise and tenon joints are needed in many woodworking projects. While mortises can be drilled out and trimmed to shape with a chisel, there are mortising machines that do the same job. There may not be a need for one in a home shop, but it is possible to adapt a drill press or a lathe for this purpose. Some combination machines have mortising attachments. The mortise is made by feeding this tool into the work a number of times to make a mortise of the required length.

The tool is a hollow, square chisel, through which an auger bit turns (Fig. 3-22). As the bit removes most of the waste wood, the chisel faces trim the hole square. Feed is controlled by a lever that may move the tool up and down, as in a drill press; in some combination machines and lathe adaptations, the tool does not move along in the mortise; instead, the wood is moved toward it or away from it with a lever.

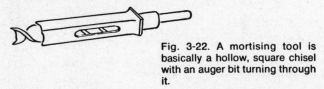

Fig. 3-22. A mortising tool is basically a hollow, square chisel with an auger bit turning through it.

While it is not impossible to make a square hole without mechanical assistance in controlling the wood, it is safer and more accurate if the machine has a means of gripping the wood and traversing it so the square holes are accurately arranged. In some machines the wood is moved by hand along a fence. When the wood is not gripped by a vise, there may be a guard above it (Fig. 2-23) to prevent it from lifting when the tool is withdrawn.

Fig. 3-23. Some mortising machines have a guard to prevent the work from lifting.

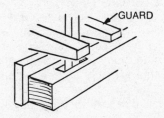

GUARD

A grinder is needed to sharpen tools. For the thin edge of a woodworking tool, a traditional slow-turning wetted sandstone has the advantage of minimizing the risk of the tool overheating and "drawing its temper." However, this type of stone has had to give way to the more compact bench grinder; it has a smaller wheel and was originally intended more for grinding engineer's tools than those of the woodworker. It is best to grind woodworking tools on a fairly large wheel. It is inadvisable to have one less than 6 inches in diameter and 1 inch thick. If it is a type that will sharpen a tool with its side, (Fig. 3-24A) as well as on its circumference, it will help in getting a flat bevel on a broad tool like a plane iron.

A satisfactory type of grinder has a motor on a stand with a means of mounting a grinding wheel at each end (Fig. 3-24B); wheels of different coarseness can be used. It is also possible to install a polishing mop for metal in place of one of the grinding wheels; or a sanding disk may be mounted.

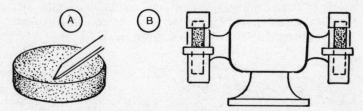

Fig. 3-24. A grinding wheel with grit on its side (A) is helpful in getting a flat bevel on a broad tool. A bench grinder (B).

It is inadvisable to mount a grinding wheel on a lathe or other machine tool. Although it may make having another electric motor unnecessary, particles of abrasive from the grinding wheel may get into the bearings and sliding parts of the machine and do considerable damage. It is possible to get a grinding head, a stand with a pulley at the center instead of a motor. One of these can be mounted far enough away from another machine to keep grit away from it, while taking its drive from a pulley.

The grinding wheels used in these machines have to turn at a high speed. Using it too slowly causes the wheel to wear rapidly and makes sharpening less effective. For the usual grit composition used, a 6 inch wheel should turn at about 3000 rpm. Some grinders have attachments, but any extra equipment intended for assisting in grinding certain engineer's tools should be avoided for woodworking tools. Usually, much of the wheel's circumference is shrouded—essential for safety. Except for this casing, there should only be a simple tool rest. It is helpful, when grinding some woodworking tools, if the motor casing does not project as far as the circumference of the wheel. In some grinders the diameter of the motor casing is greater than the diameter of the wheel; it gets in the way when grinding a tool that projects to the side of the part being ground.

4

Tool Maintenance

It is difficult—maybe impossible—to do good work with blunt tools. One difference between the attitude of a beginner and that of a skilled craftsman—the beginner often tries to continue using a tool that has lost its sharp edge; the expert takes time from the job to restore the cutting edge before continuing. A blunt tool will not do good work, may be slower, and increases the risk of it breaking grain or jumping out, making unwanted cuts.

Sharpness is a relative term. The act of cutting is actually a wedge action. At its finest stage, the wedging (or splitting) is so minute that the surface seems perfect to the eye. The sharpest edge would be two perfectly flat surfaces meeting at an *infinitely* small angle. This is impossible. But something almost as close to it is found in surgical instruments. The nearest to it in a common cutting tool is a razor. One who uses a blade knows that even in the comparatively light work of shaving, the edge will blunt after quite a short time—and if used on wood, it would crumble before it got very far in its first cut.

The angle at a cutting edge has to be a compromise between the fineness needed for a sharp edge and the strength needed to make the edge stand up to a reasonable amount of work. A tool used regularly on softwoods can have a slightly finer angle than one intended for considerable use on hardwoods. In practice, most tools are sharpened to an angle that is a good average for all woods.

No surface can be made perfect; the two sides of a cutter that meet to form an edge fall short of the ideal. If a cutting edge is examined under a microscope, it will be seen to be serrated—something like a saw. The object of sharpening is to get the serrations as small as possible, coming close to the (impossible) ideal of two surfaces meeting without flaws. How close this can be taken depends on the work and the results expected. Carving tools need a finer edge than, say, a chisel used for chopping a block of wood to approximate shape.

The size of a sharp tool's edge serrations match the size of the grit on the stone used for sharpening. (Sharpening is the process of rubbing away a tool's edge surfaces on both sides until they meet.) Unfortunately, the very fine abrasive used to get the finest edge cuts very slowly. Attempting to restore the edge of a very blunt tool on a very fine stone would take an impossibly long time. Consequently, sharpening often involves working with successively finer stones, each removing the marks of the previous one.

The two main steps in getting a sharp edge are grinding and sharpening *(honing)*. Grinding is the term for the process of removing excess metal; sharpening, the process of actually getting a sharp edge. In some tools, such as chisels, the grinding and sharpening bevels are distinct. In others, such as knives, the bevels are the same. (Sharpening can be done many times before grinding is needed.)

Oilstones are used for sharpening most woodworking tools. For some things, like the cutting tools used in agriculture, similar stones are used with water, but oil gives better control and a better edge. Of course, water and oil don't mix; the two lubricants can't be used on the same stone. Any thin oil may be used. At one time craftsmen had their preferences for oils, such as neat's-foot oil (which is still available); but thin lubricating oil has been found to be just as good. The oil lubricates and washes away steel and stone particles. It also carries away the heat generated by the friction of sharpening, which could be enough to draw the temper of a thin edge, making it brittle. Thick oil would keep the tool from making the necessary contact with the stone. If a stone gets clogged with dirt and thick oil, it should be cleaned with a solvent. Kerosene may be preferable to a thicker oil. Heating a stone in an oven or soaking it in kerosene will free old embedded oil and dirt. A stone used dry will acquire a glazed surface, which will have to be soaked.

For basic sharpening a stone about 8 inches by 2 inches by 1 inch is suitable. It should be kept in a case. Several stones may be needed, although a combination stone, with coarse and fine grits on opposite sides, may serve for most normal tool sharpening. When a stone is out of use, it should be wiped clean and its cover replaced.

At one time many natural stones were available. Because of their origin, they varied in coarseness; but most were fine. A good natural stone was treasured. They are still desirable for fine finishing, but for most purposes a manufactured stone will have to be used. They have the advantage of even grit size throughout, but tend to be coarser than most natural ones.

Besides the steel of the tool wearing away, the oilstone itself wears away. This won't matter if the wear is even. But the whole width of the stone, needed for broad tools like plane irons, becomes less effective if grooves are worn in it by narrower tools. Tools should be rubbed over as much of the stone surface as possible; this is very important for narrow tools. A slight hollow in the stone's length may not matter, but unevenness in its width will spoil the stone for broad-edged tools.

An oilstone that becomes uneven can be rubbed down on a coarser stone. Both will wear, but the high spots on the oilstone will be reduced. Final leveling can be done on a sheet of glass spread with grinding compound, preferably coarser than the grit of the stone. Coarse emery cloth held against a flat surface will work with some stones. However, this is a slow process; it is better to avoid getting a stone into this state.

A knife blade can be used as an example for sharpening. Bluntness may be obvious from its inability to cut, but it can quite often be obvious enough to be seen. If the edge is held to reflect light, a blunt part will be indicated by a white line of light along the edge. If this is apparent, it needs particular attention.

For most freehand sharpening, one hand holds the tool at the correct angle, while the other applies pressure. It is usual for the operator to keep the cutting edge facing away from him. And because a knife has to be rubbed on both sides, this means changing hands. Some workers turn a knife over, reversing the blade without changing hands, but getting the correct sharpening angles is easier if the blade points away.

Hold the knife so its blade is flat across the stone. Apply a thin film of oil to the stone and secure it (in its case) in a vise, if there is no other way to prevent it from moving. Lift the knife to see if the edge is on the stone. Spread the fingers of your free hand over the blade and rub it back and forth on the stone.

If the blade is longer than the width of the stone, move it around so all of the edge is rubbed. If the point is curved, move the blade around so the curve maintains the same angle as the rest of the knife. During the rubbing, concentrate on maintaining the angle with the hand on the handle. After a time remove the knife, wipe its blade with a cloth, and examine the result. The newly rubbed surface should reach the edge. If it doesn't, continue rubbing; try a slightly steeper angle, if the original angle does not appear likely to get to the edge.

When one side has been rubbed down, turn the knife over and do the other side. As the two surfaces are rubbed down to meet, a tiny sliver of steel will be produced on the edge. This *wire edge* (burr) may cling to the knife edge; it can be felt, but is usually too small to be seen. It will be turned over on the other side of the last to be rubbed. If you rub a finger from the back of the blade toward the edge on that side, the wire edge (Fig. 4-1A) will be felt as roughness if the knife is sharp. If you cannot detect it, or it is only on part of the edge, further sharpening is needed.

A wire edge will prevent a tool from cutting properly if it is not removed. One way is to draw the knife a few times along a leather strop on both sides. Some workers strop the edge on the palm of their hand. In either case, only draw the blade back; do not go forward (a cutting action). A simpler way is to draw the blade across the edge of a piece of scrap wood with enough pressure to make it cut (Fig. 4-1B). This will remove the wire edge, which can sometimes be seen piled against the edge of the cut wood.

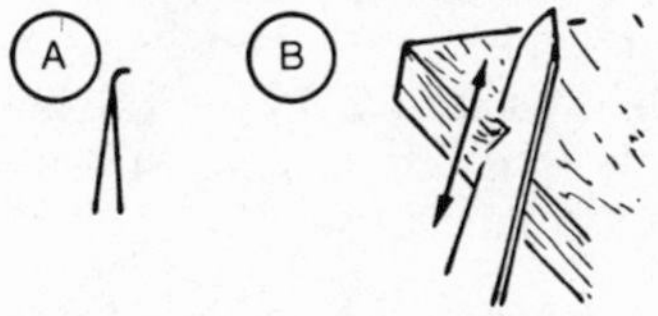

Fig. 4-1. The wire edge (A) that forms on the edge of a tool being sharpened can be removed by drawing the tool across a piece of scrap wood (B).

If the first sharpening was done on a coarse stone, sharpening should be repeated on a fine stone, but not too long; all that is necessary is enough to remove the marks of the coarse stone. If any tool is sharpened as soon as it shows signs of bluntness, only a touchup on a fine stone will be needed.

A fine knife edge may turn over in use without wearing or breaking off. Butchers and other people who use knives with fine angles employ a *steel* to straighten edges. Both sides of the knife are alternately drawn across and along the steel. The hard steel straightens curled over edges. It does not sharpen like an oilstone does, so the knife has to be returned to the oilstone when the edge wears away.

For the very finest edge, the oilstone may be followed with a leather strop, which may be stretched leather, as those used for razors, or leather glued to a piece of wood. The strop should be dressed with a very fine grinding paste. A paste can be made with crocus powder (red ferrous oxide) mixed with oil. A household porcelain cleanser may also be used on the strop. An undressed strop will do no more than straighten an edge. If it is to provide a final stage in sharpening, it must have a fine abrasive coating.

Chisels, plane irons, gouges, and similar woodworking cutting tools are sharpened on one side only. The other side is kept flat. Because beveling or rounding the second side will affect the performance of the tool, any rubbing of that side on an oilstone should be confined to removing a wire edge.

The important thing in sharpening tools is the maintenance of a correct angle during movement along the stone. Keep one hand on the handle of a chisel, or on the upper part of a plane iron, holding the tool and moving it back and forth as you maintain the angle (Fig. 4-2A). Apply pressure to the edge being sharpened with the other hand. If it is a wide tool, use your fingers or whole hand a short distance behind the cutting edge.

If the tool has both grinding and sharpening bevels, the grinding bevel should be put on the stone first, then the handle can lifted about 5° to get the sharpening bevel (Fig. 4-2B). The angle is not so critical that it can't be varied within a few

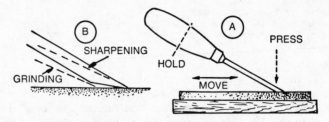

Fig. 4-2. Sharpening a chisel (A). Some tools have grinding and sharpening bevels to their edge (B); both can be restored with an oilstone.

degrees; the existing bevel will serve as a guide. The edge of a narrow tool should be moved around on the stone. This also helps if it is a wide tool, because the center of the edge is likely to be sharpened better as it moves to the side; wear on the stone will be kept even.

When sharpening by hand keep the angle as nearly constant as possible. There will be a tendency, at first, for your hands to dip at the far end of the stroke. If this isn't avoided, the bevel will not be kept flat.

It may be helpful to cut a wood pattern with the correct angles and use it to check how you hold the tool, but with a little experience you will get the angle by feel. Several devices are available that mechanically control the angle. Most consist of rollers that clamp on to the blade. When the whole stone surface is used with one of these, its top should be extended with wood (Fig. 4-3A). Even when a sharpening guide is not used, there is some advantage in having short wood sections at the ends of an oilstone; then, the tool runs over the edge onto the wood and it won't be damaged.

Bluntness in a chisel may be seen by a white reflecting edge, as described for a knife. Sharpening should be continued until a wire edge can be felt when you run a finger down the flat side toward it. Then give the flat side a few circular rubs absolutely flat on the stone (Fig. 4-3B). This will loosen the wire edge, if not remove it; but to make sure it has gone, slice the edge across the edge of a piece of wood. If sharpening has been done on a coarse stone, repeat the process on a fine stone until the coarser marks of the first stone are removed. For general use this leaves the chisel ready for cutting. But for the fine cut required of carving tools, further rubbing on a strop is needed.

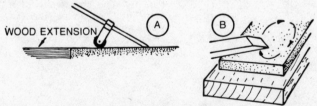

Fig. 4-3. A device that controls the sharpening angle for a tool (A). After the wire edge has been removed from a tool being sharpened, hold the tool flat on the stone and give it a few circular rubs (B).

Chisels for turning are sharpened equally on both sides. They may be given sharpening and grinding bevels, or the surfaces may blend, the flat part curving toward the cutting edge. Many carving chisels are sharpened on both sides this way. They may either have a main bevel on one side and a lesser one on the other, or equal bevels. Because carving tools of this sort are used for delicate cuts, and the carver must be prepared for frequent sharpening, it is usual to have longer bevels to give a finer edge.

Plane irons are sharpened the way chisels are, although the thin blades of most metal planes can be given only one angle: the sharpening angle, taken right across the thickness of the steel. If the cutting edge of a chisel is not perpendicular to the side, it won't matter for most purposes; but try to aim for a reasonably square end anyway.

If the end of a plane iron is far from square, it will affect the setting of the plane. Sharpening should be checked with a try square (Fig. 4-4A). A jack plane, mainly used for removing fairly thick shavings, should be sharpened with a slightly curved edge (Fig. 4-4B). This will produce a slightly ridged surface; but because this is only the preparation for finishing with another plane or sander, it is preferable. It allows quick and heavy cuts. Other planes should have their edge going straight across; but, because sharp corners would dig in and mark the surface being planed, it is better to round them slightly. Spokeshave blades may be treated as small plane irons.

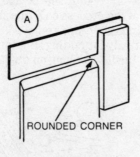

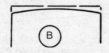

ROUNDED CORNER

Fig. 4-4. The sharpening of a plane iron should be checked with a try square (A); a jack plane should be sharpened to a slightly curved edge (B).

An externally sharpened gouge may be sharpened on a flat oilstone. Its bevels, usually similar to those of a chisel, have distinct grinding and sharpening angles. However, their curved cross section complicates sharpening. Hold the tool crosswise on the stone as you would a chisel, but roll the gouge as you rub it (Fig. 4-5A). A firmer gouge has a straight end. Because most of its cutting is done at the center, it is usually necessary to rub more toward the sides to prevent the middle from finishing hollow. Move the gouge around and vary the direction in relation to the stone, while maintaining the sharpening angle. A turning gouge has a rounded end, but except for the need to move the end around to keep the angle constant, it is sharpened the same way. Carving gouges usually have blended sharpening and grinding angles. Because carving gouges are usually thinner than others, there is no difficulty or excessive labor in giving them a long bevel on the stone.

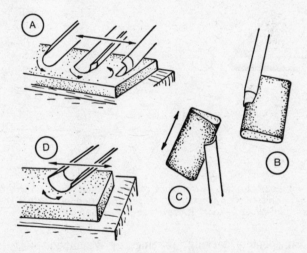

Fig. 4-5. An externally sharpened gouge should be rolled as it is rubbed on the stone (A); a slipstone (B) is needed to remove the wire edge. An internally sharpened gouge has to be sharpened on the inside with a slipstone (C), and finished on the outside with a flat oilstone (D).

A wire edge cannot be removed from a gouge on a flat stone. A *slip* or slipstone is needed. This is a piece of oilstone, usually tapered so the edges of the gouge can be given two curves (Fig. 4-5B). It is oiled and used in the hand like a file; the edge of a curve closest in degree to that of the gouge is held flat along the inside of the gouge and moved around the curve. Finally, the gouge can be sliced on the edge of a piece of wood, or pressed into the surface and turned around, to take off the loose wire edge.

Internally sharpened gouges are usually sharpened entirely with a slipstone, beginning with a filing action (Fig. 4-5C) on a coarse stone, and finishing with a fine one. The outside is rubbed with a rolling action on a flat stone (Fig. 4-5D); then the wire edge is removed by making cuts on a piece of wood. A flat strop can be used on the straight surface of a gouge. For the inside, use a piece of leather glued over the edge of a piece of wood, (Fig. 4-6A) and use it like a slip. Carving gouges are mainly sharpened on the outside, but the inside does have a slight bevel that is claimed to make the tool cut intricate shapes easier and dig in less. But for other forms of woodworking, it is better for gouges to be beveled on only one side.

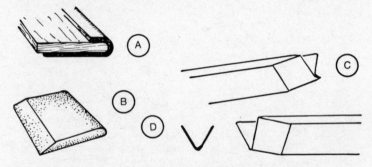

Fig. 4-6. Leather glued over a piece of wood (A) can be used to strop a gouge. A chisel-edged slipstone (B) is used on cutting tools with V-shaped edges; sometimes a "hook" (C) develops at the point of these tools.

Sharpening carving, parting, or V-shaped tools is a peculiar problem. In effect, these tools are like two chisels joined together. Basically, sharpening them is like dealing with chisels, but difficulty comes at the point. Carvers give their tools a slight bevel on the inside as well as the outside. A chisel-edged slipstone (Fig. 4-6B) is used inside. Sometimes a "hook" develops at the point of these tools (Fig. 4-6C). Treat the meeting point of the two sides as a tiny gouge rather than as a sharp angle. This will overcome the tendency to hook. If the end of a V-shaped tool becomes badly shaped, it will have to be ground or rubbed on an oilstone across the end until it is flat and true. Reflected light and variations in the end's thickness will show where most sharpening is needed.

GRINDING

Although new tools must be ground before they are sharpened, the home woodworker can use a tool a very long time before regrinding becomes necessary. A very coarse oilstone can often be used instead of a grinder, particularly for thin steel tools, like the blades of a metal plane. It is with thicker chisels that there is more of a problem, and grinding becomes necessary.

The sharpening bevel of a newly ground chisel is quite narrow (Fig. 4-7A). Further sharpening will lengthen the sharpening bevel (Fig. 4-7B) until quite a broad surface has to be rubbed away on the oilstone to bring the tool to a keen edge. This is the stage where grinding is called for. A grinder is the best tool to use when an edge has to be altered; for example, when a plane iron goes too far out of square due to uneven sharpening, or when a cutting edge has received a very deep nick upon striking a nail. It is then best to grind a completely new end and sharpen from the beginning again. A grinder is also needed for metalworking tools, with obtuse angles that cannot be sharpened on an oilstone.

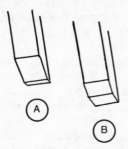

Fig. 4-7. A chisel has to be ground to a narrow bevel (A) when the sharpening bevel becomes too long (B).

If a slow-turning sandstone wheel is used, it should turn away from the tool as water drips on its surface. Water assists grinding as a lubricant and keeps the edge of the tool cool, preventing overheating that would draw the temper of the tool (making it brittle). A high-speed bench grinder turns toward the tool and is used dry. This means there is a risk of overheating; the tool has to be removed frequently from the wheel and dipped in water. There is no need to remove the tool from a sandstone wheel, except to inspect progress. If the tool overheats on a dry, fast bench grinder, a series of colors will appear on the edge, indicating the steel has softened.

Rehardening and tempering to restore hardness is not practical in a home workshop. All that can be done is to grind the edge further, past the colored part, until unaffected steel is reached. The coloring can easily be removed with an oilstone, but this would merely disguise the fact that the steel has softened.

The previous grinding bevel will indicate how the tool is to be held against the grinding wheel. The angle to the surface of the wheel should be about 25° (Fig. 4-8A). If the tool is ground on the circumference of the wheel and is kept absolutely steady, it will become hollow ground. (The smaller the wheel, the more this will happen.) In practice, moving the tool around will remove most of this hollowing. Hollow grinding produces two conflicting qualities. A hollow-ground chisel can be sharpened more than one ground flat before it needs regrinding; however, hollow grinding weakens tools slightly, because there is not quite as much stiffness immediately behind the edge. For a paring tool this will not matter. But for heavier work it may cause the tool to vibrate, perhaps even break. Try to produce a flat grinding bevel.

If the wheel is a type that can be used on its side, the ground surface will be flat (Fig. 4-8B). To allow for the different speeds between the surface grinding the inner edge and the one grinding the outer edge of a broad tool, move the tool around as it is being ground. This is important when grinding on the circumference of a wheel, but then it is to keep wear on the wheel even if the tool is narrow, or to cover the whole width of the tool if it is wider than the wheel.

Most grinding is done freehand. Holding the tool at the correct angle will come with practice. However, the frequent removal of the edge from a dry grinder, to cool it in water, makes it difficult to consistantly come back to the correct angle. If you have a grinder with the usual straight tool rest (intended for metalworking tools), keep one finger between it and the tool in the same place, so when the tool is dipped in water, your finger will act as a gage (Fig. 4-8C). This will be the controlling hand. The other hand applies pressure. For dry grinding it is better to let the stone cut lightly as the tool is moved across it. Avoid grinding the edge to almost nothing; this is when overheating occurs the quickest.

A gouge is ground the same way as a chisel, except it is rolled on the grindstone and may be held at a slight angle to the circumference. Awls and other spikes are also kept rolling during grinding. Thin pointed tools overheat quickly and must

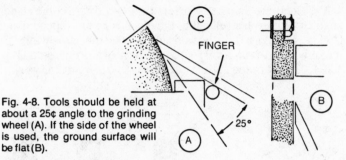

FINGER

25°

Fig. 4-8. Tools should be held at about a 25¢ angle to the grinding wheel (A). If the side of the wheel is used, the ground surface will be flat (B).

be dipped in water frequently. Knives rarely need grinding, except when the edge is damaged to the extent that a lot of metal has to be removed. (Their thin edges also overheat quickly.)

SCRAPERS

A different sort of sharpening is needed for a cabinet scraper. The cutting edge is turned over to make a hook that looks something like thick wire edge of a chisel. This edge, when correctly sharpened, will remove extremely thin shavings from most hardwoods. If the tool does not cut at all, or only produces dust, it needs sharpening.

The complete sharpening process, which is rarely needed, or the making of a new scraper, starts with getting the edge true. The two long edges produce four cutting edges. The narrow edges may be sharpened as well, if desired, but they are of little value for surface finishing.

The steel, tempered like that of a saw, is not too hard for filing. Use a single-cut fine mill file: one with only a single set of cuts across the surface. When the edge is straight, draw a file over it (Fig. 4-9A). Square the edge accurately by rubbing the edge and each side on an oilstone (Fig. 4-9B). The oilstone should remove any file marks completely. Rub each side after rubbing the edge; this will leave the edge ready for the next stage.

A *burnisher*, a hard piece of round steel in a handle, is used for sharpening scrapers. A chisel or gouge can be used if a burnisher is unavailable, but a proper burnisher is likely to be harder.

An expert may dress the edge of his scraper while holding it in his hand; but, at first, work with the scraper in a vise. With firm pressure, rub the burnisher flat along the edge (Fig.

4-9C). Continue doing this a few times, tilting the burnisher slightly with each stroke until the last stroke has dipped about 5° (Fig. 4-9D). Do the other side of the edge the same way. The effect will be to rub a very small lip or hook on each side (Fig. 4-9E). These are the cutting edges; the tool is ready for work.

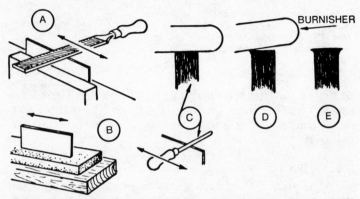

Fig. 4-9. After you get the edge of a scraper straight, draw a file over it (A) and square it on an oilstone (B). Then rub it with a burnisher (C), tilting it slightly with each stroke (D); the result should be a lip on both sides of the edge (E).

Other scrapers are made with a beveled edge, like plane irons sharpened to about 45°. They are intended to be sharpened one way only; otherwise, the work is like that for a square-edged cabinet scraper. Sharpen the bevel side on an oilstone, as you would a plane iron, and rub the flat surface to remove the wire edge. Curl the edge over with a series of rubs on the beveled side, starting at a little more than the sharpened bevel (Fig. 4-10A); make subsequent strokes progressively higher (Fig. 4-10B) to curl over the cutting edge, forming a "hook" similar to that of the cabinet scraper (Fig. 4-10C).

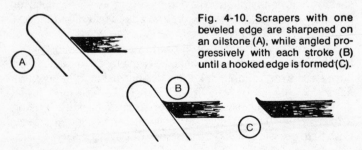

Fig. 4-10. Scrapers with one beveled edge are sharpened on an oilstone (A), while angled progressively with each stroke (B) until a hooked edge is formed (C).

130

When a scraper blunts, its trouble is likely to be a turned back hook rather than a worn or broken one. It can be restored with a burnisher. With a little experience, this can be done while the scraper is held flat with its edge over the edge of the bench; the burnisher is held point up, almost vertically. This dressing can be done several times before the edge reaches a stage where it has to be rubbed on an oilstone again to make a new hook.

There are scraper tools in which the scraper is held in a body with plane-type handles, or a pair of handles like those on a spokeshave. These blades are sharpened the same way as hand scrapers, but there may have to be some experimentation to get the right degree of hook to suit the angle of the blade.

Other types of scrapers, with a variety of handles, are made with a hooked blade that is pulled over the work. Some have disposable blades and are not intended to be resharpened. However, it is possible to get more life out of a blade by using a fine file, or a flat slipstone used like a file to restore the edge (Fig. 4-11). Work across and diagonally, preferably away from the cutting edge to avoid forming a wire edge or burr, and follow the original angle.

FILE OR STONE

HOOK SCRAPER

Fig. 4-11. It is possible to get more life out of a disposable scraper blade by restoring its edge with a fine file.

SHARPENING SAWS

A properly set and sharpened saw is a joy to use. Trying to use one that has incorrectly set or blunt teeth is not only frustrating, it can lead to poor results or even an inability to complete the job. The motor of a power saw in poor condition may be overloaded when an attempt is made to force the saw through wood, consequently risking damage.

A new saw is set and sharpened by machine during its manufacture, resulting in precision difficult to match by any hand treatment; but there are ways of restoring a saw to good condition with simple equipment and very little skill. The teeth of a saw that has been machine-sharpened during manufacture should be examined, particularly for the amount of set, how much of the tooth is bent, what angles have been filed on the front and back of each tooth, and the tooth's general form. This will give a good indication of what sort of treatment will be needed in the home shop.

Normally, the points of a saw become blunt while there is still ample set to give clearance for it as it passes through wood. A saw may be sharpened two or three times before setting is needed. When setting is needed, the teeth may also have become uneven; the saw will be in a generally bad condition. If this is so, it may be better to have the saw completely serviced by an expert.

The majority of saws are made of hardened and tempered tool steel, without any additional treatment. Some saws are made of special alloys, or the teeth are tipped. The object of these treatments is to make the saw keep its edge for a very long time. The teeth are exceptionally hard to resist wear. This means that they stay in good condition for a very long time; but when they get blunt, they cannot be sharpened in the home shop. Although a saw in this condition should be taken in for sharpening, even the specialist may not be able to do anything with tipped teeth. It may only be possible to service such a saw by cutting off the worn teeth and starting again—which may be as costly as scrapping the saw and buying another. The complete sequence of steps in reconditioning a saw is:

1. Joining: making the teeth the same height.
2. Shaping: making the teeth the right shape.
3. Setting: bending alternate teeth in opposite directions.
4. Filing: the actual sharpening of the teeth.

When a saw begins to show signs of bluntness, only filing may be needed to restore it. It may be possible to file several times before it becomes necessary to set the teeth. Filing lowers the teeth further into the saw and removes parts of teeth that were set, so the effective amount of set is reduced. How many times the teeth may be filed before setting is needed depends on the original amount of set. If the saw has been carefully filed and the teeth are still even in shape, setting and sharpening may be all that is necessary.

If teeth become damaged, due to striking nails or uneven filing, a stage will be reached where it is necessary to go back to jointing and work through the complete sequence.

Saws are sharpened with a triangular file to match the included angles between the teeth (in most saws); the three equal sides form 60° angles. Saw files, specially made for the purpose, are slightly tapered with fine, single-cut teeth. Sizes range from 5 to 10 inches in cutting edge length. It is also possible to get double-ended files that are like two files meeting at the center. Saw files do not retain their sharpeness long, because they are used on tempered steel; a double-ended file would last longer.

For jointing, a file has to be run along the teeth. You could use the same file used for sharpening, but it is easier to use one with a broader surface (but with similar teeth). A flat mill file with rounded edges can be used. It is also needed if gullets (for clearing dust) have to be deepened.

When working on a saw, hold it in a vise, supporting it close to the teeth over a reasonable length. Two boards can be used to hold the saw in an ordinary vise (Fig. 4-12A), with straight edges for hand saws, and a curved top for circular saws. It's easier to work on a saw if it is near eye level. If much sharpening is to be done, a higher second vise can be made (Fig. 4-12B) that will either clamp into the first vise or bolt to the bench. Metal vises of the right height are made, with a cam action instead of a screw; the amount of jaw movement needed is slight. To allow for backsaws there should be a space below the jaws to clear the back.

If the teeth are uneven, the first step is jointing. With the saw in a vise, run a file (without its handle) squarely along the tops of the teeth. Because the file has to be kept square and flat, use a guide. You could buy a jointer, a metal tool to hold the file; or one can be improvised by boring a hole through a block of wood into which the file can be pushed, and slotting it to fit the saw (Fig. 4-12C). Similarly, a piece can be made to hold a flat file.

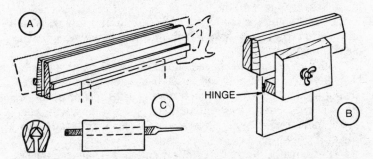

HINGE

Fig. 4-12. Two boards can be used to hold a saw in a vise for sharpening (A); an extension to the vise (B), to bring the saw to eye level, will make the job easier. A jointer, used to make all the teeth the same height, can be made out of a block of wood bored to hold a file (C).

Jointing should be done only when the file touches every tooth. If the teeth are very uneven and a considerable amount of jointing will have to be done, work in stages; otherwise, the shape of some teeth may be lost. Lower the highest teeth, then shape those that have been jointed before going on to level the teeth in preparation for the next step. Unless the saw has been very misused, most of the teeth will still be uniform in height, but those that were high will have had their tops taken off (Fig. 4-13A).

Shaping brings the teeth to the same size, but does not sharpen them. With the saw edge fairly close to the top of the vise, so the thin metal does not vibrate when filed, check the shape and angles of the good teeth. Work on those that have been leveled, restoring them to the same shape. Filing can be done straight across or approximately at the angles showing across the teeth. A cutting edge is not required yet. What is important is that the teeth are all the same shape and size. Care is needed to avoid taking off all of the back or front of a tooth, as this could result in uneven sizes. Because the file will fit the gullet between teeth, it will file the front of one tooth and the back of the next if pressed straight down. If this is not what you want, press against one side or the other as required (Fig. 4-13B).

Circular saws may be checked for tooth height by observation. Wear on the teeth will indicate which have been highest (doing most of the work); this may be a sufficient guide for jointing. Another method can be used while the blade is still mounted, projecting through the table. A sharpening stone is held lightly against the saw (Fig. 4-13C), which is turned by hand. The stone is brought progressively closer until it touches the tops of all the teeth.

After shaping the teeth, rub both sides of the saw with an oilstone to remove any burr left from filing, leaving the teeth clean for setting.

Although setting has been done in many ways, the object, basically, is to bend only the top half of each tooth outward. Trying to bend a tooth too much may break it off or cause a crack at the bottom of a gullet; this applies to any type and size of tooth, and is easily understood if a saw with large teeth is examined.

Traditionally, an expert (often called a "saw doctor") used an anvil with a beveled edge and a hammer with a narrow cross peen (Fig. 4-13D). With the skill that came with experience, he worked by eye, hammering alternate teeth one

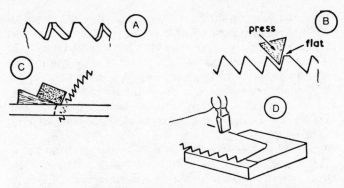

Fig. 4-13. Jointing may remove the tops of some teeth (A). Avoid taking off all of the back or front of a tooth by controlling the file's direction of pressure (B). A circular saw blade can be sharpened while it is mounted in the table (C). The traditional method of saw-sharpening involved using a beveled anvil and a hammer (D).

way, then turning the saw over and doing the same the other way—extremely quickly and accurately. This is obviously not the method for the beginner. If you have no other tool for setting, you could use a punch to direct the blows of a hammer while the saw is held with its teeth on the edge of a beveled piece of iron; but this would only work with large teeth. (It would be unsuccessful with the fine teeth of a backsaw.)

Most saw setting in home shops is done with a *saw set* that operates with handles like those of pliers. There are several forms, but the basic action is supplied by a plunger that pushes against a tooth when the handles are squeezed. It actually operates against a little anvil with a beveled edge (Fig. 4-14). An adjustable fence controls how much of each tooth comes under the plunger.

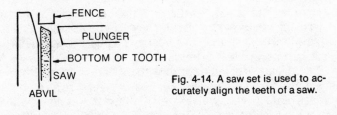

Fig. 4-14. A saw set is used to accurately align the teeth of a saw.

In use, the simplest saw sets have their handles in line with the saw edge. It is more convenient to have a pistol-grip type with handles at a right angle to the setting action, allowing the saw to be held edge-upward in a vise, and the free hand used at the side. It is helpful if the top of the set is open sufficiently for the action to be easily observed so progress can be watched. Some saw sets will fit teeth of any size. Others come in two sizes, a small one to fit the fine teeth of thinner saws up to about 10 points per inch, and a larger one for saws used away from the bench, including most circular saws. A saw set in the form of a piece of steel, with slots in the edge and handles, is of no use for shop saws.

A saw set pushes a tooth forward. To use one, first place the saw in a vise. The first teeth to deal with are those seen pointing away. Move along the saw dealing with alternate teeth; then turn the saw around and deal with the teeth in between those already set.

Once you have started, be sure to maintain the adjustment of the set, and apply the same amount of pressure to the handles each time. Check the finished job to see that the set is even and no teeth have been missed. Rub each side lightly with an oilstone to take off any raggedness or high spots.

The amount of set is affected by several factors. Excessive set makes a saw cut a kerf wider than needed to clear the saw sides, and makes cutting harder work than necessary. If the saw is ground to taper, that is, thinner at the back than at the cutting edge, less set is required because the cross section of the blade assists in clearing as it passes through wood. If the saw is intended for sappy wood, more set will be needed than required for dry woods. Hardwoods need less set than softwoods. A saw used in the shop for accurate work on properly seasoned wood should have no more set than necessary. This applies to circular saws as well as hand saws.

If there is a riving knife behind the saw, the kerf must be wide enough to clear it easily. Excessive set on a circular saw can put considerable extra load on the motor. A saw used for ripping may need more set than one used across the grain. A board being run through a circular saw lengthwise may tend to spring inward along the cut. A fairly coarse set will help to minimize this pinching on the saw.

The thickness of a file varies with its length. There is some advantage in using a larger file on coarser teeth, so as to make best use of the width available. A small file is less clumsy and its work is easier to see on finer teeth. A 5 inch file should suit any saw from about 11 to 18 points; down to 7 points, a 6 inch file may be used; to 4 points, it may be 7 inches. (The larger saw files are for larger industrial and forestry saws.) If you buy only one file, a 6 inch one will deal with most shop saws.

Saws are usually filed by hand. Filing guides are made to insure a uniform bevel on each tooth; but in practice, most workers are able to file teeth accurately and uniformly enough without any mechanical control of the file. For a first attempt, sharpen a saw with fairly coarse teeth, so the angles can more easily be seen. The saw should only project a little above the vise jaws. It will probably have to be moved at intervals to keep the part being worked on near the center of the jaws.

There are two shapes of teeth found in hand shop saws. For the special shapes of some circular saws, filing should follow existing tooth shape and angles. Concentrate on the fronts of the teeth—they do the cutting. If a ripsaw or crosscut saw is being sharpened, remember that it is the front of each tooth that does the cutting; its correct shaping should be your primary concern. Because the inclusive angle between the teeth is the same as that of the file, shaping the back of a tooth will come almost automatically. For crosscut saws the file has to cross the saw edge at the appropriate angle. For ripsaws it crosses at a right angle to the length of the saw. Except for the angle across the saw when viewed from above, the file should be level and parallel with the floor.

A good guide to the correct angle can usually be found at the handle end of a hand saw, where there will be a few teeth that rarely see wood, and are therefore likely to still have their original shape. Putting a file between these teeth and moving it around until it matches the angles will show you how to set the angle of the file. The front of the teeth pointing toward you have to be filed. When these are finished, turn the saw around to file the others. By working in this way the file takes metal off the front of each tooth away from the cutting edge, and so does not form a burr there.

For a crosscut saw, put the blade end away from the handle in a vise. Locate the first tooth pointing toward you, and put the file in the gullet in front of it. Let the file settle at an angle that matches the existing bevel of the tooth, while holding it level. Position yourself behind the file. Note how flat the top is on the tooth from jointing. File enough of the front of the tooth to remove half of this flat (it will look white against the light).

Skip the next gullet going toward the handle and repeat the process. Once you have started, maintain the file at the same angle all the way along the saw as you progress with alternate teeth. As you file the fronts of the teeth pointing toward you, the other side of the file will be filing the back of the adjoining tooth pointing away from you. Normally, this will be about the right amount, but if the tooth has an extra large flat surface or has no flat, regulate the amount of pressure on that side, so a reasonable amount is taken off.

Once the teeth pointing toward you are sharp, turn the saw around and work the other way in exactly the same manner, using the same angles and actions. Start with the front of the first tooth pointing toward you. After going into alternate gullets to sharpen the fronts of the first few teeth pointing toward you, examine the teeth. Your filing should have brought all these teeth to points, with bevels on both sides of all teeth pointing both ways (Fig. 4-15A). If this is not the case, adjust your filing accordingly. Just remove flat tops; don't continue longer on a tooth, or it will finish too low. Go along the whole length of the saw, filing all teeth pointing toward you on the second side.

A ripsaw is sharpened in exactly the same manner, except the file is used straight across the saw (Fig. 4-15B), and the fronts of the teeth are upright, or very nearly so. Work only on the fronts of the teeth pointing toward you, then turn the saw around to do the others. Although it may seem reasonable to do all the teeth from one side, because you are filing straight across, this is unsatisfactory and could result in the saw cutting to one side.

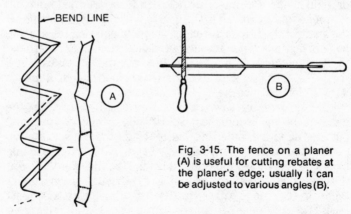

Fig. 3-15. The fence on a planer (A) is useful for cutting rebates at the planer's edge; usually it can be adjusted to various angles (B).

Filing is the most important part of setting and sharpening. Care is needed to keep the angles the same in both directions, and to keep both sets of teeth the same size. This can be seen by looking along the saw edge. Looking at it from the side may give the impression of different sizes, due to the beveled edges of a crosscut saw. It is satisfying to let a needle, or a pin with its head cut off, slide along the edge of a saw without falling off the side at any point, indicating success. But satisfactory setting and filing can usually be seen without doing this.

Circular saws may be filed the same way. To avoid missing any, or going over some twice, mark a starting point. As with hand saws, support the blade so it only projects very slightly above the vise. Too much projection will cause the saw to vibrate. Apart from the noise, the chattering of the file will blunt the saw quicker than it would cutting steadily.

The final test of a newly serviced saw: use it. Spiky teeth will soon become obvious when they catch in wood fibers. File them down. A tooth that is too low may not affect performance very much, but it will not do its share of work; it can be corrected during the next sharpening. Observe a hand saw's direction as it goes through wood. If it tends to wander, and this cannot be attributed to the way it is handled, the teeth leaning one way may be larger or set further than those leaning the other way. Normally, once this fault is known, it can be corrected by handling the saw to compensate for it, but it is something that should be rectified during the next sharpening. Light cuts made with a circular saw will uncover any tendency to wonder; but usually the high blade speed, and the fence, will cancel any minor discrepancies between teeth.

Most shop saws only cut one way: on the push stroke. Saws used for cutting logs, pruning branches, and the like, may have teeth that cut both ways. Such saws usually have deep gullets between groups of teeth to clear sawdust. The teeth are usually much larger than those of shop saws, but are set the same way—often quite wide to give enough clearance in wet wood. Teeth are sharpened on both edges, so their points are outward. After repeated sharpening, which reduces the overall depth of the blade, the gullets may have to be deepened with the rounded edge of a mill file. Some saws have *raker* teeth (Fig. 4-16). They do not cut, but are there to rake sawdust into the gullets, which carry it to the outside of the log to drop off. Raker teeth should be kept slightly shorter than cutting teeth, so they do not interfere with cutting; they should be filed straight across.

Sharpening band saw teeth is only justified with very large saws. Usually, home shop saws are replaced when they

SHARPEN BOTH WAYS

GULLET

RAKERS

Fig. 4-16. The teeth of log-cutting saws are sharpened on both edges, so their points are outward; raker teeth rake sawdust into the gullets for its removal.

become blunt. This also applies to saber saws and other small saws. A compass saw, and its cousins, may be sharpened like any hand saw, but it gets comparatively little use and only needs to be sharpened rarely.

SHARPENING DRILLS

Woodworking bits and drills are mostly sharpened by filing, although a slip stone may follow the file or be used in place of it. Usually, a woodworking bit is only able to accept a limited amount of sharpening. Whatever its type, the central point must extend furthest to guide the direction of the bit; the spur must project far enough ahead of the cutter to sever fibers before the cutter lifts out waste wood. It is usually the spur that wears away and has to be sharpened the most. When it gets too short to keep ahead of the cutter, the bit has to be discarded. Consequently, just sharpen enough to restore the edge.

A small, thin, fine file is used. It could be a *warding* file, intended for locksmith work, or a needle file. Restore the cutting edge by filing inside the spur, tapering toward the clockwise direction of cut (Fig. 4-17A). Never file the outside of a spur; it will affect the size of the hole. For the finest cutting edge, follow the file with an oilstone slip, using one with a square or knife edge.

The cutter has a small amount of *relief angle* underneath (Fig. 4-17B) and a cutting angle on top. If it has already been sharpened back very far, it can give a sufficient cut by filing it on top, possibly with a second bevel (Fig. 4-17C). A bit that is reaching the end of its useful life, that is, the spur is almost back to the same depth as the cutter, can have its cutter filed back on the underside to give the spur a little more lead.

Countersink bits can't be practically sharpened, but a rose bit can be filed with a saw file, and a snail bit may be sharpened with a small, round file.

Power woodworking bits with spurs present the same sharpening problems as brace bits. Spade bits depend on the backed-off angle meeting the flat side at a sharp angle. This

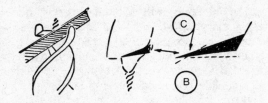

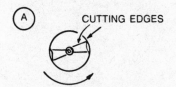

CUTTING EDGES

Fig. 4-17. A woodworking bit is sharpened on the inside of the spur (A); the cutter has a small relief angle (B). A previously sharpened bit can be filed on top, adding a second bevel (C).

can be restored by sharpening with a flat oilstone (Fig. 4-18A). Be careful to avoid rounding the outer corner that cuts the circumference of the hole.

Morse-pattern twist drills intended for metalworking, but used in the smaller sizes for making holes in wood, are sharpened on a grinding wheel. They are too hard to be filed and are unsuitable for sharpening with an oilstone. Each cutting edge is backed off 12° to 15° (Fig. 4-18B). This angle has to be maintained in sharpening, usually with the side of the stone (Fig. 4-18C), with frequent removal to dip in water to prevent overheating and drawing the temper. It is fairly easy to see this angle in a large drill, but not in the small sizes used for woodworking. Grinding jigs that mount on the grinder may

Fig. 4-18. Spade bits can be restored to sharpness with a flat oilstone (A). When sharpening a Morse-pattern twist drill, the "backed off" angle of the cutting edges (B) has to be maintained with the side of the stone (C).

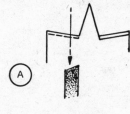

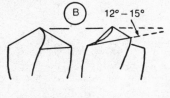

12° – 15°

be advisable, but some will not take very small drills. Fortunately, for drilling wood the angles are not critical; but some backing off is essential; if if there is not, or the angle goes the other way, there will be no cutting action and the only way the drill can be made to enter is by force. Grinding should be even. If one side is ground longer than the other, a new center will be made; a hole larger than the drill will be made, with the edge on the longer side doing most of the cutting.

5
Using Tools

The way to handle most tools may seem obvious—and it probably is—yet the experienced craftsman gets a result very different from that of the beginner. Some of this may be due to experience. But it is also affected by the way the tool is used and looked after. A tool should be used as if it were an extension of its operator, whether it is a hand tool or a power tool. There has to be an affinity with the tool and with the material being worked. This comes with experience. But the basic techniques provide a correct foundation on which skills can be mastered.

A great many people, particularly those not regularly engaged in hand work, tend to use one hand for almost everything, leaving the other virtually unemployed. A successful craftsman uses both hands. Of course, many tools require that both hands be involved; but in many cases, one hand is dominant; it may provide control, while the other applies pressure. It is often helpful to be able to change hands. If the tool can be used equally well with either hand, work on the ends of a long heavy piece may be done without turning it around, as would be necessary if the tool could only be used one way.

Since most people are right-handed, some tools only suit right-handed use, and may be inconvenient for the left hand. Some suit either; fortunately, they are in the majority. However, a wise craftsman learns to saw, plane, or do other tasks with both hands from the start. The aim should be to become as ambidextrous as possible. Most of us favor one hand, but the other can be brought to very nearly the same degree of dexterity.

SETTING OUT

The best method of measuring two parts that have to match is to compare one against the other. Of course, there are many situations where this cannot be done, and some sort of measuring instrument has to be used. Whether it is marked in inches and feet or metric measures is of little importance—it merely has to provide units for comparison. Sometimes it is better to transfer the measurement to the edge of a piece of wood, then transfer that to another part. When this is done, it may be sufficient to put a short pencil mark in each place, but it is more obvious, and often more accurate, to "peck" the marks out in the form of a rough *V* shape, with the point at the actual measurement (Fig. 5-1A).

This is sometimes a good way to transfer measurements along the edge of a rule onto a piece of wood. If measurements have to be taken from a point or an edge, and the distance is within the length of the rule, it would be accurate to put the measurement on the rule at the point or edge, and mark the distance across the end of the rule (Fig. 5-1B).

If the rule is thick, any errors of parallax can be avoided by standing the rule on its edge, so the actual marks are close to the surface being measured (Fig. 5-1C). If a series of distances have to be marked, add them together and mark them along the rule; measured individually, accuracy will be lost. As a simple example, suppose several points 3 inches apart are needed. If each is measured from the next (inches at a time), by the time six are marked, the total could be as much as ⅛ inch off. Instead, keep the rule still and measure 3 inches,

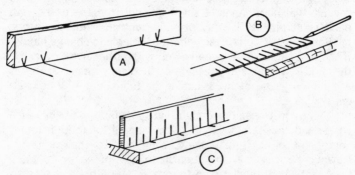

Fig. 5-1. When transferring measurements with a piece of wood as a gage, more accuracy can be had by making V-shaped marks (A); when marking a distance from an edge, make the mark across the end of the rule (B). To eliminate the inaccuracies caused by parallax in using a thick rule, use the rule on edge (C).

6 inches, 9 inches, and so on. If the series of measurements is more than the length of the rule, and an expanding rule or tape is not available, measure all that comes within the rule's length, then let the rule overlap at least the last space marked, before extending the marks. In this way the risk of the overall measurement "growing" will be reduced. (The total nearly always increases when individual spaces are measured.)

A series of even spaces can be "stepped off" with dividers or compasses, or with trammel heads for larger distances. These tools are also useful for comparing measurements. If dividers have to be set to a distance on a rule, it is easier and more accurate to get the distance from the 1 inch mark, instead of the end of the rule—allowing for the extra inch, of course. This gives the divider point a groove to settle in, instead of slipping over the end of the rule.

If many parts have to have identical measurements, it is wiser and quicker to mark them together. If there are four corner posts to a cabinet that extend to form legs, and other upright members, they can all be put together and key distances marked across them with a try square (Fig. 5-2A). Distances marked this way are more likely to match than if marked individually. Any construction that has to be squared up cannot finish with all corners being right angles if there are any uneven distances in parts that should agree.

When a try square is used, its stock should be pressed tightly against the wood. For the greatest precision, the same edge should always be used for further marking as the work progresses. In some machine construction this may not be so essential, but for hand work it is always advisable to plane a *face* side and edge as a reference point from which all marks are made. There is a traditional *face mark*: a pencilled loop on the face that meets a matching *vee* on the face edge (Fig. 5-2B). All measurements are taken from this edge, and try squares, marking gages, adjustable bevels, or other marking tools are used from this edge, whenever possible, to insure uniformity—even if there are slight inaccuracies in the other surfaces. Normally, the face side and edge come at the important part of the construction when the wood is incorporated, such as when the top and front of a shelf are made.

A lot of marking is done with a pencil, but for greater accuracy, use a knife. If a line is to be taken all around a piece of wood, whether with a pencil or a knife, place the try square stock first against the face edge to mark the face side. Then use it on the face edge while keeping it against the face side, followed by the other edge and, eventually, the opposite side; always place the stock on the surface with the face mark (Fig. 5-2C).

If the mark is to be sawed and the greatest accuracy is needed, sever the fibers all around with a knife, then use a paring chisel along the waste side of the cut (Fig. 5-2D). This will act as a guide for a fine saw, which can follow through on the waste side of the cut lines.

For important work, mark all around the wood for any cuts or joints to go right through. It is also advisable to do all the marking you can before starting to cut or shape. This is not always possible, such as for a piece curved in two directions where one has to be worked before the other can be marked. Marking out is a very important part of any woodworking project; the time spent on it is always worthwhile. After the wood is marked, do not be in too great a hurry to cut the ends to length. It is often better to leave them too long, while joints are cut or other work is done in the body of the wood. The excess wood can take knocks or wear, and need not be cut off until that is the only job left.

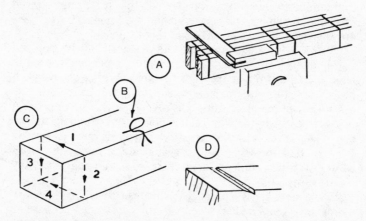

Fig. 5-2. Parts can be held together and marked at the same time with a try square (A). The traditional **face mark** (B), from which all measurements are taken. Always place the stock of the try square on a surface with the face mark (C). Using a paring chisel along the waste side of a cut will create a guide for a fine saw (D).

Marking gages are useful tools, but are not always easy to control. Set a gage by placing the end of a rule against the stock, and set the point to the proper measurement (Fig. 5-3A).

Set a mortise gage the same way, but if a chisel is to be used to cut the mortise, use it to set the width between the points. To use a gage, hold it in one hand with the palm over the stock and the first finger hooked over it. Position the thumb to push behind the point, and curl the other fingers around the other side of the stem (Fig. 5-3B). Tilt the gage forward, with the stock against the edge of the wood, then lower the point onto the wood. Push inward with the fingers and forward with the thumb (Fig. 5-3C). By adjusting the forward tilt, the amount the point scratches can be controlled.

Many assemblies can be checked for squareness by measuring (*comparing*, remember) their diagonals. This can be done by measuring with a rule, or by marking the edge of a strip of wood with the measurement (Fig. 5-3D). Testing in this way can form a final check after using a large try square, although it is also suitable for testing tapering structures, like splayed stool legs.

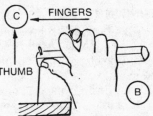

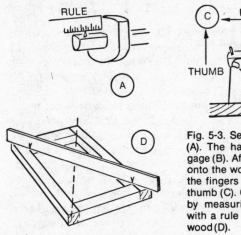

Fig. 5-3. Setting a marking gage (A). The hand's position on the gage (B). After lowering the point onto the wood, push inward with the fingers and forward with the thumb (C). Check for squareness by measuring diagonals, either with a rule or a marked piece of wood (D).

Like a broad board, an assembly can appear to be accurate when tested diagonally, yet have a twist in it. This can be checked with a sufficiently large surface known to be flat. If there is any twist, diagonally opposite corners will be above the surface.

"Measure twice before cutting once," is not just another clever remark. There is a lot of sense in it. When marking out wood, always do as much as possible before sawing, making joints, or otherwise working the wood; then check everything that has been marked by using a method different from the first employed. Check the location of a mark by calculating the distance between the opposite end and a first mark. If several measurements have been made, check their overall total, or what the gap between them should be.

If there are many marks, make sure there will be no confusion later. Scribble on what will be waste wood at the ends, or what will be cut out of joints. If there are two neighboring lines that might be confused, write something lightly alongside one or both of them that will tell you what they are. If you are marking a group of pieces together, it may be some time before you actually work on some of them; it would be a pity if you made the mistake of forgetting what the marks indicate. Watch the pairing of parts. You might not be the first woodworker to make two lefthand sides instead of a pair for a bookcase, but it wastes wood as well as being annoying.

USING SAWS

The best control of most handsaws and backsaws is obtained by having the first finger positioned alongside the handle, pointing along the blade. The other hand is not used on the saw, except when using a ripsaw on thick wood when it may help in applying pressure over the back of the handle.

It is important when sawing that the wood does not move or vibrate. Small pieces can be held against a bench hook for cutting with a backsaw. Large pieces can rest on one or two saw horses for cutting with a hand saw or ripsaw. It is usually convenient, both for getting into the best sawing position and for holding the wood, to kneel on it. Vibration can waste effort and may make the saw wander from the line, or leave an excessively rough edge. Plywood, in particular, should be supported fairly close to the line being cut to reduce vibration.

When cutting wood flat on the bench with a backsaw, it is often possible to merely start cutting with a forward push. To start exactly in the right place, draw the saw back a few times over the far edge; then change to forward cutting, bringing the saw to a flatter angle with each cut (Fig.5-4A).

Ripsaws and handsaws are held the same way, and the cut is directed the same way; but for ripping, saw at a more upright angle than when crosscutting. Precise angles are not important, but 45° for crosscutting and 60° for ripping is about right (Fig. 5-4B). The more upright the saw, the shorter the

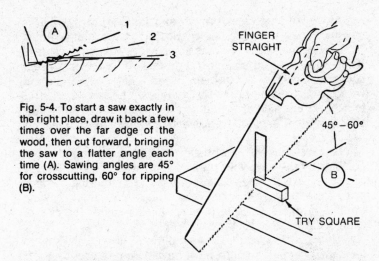

Fig. 5-4. To start a saw exactly in the right place, draw it back a few times over the far edge of the wood, then cut forward, bringing the saw to a flatter angle each time (A). Sawing angles are 45° for crosscutting, 60° for ripping (B).

length of blade actually cutting. On thick wood this lessens the effort needed for each stroke. On thinner wood, control may be better if the angle is flatter, so more teeth contact the wood.

Start sawing by pulling the saw back a few times, using the thumb of the other hand as a guide. Some ripsaws have a few smaller starting teeth at the end. Draw the saw back slowly, to get the saw's cut, or *kerf*, correctly located and to keep the saw from jumping—and damaging your thumb.

Once the saw has been started, start the first full cuts with the teeth near the handle (the *butt end*, as distinct from the point). By doing this the first real power is applied under the hand, at a point where the saw blade will not buckle. As you continue cutting, use as much of the saw's length as possible. Most workers find cutting easier, truer, and faster with long swings of the arm, rather than if only a part of the saw is used with short strokes. This also reduces local wear on the teeth, thus keeping the saw sharp longer.

Use the whole length of your arm when sawing, whether you are working with a backsaw on the bench or a handsaw on a saw horse. For heavy cuts, get into a position where you can swing your shoulder as well, using more of your body to provide pressure. Using this technique, muscles will not tire as quickly. The effort of sawing is lessened and better applied if you are behind the saw rather than beside it. Even if you are not able to get completely behind it, your shoulder should be in line with it. This also allows you to sight over the top of the saw blade and direct its movement.

As the cut progresses, provide extra support to prevent the free part from dropping and cracking. But the support must not be such that the kerf closes and pinches against the side of the saw. Support a short cut by hand. It is unwise to cut between supports, because the wood will bend as the cut weakens its length, and the kerf will pinch the saw. It is better to support one side of the cut firmly, while at the other side only sufficient support to prevent the wood from falling is needed.

Be careful as the saw breaks through at the end of a cut. Cutting too fiercely, with the same pressure needed for the body of the wood, may cause splitting and splintering. Reduce pressure and make the last few strokes quite light. Sawing through on the surface of a bench hook reduces the risk of splintering at the end of the cut.

After a little practice, it is not difficult to control a saw so it cuts where you want it to. Saws have their own peculiarities. Sharpening a saw slightly differently one way may cause it to run one way. Slight differences in setting will have the same effect. This may not be enough to matter, providing you know about the peculiarity and make the necessary correction by pressing or tilting slightly the right way. For cuts of any depth, the line on the surface should be *squared* down the front edge (Fig. 5-5A) as a guide for vertical sawing. Careful sawing close to the final size indicated by marking can reduce the amount of further work (Fig. 5-5B). Allow time for some practice on scrap wood to get used to a new saw, or one that has been newly serviced, before using it on an actual job.

A try square standing on its stock can be used to check whether the saw is vertical or not (refer to Fig. 5-4). A piece of scrap wood with a square edge can be clamped over a piece of wood being cut with a backsaw, to guide the saw's direction and to verify that the cut is vertical (Fig. 5-5C).

When ripping a long board, support the cut part on another saw horse. Any tendency of the kerf to close and bind on the saw can be reduced by putting a wedge into the end of the cut (Fig. 5-5D).

There are a few other points to watch. If you are working on old wood, check for nails or other metal. If a woodworking saw meets a nail with any force, you will have several inches of blunt teeth along the saw, because the steel is not hard enough to withstand this sort of abuse. When this happens, the whole length of the saw will have to be sharpened. If your saw wanders from the line, do not be too forceful in trying to bring

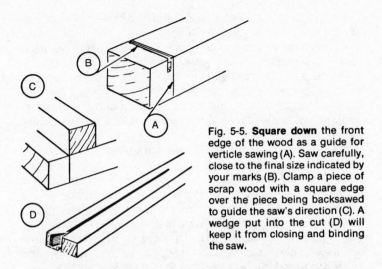

Fig. 5-5. **Square down** the front edge of the wood as a guide for verticle sawing (A). Saw carefully, close to the final size indicated by your marks (B). Clamp a piece of scrap wood with a square edge over the piece being backsawed to guide the saw's direction (C). A wedge put into the cut (D) will keep it from closing and binding the saw.

it back. Continue cutting while twisting the handle until you have returned to the line. If the line marks a finished edge, cut on the waste side to allow for planing or finishing to size. If you cut directly on the line, half the kerf will be on the wanted side, which will finish undersize. Thin plywood, wallboard, and several other manufactured boards may crack or splinter if sawed freehand and allowed to flex—even slightly. It is better to clamp strong boards on each side (Fig. 5-6A).

Many of the precautions for handsawing also apply to power sawing. Allowing a kerf to pinch a power saw may stall and damage the motor. Sometimes it is better to start a cut with a handsaw, before using a power saw freehand, to insure accuracy.

Internal cuts should be planned so that they suit the tool and the shape. Some saber saws can be made to cut in from the surface, but it is usually better for them—and essential for other power- and hand-saws—to drill at least one hole in the waste part, far enough away not to mark the final edge; but it should be in a position where the saw can swing into the line with a minimum of wasted cutting (Fig. 5-6B). For tight curves a coping- or fret-saw can be kept working up and down without being pressed forward, in this way easing out a corner of a diameter no more than the width of the blade. There is a limit, however. With these saws, and the wider saber- and compass-saws, a sharp internal angle has to be made in two cuts. One line is cut into the corner, then the saw is backed out and run in along the other side. Similarly, an internal point can be kept with two cuts (Fig. 5-6C).

Traditionally, much cutting was done by chopping with a chisel and mallet. Power saws have reduced the need for heavy chisel work. For instance, a band saw or saber saw can be used to remove a lot of the waste in a dovetail joint by making a series of cuts (Fig. 5-6D). The last part is a series of straight cuts, leaving only simple paring with a chisel to finish the job.

It is possible to work out shapes with a series of cuts. For an external curve too tight for a blade (Fig. 5-6E), the blade can follow the line a short distance then, when resistance prevents it from going further, the saw can run off and a little more can be done. With a tight internal cut, the saw cannot run outward; but by making several cuts toward the line (Fig. 5-6F), the line can be followed fairly closely. The kerf toward the line will close under the sideways pressure of the saw, and allow it to travel in a tighter curve than it could otherwise.

For general cutting, the most efficient way of working a table saw, or any other tool that uses a circular blade, is to have as much blade projecting through the table as possible. This makes the actual cut more like that of a handsaw kept nearly upright, bringing a smaller number of teeth into contact

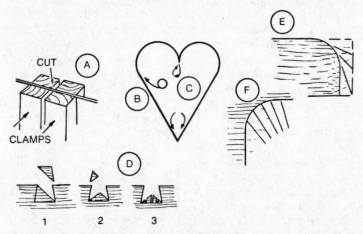

Fig. 5-6. Some materials, both natural and manufactured, may splinter unless the cut is supported between two boards (A). The starting hole for an internal cut should be located so the saw can swing into the line without wasted cutting (B); an internal point can be kept sharp with two cuts (C). A saber saw can make a series of cuts for a dovetail joint (D). A series of cuts can also be used to rough out external curves (E) and internal curves (F).

with the wood at one time, and thus reducing the load on the motor. At the other extreme, if the saw only just breaks through the wood, a large number of teeth are in contact and the load is much greater. While this may be necessary for cutting dadoes, or for other special work it is wrong for general cutting.

It is important that wood being cut with a circular saw blade does not swing. If it does, it will twist the blade and either cause it to wander from the line, or seize and maybe stall the motor. This means large pieces of wood should be supported away from the actual table on improvised supports, both before coming onto the saw and after leaving it. It is also helpful to have an assistant take the cut end as it comes off. However, devise a work plan between you. One could feed the wood onto the saw, while the other merely supports it without attempting to control or pull the wood, unless instructed to do so.

HANDLING CHISELS

Of the woodworking cutting tools, chisels and gouges are the ones most likely to cause accidents when improperly handled. As far as possible, the work should be fixed with a vise, holdfast, clamp, or other securing device. Both hands should be behind the chisel. There are a few occasions when this may be impossible, but holding wood with one hand while using a chisel in the other is inviting trouble. (Never chisel toward yourself.)

For successful chiseling, the grain has to be considered first. Except when cutting directly across the grain, its direction should be noted. If a chisel is used against the grain, splits and roughness will develop, and it will be difficult to control the chisel. Consider grain to be a bundle of loose straws. A cut against the way they are laid will lift and disturb them (Fig. 5-7A); strokes in the direction in which they are laid will cut them without lifting them (Fig. 5-7B). The direction of the grain can nearly always be ascertained by observing the edge perpendicular to the surface to be cut.

Chisel cuts should be directed away from the marked line and into the waste wood. Make initial cuts away from the line, so the direction of any splitting can be seen and further cuts can be made accordingly. In any case, the best chiseled finish is obtained by removing progressively finer shavings. Whenever possible, use the chisel with a slicing action. A direct cut, a wedge action, may roughen the surface, even when cutting correctly with the grain. If the chisel's edge attacks the wood at an angle, and is moved across the surface as it cuts (Fig. 5-7C), the effect will be more knifelike, resulting in a better surface.

When chiseling, grip the handle and push with one hand; the other may be on top of the blade to apply pressure and control for a heavy cut. For a lighter cut, having the thumb on top may be only necessary.

Use the chisel bevel-downward; the shape of the cutting end will resist going deeper, and will tend to lift the wood toward the surface—the safe way to remove a lot of wood. A chisel pushed by hand or tapped with a mallet breaks wood without causing splits below the line (Fig. 5-7D). The chisel is then turned over and used for hand paring with light slices until the line is reached.

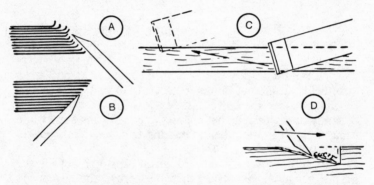

Fig. 5-7. A cut against the lay of the grain will lift it (A); going with it, it can be cut without being lifted (B). If a chisel enters the wood at an angle, and is moved across the surface as it cuts (C), a better surface will result. The safe way to remove a lot of wood with a chisel is with the bevel facing down (D).

Chiseling in this way can be used for any angle directly along the grain, and at a fairly steep angle to it. If much wood has to be removed, bring the edge close to the line with a saw, so little will be left for the chisel to pare. If there is a curved edge, the saw can make a series of straight cuts, and the chisel can pare them to the curve.

With difficult grain it may be impossible to work successfully, either with or across the grain. If this is the case, it may be better to work diagonally across the grain with a slicing action. It is usually a good idea to avoid cutting directly across the grain, but in some circumstances it is necessary. A direct cut across the grain, without any slicing, will not produce a good surface. This occurs in the *dado* (groove) found in several kinds of joints. Fortunately, the quality of surface at the bottom of the dado is not important.

For this sort of work, the sides are sawed, then the chisel is used bevel-downward to lift out most of the waste wood. A mallet may be needed in all but the smallest work. When the work gets close to the bottom of the dado, light cuts are made with the chisel, flat-side down, and with hand power only, to get the surface as smooth and level as possible. Attempting heavy cuts across the grain will lift it and leave a rough surface that may go deeper than needed.

A chisel can be used inside a curve, but there is a limit. It will not follow too small a radius. If it is a hollow area, cut from both directions toward the center (Fig. 5-8A), working a little at a time from each side.

Vertical chiseling, a different technique, is used to remove wood and get it to shape; but the surface it leaves cannot compare to one pared with the grain. Both hands are usually around the chisel (Fig. 5-8B), or one around the handle, if a mallet is used.

When vertically chiseling a part wider than the chisel, observe the grain, so if there is any splitting it is into waste wood. When following a curve or angle that goes from side to end grain, cut from the side so each cut overlaps the previous one (Fig. 5-8C), the edge of the chisel projecting over the cut just made. Any breaking out will then be away from the final shape. Starting at the other end, or burying both sides of the chisel, might cause splitting into the wanted part.

As far as possible, a shearing cut should be made by tilting the chisel with the grain when paring vertically. There is a risk of the far side of the wood breaking out, if it is unsupported during vertical paring. A piece of flat scrap wood should be put under the work, which should be clamped down. This is particularly important when cutting directly across end grain and a slicing action is next to impossible.

Gouges are used somewhat like chisels. An outside-ground gouge is used mainly for hollowing. Its action is like a chisel used bevel downward. Watch the grain form, and be careful to avoid digging a corner of the gouge into a place where it could start a split into good wood. When hollowing a bowl-like depression, make most of the cuts diagonally across the grain. Keep them light, so the corners of the gouge are always above the surface; this will reduce the risk of splitting. Always cut from the outside toward the center of a hollow. Cutting the other way, even diagonally, will tend to lift the grain.

An inside-beveled gouge is a hand paring tool that is not used with a mallet. Most of its work is trimming the insides of curves by vertical *paring*. This is done by making light, overlapping cuts. Keep the corners of the gouge above the surface; if this is impossible, make the cuts in steps, starting from an across-the-grain position (Fig. 5-8D) so any breaking out will be toward the center.

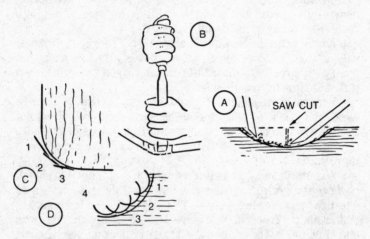

Fig. 5-8. Make the chisel cuts for a hollow from opposite directions, toward the center (A). Vertical chiseling (B) requires that both hands be around the chisel (if a mallet isn't being used). When following a curve that goes from side to end grain, make overlapping cuts with the edge of the chisel projecting over the last cut (C). When using a gouge to trim the inside of a curve, and you can't keep its corners above the surface, cut in steps, starting from an across-the-grain position (D).

PLANING

Except when using a few of the small planes, both hands are needed on the tool. This means that the wood being planed has to be held in a way that resists the thrust of the plane, either by being clamped or held in a vise, or worked against a stop. A plane that can move will vibrate and mark the surface of the wood. When heavy cuts are being made, the thrust from a plane blade can be considerable.

It is as necessary to consider the direction of the grain when using a plane as it is when using a chisel; the cutting action is very similar. Nearly all woods will tear up, at least slightly, if planed against the grain. If there is any doubt, set the plane finely and test it on a less important surface. The directions of the grain on opposite sides of a board are almost always opposite to each other. When planing approximately parallel to the grain, use the lines viewed at a right angle to the surface as a guide. If the lines are wavy or very nearly parallel to the edge or surface, only a trial will determine the best way to plane.

When planing diagonally to the grain, there is no question about its direction. An experimental cut the wrong way down a slope will demonstrate that the blade will dig in and tear. Always plane as if the wood fibers were hairs that have to be stroked straight. A low-angle plane is best for work directly across the grain, but an ordinary smoothing plane can be used. The risk of breaking out at the far side of the cut (Fig. 5-9A) can be overcome by planing an end from both sides toward the middle (Fig. 5-9B). If the cut has to be made right through in one direction, a bevel at the far side (Fig. 5-9C) will reduce the risk of splitting, because not until the final cuts will the blade be going right through. Another form of protection is a piece of scrap wood held against the side (Fig. 5-9D); but it has to be held very close to be effective.

The sides of modern planes are perpendicular to their soles; they can be used on edge. The cut will be square with the base. This is convenient for working on a shooting board, but for small, thin pieces, such as plywood parts, use a block plane on its side, with the work held against a bench hook (Fig. 5-9E).

Planing by hand can be fairly strenuous work, so it is important to use muscle power to the best advantage. The plane has to be swung with both arms; at the end of a stroke they should be almost extended. This cannot happen if the bench is too high. For planing, it is better to have a bench too low than too high. But there has to be a compromise, because a very low bench may be less suited to other purposes.

Stand so that the plane is pushed away from your body. This cannot be a direct, central push, but stand comfortably behind the starting point. For right-handed planing along the bench, or with the wood held in a vise, keep your right shoulder over the line that the plane is to follow, and lean your body over accordingly. The stroke then starts with the heel of the plane almost under the right shoulder; the stroke will be as long as the left hand will reach. The right hand, which controls

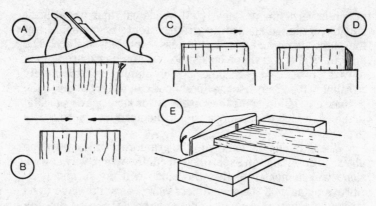

Fig. 5-9. Having the wood break out at the far side of the plane's cut (A) could be avoided by planing from both sides toward the middle (B); a bevel at the far side (C) will also reduce the risk of splitting. A piece of scrap wood held against the side (D) can provide similar protection. For plywood parts, use a block plane on its side, with the work held against a bench hook(E).

the plane, should be kept firmly on the handle. The left hand can swing around on the knob at the front, but it should maintain downward pressure. The thrust of the right hand on the handle will be like that on a saw. The push is directed toward the cutting edge, and the left hand gives supplementary pressure. For a flat surface, put more weight on the front of the plane at the start, and more on the back as the cut is finished.

Normally, the plane should be kept in line with the work, to get the full benefit of the length of the sole in keeping the surface flat. Turning the plane can shorten effective sole length considerably (Fig. 5-10). However, there are occasions

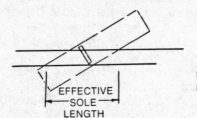

EFFECTIVE
SOLE
LENGTH

Fig. 5-10. Turning a plane can shorten its effective sole length.

when this may be worthwhile. When used this way, the cut becomes a slice. It may be the only way that difficult grain can be brought to a smooth finish.

If a full range of planes is available, the first one to use is the jack plane, set fairly coarsely, and with its cap iron not too close to the edge of the cutting iron. It will remove saw marks and other roughness. A straightedge can be used to test the surface, both in length and width, but perfection is not necessary at this stage. The jack plane, with a slight curve to its cutting edge, is used to get approximate flatness.

The jack plane is followed by a jointer, or a fore- or try-plane. Its longer sole reduces the high spots. Use the try plane along the wood for most of the work, but sweep it diagonally as well to get flatness in all directions. Use a straightedge to bring the surface to as near flat as possible. Do this checking while looking toward a light; bits of light below the edge of the rule will disclose hollowness. If you are planing a broad board, test with winding strips too. If the try plane is set finely and has a straight cutting edge, it should produce a good finish. Follow the try plane with a very sharp, finely set smoothing plane. It will remove tiny inequalities left by the try plane. If the smoothing plane has to be used heavily, it is a sign that the try plane stage has not been done properly.

If the wood has been machine-planed, further planing will depend on the accuracy of the surface. A good machine with sharp cutters, and fed slowly, may produce an acceptable surface, except perhaps for sanding. Planing in haste with an imperfect machine may call for considerable hand work. If machine-plane marks are very evident, but the surface is generally true when tested with a straightedge, it may be sufficient to go over it with a smoothing plane, taking off just enough to get through the ripples left by the machine. If there are inaccuracies, as well as a poor surface, it may be necessary to use a try plane before a smoothing plane. Machine planing, then, will have replaced the laborious jack plane stage; but a properly set planing machine, used without haste, should take the work further.

In most woodwork of any importance, the first planing job is to get a true, broad surface that will become the face side or surface from which other measurements are taken. The next step is to produce a face edge that is at a right angle to the face side. If the wood is considerably thinner than it is wide, it will have to be held in a vise; otherwise, it can rest on the bench against a stop.

Use a jack plane to get the edge reasonably straight. Its length can be tested with a straightedge, but it is easy enough to sight along it to see high spots or hollows. The jack plane should be kept reasonably square to the face side, but an exact right angle is not important at this stage. Change to the try plane. Keep it straight and use its whole length. Some workers, when working on a narrow edge, prefer to have their thumb on top and their fingers curled underneath, forming a guide (Fig. 5-11A). Sight along the work as a check for straightness. Check for squareness with a try square at several points (Fig. 5-11B). It is very easy, at first, to swing off toward the full reach of your arms, making the edge develop a curve. If the edge is true enough from the try plane it may be unnecessary to follow with a smoothing plane. If the grain is difficult and the smoothing plane is necessary, be careful not to plane unevenly and spoil the trueness obtained with the try plane.

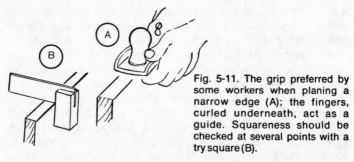

Fig. 5-11. The grip preferred by some workers when planing a narrow edge (A); the fingers, curled underneath, act as a guide. Squareness should be checked at several points with a try square (B).

The accuracy of a machine-planed edge is dependent, to a certain extent, on the size of the machine in relation to the wood. In effect, the machine acts like a try plane. Its degree of accuracy depends on the squareness of the fence and the length of the bed, coupled with how carefully the wood is passed over it. If the machine-planed edge is found to be true when tested, a stroke with a try plane to remove machine plane marks may be all that is necessary. This is better than using any sort of sander on an edge, because a sander may round out the angles slightly. In any case, do other work on the wood before sanding; there may be tiny particles of abrasive left that could blunt tools.

When the face side and face edge are true, mark them and use them as bases for further measuring and marking. Use a marking gage to mark the width over the face side, and the one opposite it, from the face edge. After this is planed, gage the thickness from the face side at both edges, and across the ends if the wood is very wide. Plane to the desired thickness to the gage lines around the edges, then plane to match the center. If done accurately—the surface finishes by splitting the gage lines—the second side should be as flat and true as the face side.

Sometimes a broad surface, particularly one made up of several pieces glued together, has grain that will not plane all the same way. The best way to deal with considerable unevenness here is to use a very sharp, finely set plane almost perpendicular to the grain. As the surface gets flatter you will discover portions of grain less likely to tear up in one direction. As you make the final cuts, swing the plane to make slicing cuts in the right direction over these places, possibly varying the angle of the plane several ways as it progresses across the surface. This sort of surface may have to be finished by scraping, followed by sanding. If you go directly to sanding, awkward pieces of grain and fiber ends, that may have been bent or pressed down, will stand up again, appearing as roughness when polish or stain is applied. A scraper is much more likely to remove, rather than bend, such imperfections.

A shooting board is a useful device for squaring edges being planed, providing the wood is no longer than the board. It is also valuable for planing ends across the grain with a low-angle plane. As you gain skill in handling planes, you will be able to do more of this sort of work freehand with confidence. A plane is something like a saw in that it does better work if you are used to its peculiarities. Although modern planes are mass-produced, there are still subtle differences that make a craftsman prefer to use the planes he knows.

The accuracy of a plane depends on the flatness of its sole. A metal plane is unlikely to distort. If it is found to lack trueness, there is little that can be done about it. However, there are other points that may be overlooked. The sole may pick up things that cling to it, affecting its flatness. If a glued joint is planed before the glue has fully hardened, or painted wood is planed, there can be blobs and ridges that will affect flatness. These things can usually be scraped off. It is a good idea to remove the plane iron and rub the sole on a piece of abrasive paper or cloth supported on a level surface.

Wooden planes have to be trued periodically by planing their soles with another plane. Craftsmen used to lubricate their planes by drawing them across a block of wood with a hollow, containing a cloth pad soaked in light oil. One of these would be worth having when planing resinous or otherwise sticky wood.

A hand-held power plane is an example of a machine adapted to be used almost as a hand tool. Hold it as you would a jack plane, and use it the same way. Get plenty of practice on waste wood before starting on a special job. When the tool is mastered and understood, it will do many planing jobs with considerably less labor than equivalent hand methods. A smoothing plane and scraper may still have to follow, however.

Special hand planes, such as those for cutting rebates, following curves, or cutting dadoes, should be understood, as well as basic planes. Most of them are much lighter and have single irons. They must be held very firmly, because their light weight cannot counteract vibration. Because a single iron also has a tendency to vibrate slightly, and tear up the surface more than a cutter having a cap iron would, it is important that it be sharp. It should not be set too coarsely, unless the surface produced is not important, like the groove for a plywood panel. It is particularly important to keep low-angle planes very sharp and finely set. They are intended only for finishing work across the grain. The bulk of the wood should be removed by other tools before they are used.

Spokeshaves are particularly susceptible to changes in grain direction as they follow curves. As with chisels and planes, a spokeshave must be used as if you were stroking the "grain hairs" into place (Fig. 5-12A).

Normally, a plane has an evenly projecting cutting edge. When viewed from the front with its sole held upward, a jack plane's cutting edge can be seen to be curved (Fig. 5-12B). Other planes will show a straight line (Fig. 5-12C); their blades should not project enough to expose the corners. If there is uneven projection (Fig. 5-12D), there will be uneven cutting;

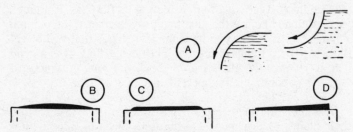

Fig. 5-12. A spokeshave must be used as if it were stroking "grain hairs" into place (A). A jack plane has a curved cutting edge (B); the straight cutting edges of other planes (C) should not project enough to expose their corners. Uneven plane-blade projection (D) will cause uneven cutting.

but occasionally this may be necessary, as when the plane has to get more off in a restricted place.

In many bench planes the lever cap is held by a cam that locks everything firmly. Although blade adjustment is sometimes made with the cam under full pressure, it is better to release the cam slightly. With the plane inverted and sighting across the cutting edge along the sole, turn the adjusting nut to move the edge in or out, and the lateral adjusting lever to bring the projection even. After preliminary setting has been done in this way, minor adjustments can be made while the plane is in use. How far the cap iron is kept from the edge will depend on how coarse a setting is used and the type of wood being planed, but try it quite close at first.

Other planes may not have both adjustments. Block planes and some others have a screw adjustment to move the blade up and down, without a means of adjusting the angle of the cutting edge. If the cutting iron is long, as it is in a shoulder plane, there can be very little sideways adjustment. With these planes it is important that the edge be kept sharp straight across, or at the correct angle if it is a skew cutter. There is not as much room for adjustment in these planes as there is in ordinary planes.

If there is no screw or lever adjustment provided, position the plane iron by eye, sighting along the sole, before tightening the wedge. If there is an up and down adjustment, set the edge without tilt, then use the screw adjustment to get the correct projection of the cutting edge.

Getting the correct setting for any plane is a matter of experience. Try the plane on a piece of waste wood after setting it. Even if the iron has been removed for sharpening, without disturbing the adjustments, it is unlikely to cut exactly as it did before.

The successful performance of a power planer depends on sharpness and setting. Cutting edges should be square and project by the same amount, otherwise one blade may do all the cutting; apart from causing excessive wear on its edge (while the other edges are unaffected), this also gives a poorer finish. If only one of two cutters are working, the effect is the equivalent of running the machine at half-speed with both cutters working. Of course, if there are three or four cutters and only one is working, the result is proportionately worse.

The rear table should be tangent to the cutting circle of the knives. This can be tested with a straight-edged piece of wood. If its edge is rubbed with chalk and it is moved to various positions on the table, maladjustment of the cutting edge can be seen. Any testing and adjustment of the machine should be done with the power supply disconnected. This method of checking insures that the table and cutting circle are at the same height. Some workers favor a cutting circle very slightly above the rear table level. This can be tested by marking the edge of the wood with lines about ⅛ inch apart. If the first line is put at the edge of the table and the cutter block is rotated by hand, the cutting edge will move the wood toward the next mark (Fig. 5-13A). How much the wood moves indicates how much the cutting circle is above the rear table level. For small, home-shop planers, it is probably better to set the cutting circle level by the first test; but find out what the makers of the particular machine suggest.

How the knives are held on cutter blocks varies with different makes. A screw adjustment allows some precision in setting after the securing screws are slackened. One way to bring the cutting edges to the level of the rear table is with a flat-sided magnet. If the magnet is used to hold each knife in turn while its screws are tightened (Fig. 5-13B), they should all be at the same height.

The cutting angle is important. If a cutter is damaged, get a replacement, rather than trying to grind it by freehand methods; it is difficult to maintain the correct angle and keep the edge straight with ordinary shop equipment. It is wiser to have a second set of planer knives on hand to use while the other set is being serviced.

Evenly blunted knives can routinely be sharpened in the machine. Disconnect the power. Lay an oilstone over the edge of the front table, and lower the table until the stone rests across the bevel of the blade (Fig. 5-13C) when the cutter block is turned into position by hand. Wrap a piece of paper around the oilstone, but leave enough of the stone projecting to contact the cutting edge. Hold the cutting block steady with one hand, perhaps by gripping the drive pulley, and rub the stone on the blade. Use oil on the stone. After a few rubs, check to see that the whole width of the bevel is being rubbed. If it is not, adjust the front table accordingly. The original angle must be maintained if the planer is to work properly.

If you intend to use the planer to work rebates over the edge of the table, the knives should project slightly from the end of the cutter block to avoid leaving a torn or rough surface on the wood. If the knives are removed or adjusted, make sure the amount of side projection is the same for all knives.

Keep the cutting edges in good condition for as long as possible. This means you should constantly check wood for embedded nails, stones, or grit before feeding it on to the planer. If wood left in a rough state is to be planed, make the first cut deep enough to go through to a new surface, removing all of the dirty part in one pass. Grit may become embedded in the end grain of wood stored on end; it is better to cut off these ends before planing the wood.

The high-speed cutters rotating of a planer can be dangerous if carelessly handled. Any guards should be kept in position whenever possible. When the job makes it necessary to remove them, keep your hands away from the vicinity of the cutters. Short pieces of wood present the greatest problem—and the greatest possible danger. Do not attempt to machine plane a piece of wood less than a foot long without the safe control of a pusher block (Fig.5-13D).

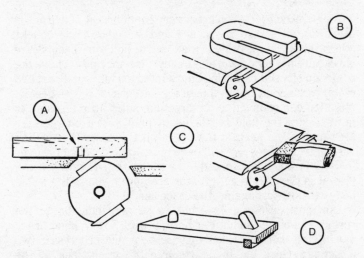

Fig. 5-13. By marking a piece of wood with lines ⅛ inch apart, and feeding it onto a power planer, you can check the height of the cutting circle (A) by noting how far it moves. A flat-sided magnet can be placed on the planer's table to hold each knife while its screws are tightened, thereby insuring uniform height (B). Blunted planer knifes can be sharpened on the machine with an oilstone (C). Pieces less than a foot long should be fed onto a planer with a **pusher block** (D).

With any length of wood, be careful of *kickbacks*, where the cutter rejects wood brought to it. This could be caused by bluntness, too fast a feed, or both. The small planer is designed so the left hand presses the wood down on the rear table, while the right pushes forward without pressing. As you plane, and sufficient wood carries over to the rear table, transfer your left hand to that part while still pressing down. As you approach the end of the wood, move your other hand around to join the first, so both hands complete the job over the rear table.

As with hand planing, the direction of the grain must be taken into account. If it is not obvious from side markings, plane a short distance, withdraw the wood, and examine it. Turn it end over end if necessary. It is usual to work in a sequence similar to hand planing. Get a broad surface true, then hold it against the fence while planing an edge. Check the squareness of the fence with a try square standing on the table, rather than relying on any calibration on the fence adjustment, which may be small and therefore liable to error.

USING OTHER TOOLS

Making holes in wood is not very complicated. If a brace is used, the bit should be secure and straight in the chuck; otherwise, it is impossible to make a true hole very deep. Some chucks are not very accurate. In any case, they do not have the precision of a self-centering chuck intended for round-shanked metalworking drills. If the brace bit has a screw center, attention can be given to its direction, since little pressure is needed once the hole is started. A plain brace bit requires pressure on the head of the brace all the time. For drilling vertically, this pressure will have to be applied by leaning over the brace. When horizontally drilling work held upright in a vise, it is possible to get greater pressure because the whole body can be thrust against the brace head.

In most cases the hole has to be perpendicular to the surface the bit starts on. For normal work with a hand brace and bit, this can be checked by observing your progress in two directions. Once the bit starts into the wood, look at the brace—or get someone else to—first from one side, then from a position at a right angle to it (Fig. 5-14A). Adjust the angle of the brace as required before the bit goes more than a few turns into the wood. A small try square could also be used to check that the bit is upright.

Although the point of a bit is supposed to make it start in the right place, make a dent first, either with an awl or a center punch. If there are many pencil lines, possibly indicating joints or other work to come later, lightly mark around the hole positions with a pencil; otherwise, you may enter the bit at the wrong crossing of pencil lines, in a place intended for something else.

A brace bit is designed to cut into wood. The pressure of the center screw's pull, or the operator's thrust on the head of the brace, can make it break through the far side violently tearing out wood around the hole—if nothing is done about it. One thing that can be done is to have a piece of scrap wood clamped tightly behind the work. Another is to watch for the point's emergence, then turn the wood over to drill back the other way; the nibs or spurs will sever the surface fibers (Fig. 5-14B), and a clean hole will result.

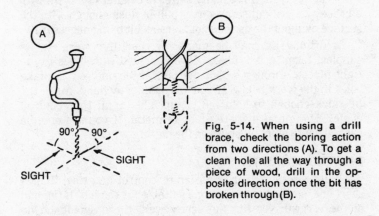

Fig. 5-14. When using a drill brace, check the boring action from two directions (A). To get a clean hole all the way through a piece of wood, drill in the opposite direction once the bit has broken through (B).

When power drilling freehand there is a similar need to watch direction, and deal with the risk of wood breaking out. One problem with a hand-held power-drilling tool is its very rapid penetration. Restraint is needed to keep the hole from going right through. This is particularly important for screw holes. Use a hand drill for small holes; they are easier to control, and certainly not laborious to use with screw-size drill bits.

Deep holes, whether made by hand or power, bring the risk of shavings jamming up around the bit. This phenomenon varies in degree between woods, but if the flutes or neck of a drill become tightly jammed with waste, the bit may cease to work, the hole's shape may become distorted, and, in extreme cases, the bit may seize and break. When drilling deeply, withdraw the bit occasionally; with a power drill, pulling out the bit without stopping it will clear wood chips automatically. With a screw-center bit in a brace, it will be necessary to reverse rotation to free the screw, then change to the normal clockwise direction as the bit is pulled further out.

For accurate drilling it is better to have an electric hand drill in a stand, or a drilling machine. The cut will be better at a moderate speed, particularly for larger holes. If the machine has a feed lever, regulate the pressure to suit the cut, while keeping the edges cutting without force. A clean hole can usually be made by machine drilling, if the bit goes through into a piece of scrap wood.

Countersinking should be done by hand or with a slow-turning power drill. Even if screw holes have been made with a power drill, it is usually better to countersink them with a brace. Very small screws may pull in flush enough with the surface, without the use of a countersink bit being necessary.

A drilling jig may be made for repetitive work. In its simplest form, it is a piece of wood drilled with holes in the right places, through which the bit can be entered to make holes in the work below. If you are drilling by hand, make the jig thick enough to hold the bit upright (or at the required angle). Dowelling jigs are made of metal. If you use one, be careful not to blunt bit spurs on the metal.

DRIVING SCREWS

A long screwdriver is easier to control and turn than a short one, so use the longest one suitable for the job. If the end of the screwdriver fits the screw well, there should be no difficulty driving or withdrawing the screw. When withdrawing a tight screw, apply maximum pressure to the screw in the first turn. If the end of the screwdriver is allowed to ride out of the screw's slot, the edge of the slot will become rounded and may make it impossible to get a firm enough hold on the screw to remove it.

There are screwdrivers fitted with screw-gripping devices for directing screws into almost inaccessible places. For steel screws it may be sufficient to magnetize the screwdriver, so it can carry the screw into place. Another method is to put the screw through the sticky side of a piece of masking tape, then tape the screw onto the end of the screwdriver (Fig. 5-15); the

SCREW THROUGH TAPE

Fig. 5-15. One way to hold a screw before starting it is to tape it to the screwdriver blade; use tape that will break easily once the screw is started.

tape will break away from the screw once it has started into the wood.

Extra torque can be put on a square-necked screwdriver by using a wrench. For large, long screws, it is better to use a screwdriver bit in a brace. If holes are correctly drilled for size and length, you should be able to drive any screw without it giving excessive resistance. If a screw becomes almost impossible to turn, withdraw it to see what is wrong—almost always the drill was too thin or not taken deep enough.

Pump-action and ratchet screwdrivers are useful when many screws have to be driven; but, in general, a plain screwdriver is a more sensitive tool. It allows a more careful feel of your progress in pulling parts together. Some screws, particularly brass ones, may shear within the wood if they are torqued too hard. Similarly, screw-driving attachments for drills and self-powered screwdrivers are valuable when a great many screws have to be driven, but they are not often justified for home shop projects. If a series of screws have to be driven, drill all the holes, start the screws with light hammer taps then use a pump, ratchet, or power screwdriver.

Screw-driving is mostly a two-handed operation, one hand on the handle to provide thrust and torque, the other gripping the blade just above the screw head to keep the tool in place. Keeping the end of the screwdriver in place is particularly important when the surrounding wood is already finished; the screwdriver end should not be wider than the screw slot, or off-center, projecting to one side. Phillips head screws are designed to reduce the risk of screwdriver movement marring the surrounding surfaces.

HAMMERING

Mallets and hammers require the confidence to hold them by the end of the handle. A craftsman swings a hammer while gripping the end of the handle, the pivot point being mainly around his elbow; but both wrist and shoulder will move for a heavy hit. A beginner does not usually trust his aim, and therefore moves his grip closer to the head. He may gain something in control, but he loses a considerable amount of power, as well as experiencing an uncomfortable jarring of his wrist.

A nail is started with light taps while it is held between index finger and thumb. The advantage of a cross peen is its ability to get at very small nails held between the fingers.

Using a hammer with a curved face, a skilled worker can drive a nail flush without marking the surrounding surface (Fig. 5-16A); the skill is in directing the blow. The alternative, if you do not trust your hammering, is to make the last blows with a punch (Fig. 5-16B). This is necessary in any case, if the nail is to go below the surface. Choose a punch about the same size as the head of the nail.

When using a claw hammer to withdraw a nail, a thin pad of scrap wood may be used for leverage under the claw if there is risk of damaging the surface. If the nail is long, it may be necessary to use a thicker block to get enough leverage for the last pull (Fig. 5-16C). This would also apply to the use of pincers.

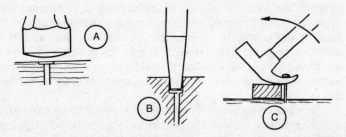

Fig. 5-16. Using carefully directed blows, a hammer with a curved face can drive a nail flush with the surface (A); the alternative is to make the last blows with a punch (B). When using a hammer to withdraw a nail, putting a small block of scrap wood under the claw (C) will provide more leverage.

If a hammer head gets loose, you can use the difference in inertia between wood and steel to tighten it. Instead of trying to hammer the handle further into the head by hitting it directly on the bench, head down, hold the hammer in one hand with the head down, then hit the end of the handle with a mallet. A similar effect is obtained by knocking the end of the handle on the bench. This will drive the head further onto the tapered handle, tightening it.

It will then be necessary to tighten the wedges to prevent the centrigugal force of the swinging hammer from loosening the head again. If it was only slightly loosened, it will probably be sufficient to drive the metal wedge in further. After a considerable amount of tightening, it may be necessary to remove the metal wedge with pliers, then pick out the remains of the wooden wedge and drive in another hardwood wedge, followed by the metal wedge again.

Tightening the head of a hammer or axe by soaking it in water is inadvisable, except in an emergency or for an immediate job. Soaking causes the wood to swell, making it grip the head; but when it dries out the head is liable to be looser than ever.

If a new handle has to be fitted to the head, make saw cuts for wedges in the end before driving on the head. Drive a wooden wedge the long way across its cross section as tightly as possible, then trim it off with a saw and drive in a metal wedge across the wooden one.

METALWORKING

A woodworker has to do a certain amount of metalworking, even if all he has to do is cut off the ends of nails, or take the roughness off a fitting. A metalworking hacksaw has a replaceable blade, held taut by a wing nut. Adequate tension is important. A hacksaw is held with one hand on the handle, and the other at the crook in the far end of the frame (Fig. 5-17A). Both hands share in control, but the hand on the handle provides direction. Release pressure on the return stroke. A long, slow stroke, one using most of the length of the blade, is more effective than short, quick ones that use only a few teeth.

Files are used in a way very similar to saws, that is, with a hand on each end. If you have to remove metal from an edge wider than the file, make the edge go along the length of the file, as the file moves the length of the edge (Fig. 5-17B). To

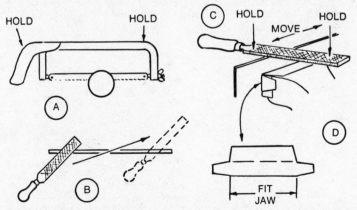

Fig. 5-17. The correct hacksaw grip (A); cross-filing (B); draw-filing (C). Vise clamps provide a malleable backing to protect metalwork in the vise (D).

remove the crossfiling marks, hold the file square across the edge with both hands and move it sideways to "draw file" the edge (Fig. 5-17C).

If you have to drill holes in metal, use a center punch to locate the position accurately. A Morse-pattern drill may wander some distance before entering the metal, if there is no center-punch mark to take its center. Center-punching thin metal on the wood surface of a bench will buckle the metal. A block of iron with a flat top should be kept as an anvil for punching and other similar metalwork; a small section of railroad track makes a nice little I-sectioned anvil, if you can find one. It needs to be strong enough to do its job; but if it is also light enough to hold in one hand, it can be used to support nail heads when their projecting ends are clenched, or for similar jobs.

If a metalworking vise is used to hold things like ornamental brass hinges for sawing or filing, something must be done to cover the rough, sharp vise jaws to prevent them from damaging the softer brass. Sheet-metal vise clamps are the answer (Fig. 5-17D). Copper is also suitable for this, being softer than most metals you are likely to hold in a vise, yet hard enough to provide a good grip; one of the softer aluminim alloys might also be suitable.

6 Fasteners

Wooden parts are joined in many ways. Parts may be fitted into each other, requiring no other fastening. Often, joints are glued—a technique that has been used from earliest times. Parts may be held by wooden pegs, like dowels; such *treenails* held Viking longships together for Atlantic voyages. Glue is still favored in good quality work, but a lot of woodwork is nailed or screwed, either in place of or in addition to being glued.

Screws are considered the superior fasteners. Nails are one-time fasteners, because they are difficult to withdraw without damaging the wood. A screw, of course, can be withdrawn and replaced; but it also clamps parts together, and is generally more secure than most nails. For rough woodworking, the use of screws would not be justified: screws cost more than nails, it takes more work to drive them, and more tools are needed.

For things attached to wood, such as hinges and locks, it is usual to use screws, although some plastic edging and other things require nails. Fine nails have their uses in cabinetwork, where they can be punched below the surface and covered with stopping, but nails are usually only used for rougher, less important work.

NAILS

All general-purpose nails are made of *mild steel*, often incorrectly called "iron." The steel may be protected by plating. Zinc has been commonly used on nails intended for exterior use. Nails are also made of metal less susceptible to corrosion, such as aluminum, brass, and copper. Copper, having a good resistance to salt water, has been used extensively in wooden boat construction. None of these other metals make nails as stiff as does steel, so care is needed in driving them. Some special nails are made of tool steel, sometimes hardened and tempered, for such tough work as penetrating directly into masonry. For nearly all woodworking purposes, mild steel nails are the usual choice.

Ordinary nails are round, with parallel sides and flat heads. Some have ridges below the head to increase their grip slightly. The point is formed by several flats, meeting in a diamond form (Fig. 6-1A); the angle of the point varies between types. Some larger nails for masonry work have chisel- or wedge-like points; some very fine nails, which are little more than pins, have needle points (Fig. 6-1B). It is not usually possible to specify the type of point required, because only one type of point is used with a particular nail.

Common nails may be collectively called *wire* nails, distinguishing them from earlier *cut* nails (Fig. 6-1C), which were made from sheet iron. Cut nails, which may be found when dismantling old woodwork, are of historic interest, but they cannot be bought today. General-purpose nails are described as *common* or *box* nails. The thickness of a nail varies with its length; most common nails are slightly thicker than box nails the same length.

Common nails may be ordered by length, but the system of *penny* sizes is applicable to other types of nails as well, although thicknesses will differ. Appendix A shows penny sizes compared with lengths, the gage thickness, and an approximate indication of how many nails may be expected in one pound.

Similar in form to common nails and box nails, wood shingle nails are slightly thicker and have slightly larger heads. These and some others may be made with grooved or barbed shanks to increase their grip (Fig. 6-1D). Roofing nails have wider heads (Fig. 6-1E).

Nails with fine heads are used in places where they are to be punched below the surface, or otherwise made inconspicuous. A fine head will not easily resist the tendency of wood to "pull back," but it will hold adequately in light construction. The heads of smaller nails of this type, called *panel* or *veneer* pins (Fig. 6-1F), are countersunk deeply. Common types, from sizes 4d to 16d (*d* denoting *penny*), are called casing nails. Flooring nails (6d to 12d) have similar heads and may be grooved, a feature claimed to reduce squeaking in floors. A variation on the steep countersunk head, the *brad head*, is seen on finishing nails (Fig. 6-1G), which are thinner than casing nails but come in similar lengths. Even thinner than these are the needle-point nails for insulation board and fiberboard.

The plain, parallel-sided wire nail does not grip well with its smooth surface. Besides grooves, nails may be given a twisted, square-shank pattern, giving them the name *screw nail* (Fig. 6-1H). A ringed-shank nail (Fig. 6-1I) gives the best grip, particularly when the barbed rings are shaped to resist their removal. (Bronze versions are used in boatbuilding.)

Besides the foregoing types used in wood-to-wood construction, the woodworker should know about other nails. For fixing corrugated roofing, there are nails with extra large heads (Fig. 6-1J). Some large nails for heavy construction have countersunk heads (Fig. 6-1K), usually at a flatter angle than the countersink of a screw head. Heavy, galvanized nails used for construction work have wedge-shaped points, and either countersunk or round heads (Fig. 6-1L).

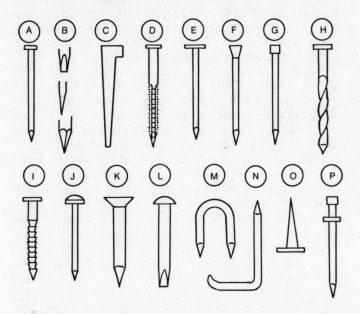

Fig. 6-1. The variety of nails available to the woodworker. (See text for descriptions.)

A staple is a double-ended nail (Fig. 6-1M). Usually, the points are the same length, but an electrician may use a staple with not much of a second point (Fig. 6-1N). A tack is a small tapered nail (Fig. 6-1O). The tack's taper does not give a very good grip, but it is useful for holding canvas and upholstery material. (Their resistance to the sideways pull of stretched fabric is adequate; but a direct pull will lift a tack.)

Most nails are not intended to be removed. Those with ringed shanks offer so much resistance to withdrawal that considerable damage to wood fibers occurs when they are forced out. When an ordinary nail is driven flush with the surface, it is necessary to cut into the wood to get pincers under the head. For temporary construction, when you know the nails will be removed, there are *scaffold* nails with double heads (Fig. 6-1P). The lower head holds the wood, while the upper head stays above the surface to provide a grip for pincers or a claw hammer.

One advantage a nail has over a screw is that in many circumstances it can be driven directly into the wood without having to drill a hole for it. Practice is needed in getting a direct hit to drive in a long nail without it bending. If a nail bends, it is often difficult to straighten; it may bend again the same way. Even if an unbended nail appears to be straight, it may be weakened. For these reasons, it is better to withdraw a bent nail and replace it when doing important work.

Bending can be made less likely if holes are drilled for nails. They can be slightly undersize, and not as deep as the length of the nail. A nail guided well into the wood is unlikely to bend. This drilling is also essential for nails being driven near an end-grain edge, where a split might be made by driving the nail directly. Close-grained hardwoods will need holes drilled almost the same diameter as the nail, and almost as deep, while the softwoods can take quite large nails without drilling.

There is also a case for drilling if the nail is used to pull parts together. In ordinary nailing, the shank of the nail grips the wood the same way all the way down if there has been no drilling. If a hole is drilled only slightly undersize in the top of a piece of wood, and the nail is driven, the top piece will be squeezed against the lower piece, between the head and the grip of the nail in the lower piece.

For most purposes nails are driven perpendicular to the surface. But to hold a broad piece of wood, a series of nails can be given a better collective hold if they are driven at different angles, in a dovetail form (Fig. 6-2A). Because the edges of a board are more likely to loosen than the center, arrange nails slightly closer toward the edges (Fig. 6-2B). Nails do not hold as well in end grain as they do across the grain. Construction should be arranged so that end grain nailing is avoided as much as possible. Where nails have to be driven into end grain, use "dovetail" nailing.

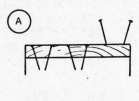
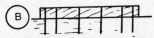

Fig. 6-2. Increase the collective hold of a series of nails in a broad piece of wood by driving them in dovetail fashion (A); have more nails near the edges (B) where the board is more likely to loosen.

If metal parts have to be nailed to wood, particularly outdoors. use nails that match the metal if possible (aluminum nails for exterior aluminum parts, e.g.). For some parts it may be necessary to get plated steel nails. When some dissimilar metals are in contact or close to each other, a corrosive action (electrolysis) takes place that eats one of the metals away; this action is encouraged particularly by a salty atmosphere. Nails made of the softer metals require slightly undersize holes, drilled almost full length in nearly every position.

In some constructions, particularly in garden woodwork, it is convenient to let the nail point go right through, then *clench* it for a stronger grip. The simplest way is to merely support the head with another hammer or an iron block, while the point is knocked over and buried in the grain. The grip will be even stronger if the point is curved over a spike (Fig. 6-3), then driven across, or diagonally to, the grain. This method is also safer. Curving the end insures that the point is buried and cannot be a danger to anyone.

Fig. 6-3. Curling the end of a nail over a spike and hammering the point back into the wood will give the nail a tighter grip and make the assembly safer to handle.

In some lapstrake (overlapping planks) boatbuilding, plank edges were held by clenched nails. Such boats were sometimes called "clenche-build," from this method. However, better lapstrake boats had plank edges held by riveted copper nails, a method that has uses in other types of woodworking. The boatbuilding nails for this work were square, and were used with conical washers called *roves*.

This method will draw parts together, and could also be used in other wood assemblies where one part has to turn against another. For today's woodworking, round nails used with flat washers will do just as well as the traditional method.

Drill an undersize hole for the nail and drive it through. The washer's hole should be just too small to push on to the nail by hand. Support the nail head with a hammer or iron block. Use a hollow punch, or a piece of wood with a hole in it, to drive the washer onto the point of the nail (Fig. 6-4A). Cut off the end of the nail a short distance above the washer. The length left should be about 1½ times the thickness of the nail (Fig. 6-4B). While still supporting the nail head, lightly hammer around the end to rivet it onto the washer (Fig. 6-4C). It is important to hammer lightly. Heavy blows might buckle the soft copper nail in the thickness of the wood (Fig. 6-4D); later it would straighten under a load and loosen the joint (causing a leak, if it is were in a boat).

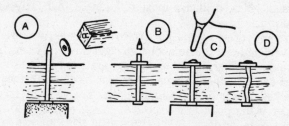

Fig. 6-4. Riveting sequence for wood: A washer is driven onto the project-ing point of a nail with a hollow punch (or a piece of wood with a hole) (A); the point is cut off, leaving a length above the surface 1½ times the thick-ness of the nail (B); the nail end is flattened by light hammering, complet-ing the rivet (C). Heavy hammering might buckle the nail (D), which would then straighten under stress, loosening the joint

SCREWS

The word *screw* used without qualification could be misinterpreted. The screws driven into wood should be described as *wood screws*. A *machine* or *metal thread* screw is what many people would call a bolt. But a machine screw has threads running almost to the head; a bolt's threads go only a short distance. Both, of course, usually have nuts and are not intended for wood. Sheet-metal screws (self-threading and self-tapping), which can take several forms, are designed to cut their own threads in metal.

A wood screw has a parallel shank for a short distance below the head; the thread has a sharp edge and tapers to a point (Fig. 6-5A). Commonly, the head is flat and countersunk (Fig. 6-5B) to finish level with the surface. Next in popularity is the round head; it is almost semicircular and stands above the surface (Fig. 6-5C). An oval head (Fig. 6-5D) is like a flat head, but is slightly domed on top. It can have a deeper slot than the other two, making it easier to grip with a screwdriver. An oval head may also be considered more attractive than a flat head, as it doesn't project as much as a round head. The less common fillister head (Fig. 6-5E) is considered better for driving; there is less risk of the screwdriver slipping out of its slot and, possibly, marking the surface. It is also more suitable for power screwdrivers.

Besides slotted heads, which have been used for a very long time, there are heads with special recesses for power driving in quantity production. The star-shaped socket of the Phillips head (Fig. 6-5F) is one example of these; except for this difference, these screws have the same characteristics as slotted screws. Very strong *coach* or *carriage* screws have square or hexagonal heads that are turned with a wrench.

The length of a wood screw is measured from the part that would contact the wood at its surface to its head (Fig. 6-5G); thus a flat-headed screw is shorter than any type with a raised head. Screws are usually no shorter than ¼ inch. Screw lengths are designated in ⅛ inch steps up to an inch; from 1 to 3 inches, they come in ¼ inch increments, while larger screws may be measured in ½ inch intervals. A screw's diameter is the thickness of its parallel-sided shank, but it is given in gage sizes (which are peculiar to each manufacturer). The lower the gage, the thinner the screw. Appendix B relates each gage number to shank diameter, and gives pilot (starting) hole dimensions for the screws used in all woods.

No hardware store carries the complete range of screws, so the following is a guide to the ones most likely to be available: gages 2 and 3 are no longer than ½ inch; gages 4 and 5 are usually between ⅜ and ¾ inch; 6 and 7, from ½ to 1½ inches; 8, from ½ to 2 inches; 9, 10, and 11 cover the range to

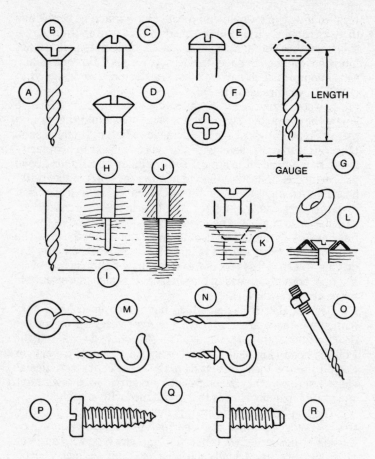

Fig. 6-5. Threaded fasteners. (See text for descriptions.)

2¼ inches. Higher numbers extend the range; anything over 3 inches is at least 18 gage.

Steel is the usual metal for screws, but brass is also used. Screws made of either metal are available in the whole range of sizes. Aluminum, bronze, and stainless steel screws cost considerably more than steel screws, and are used in metal of the same type to avoid corrosion, due to dissimilar metals being in contact. Steel screws rust rapidly in damp conditions. Brass resists corrosion much better, and looks better, being particularly attractive in high-class work. Although brass is not as strong as steel, brass screws are strong enough. (If there is any doubt, use more of them.) Steel screws can be plated in many ways to protect the steel from corrosion, and to match the metal of most of the fittings that might be screwed to wood.

A screw joins two parts by pressing the top piece down with the head as the threads bore into the bottom piece. Therefore, nothing is gained by making the threads bore their way through the top piece. To avoid this wasted effort, two different-sized pilot holes are drilled (Fig. 6-5H). One is drilled through the top piece to the same diameter of the screw, allowing the screw to slide through easily while still pressing down with the head. The second pilot hole is drilled into the other piece, to the diameter as indicated in Appendix B.

How much drilling is needed depends on the size of the screw and the hardness of the wood. When using short screws, up to about gage 4 in softwoods, it may be sufficient to put the screw in the shank hole and give the head a light tap to enter its point in the lower piece of wood, then drive it in with a screwdriver. For larger screws (in a softwood), the pilot hole can be much smaller than the core diameter at the bottom of the thread, and need only be as deep as perhaps half the length of the screw (Fig. 6-5I). There are no hard and fast rules. Drilling out too much may result in the screw gripping improperly; not drilling enough may mean the screw will not go all the way, or that the effort needed to drive it shears it off. With hardwoods the pilot hole should be closer to the core diameter of the thread and taken to the full depth of the screw (Fig. 6-5J). (Appendix B provides a guide to drill sizes, but only experimentation will show the best sizes to use for a particular combination of screw and wood.)

For flat-headed screws, the mouth of the hole may have to be countersunk (given a funnel shape); however, small gage flat-headed screws may pull in enough in many woods without the use of a countersink bit. Theoretically, it would be appropriate that the angle of the countersink bit be the same as the angle of the screw head; but in practice, it is better if it is steeper (about 60°). The compressive effect of the head as it tightens makes it bed down neatly in a countersunk hole (Fig. 6-5K). A hole matching the countersink of the screw head might be forced open, leaving an ugly space around the screw head.

If you install a screw that has to be removed occasionally, say, for an inspection panel, use a cup washer under a flat-headed screw (Fig. 6-5L) for neatness, and to avoid marking the panel surface. Screws are affected by some woods. Oak may attack steel screws, corroding them and making them difficult to withdraw. It is sometimes helpful to lubricate a screw with oil, wax, or graphite to aid in driving it, and to provide some protection for the metal. Brass screws do not suffer as much, and are a better choice for places where it is known they will have to be backed out later. However, brass (a copper/zinc alloy) does not stand up very well to salty conditions, because a chemical action takes the zinc out of the alloy. For use on or near the sea, it is better to use salt-water-resistant bronze or stainless steel screws.

Other hardware, besides screws, have ends that screw into wood. There are hooks and eyes (Fig. 6-5M). Straight hooks, and others with shoulders, are called cup hooks (Fig. 6-5N). If a threaded stud has to project from the wood, a hanger bolt is used (Fig. 6-5O); it is driven by tightening two nuts against each other with wrenches, then a wrench is used on the top one to drive the screwed end into the wood.

Sheet-metal screws have no direct woodworking application, but they may be needed for metal parts connected to wood. Some industrial screws are intended for driving with a screwdriver. All are made of hardened tool steel and will act like metal taps, cutting their thread as they enter the metal. Some are available with plated surfaces, so they can be matched to the surrounding metal. For hardness, there are no alternatives to steel.

Sheet-metal screws are not driven into thick metal. Their usual purpose is to pull one piece of sheet steel tightly against another. Gage sizes similar to wood screws are used; lengths are from ¼ inch upward. A shallow, flat "cheese" head (Fig. 6-5P) provides good pressure on sheet-metal joints. The makers describe the screws by letter. Type A (Fig. 6-5Q) is tapered, and is particularly suitable for joining thin metal sheeting up to about $1/_{20}$ inch thick. Type B (Fig. 6-5R) is similar, but has a *pilot end* instead of a point. (The tapping hole should be the same diameter as the end.) These screws will cut their way into sheet metal up to 0.20 inch thick. Type C is a finer-thread version. Type F can cut into thicker metal.

NUTS AND BOLTS

The threads of machine screws reach to their heads. The screw threads are intended to be driven into tapped holes in metal, or they may take nuts. These are precision screwed fasteners for engineering applications, but they have uses in woodworking. Their dimensions are taken like those of wood screws. but are given by measurement rather than gage, and different types of threads may be available.

A machine bolt, a similarly precise fastener, has threads for only a short distance; both head and nut are square or hexagonal to take a wrench. Carriage or coach bolts are more useful for woodworking. They have a shallow round head with a square neck or shoulder under it (Fig. 6-6A). This pulls into the wood and prevents the bolt from turning. These bolts usually have a fairly coarse thread, and the nut is usually square. If a finer thread is needed, a machine bolt should be chosen.

Stove bolts have round or flat heads (similar to wood screws). They lack the square shoulder of the coach bolt and are usually threaded over a greater part of their length (Fig. 6-6B). A good range of diameters and lengths make them useful for many woodworking jobs. Their diameters are from $3/16$ to $1/2$ inch, and may be anything up to 6 inches long.

If a nut has to be secured to a bolt (or screw) where it is likely to vibrate loose, or turn and loosen if it is a rotating joint, a self-locking type (friction-fitting) , or one secured with epoxy resin glue, is the kind to use. Alternatively, two nuts may be used: one held by a wrench, while the other is turned against it with another wrench, jamming the two together (Fig. 6-6C); the lower nut, turning back against the upper one, does the locking.

For most bolting to wood, use washers under a small head and under the nut. Standard washers are not much bigger than the distance across the points of a nut. Oversize washers are

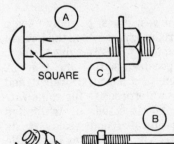

Fig. 6-6. Carriage bolts have square necks (A) to prevent them from turning in the wood. Stove bolts (B) are threaded over a greater part of their length. Two nuts may be tightened against each other (C) to better secure the bolt. A **drift** (D) is a tool used to clean out a series of holes for bolts.

better, because they spread the pressure over more wood fibers, reducing the tendency to pull into the wood.

It is sometimes difficult to drive a bolt very far into wood through a hole of the exact size; but for most purposes, it is better not to make the hole very much oversize. The bolt can be lubricated with wax or graphite. If many bolts the same size have to be put in, it would be worthwhile making up a *drift*: a round steel rod the same diameter as the bolts, with a filed or turned taper at one end (Fig. 6-6D). It is driven through the bolt holes to clean them out for the bolts.

GLUES

Throughout history man has used a variety of substances as glues. Many have had to be supplemented by mechanical fasteners. Many natural resins have been used, but for many centuries the most successful glues have been animal or vegetable products that usually had to be melted for use. Wood glues made from animals hooves and bones, in regular use up to World War II, had to be prepared in a double glue pot (one inside the other). Water was heated in the outer pot, with the glue in the inner pot. The water in the outer pot prevents the temperature from going past the boiling point and boiling the glue. The glue was applied hot, and the glued assembly had to be clamped tightly until set.

Some of the developments that came out of the war were plastics and synthetic resins. They have made possible a whole range of new and better glues. The traditional glue-pot stickum is just about obsolete, and might only be useful for repairing old or antique furniture, when matching existing glue would be desirable.

Before the coming of the newest glues, the only plastic glue in use was *casein*, a milk product; it comes in the form of powder to be mixed with water into a paste. The glued joint is clamped until the water evaporates, setting the glue. A properly made close-fitting casein joint has good strength and is water-resistant. It is not fully waterproof, in the same way many more recent glues are, but it stands up to limited dampness; and if it becomes saturated and weakened, its strength is restored when it dries out. Casein may have little use in the home shop today, but it still has industrial applications, as in laminated indoor beams.

Some modern glues, although they have complex chemical names, are only known by trade names, making it difficult to identify what is available. Their strength and particular suitability for wood may not be immediately obvious. If a glue or adhesive is described as being suitable for wood as well as cloth, paper, leather, or other materials, its application to woodwork is only likely to be for light construction. It will probably not have enough strength for furniture or other comparable wooden structures. If it is a very strong wood glue, it will probably not be described as suitable for other materials. If the glue is for fabrics or other flexible materials, it will not be one that sets rigidly. Most specialized wood glues set hard and stiff. A glue supplied in two parts can be considered a high-strength waterproof wood glue.

Most glues supplied in one part depend on evaporation to make them set. This means the parts have to be held in contact until the glue sets. But the setting time of some can be shortened by warming the joint. Read the directions; overheating may spoil some of these glues. Some are supplied in convenient container/applicators.

The stronger synthetic resin glues are also waterproof to various degrees, but all are much more waterproof than casein. These glues have revolutionized boatbuilding. Until their coming, there was no satisfactory glue for boats that could be trusted to maintain its strength after long immersion. Now all are adequate for boats stored out of the water, and some, fully waterproof for all practical purposes, no matter how long their immersion.

Urea-formaldehyde (resin) glues usually come in two parts, a resin, or a powder that mixes with water to form a resin, and a liquid hardener, a mild acid. In using some brands, the resin is applied to one surface, the hardener to the other; when they are brought together, a chemical reaction starts, and the glue begins to set. The hardener may also be a powder mixed with a resin powder. While the mixture is dry, nothing happens; but when water is mixed in, the reaction commences; at normal temperatures, there may be about an hour during which the glue must be applied. (Any excess mixture will harden in the pot.)

Resorcinol glues—with other chemical names following that word—are found in plywood construction. Some have a pronounced red color that may not be acceptable for some work. The hardener is mixed with the resin before use. Several hardeners may be available to give a *pot life* (how long the mixture is workable) from 1 to 5 hours.

Both glues are unsatisfactory when the line of glue in a joint is uneven and more than a few thousandths of an inch thick, unless the glue is described on the container as "gap-filling." The snag with a glue that is not gap-filling is that when it has set, it is liable to craze anywhere it is thick, the minute cracks destroying much of its strength. Fortunately, this can be avoided in an open joint by mixing sawdust with the glue. The glue then bonds wood particles, instead of trying to span wider spaces.

Epoxy glue (epoxide resin) is the strongest, most waterproof of this group. Besides sticking wood to wood, it will join most other materials. Epoxy glue comes in two parts, mixed just before use. Some epoxy glues need a very long time to set—maybe 3 days—but there are quicker-setting versions. It's a good idea to check the setting time before buying an epoxy glue.

With traditional animal-byproduct glue, it was recommended that both parts be coated, rubbed together, and clamped tightly. Read the instructions. Usually, it is sufficient to coat one or both surfaces, then bring the parts together, clamping them just tightly enough to maintain contact. (Overtightening will squeeze out glue and "starve" the joint.)

The strength of many adhesives builds up progressively. Instructions with the glue may provide clamping times: the period after which the clamps can be removed and work continued. Although the glued assembly may stand up to planing and other work when the clamps are removed, the full strength of the bond may not be reached for several days; full loads should be avoided for awhile.

Because glue obtains its grip by penetrating wood, its pores must not be obscured. If glue is used over paint or varnish, it will adhere only to the film of paint or varnish; its strength will depend on the security of the coating underneath. Even if the wood is apparently bare, grit may prevent the glue from entering the wood pores. Machine-planed wood, "case-hardened" by blunt cutters, is less obvious. If the cutters are not as sharp as they should be, the pounding of the edges against the wood will tend to close the pores. Follow power planing with hand planing or sanding, if the surface is to be glued.

End grain does not glue well. Strong joints are only made when the grain runs across the joint. If possible, construction should be arranged so end grain does not have to be glued. But if it does, it should be supplemented by other side grain gluing.

Some woods are naturally "greasy" or resinous, teak and some of the pines, for example. Resorcinol glues may not be affected by this condition, but urea glues will. If they are to be used, the surface should be wiped with a degreasing agent, sanded or scraped clean, then degreased again before applying glue. Clamping may require more pressure than would be necessary for nongreasy wood, and the application of heat to speed setting, before the grease or resin has time to soak back into the glue line, is advisable.

Some urea glues react with metal and stain surrounding wood. Avoid using a brush with a metal ferrule (holding the bristles), as it may deposit stains in the wood. Screws or nails in contact with the glue may cause staining. The glue should not be in a metal container. Disposable plastic containers are best.

You can remove glue stains with a weak solution of oxalic acid (3%), but be careful with it; wear rubber gloves and use the diluted acid on a pad. Protect your skin and eyes, and keep the acid away from food.

Contact adhesives are suitable for fixing hard plastic sheets to wood tops and panels. Many give an immediate bond: the two surfaces cannot be separated or moved when they come into contact (hence the name). Follow the manufacturer's instructions carefully. Usually, both surfaces are coated and left until tacky; when they come together, they have a bond instantly. The plastic sheet can usually be flexed and lowered correctly at one edge, then straightened slowly to make complete contact.

Stoppings are allied to glues. Rather than join surfaces, they fill holes and cracks. These putty-like products are thick pastes, either squeezed from a tube or used with a knife from a can. They set without expanding or contracting. Most brands set in a few minutes, leaving a surface that can be sanded level with the surrounding wood. It is usual to fill a hole over a nail, so a little stands above the surface to allow for leveling. The material has no strength for filling wide gaps, but for small imperfections, it can be leveled and treated with polish or stain, in the same way as the wood. Colors that match popular woods are available.

If strength is required as well, sawdust mixed with synthetic glue makes a filler for cracks and holes. It is possible to make a mixture that sets to match the surrounding wood. A glue/sawdust mixture should stand above the surface a little, to allow for slight shrinkage, and for sanding after setting.

There are occasions when the wood being stopped is liable to expand and contract, particularly in damp conditions; it can be a problem with a boat that is sometimes afloat and sometimes stored ashore. Flexible stoppings, applied from a special gun or squeezed from a tube, go on like putty and can be smoothed with a wet knife. They never completely harden and will remain sufficiently flexible to allow for slight wood movement, yet the surface may be good enough to take paint.

When using any glue, use enough to coat all surfaces to be brought together. Along with this, avoid excess wherever possible. Most modern glues set as hard as glass and adhere exceptionally well. This means that any hardened excess may break away wood fibers or otherwise mark the surface when an attempt is made to chip the glue off.

Small areas can be coated, using the applicator provided with some glue containers. The alternative is a brush (without a metal ferrule). Better than a brush, however, is a piece of wood with cloth tied to the end, making a disposable applicator.

Excess nonwaterproof glue can be wiped off with a cloth soaked in hot water. This may be effective with some synthetic resin glues before they have fully hardened, but the diluted glue may smear, marring the surface. It is better to let the glue *gel*: partially hardened—no longer runny, but soft to the touch. Then, a knife or chisel will lift off the excess glue without spreading it over the surface or damaging the wood. If the surplus glue has become fully hardened, work carefully with the chisel to avoid the risk of glue pulling away wood fibers. If a sander can be used, wear away the hard glue with an abrasive, but take care not to wear away the wood unevenly.

Sometimes a joint has to be glued temporarily, as when certain parts have to be turned in a lathe. Ordinary glue is used, but paper is put in the joint. Glue one surface and lay a piece of paper on it; then glue the other piece and press it into place. When set, the joint will have adequate strength, but when you want to separate the parts, run a knife or chisel into the joint to split the paper (which can be sanded off).

There are also temporary glues. When a sanding disk, fixed to a metal backing, has to be removed because its surface has worn away, the rubber-like glue used allows the disk to be peeled off; the disk makers supply the adhesive. Flexible, temporary adhesives used for upholstery may be used for fixing canvas and other fabrics to wood.

Adhesive suppliers provide information on their products. It is important to check the strength and suitability of a glue for a particular purpose. There are a great many adhesives available, each with individual characteristics. It would be a pity to spoil something by using an incorrect adhesive.

In general, the word *glue* means it is for wood—but not always. The word *adhesive* could mean it is applicable to one or more of many materials—which may or may not include wood. Always read the label to be sure you are getting what you need.

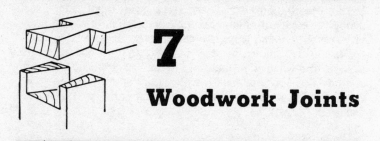

7

Woodwork Joints

Although the simplest assemblies are made by merely nailing one piece of wood to another, or by screwing them together in slightly better construction, most quality woodwork involves joints: one piece of wood fits into another; two or more parts are cut to interlock. When glues were less reliable, much of the strength of a construction came from the careful design and fitting of joints. Because newer glues give a very strong bond, joints are not needed in such great variety, and the more complex ones are not required; neither is extreme accuracy in fitting them quite as vital. However, anyone who wants to claim to be a competent woodworker needs to be familiar with a number of joints, and to be able to make them with reasonable accuracy.

Certain joints and their variations may be regarded as traditional. They date from the days when all joints had to be cut with hand tools. These joints are still with us today in an age of power tools. Many are formed in the traditional way, the power tool merely doing it more accurately and with less effort. Other joints have been devised with power tools in mind.

To give the best conditions for strong gluing, arrange joints so they present broad surfaces along the grain, in contact with each other. A joint made without glue may have little mechanical strength. Other joints, because their shape usually incorporates a wedge, will resist pull in at least one direction, without glue.

EDGE JOINTS

One of the simplest joints, although not necessarily the easiest to make, is the edge-to-edge joint made to make up a width. The old-time carpenter may call it a rubbed joint, but that name dates from the days of animal glue, when the edges were rubbed together to squeeze out surplus glue. This is not done with modern glue.

If the two edges are planed accurately, there should be no trouble in making this joint; but there are a few points to watch. One board should be stood on the other, to check that they will finish in the same plane (Fig. 7-1A). Warpage can be reduced throughout the whole width by alternating the end grain (Fig. 7-1B). Difficulty is sometimes experienced when the ends of the joints open. This can be counteracted by planing the edges very slightly hollow in their length (Fig. 7-1C). When the boards are clamped, the greater compression at the ends will keep those edges close. It may be helpful to use joiners dogs (Fig. 7-1D) to hold the ends while the glue sets. Check for twists when clamping. It is helpful to assemble the joint on a surface known to be flat.

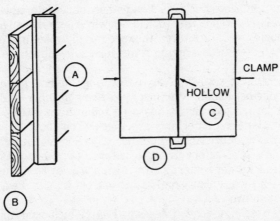

Fig. 7-1. Before joining two boards edge-to-edge, stand one on the other to make sure they will finish in the same plane (A). Warpage can be reduced by alternating end grain (B). The ends of the joints can be prevented from opening by first planing the edges slightly hollow throughout their length (C). Joiner's dogs (D) can be used to hold the boards together while the glue sets.

Put paper under boards being clamped, flat on the bench or resting on the bars of bar clamps, as protection against damage from surplus glue. Do not tighten the clamps excessively. Although it is usual to plane the boards to the desired thickness before gluing made-up widths, some planing or power sanding will be needed later to remove unevenness. If the wood is one that tears up a lot when planed the wrong way, make sure all the boards have the "better" direction of the grain going all the same way. This may be marked with penciled arrows. Where several boards are involved, use crossing pencil marks to insure assembly as planned. (Fig. 7-2.)

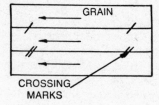

Fig. 7-2. When joining boards made of wood that tends to tear when planed the wrong way, mark the boards with the correct planing direction first; if several boards are involved, use crossing pencil marks as a guide to correct assembly.

The need to make up widths by gluing many boards has almost disappeared. Plywood and other manufactured boards make better broad, flat panels. However, for repairing or reproducing old furniture, the use of plywood and other modern materials is inappropriate; instead, widths have to be built up.

Secret slot screwing, an interesting method of pulling edges together, dates from the days when glue alone could not always be trusted. But it has uses today for making joints without clamps. Centerlines are marked on the edges, and screw positions are marked on the centerlines at intervals; 9 inches is a satisfactory average distance (Fig. 7-3A). On one board, mark other centers a short distance away from the first marks—½ inch is plenty for hardwoods, but it might be a little more for softwoods.

Use steel flat-headed screws. For ¾ inch boards, they could be 1 by 8 inches. Drill holes for the screws and drive them into the board with single marks, until about ¼ inch projects (Fig. 7-3B). On the other board, drill holes at the second marks that are just large enough to clear the screw heads (Fig. 7-3C). At the first marks, drill holes that will clear the necks of the screws. These holes should be slightly deeper than the screw heads project. Drill between the holes, and chisel out slots (Fig. 7-3D).

Bring the boards together so the screws go into the holes, then drive one along the other until the screw heads have cut their way along the bottoms of the slots to the other ends. If the

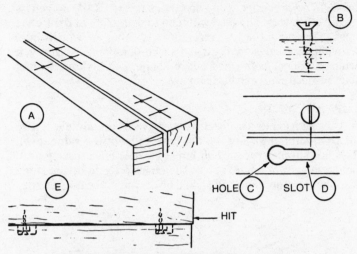

Fig. 7-3. **Secret slot** screwing. (See text for details.)

assembly is satisfactory, drive the boards back again until the screws lift out. Give each screw a quarter-turn. Apply glue to both edges and drive the boards together again (Fig. 7-3E).

When boards are used to make up widths, with others going across them to hold them together, the screw holes may be slotted to allow for expansion and contraction (Fig. 7-4A). In this kind of assembly, commonly used for a door, include diagonal braces (Fig. 7-4B) in the direction that will put the

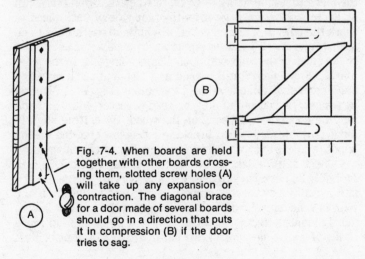

Fig. 7-4. When boards are held together with other boards crossing them, slotted screw holes (A) will take up any expansion or contraction. The diagonal brace for a door made of several boards should go in a direction that puts it in compression (B) if the door tries to sag.

brace in compression if the door tries to sag. If the diagonals go the other way, any load will tend to pull joints at their ends open. *Triangulating* a structure is always worthwhile. Providing the sides are rigid and the corners joined securely, a triangle cannot be pushed out of shape; but a shape having four or more sides can be distorted.

LAPPED JOINTS

Lapped joints are used frequently. In the simplest, two strips of similar size cross, but have to be at the same level. This is a simple *cross* or *half* lap (Fig. 7-5). The crossing need not be at a right angle, nor do the strips have to be the same size; but no more than half should be cut out of the thicker one.

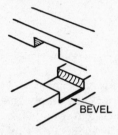

BEVEL

Fig. 7-5. The parts that join to form a simple half-lap joint. Bevel the inner edges for a joint that has to be very tight.

In making a simple lapped joint, place both face sides upward, and mark the position of the joint on each piece. Use the piece that is actually to go there when marking the width on each part. Use a gage from the face side of each piece to mark the bottom of the cutout. Use a knife to mark lines to be sawed, and mark the waste parts with a pencil. Saw on the waste sides of the lines with a backsaw, going just to the gage marks (Fig. 7-6A). Put the wood in a vise and use a chisel to cut diagonally from each side of the cutout (Fig. 7-6B). It may be necessary to use a mallet, or hard pressure with the hand may be enough—it depends on the wood. By cutting slightly diagonally upward, wood breaking out below the line on the opposite side is avoided. After chiseling, trim straight across.

Check the flatness at the bottom of each cutout. It will probably be necessary to chisel straight across the grain; the surface may not be very smooth, but it won't matter. If the joint is wide, chisel with a slicing action at the last strokes, to get a cleaner effect. The waste part can be broken up more easily if extra saw cuts are made (Fig. 7-6C). For a first

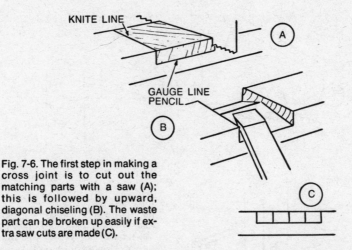

KNITE LINE

GAUGE LINE
PENCIL

Fig. 7-6. The first step in making a cross joint is to cut out the matching parts with a saw (A); this is followed by upward, diagonal chiseling (B). The waste part can be broken up easily if extra saw cuts are made (C).

attempt, you may want to make some trial assemblies, but neater joint edges are obtained by the craftsman who is confident in his work, whose first assembly is also his last. If C clamps are used, have scrap pieces of wood above and below the joint as it is squeezed together. It may help, for a very tight joint, to bevel the inner edges slightly (refer to (Fig. 7-5), but all other edges should be left square, because they will visible in the finished joint.

An end or corner lap (Fig. 7-7A) and a middle lap (Fig. 7-7B) are similar joints, both without pieces projecting. They are made in a similar way, but the open-ended part can be

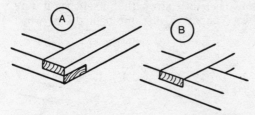

Fig. 7-7. An end or corner lap joint (A); a middle lap joint (B).

sawed both ways, without having to use a chisel. The best way to do this by hand is to saw diagonally one way, while watching the end and side line from one side (Fig. 7-8A), then the other way (Fig. 7-8B), and finally straight through (Fig. 7-8C). The same cut can be made accurately with a table saw (Fig. 7-8D).

195

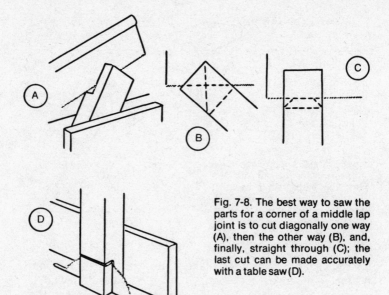

Fig. 7-8. The best way to saw the parts for a corner of a middle lap joint is to cut diagonally one way (A), then the other way (B), and, finally, straight through (C); the last cut can be made accurately with a table saw (D).

The three lap joints mentioned will serve most needs, either for rails crossing in exposed positions, battens backing plywood, or hardboard panels. Of course, strips do not necessarily cross flatly; they could be on edge (Fig. 7-9A). A narrow strip crossing a much wider one need not be cut (Fig. 7-9B).

A half-lap joint can be used for two end-to-end pieces (Fig. 7-9C); this sort of splice has little strength in itself, but it may be adequate if the wood is part of a frame behind a plywood panel.

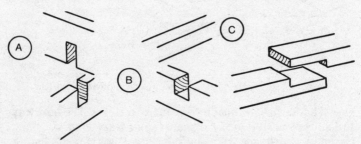

Fig. 7-9. Strips could be joined with notches in their edges (A), or only one might be notched (B); a half-lap joint can be used for two end-to-end pieces (C), but the splice won't be very strong.

These joints, excluding the glue used, have no mechanical resistance to being pulled apart. It is possible to nail, screw, or dowel the joint. A half-lap dovetail joint resists pulling on the cross piece (Fig. 7-10A). Do not cut too much from the dovetail piece, as this will weaken it. A taper of about to 1:8 at each side is satisfactory (Fig. 7-10B). From the full width of a 2 inch piece, this would be ¼ inch in at each side. If the parts are thick enough, the underside of the dovetail may slope slightly (Fig. 7-10C) to make up for the width lost at the bottom of the dovetail. This type of joint is used at the ends of cross beams on the cabin tops of yachts, and in other places where sides likely to spring have to be held in.

Fig. 7-10. A half-lap dovetail joint resists pull on the cross piece (A); the taper of the dovetail should be about 1 : 8 (B). If the parts are thick enough, the underside of the dovetail may slope slightly (C).

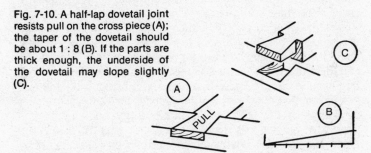

DADO JOINTS

Dado joints are related to lap joints. In the basic form, a groove (*dado* or *housing*) across one piece accepts the end of another. This can be seen where a shelf is attached to an upright (Fig. 7-11). The simple dado joint is sometimes used to connect two comparatively narrow pieces in a structure, but usually they are wide (other joints are better suited to narrow parts).

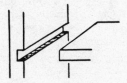

Fig. 7-11. The simple dado joint is commonly used to hold shelving between uprights.

Making a dado joint by hand involves work similar to cutting lap joints. For a neat finish, the sides of the part to be cut out should be marked from the actual piece that is to fit, and the wood fibers should be severed with a knife before sawing. As the board is usually wider than those in which a lap joint is used, the chisel may be followed with a router plane. If many dadoes have to be cut, use a radial arm saw or a table saw set to the required depth, with a sliding support to keep the cut at a right angle. The radial arm saw is easier to keep exactly where you want it, because the surface being cut is above it. But by using stops to locate the wood, the work can be done on a table saw. A power router can be used to remove the waste between saw cuts; in hardwoods that cut cleanly across the grain, the router may be guided by a strip of wood temporarily clamped on to cut the dado without sawing first. With most woods, particularly softer ones, a better joint is made if the sides are sawed first.

For rougher carpentry, a dado joint can be reinforced with a strip below it (Fig. 7-12A). For the crudest of requirements, as in some outdoor or temporary assemblies, it may be sufficient to merely fix the shelves to the strips without cutting into uprights at all. Because a dado joint brings side and end grain together for gluing, conditions for gluing are not conducive to the best results. In practice such joints are adequate, particularly if there is some part to brace the assembly. Screws visible in the finished job could be undesirable. They can be hidden by driving them in diagonally from below (Fig. 7-12B). If there is a piece strengthening the rear end of the joint, it might be enough to have just one screw, located a short distance back from the front edge.

A dado joint cut right through an upright, with joint details visible at the front, may not matter for some work, but in better items, such as a bookcase, it would be better to avoid this unsightliness. The joint to use is a *stopped* dado (Fig. 7-12C). The dado finishes a short distance from the front edge, and the shelf is notched to fit into it. This complicates sawing, of course. After marking the outline of the slot, chop out a distance of about an inch with a chisel. Cut on the waste side of the line at first (Fig. 7-12D), until most of the waste has been lifted out with the chisel (used bevel downward). Pare the waste to the *sides* of the slot; leave a little waste in place in the front end of the slot.

Saw the sides of the dado, using a short stroke—the point of the saw will be restricted by the chopped-out part. The saw will almost certainly hit the front of the slot occasionally; a small amount of waste was left there for this stage, to avoid damage to what will be the front of the dado. Remove the

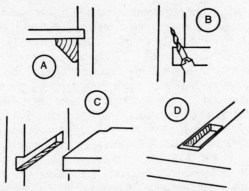

Fig. 7-12. The dado joint can be reinforced with a strip of wood below it (A); screws in the joint can be hidden by driving them in diagonally from below. The stopped dado joint (C) is invisible from the front; waste wood is first chopped out with a chisel to begin the dado (D).

waste with a chisel and router, then trim the front end of the dado to the line.

With a power router, it is possible to cut a stopped dado completely, except for squaring the corners of the front end of the recess. For a neat finish, use a knife before cutting the front of the notch in the shelf. Be careful not to make the notch deeper than the depth of the dado. Ideally, the shelf and dado match exactly; but if the notched edge meets the upright just before the end of the shelf touches the bottom of the dado, it will be acceptable.

The dado can be strengthened against sideways pull by giving it a dovetail section. It may be on the top and bottom, or on the bottom only (Fig. 7-13A). While dovetailing both top and bottom should make the joint stronger, it is easier to make a neat job if only the underside is cut. While the side of the dado can be made with a saw (power or hand) used at a suitable angle, the bevel on the end of the shelf can be pared better with a bevel-edged chisel.

It is possible to get additional strength by tapering a dovetail dado, that is, making the dovetail slightly narrower at the front than at the back. Of course, the shelf remains the same thickness throughout (Fig. 7-13B). Dovetail dadoes may go right across the uprights, or they may be stopped. Obviously, a stopped and tapered dovetail dado calls for skill and practice—but the result is a very strong assembly.

Tapered dovetail-dado joints are particularly suitable for fixing treads in stepladders. If simple dadoes are used for this purpose, strengthening blocks under the joints will give stiffness; threaded rods are sometimes bolted through the uprights to prevent the joints from pulling apart (Fig. 7-13C).

The dado joint, in traditional woodwork, was only used for shelf-type assemblies, but adaptions of it are found in framing joints. These joints usually involve rather short pieces of end grain that could break away in a solitary joint; but when a framework is glued, and the joints are mutually supporting, there is adequate strength. Besides a plain dado at intermediate points, there can be a dado joint and rebate at the corner of a frame (Fig. 7-13D). Leave some waste on the end of the part with the dado, at least until the dado is finished, and possibly until after the joint has been glued, to reduce the risk of short end grain breaking away.

A corner joint can be made with two interlocking rebates. This is not a cabinet joint, but in less important woodwork it allows nailing both ways (Fig. 7-13E) so the joint cannot be pulled apart. Taking the dado and rebate a step further, try giving the rebated piece a tongue (Fig. 7-13F) to cover the end of the piece with a dado. The tongue will not contribute much strength, but it will hide the end grain and give a better appearance where that part of the joint is exposed.

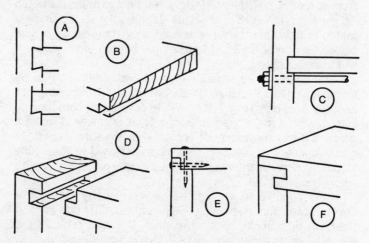

Fig. 7-13. The dado will resist being pulled apart if it is dovetailed (A); additional strength can be gained by tapering the joint (B). The dadoes used in stepladder construction are often strengthened with bolts (C). The corner of a frame might use a rebated piece that fits into a dado (D), or two interlocking rebates nailed together (E); taking the rebate/dado joint a step further, the rebated part could have a tongue (F) covering the dadoed part.

MORTISE-AND-TENON JOINTS

Mortise-and-tenon joints go a long way back in history. Early woodworkers used them to join the roof timbers of buildings, buildings that have stood for hundreds, even thousands of years. In traditional furniture, the mortise-and-tenon joint is the one most frequently used.

In the basic mortise-and-tenon joint, two parts of similar thickness meet. One has a slot cut in it (the mortise); the other, a tongue (the tenon) to fit into it. Customarily, the mortise and tenon are one-third the thickness of the wood (Fig. 7-14A), but if the mortise is to be chopped out with a chisel, it is usual to vary the width slightly to suit the nearest available chisel size.

Careful marking is an important part of making such a joint by traditional hand methods. Always use squares and gages, from the face surfaces. On the piece with the mortise, mark the position and width of the other piece with a pencil and try square, taking the marks around the piece to give the location for the top and bottom (Fig. 7-14B). Allow a little excess length on the piece with the tenon; it will be trimmed after the joint is assembled (Fig. 7-14C).

Set the points of a mortise gage to the width of the chisel, then adjust the gage so its points will scratch two lines centrally on the wood against the face side (Fig. 7-14D). Mark these lines on the top and bottom of the mortise. Use the gage to take measurements all around the end of the tenon (Fig. 7-14E). Pencil the gage lines on the waste parts. Use a knife to cut in where there will be saw cuts across the grain of the part with the tenon.

Cut the tenon by sawing across the two shoulders, making the kerf on the waste side of the line; take care not to cut into the tenon. Saw down the sides of the tenon in three stages, watching end and side lines, the way you would for a lap joint (refer to Fig. 7-8A through 7-8C). Careful work with a fine-toothed backsaw should produce a tenon that needs no further treatment. If necessary, correct unevenness with a chisel.

The traditional method of chopping out the mortise with a chisel to the same width as the mortise calls for a square-edged chisel. For heavy work a thick mortise chisel is needed, but for lighter work a firmer chisel will do. Start the cuts at the center, driving the chisel with a mallet and moving toward the ends of the hole in small steps. Use the chisel bevel-downward to pry out the waste in stages (Fig. 7-14F). Do

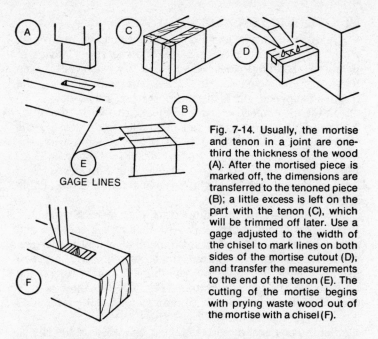

GAGE LINES

Fig. 7-14. Usually, the mortise and tenon in a joint are one-third the thickness of the wood (A). After the mortised piece is marked off, the dimensions are transferred to the tenoned piece (B); a little excess is left on the part with the tenon (C), which will be trimmed off later. Use a gage adjusted to the width of the chisel to mark lines on both sides of the mortise cutout (D), and transfer the measurements to the end of the tenon (E). The cutting of the mortise begins with prying waste wood out of the mortise with a chisel (F).

not cut right to the ends yet. Cut from both sides, until the cuts meet in the middle. It is better to have the wood on the bench rather than in a vise; if the wood is held in a vise, the unsupported surface underneath might break out under hitting.

Chop out the center of the mortise, then chop or pare the ends true, working from each side alternately. Do not cut the ends until most of the waste wood has been cut and removed, otherwise a cut intended to be on the line may finish beyond it, due to the compressive effect of the wedge-shaped end of the chisel as it goes into fairly solid wood.

Although small mortises may be cut this way by hand, it is usually better to remove some of the waste wood by drilling. When drilling with a hand-held drill or brace, go only about halfway from each side, in case the direction is inaccurate. Use a drill that is undersize, in case it wanders a little. Greater accuracy can be expected if a drill press is used; the drill may be closer in size to the width of the slot. If the drill can be sufficiently controlled by a jig or other means, drill slightly overlapping holes, leaving very little to be cleaned out by chiseling. If a mortising machine or mortising attachment is available, use it.

A skilled worker will only have to assemble a mortise-and-tenon joint once; but a beginner may need to make trial assemblies at first. Even then, drive the tenon in fully. Dismantling will loosen the parts and may round edges that will show in the finished part.

In a normal, full mortise-and-tenon joint, glue is applied and the parts are assembled, either driven together in a single joint or, more usually, pulled together with bar clamps as part of an assembled frame. Plane any excess wood from the tenon, and sand to complete the joint. Extra strength may be given by wedges. Saw cuts are made in the tenon before the joint is assembled, then wedges are glued and driven into the cuts to expand the tenon (Fig. 7-15A). The mortise may be slightly dovetailed to allow for this, but letting the tenon expand too much could cause splits; it is usually sufficient to make the sides of the mortise parallel.

Another way of securing the joint, in addition to gluing, is to install a dowel through its center. This method makes it possible to pull the joint together without using a clamp. Drill a hole through the mortised piece and the tenon—slightly closer to the shoulder, so when the joint is first assembled, they are not quite in line (Fig. 7-15B). Taper the end of a dowel and drive it in, so the wedge action pulls the joint together.

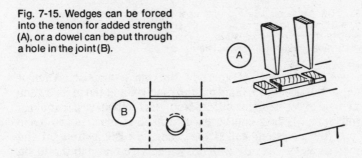

Fig. 7-15. Wedges can be forced into the tenon for added strength (A), or a dowel can be put through a hole in the joint (B).

At one time tenons were held by wedges or *keys* (Fig. 7-16A). This can be seen in such things as the rails of Tudor tables. This version of the mortise-and-tenon joint still has its uses. It gives a tight joint without glue and is suitable for some outdoor furniture and anything that may have to be dismantled for storage. The tenon goes through the mortise, and a slot is cut in it. The outer edge of the slot matches the taper of the key, which can be slight—not more than 1:8. The inner end of the slot is cut so it is within the mortise. By doing this, the key pulls the joint against the face of the mortised piece, and tightens it before it can touch the inner end of the slot. The key and the end of the tenon may be decorated to provide an attractive feature in a piece of furniture.

Mortises have to be made with their larger dimension going with the grain. This means that with thicker parts, it may be necessary to make twin mortise-and-tenon joints (Fig. 7-16B). In a place where a deep rail has to be joined with a leg, the leg would be weakened if a single, deep tenon were cut. Instead, there should be two or more tenons with a small *haunch* between them (Fig. 7-16C).

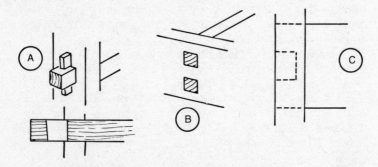

Fig. 7-16. A key going through the tenon (A) will give a strong joint without glue. Thicker parts may require twin mortise-and-tenon joints (B). Where a deep rail has to be tenoned into a leg, there should be two or more tenons with a small haunch (C) between them.

A tenon need not go right through a mortise. When it doesn't, it is called a *blind* or *stub* mortise-and-tenon joint. The method of construction differs from the method used to make a full joint. Wedges can be used in a blind mortise-and-tenon joint by a system called *fox wedging*. The bottom of the mortise is cut slightly wide. Saw cuts are made in the tenon and wedges are fitted in them; as the joint is hammered or clamped together, the wedges press on the bottom of the mortise and expand the tenon (Fig. 7-17A).

At a corner, a mortise-and-tenon joint may be open (Fig. 7-17B). Sometimes this is called a *bridle* joint. Used elsewhere, it is like a mortise-and-tenon joint with the functions of the parts reversed (Fig. 7-17C). A bridle joint has its uses occasionally, but in most situations it is preferable to use mortise-and-tenon joints.

204

The open corner mortise-and-tenon joint exposes end grain on both sides of the corner. It can be hidden one way, using a half blind joint (Fig. 7-17D), but neither of these joints are what the cabinetmaker would use. His corner mortise-and-tenon joint is haunched. There may be an exposed haunch

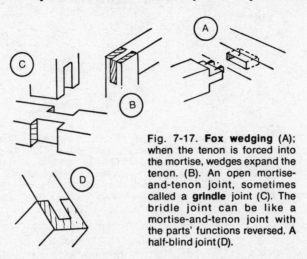

Fig. 7-17. **Fox wedging** (A); when the tenon is forced into the mortise, wedges expand the tenon. (B). An open mortise-and-tenon joint, sometimes called a **grindle** joint (C). The bridle joint can be like a mortise-and-tenon joint with the parts' functions reversed. A half-blind joint(D).

(Fig. 7-18A) or a concealed one (Fig. 7-18B). The concealed haunch is normally used, but the exposed haunch is appropriate where the parts have grooves to take a panel. In mortise-and-tenon joints at the corner of a grooved frame that is to go around a panel, the grooves are made first, then the tenon is cut back to the bottom of the groove. A haunch is made at the other side that is as deep as the groove in the other piece (Fig. 7-18C).

In tables, stools, and similar objects, rails at the same level meet perpendicularly to each other (at legs or other uprights). At the top, each tenon can be haunched—either exposed, if it will be covered later, or concealed, if the top of the leg will show in the finished article. To get the maximum strength, cut mortises into each other and miter the ends of the tenons (Fig. 7-18D). However, do not cut the miters so closely that they meet before the shoulders are fully tightened on the surfaces.

In roofing construction, an inclined member is notched and fitted into a horizontal or upright member with a *birdsmouth* tenon joint (Fig. 7-18E). The shouldered part takes the thrust of the inclined end against the notch, then the tenon

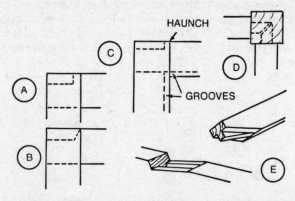

Fig. 7-18. The cabinetmaker uses a haunch in his mortise-and-tenon joints, which may be exposed (A) or concealed (B). If the joint is in the corner of a grooved frame, the grooves are cut first, the tenon is cut back to the bottom of the groove, and a haunch is made at the other side (C). For maximum strength, cut mortises into each other and miter the ends of the tenons (D). Birdsmouth tenon joints (E) are used in roofing construction.

goes slightly deeper, without too much wood having to be removed from the main part (so as not to weaken it).

Mortise-and-tenon joints have to be adapted to suit various circumstances. They will not necessarily form right angles. A horizontal rail going into a tapered leg needs sloping shoulders. The shoulders may have to be rounded to match a shaped part, or the mortised piece may have to be cut away to give the shoulders a flat bearing.

If the tenoned piece is thinner than the mortised piece, it may have a shoulder on only one side. If the other side is on the same level as the side of the tenon, it is called a *barefaced* tenon. If two rails have to meet end to end in a mortise, as it is with fence rails, they should be mitered together in their width.

DOWELED JOINTS

Wooden pegs and dowels are found in many pieces of old woodwork. They were individually made, and were only approximately round, or shaped more accurately by driving short pieces of wood through holes in a steel plate. Modern machine-made dowels have made a different kind of construction possible. Dowels were used to reinforce joints, as alternatives to nails or screws, when glue could not be trusted. But dowels can be used as a sort of inserted tenon. Accurately sized dowels, combined with precision drilling, can give a form with the strength of a mortise-and-tenon joint, yet be easier and quicker to make.

If a dowel is to be glued into a hole, driving it in would be something like forcing a piston into a cylinder; if air cannot escape, there could be a bursting action that would split the wood. The end of a dowel should be beveled, and a shallow cut should be made in the length of the dowel to allow air to escape (Fig. 7-19A). The dowel should be slightly shorter than the combined depths of the holes in the two parts to be joined (Fig. 7-19B), but not so much shorter that too much of the dowel goes into one hole, and not enough into the other.

Accurate doweling depends on the careful marking and accurate location of drilling points. To reinforce an edge-to-edge joint with dowels, first place the two pieces in a vise high enough to clear a marking gage. Mark them out with their face sides outward (Fig. 7-19C). Insert a spick or use a center punch at each position to be drilled.

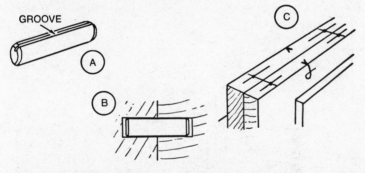

Fig. 7-19. Beveling the end of a dowel and cutting a lengthwise groove in it (A) allows air to escape as the dowel is forced into a hole. The holes in the two parts to be joined with a dowel should be slightly longer than the dowel in combined length (B). The parts to be joined are first placed in a vise and marked out with their face sides outward (C).

The holes drilled for dowels should be at a right angle to the surface. Using a brace or electric drill freehand may be successful; but this depends on estimating angles in at least two directions. It is better to use a drill press or a combination machine that will hold the wood square to the drill. Inaccuracies in a series of dowel holes can make the final joint weak. Doweled joints depend on accuracy and close fits for their success.

If dowels are to be used in place of mortise-and-tenon joints. it is usual to have two dowels that fit the end of a rail in to another piece (Fig. 7-20A). The dowels will have to be a stock size. but they should be thicker than the tenon for the job. For a deep rail there may be more than two dowels. Accuracy will be better if a gage is made to mark all the parts. This will insure matching hole spacing (Fig. 7-20B). The points can be nails driven in and cut off. with their ends filed.

Use dowels in oblique joints (Fig. 7-20C) where the only way to cut a tenon would be diagonal to the grain. therefore making it weak. This happens in a miter. Broad pieces of wood under a cabinet may meet with a miter that needs something besides glue to hole the joint. Dowels. with their grain perpendicular to the meeting surfaces, will make a strong joint.

In general, glue all the dowels in one piece of an assembly. Spread glue on the meeting surfaces, and in the mating holes of the other piece; then bring the parts together with enough

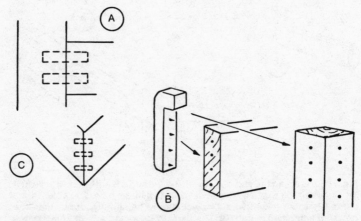

Fig. 7-20. In place of a mortise-and-tenon joint, two dowels can connect the parts (A); a gage can be made to insure that corresponding holes match. (B). Use dowels in oblique joints (C) to avoid cutting a tenon diagonally to the grain.

pressure to close the joint. If there are many dowels involved, it may be easier to put alternate dowels in opposite pieces before bringing them together. There should be no roughness from sawing left on the exposed ends of dowels. It is helpful to bevel them all round. (When the glue has been applied, it is too late to attempt to ease in a reluctant dowel by chiseling.)

SCARFED JOINTS

When two pieces of wood have to be joined end to end, it is difficult to make a joint as strong as the solid wood without increasing the width or thickness of the joint. If the increase is acceptable, the splice may be *fished* with wood or metal on both sides (Fig. 7-21A). The pieces may be glued and screwed, or bolted together, depending on the purpose of the fish joint. In any construction, avoid an abrupt change in section, particularly if the resulting assembly is subject to strain and has no other support. When the ultimate strain is reached and the wood breaks, the break is most likely to occur at the point of change in section (Fig. 7-21B). If the *fishplates* (the supporting pieces) are tapered at the ends (Fig. 7-21C) to give a more gradual change of section, the joint will be less likely to break. If the joined pieces are supported in other ways, this is not such an important consideration.

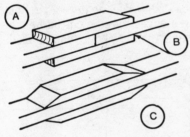

Fig. 7-21. Because a fish joint (A) could break at the change in section (B), it would be better to taper the ends of the fishplates (C).

The simplest end-to-end joint is a *half lap*, which is satisfactory in such places as the framing behind plywood or the studding on a wall. It may be given some strength against elongation by tapering it in a dovetail fashion (Fig. 7-22A). Another way to get strength in the same direction is to make a *squared splice*: the parts are cut to hook over each other (Fig. 7-22B). In roof construction, metal fishplates are often put on each side of a joint and bolted on, although a joint that has a tapered *scarf* (Fig. 7-22C), instead of a plain butt between the ends, is better.

A good end-to-end joint that resists both tension and compression is the tenonned scarf joint (Fig. 7-23A). The two parts have tenons and grooves across the full width of their ends that fit into each other. A gap is left at the center to allow the parts to be mated. After assembly, a pair of folding wedges is driven into the gap to force the grooves and tenons together.

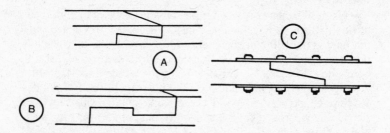

Fig. 7-22. The half-lap joint can be made to resist elongation by being dovetailed (A); the squared splice (B) offers the same kind of resistance. In better roof construction, the tapered scarf is used (C).

A variation on this is to cut the ends at an angle, either straight across, or to a slight *V* at the center. Again, the joint is tightened with folding wedges (Fig. 7-23B).

Where the scarf takes a load edgewise, as in roof purlins (horizontal rafter supports), the edges may be cut into each other at an angle (Fig. 7-23C), then folding wedges can be used to tighten the joint.

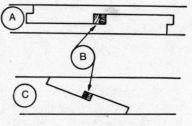

Fig. 7-23. A tenonned scarf joint (A) resists both tension and compression. It is tightened with folding wedges inserted into its central gap (B), as are similar joints used in horizontal rafter supports (C).

With the better synthetic resin glues, it is possible to use a much simpler splice that can depend on the glue alone to provide strength. Such a splice is considered satisfactory in the boatbuilding industry for making up a length by joining two pieces, which may be alone or part of a laminated structure. The rise of the scarf should not be less than 1:7 (that is, 7 inches in length for each inch of thickness, for example). The parts are planed to this angle and glued. For light work, paper can be put on each side of the joint as it is clamped between boards (Fig. 7-24A). The boards should extend over each side of the joint, then clamped to prevent the meeting surfaces from slipping against each other.

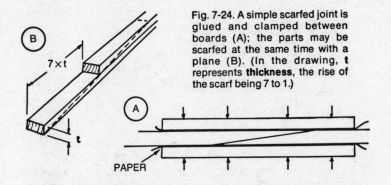

Fig. 7-24. A simple scarfed joint is glued and clamped between boards (A); the parts may be scarfed at the same time with a plane (B). (In the drawing, **t** represents **thickness**, the rise of the scarf being 7 to 1.)

A simple scarf joint can be planed without having to make any marks beforehand. The two pieces are held on the bench top, the top one set back by the length of the splice (Fig. 7-24B). The two are planed together until both are feather-edged. If the plane is kept straight, the surfaces will match.

DOVETAIL JOINTS

Of the many families of joints used in woodworking, the dovetail joint is superior. If there is any choice in a particular situation, and a dovetail could be used, that is the one the woodworker with pride in his craftsmanship will choose. Drawers with dovetail joints are better than those made with other joints. Handmade dovetail joints are considered superior to machine-made ones, although there is little real difference in strength. At one time the expert cabinetmaker was proud of how narrow he could make the *pins* between dovetails. This can be seen in the sides of drawers in old furniture. Except for showing skill in technique, this did not appear to have any advantage. Actually, a joint should be stronger with wider pins.

The basic form of the *through* dovetail used for a corner joint is shown in Fig. 7-25. When a dovetail joint is spoken of, it is usually a corner joint that is meant. The dovetail is the wedge-shaped part; the parts to the side of it, the pins. There is no firm rule about the angle of the sides of a dovetail, but somewhere between 1:6 and 1:9 will serve. For softwoods, the dovetails may splay at wider angles (lower end of the range), while hardwood dovetails may have more upright sides (upper end of range); 1:7 for softwoods and 1:8 for hardwoods are reasonable figures. These angles can be marked on the edge of

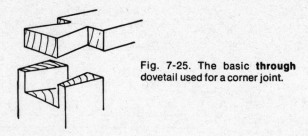

Fig. 7-25. The basic **through**
dovetail used for a corner joint.

a piece of wood, and an adjustable bevel set to them (Fig.
7-26A). If much dovetailing is to be done, standard templates
can be used to set the bevel, or a metal template can be made
for marking dovetails (Fig. 7-26B).

Fig. 7-26. Setting an adjustable
bevel to the taper of the dovetail
(A); a template for marking
dovetails (B).

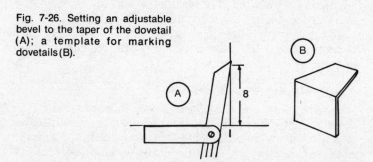

Dovetails are usually formed across wide boards.
Deciding on the number of dovetails and their spacing is a
matter of experience, and often personal choice. A large
number of narrow dovetails may be stronger, in theory, than a
smaller number of wider ones, because of the greater glue
area. But wider dovetails may have more than enough
strength in any case, providing they are not excessively wide.
For most purposes, the width of the dovetail may be
somewhere between the thickness of the wood and 1½ times
that. To a certain extent, the width of the pins is governed by
the space needed to easily pass a bevel-edged chisel. The base
of the slot into which the pin goes may be somewhere between
one-fourth and one-half the width of the dovetails.

Some craftsmen mark out dovetails by eye. It could be
argued that uneven dovetails may produce a joint just as
strong as even ones; but if the joint is visible, it ought to have a
uniform appearance. Dividing an end into dovetails will have
to be done experimentally. For example, a piece of wood ⅝

inch thick may appear to be suitable for four dovetails about 1 inch wide in its 5⅞ inches width (6 inches planed). With pins ⅜ inch at the wide part and ¼ inch at the narrow part, this gives (across the end): ¼, 1, ⅜, 1, ⅜, 1, ⅜, 1, and ¼ inches, making a total of 5⅝ inches, which is not quite enough. Adding ¹⁄₁₆ inch to each dovetail, we get a reasonable spacing (Fig. 7-27A).

If two sides of an article are to be dovetailed the same way, mark them out together. The ends of the pieces should be planed or machined square. It is usual to cut these joints without an excess of wood (to be planed later), but when marking the width of the other piece, allow a very small amount; when the joint is assembled, the ends of the dovetails or pins will be slightly above the surface, and can be planed off. This is better than having them below the surface. Grip the matching parts in a vise and mark them together (Fig. 7-27B). Some craftsmen mark and cut the dovetails first. Others complete the pins before the dovetails.

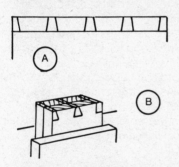

Fig. 7-27. The spacing for four dovetails across a piece of wood 5⅞ inches wide and ⅝ inch thick (A). The matching parts are placed in a vise and marked together (B).

The depth of the cut for the other piece of wood can be marked across the end with a cutting gage, leaving a cut line showing across the exposed parts of the dovetails. This may not matter; if it does, use a try square and knife and cut only where the wood will be sawed or chiseled. Mark the parts that will be cut out.

If the dovetails are to be completed first, put the wood in a vise, with no more projecting than necessary, and use a small, fine backsaw to cut down the sides of the dovetails, following the waste side of each line. Be careful not to go below the line marking the width of the other piece. Keep an eye on both sides of the wood. Turn the wood on edge and cut each side. The spaces between the dovetails have to be chopped out with a bevel-edged chisel, while the wood is resting on a fairly strong piece of scrap wood on the bench. Because of the taper, the waste will not break away easily. If heavy blows are used in an effort to remove thick pieces, the corners of the dovetails might be damaged. Instead, chop out small pieces, working from each side. Pick out the waste as it breaks off. The last cuts (to the line) should be by vertical paring, with hand pressure from each side on the bench. Check that the final cuts go straight through and that there is no lump in the middle. (A very slight hollow is preferable to an outward curve.)

This completes the dovetail part. Now it is time to mark out the pins. Although the pieces may have been sawed together, it is unlikely that they will finish so uniform as to be interchangeable. From this stage on, each joint is individually matched. Have the face sides facing outward, and the face edges together. Pencil a number inside each piece, or otherwise mark them, for correct reassembly.

Mark the thickness of the dovetail piece on the one that will have the pins. Put it in a vise to hold the dovetails in position. Use a very fine pencil or a slender steel point to mark the shapes of the dovetails on the end (Fig. 7-28A). Remove the dovetails. If necessary, go over the lines to make them clearer, then square them down to the thickness line with a try square.

Pencil on the waste part of the joint between the pins, and saw downward at each position on the waste side of the line. Some of the waste can be removed by sawing toward the sides (Fig. 7-28B). If the dovetails are fairly wide, a few more cuts in the body of the waste part may help in removing it.

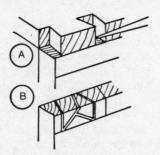

Fig. 7-28. Use a very fine pencil or steel point to transfer the shapes of the dovetails onto the pin part (A). Some of the waste between pins can be removed by sawing toward the sides (B).

Chop out the waste in a way similar to that used for getting between the dovetails. A wider chisel can be used, since the shape is not a restriction in gripping waste as it is removed. Work from both sides.

214

Make sure that wood particles do not remain in the angles of both parts. As it is with mortise-and-tenon joints, a skilled craftsman does not have to make a trial assembly; his first assembly is his last. If a trial assembly is made, only enter the dovetails a short distance. This will show if slight paring with a chisel is needed anywhere.

If you want to make the pins first, mark the end of the pin piece (Fig. 7-29A). Square down the lines and cut out the spaces between the pins as already described. Stand the pin part on the part for the dovetails, then mark the shapes (Fig. 7-29B) and cut them out as already described. One advantage of this sequence for small work is that there is more room to use a pencil or marking awl than there is in the restricted space between the dovetails.

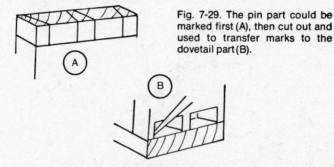

Fig. 7-29. The pin part could be marked first (A), then cut out and used to transfer marks to the dovetail part (B).

Another way of marking pins from dovetails is to saw the sides of the dovetails, then put the wood in position on the other piece and draw the saw back a few times in each cut, scratching the dovetail part (Fig. 7-30). Of course, the saw marks should be on the waste sides of the dovetails. Cuts for the pins must be made on the dovetail side of each line, otherwise the joints will be loose because of the waste removed from the kerf.

This type of multiple dovetail is common for corners of boxes. Most people see a certain beauty in exposed dovetails

Fig. 7-30. Another way of marking pins from dovetails: Saw the sides of the dovetails, put the dovetail piece over the pin piece, and scratch the marks for the pins with a saw.

that are neatly made, then planed and sanded after gluing. Many pieces of old furniture have exposed dovetails at the corners, particularly chests and similar items. However, there are many places where exposed dovetails would not be the correct finish. There are several special variations that give the strength of dovetails while hiding them.

In a drawer, it does not matter if the dovetails are exposed at the side, but they should be hidden in front. The joint for this is a *half-blind* or *lap* dovetail (Fig. 7-31A). The drawer front should be thick enough to overlap the dovetails—at least by $^{3}/_{16}$ inch. For a neat finish, the remainder of this thickness should be about the same as the thickness of the side.

Mark the overall sizes, including the thickness of the side on the end (Fig. 7-31B). From this, mark the line at the bottom of the dovetails on the other piece. If the dovetails are to be marked first, mark them on the side, then cut them out. Put this part in position on the other piece, transfer the marks, and continue each line, using a try square.

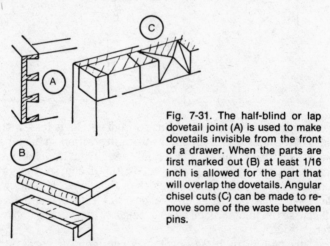

Fig. 7-31. The half-blind or lap dovetail joint (A) is used to make dovetails invisible from the front of a drawer. When the parts are first marked out (B) at least 1/16 inch is allowed for the part that will overlap the dovetails. Angular chisel cuts (C) can be made to remove some of the waste between pins.

Cutting between the pins involves more chisel work, but diagonal cuts can be made as far as the lines, and angular cuts can be made to remove some of the waste (Fig. 7-31C). More of the waste can be removed by chopping at an angle in each space (Fig. 7-32A), followed by vertical cuts a short distance from the line (Fig. 7-32B), then cuts with the grain to break out the waste (Fig. 7-32C). Continue in each space, always cutting across the grain before making any cut with the grain. Be

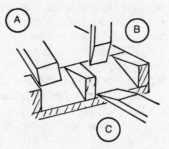

Fig. 7-32. Finishing the pin portion of a half-blind dovetail joint: chopping out waste at an angle (A); vertical cutting (B); cutting with the grain to break out waste (C).

careful not to hit so hard that the wood, which has to remain solid, is broken through. Final trimming to the base line should be by hand paring. The corners may be cleaned out with the point of a knife. Remove some of the waste between the pins by drilling a row of holes close to the base line. A depth stop should be used to prevent the drill from going too far.

The pins can be marked and cut out first if you prefer. Mark the shapes as before, but make them come only to the line on the end. Cut them out as just described, then mark the shapes of the dovetails. The rear corners of a drawer are made with through dovetails (Fig. 7-33A). It is usual to provide a groove for a plywood bottom. If the groove is kept high enough, going into the bottom dovetail, it will be hidden when the joint is assembled. At the back, a crosswise member above the bottom is glued and screwed to it. An extra piece below the bottom at each side gives an extra surface on the runner (Fig. 7-33B). It is important that the back of the finished drawer be no wider than the front. It may be very slightly narrower, however.

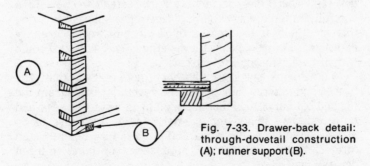

Fig. 7-33. Drawer-back detail: through-dovetail construction (A); runner support (B).

If the dovetails are to be invisible from both sides, but a narrow strip of end grain being visible is allowable, the

217

stopped lap (or blind lap) dovetail can be used. This is best visualized as a through dovetail with an extra layer on the outside of the adjoining sides, one overlapping the other (Fig. 7-34). The piece that does not overlap is made first. It could be either way, but the direction of strain is likely to come from the one that covers; the dovetailed part does not overlap.

Mark both pieces with the thickness that is to overlap, and cut the pin part back by the amount of the overlap. Marking out is similar to that for through dovetails, but not much sawing can be done on either part; most of the waste has to be chopped out with a chisel.

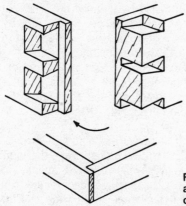

Fig. 7-34. The construction and assembly of the stopped-lap dovetail joint.

The narrow end-grain piece that is exposed when the joint is assembled can be eliminated by using a *housed-and-mitered* dovetail, where the overlapping parts extend to meet in a carefully mitered corner (Fig. 7-35A). The safest way to do this accurately is to clamp a thick piece of wood, carefully planed to a 45° angle, below the dovetail (Fig. 7-35B) as a guide to maintaining the angle of the chisel.

For many purposes, it does not matter that the housed-and-mitered joint leaves the dovetails visible from the top and bottom of the adjoining members, as for the recessed base under a cabinet, for example. But if they have to be hidden completely, the construction has to be taken a step further, to the development of a *secret* or *blind* mitered dovetail joint.

The secret variant looks like a through dovetail with the addition of narrow strips mitered at the top and bottom (Fig.

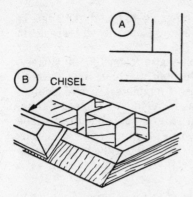

Fig. 7-35. The housed-and-mitered dovetail joint. The top view of the completed joint (A). A planed piece is clamped to the work as a guide to chiseling a precise angle for the finished corner (B).

7-36). Both pieces are marked and cut to allow for overlap (like the housed-and-mitered dovetail), while enough for cutting a miter is left at each edge. Cutting a joint for proper fit is mainly a test of a worker's accuracy with chisels; not much in the way of sawing can be done here.

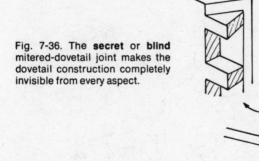

Fig. 7-36. The **secret** or **blind** mitered-dovetail joint makes the dovetail construction completely invisible from every aspect.

Dovetailing is nearly always used for a square corner, but the same method can be used for a sloping corner. The angles of the dovetails should be related to the horizontal (Fig. 7-37).

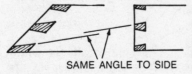

SAME ANGLE TO SIDE

Fig. 7-37. When the corner formed by a dovetail joint slopes, rather than begin truly vertical, the angles of the dovetails should be related to the horizontal to prevent weakened grain.

This is better than sloping the dovetails to match the angle of the surface; if there is a severe slope, it will result in weakened grain.

Dovetails made by machine are restricted in variety, relative to handmade ones. Dovetail machines and dovetail attachments for drill presses use a template/guide to locate a router-like tool that cuts pins and dovetails at the same time. The dovetails may be rounded (Fig. 7-38A), but their shape cannot be seen after assembly. In a machine-made joint, pins and dovetails are the same size (Fig. 7-38B), due to the cutting method, a reliable clue to identifying machine work in a finished article.

When several boards are used to make up a width, they have to be stiffened to prevent the assembly from warping, while allowing a certain amount of expansion and contraction. Stiffness can be given by dovetailed *keys*. A dovetailed-section dado (tapering slightly in its width) is cut across the width of the boards, and a key (Fig. 7-38C) is made to fit it. After the key is driven in, it is fixed near its wide end to allow for subsequent movement.

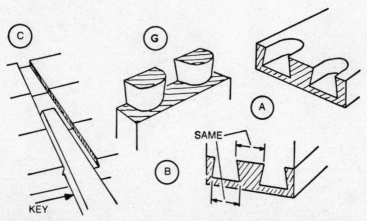

Fig. 7-38. The rounded, machine-made dovetail's shape (A) cannot be seen after the joint is assembled, but can still be indentified as machine-made because the pins and dovetails will be the same size (B). Several boards used to make up a width can be stiffened by inserting a dovetailed key into a matching slot (C).

EXPANDING JOINTS

Because wood may expand and contract in its width according to the type of wood, the thoroughness of its seasoning, and variations in humidity, the joints between boards used to make up a width have to allow for the wood's movement. Expansion and contraction in the length of grain is so minimal, it can be ignored.

Tongue-and-groove joints are used for floorboards and similar construction. The tongue prevents a gap from being formed when the wood shrinks (Fig. 7-39A). If the two sides of the groove are staggered (Fig. 7-39B), nails can be driven as the floorboards are laid so they are hidden in the finished floor. The variation shown in Fig. 7-39C for hardwood floors aids in "secret" nailing. For similar joints, in wall paneling or other places where the joints are visible, the opening and closing due to natural expansion and contraction can be made less obvious by working a *bead* (Fig. 7-39D) into the tongued piece. A simpler way of disguising the joint is to bevel the meeting edges (Fig. 7-39E).

In the days when this was done by hand, there were matching planes for making the tongues and grooves for joints. But with modern equipment there are several ways of making the joint. Suitable spindle-mounted cutters will make both parts. A planer can be used to cut rebates to form a tongue on one part, a *wobble* saw or dado cutter will make the grooved part.

Fig. 7-39. Tongue-and-groove joints: for floorboards (A) the simplest of the joints; staggered groove sides allow hidden nailing (B). Secret nailing technique for hardwood floors (C). For wall paneling, a beaded tongue section disguises wood movement due to expansion and contraction (D); Beveled tongue and groove sections achieve the same effect more simply (E).

Thick boards can be given double tongues and grooves. Tongues and grooves worked into the boards' edges are used for building carpentery rather than cabinetwork. To strengthen an edge-to-edge joint in this manner for cabinet construction, it is more usual to insert a *cross* tongue. Traditionally, the cross tongue was a cut, cross-grained piece; today it is more likely to be a piece of plywood. Cross-grained tongues have to be limited in their length, because of the width of the board from which they are cut. Of course, several can be put in a joint end-to-end, but longer tongues can be made by cutting them diagonally instead of straight across. In cabinetwork these joints are glued; there is no allowance for expansion and contraction.

If a broad board is used as a panel to be enclosed by a frame, there must be an allowance for lateral movement. This can be made unnecessary by using plywood. Although attractively veneered plywood panels can be bought, the only craftsman-like way to make some pieces of cabinetwork look right is to make the panel match the surrounding wood.

A panel, whether of plywood or solid wood, is most simply installed by fitting it into a groove (Fig. 7-40A). However, it should not reach the bottom of the groove and be glued. While this joint is suitable for wood of even thickness—and is particularly appropriate for plywood—solid wood is better left thicker, to reduce the risk of splitting or distorting. A thick panel may be beveled toward its sides to fit the groove (Fig. 7-40B). If the flat (unbeveled) side is to face front, the beveling need not be very precise; but if the bevels are at the front, they can be decorative (if made carefully). The bevels could be hollow instead of flat, for example.

A better appearance, often seen in period furniture, is obtained by using a *beveled and fielded* pane' (Fig. 7-40C): a broad rebate is cut all around the panel before it is beveled.

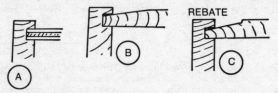

Fig. 7-40. The simplest way of installing a plywood panel is to fit it into a groove (A); a thick panel may be beveled toward its sides to fit the groove (B), but a **beveled and fielded** panel (C) is more attractive.

Sometimes a broad cabinet top or a vertical corner joint has to be made, so as to allow for movement, yet remain unspoiled in appearance when the parts move. This can be done with dado, tongue, and rebate (refer to Fig. 7-13F), but if the edges are decorated with molding, any movement will be disguised (Fig. 7-41A). Another way of disguising movement in a panel that is flush with the edge, is to work a bead into it (Fig. 7-41B).

The tongue-and-groove joint can be adapted to other things, besides flat panels. At a corner the bead can be a decorative feature (Fig. 7-41C), while the tongue at the side could be set at any angle.

Fig. 7-41. Wood movement in a corner joint can be disguised with decorative molding (A). A bead worked into the tongue part will do the same job for a right angle corner (B), as well as for corners that form other than right angles (C).

HINGED JOINTS

A surface-mounted door hinge presents no difficulty, as far as unrestricted door movement is concerned (Fig. 7-42A). But if the hinge is set into the joint, there are several possible faults that can make the door "hinge bound." A door swings around the center of the hinge *knuckle*. If the door is to swing back against a wall, the center of the knuckle (of an inset hinge) should be at about the same position it would be when surface-mounted (Fig. 7-42B). If the hinge is set in too far, the door will be hindered in movement by the doorjamb (Fig. 7-42C). If the hinge is set into the wood too much, the door will not close (Fig. 7-42D). This will also happen if the screws

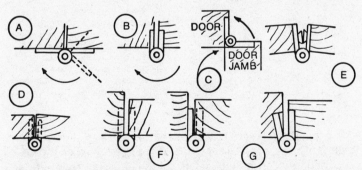

Fig. 7-42. Door hinges mounted with the hinge knuckle in the positions shown at A and B offer completely unrestricted door movement. If the hinge is set in too deeply between the wooden parts, the door could strike the doorjamb (C); if the flaps are set too deeply into the wood, the door won't close fully (D); nor will the door close fully if screw heads protrude (E). The arrangements shown at F are satisfactory, but it is better to angle one flap into the doorjamb (G).

project (Fig. 7-42E). Trouble also comes if the knuckles of the hinges are not in line, especially if there are three or more hinges: one or more will be seen to distort or pull on its fasteners as the door is moved.

A hinge may be set partially into the edge of the door and the doorjamb. Or the whole thickness of one hinge flap (the part that takes the screws) may be set into the door edge, and the other fixed on the surface of the doorjamb (Fig. 7-42F). The second arrangement involves less work and allows the door to swing wider than the first method. But for quality cabinetwork, set the hinge equally into each part, or position the knuckle over the door edge and angle the flap into the doorjamb (Fig. 7-42G). This gives better clearance for the screw heads.

Recesses for hinges should be carefully marked. Use a marking gage set to the width of the hinge from the center of the knuckle (Fig. 7-43A), or slightly less than that. Mark the ends of the recess with a knife. At first, the depth of the recess should be no more than the thickness of the hinge flap. Saw diagonally at the ends of the recess and at a few intermediate points (Fig. 7-43C). Use a mallet lightly on a chisel to cut in the outline of the recess, taking the saw cuts to the full depth. Pare out surplus wood. Even for a large hinge, the amount to be removed will not be much, so be careful not to cut too deeply or go outside the lines.

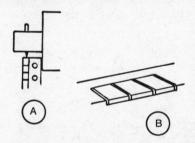

Fig. 7-43. Recesses for hinges should be marked with a gage set to the width of hinge, measured from the center of the knuckle (A). Begin cutting out the recess by making saw cuts at the ends of the recess, and at a few intermediate points (B).

After the recesses have been cut, make a trial assembly, using only one screw in each flap. If the gap left when the door is closed is wider than intended, set the hinges further into the door. If a recess has been cut too deeply, the hinge can be backed with paper.

Make sure the door matches its surrounding frame when closed. It may be necessary to move one hinge in or out by slackening the temporary screw, pulling the hinge to the new position, putting a screw through another hole, and removing the first screw.

It is inadvisable to depend on binding at the hinge to restrict the movement of a door. This puts too much strain on the hinge. Instead, fabricate a stop that the body of the door can go against, or use a restraining chain. One place where the hinge itself can act as a stop is in the lid of a box, if it does not swing past the vertical. In this special case, the hinge is set further into the parts, and the edges of the wood at the back are beveled to form stops (Fig. 7-44A).

There are a great variety of hinges in use. When fitting them, the approach to their installation is usually obvious when the pivot point at the center of the knuckle and the movement about that point is understood. A sectional drawing may help to make the movement clearer. An example is the back-flap rule-joint hinge used for the drop leaf of a table (Fig. 7-44B), as well as folding rulers.

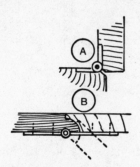

Fig. 7-44. If a box and its lid are beveled near the knuckle of the hinge that joins them (A), the hinge can act as a stop. A drawing depicting the range of movement of hinged parts can be helpful in the proper installation of the hinge (B). (This drawing shows the hinge for a drop leaf table.)

OTHER JOINTS

Plywood and other manufactured boards are useful materials; but in most cases, their edges have to be covered to improve appearance and provide protection. For such construction as doors, it is usually advisable to panel both sides; otherwise, uneven stresses may cause warping or twisting. Door edges can be covered with narrow strips of solid wood (Fig. 7-45A). For a counter or other work surface, there are plastic strips that can be taken around curves, that solid wood edging could not follow.

Plywood makes good shelving, and can have enough strength without being as thick as a solid wood shelf; but its front edge should be stiffened for an appearance of greater solidity (Fig. 7-45B).

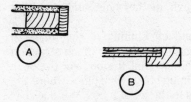

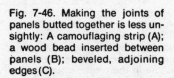

Fig. 7-45. The edges of doors made from manufactured materials, rather than solid wood, can be covered with strips of solid wood (A); the front edge of plywood shelving should be stiffened for an appearance of greater solidity (B).

Panels can be simply butted together, but the joint will remain visible even through paint and other finishes. It is sometimes possible to cover these joints with strips to make a pattern (Fig. 7-46A), or plastic and metal moldings can be used. A bull-nosed wood bead can be inserted between the panels (Fig. 7-46B). An alternative is to bevel the meeting edges slightly, so what will be obvious will at least be more pleasant to look at (Fig. 7-46C).

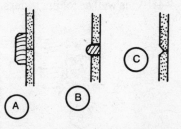

Fig. 7-46. Making the joints of panels butted together is less unsightly: A camouflaging strip (A); a wood bead inserted between panels (B); beveled, adjoining edges (C).

Comb joints are commonly used at the corners of boxes (Fig. 7-47). A comb joint is something like a dovetail joint without the wedge-shaped tails. Although it could be made by hand, it is usually a product of machine woodworking. Fittings or adaptors to make small power machines cut combs are available, using a guide or template to locate a cutter, but this type of joint is really more suitable for industrial production.

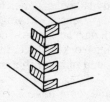

Fig. 7-47. The comb joint, commonly used at the corners of boxes, is somewhat related to the dovetail joint, but is usually only found in industrial production.

Veneer is sometimes glued into saw cuts to strengthen a joint. The mitered corners of a box may have saw cuts made at different angles, then pieces of veneer with grain going across the joint can be glued in and trimmed flush (Fig. 7-48A). This can also be done at the corners of a picture frame (Fig. 7-48B).

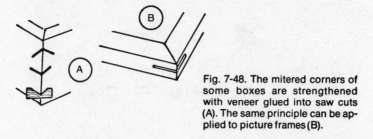

Fig. 7-48. The mitered corners of some boxes are strengthened with veneer glued into saw cuts (A). The same principle can be applied to picture frames (B).

In roofing work, a spar or rafter may have to be notched over a wall plate (Fig. 7-49A); the simple notch is called a birdsmouth notch.

A table top made from plywood, or other manufactured board not subject to expansion and contraction, may be held to the rails by *pocket* screwing (Fig. 7-49B), as well as glue.

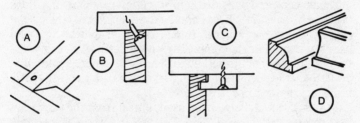

Fig. 7-49. Miscellaneous joints: the birdsmouth notch found in roofing construction (A); **pocket screwing** in a table top (B); a **button** used in a table top (C); the mating parts of a coped joint (D).

Additional strength may come from blocks glued inside. If the top is solid wood, and some movement is anticipated, *buttons* can be used (Fig. 7-49C). The rail may be grooved for its whole length or only at the button position.

A *coped* joint is an alternative to a miter. Instead of the moldings cut to meet at a 45° angle, one is shaped to fit over the other (Fig. 7-49D). In a situation like putting molding around a ceiling, slight errors in making this joint are less likely to be as obvious as a miter that does not fit properly.

8

Turning Wood

There is a tremendous satisfaction in shaping wood while it revolves in a lathe. While there is plenty of scope for an enthusiast to become skilled in producing articles of increasing complexity, the basic work is fairly simple. A beginner can produce satisfactory, simple items with a little practice. Turned woodwork can be used as part of other wood constructions, but several things, such as bowls and tool handles, can be made completely on the lathe. Turning wood may be only part of the activities of a woodworker; while some craftsmen find such fascination in the lathe, they do very little besides turn wood.

Lathes seem to have been used almost from the time man first mastered the use of tools. The potter's wheel is a simple lathe on which clay is hand-formed as it revolves on a platform, which many potters still prefer to drive with foot-power rather than an electric motor. Many early lathes revolved in alternate directions; craftsmen in India still use this type.

Indian craftsmen and others who prefer to work in a crouched position use a lathe close to the ground, turned by a bowstring (Fig. 8-1A). An assistant moves the bow back and forth, or the turner himself moves it with one hand while using a foot to help the other hand control the tool.

Lathes have been set up to use the power that can be stored in a springy tree branch to provide a return stroke for a foot-operated lathe (Fig. 8-1B); they used the alternate rotation idea of the Indian turner, but the work was done at a height better suited to the Western worker. This type of lathe

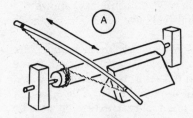

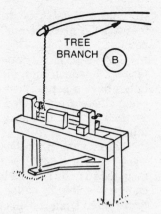

Fig. 8-1. Two primitive lathes: a bowstring-operated type (A) still used in India; a portable type (B) in which a tree branch provided power for the return stroke.

was still being used in some parts of Great Britain up until World War II to make chair rails and legs amongst the trees where the wood was cut. These "chair bodgers" used only a few simple pieces of metalwork, and were moved on to a new site when the local supply of wood was depleted.

When the work was only rotated in one direction, thus permitting cutting for only half the working time, the lathe could only be regarded as 50% efficient. But craftsmen, adept at using these lathes at high speeds, made a living by working at piecework rates. Obviously, a lathe that rotates in only one direction is more efficient and easier to use. Before electric power was available, many lathes were treadle-operated by the turner. Most included a heavy flywheel to regulate the speed. Another way, used by wheelwrights to turn large, heavy wheel hubs, was to have one or more assistants turn a large-diameter hand wheel, with a belt driving a small pulley on the lathe. The electric motor has taken over; its even, regular speed permits much more precise work and allows the turner, who now doesn't have to provide the power, to concentrate on his work fully.

In principle, the work is supported between points in the lathe called *centers*, one usually providing the drive. The work rotates with its "top" turning toward the operator, who holds a tool against the surface to cut it. In metal turning, the tool has to be securely mounted in a post, its direction controlled by hand wheels. But in wood turning the tool is supported on a rest and its movements are controlled by hand. This is called *turning between centers*. A lathe for this work can be quite basic. In many ways, simplicity is an advantage: freedom from projections, hand wheels, and adjustments, allows the unrestricted movement of hand tools over as big an area as possible.

Besides turning-between-centers work, there is *faceplate turning*, in which thin, large-diameter work is turned. Some lathes have a gap in their bed to facilitate this kind of work, while others are provided with a mounting for a faceplate at one end of the spindle, where a tool-rest extension can be fitted.

Lathes vary in construction, but all contain the basic parts shown in Fig. 8-2. The *bed* on which the other parts are mounted may be solid, a large tube, or two rods. The driving end to the left is called the *headstock*. Power is usually transmitted from the electric motor by a cone pulley, which provides three or more speeds by being moved to various positions. The headstock is likely to be enclosed for safety and to keep out flying wood dust and chips. The spindle runs in bearings that may need frequent lubrication because of the considerable load they are subjected to in heavy turning. Some larger lathes have hollow spindles that take Morse-tapered shanks. The spindle (*mandrel*) nose is threaded to take a variety of centers and faceplates.

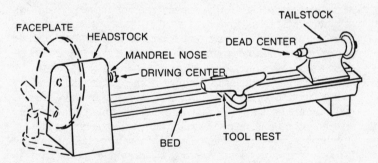

Fig. 8-2. The basic parts of a modern lathe.

The ordinary right-hand thread on a normal spindle nose will tend to tighten under a load. At the opposite end of the spindle, the load is applied in the opposite direction, so a faceplate with a right-hand thread mounted there would tend to unscrew—and come off. This means that faceplates and other accessories intended for the left-hand end of the spindle are not interchangeable with those for the right-hand end.

For work between centers, a *tailstock* supports the right-hand end of the work. The tailstock can be locked anywhere on the bed, and there is usually a fine screw adjustment for the center, which is at the same height as the center in the spindle nose. The center at the driving end is called the *driving* or *live* center, while the one in the tailstock, which does not normally revolve, is called the *dead* center.

The tool rest is mounted on the bed in such a way that it can be moved to any position and locked. It can also be moved in and out and has a limited height adjustment. In can be set at any angle to the work (when viewed from above). Some lathes can take a range of interchangeable rest sizes. A large lathe may have a long rest mounted on two supports. (For good work, a turner needs to be able to position his rest quickly without trouble.)

For turning at the other end of the headstock, there is usually a substantial bracket for the tool rest; the whole assembly may be removable.

The size of a lathe may be described by the height of the centers above the bed, or by its *swing*: the diameter of the largest piece of work that will clear the bed (Fig. 8-3). The work is held above the bed, but the thickness of the part of the tool rest that goes over the bed will limit the size of work that can be turned above that. If there is a gap in the bed, the

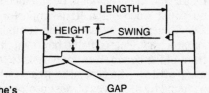

Fig. 8-3. Terms related to a lathe's dimensions and capacity.

maximum size that can be turned will be indicated. In modern lathes it is more usual for large, shallow items to be turned at the other end of the headstock. The maximum length that can be accommodated is demonstrated per the following example. A lathe described as 30 inches by 7 inches (swing) has the capacity to hold a cylinder 7 inches in diameter and 30 inches long. American lathes are usually described only by their swing. British lathe sizes are given as the height of the centers above the bed. Some lathes may have an extension bed as an option that can be attached to accommodate greater lengths.

Rigidity in the lathe and the way it is mounted is important. While a light lathe may produce acceptable items of moderate diameter, heavy construction prevents the vibration and movement that would spoil the finish on the work. This applies to slender parts as well as large parts.

A lathe may be mounted on an iron stand, but there is some advantage in rigidity and noise-deadening to having a lathe fixed to a sturdy wooden bench top. A wooden top is also kinder to the edges of tools. The stand should be firmly affixed to the workshop floor, preferably bolted down, but not so tightly that the stand or the lathe bed is distorted. It is better to use packing than to try pulling the parts into position by their bolts.

The lathe stand or bench may also be braced to the wall to make the whole thing as rigid as possible. The positioning and mounting of the lathe will have to be related to the position of the electric motor and to lighting. In some lathes the motor is included in the assembly, with its platform and drive as part of the lathe. If it has to be mounted separately, there is a choice of position. It is usually convenient to have the motor below the lathe, either in the stand or below the bench. When flat drive belts were used, it was necessary to have the centers of motor and lathe fairly distant to insure that the belt had a good grip, but with V belts the distance can be short.

The motor may be behind or above the lathe, but both the motor and the belt should be shielded for safety and to keep out dust and wood chips. It is important to have proper power switching; trailing wires and temporary switches are never satisfactory. There should be a switch within easy reach on the front of the bench. It is dangerous to lean over rotating work to use a switch. The type of switch in which the OFF position can be found by feel gives utmost protection in an emergency.

There are a few occasions when it is convenient to be able to reverse the lathe. This occurs when sanding, for example. Final sanding in reverse direction takes care of minute fibers that have been bent instead of being sanded away. Many electric motors can be reversed easily, without harming the motor. When the machine is being installed, it is worthwhile having a reversing switch included in the electrical system.

Natural lighting should come from above and in front of the lathe. It is also helpful to be able to look across the work toward a light source that highlights edges and angles. For this reason it is best to have a light that can be moved around on an arm or by some other means. Besides general lighting, the addition of a reading lamp, or some other adjustable light source in a metal shade, is helpful.

EQUIPMENT

The standard center (Fig. 8-4A) has a 60° point, and tapers at the other end to fit the headstock's and tailstock's hollow spindles. Some turners prefer a more obtuse point angle, maybe up to 90° (Fig. 8-4B); this is particularly suitable for softwoods; it does not have such a tendency to work into the wood bearing on it. Another center for softwoods is the *cup* center (Fig. 8-4C); a ring prevents the center from penetrating the wood too far.

A rotating center (Fig. 8-4D) has an enclosed bearing that allows it to rotate with the work. It is less likely to work its way further into the wood, thereby making frequent adjustment of the tailstock unnecessary; but satisfactory work is dependent on the bearing running true without slackness. Looseness or movement in the bearing will be reflected in the finish of the work. A rotating center is bulky. It cannot be used when the end of the wood being turned has to be worked to a small diameter: the tool would come against the center.

For most work there is a driving center (*prong* center or *prong chuck*) at the headstock end of the lathe. It takes its drive through the friction fit of its tapered end in the spindle. In its simplest form, there are two knife edges on either side of a central point (Fig. 8-4E). Another type has four knife edges (Fig. 8-4F). The latter makes a more positive connection with the work, but the former type is most commonly used. There are other variations, but all have a central point to locate and hold the wood in a central position, along with teeth or jaws to transmit drive.

Most lathes have their mandrel nose screwed in the same way as in a metal-turning lathe. This allows fittings to be screwed on. It is convenient to have a metalworking type of self-centering chuck to hold pieces of wood within its capacity, as well as for holding metal to be hand-turned in the wood lathe.

A driving center is used for all turning between centers, but there are many things that can only be held at one end. For small, eggcup-shaped items, there are screw centers (Fig. 8-4G) in which a screw is permanently fixed to the center of a fitting that goes in the tapered hole or screws on the mandrel nose. This means that when the screw becomes damaged, the whole fitting has to be scrapped. Another version takes a strong, replaceable wood screw (Fig. 8-4H). Besides allowing the replacement of worn screws, it also permits using screws of different lengths.

There are occasions when a lathe is used as a drilling machine. Large twist drills with suitably tapered shanks can be mounted directly to the lathe without a chuck. A drill chuck with a tapered shank (Fig. 8-4I) can be put in the tailstock to drill revolving wood with parallel shank drills, or it can be used at the headstock end to drill wood held stationary. For this purpose a drill pad (Fig. 8-4J) can support the wood.

Large disks are supported by faceplates. They are available in many sizes. Each has a broad, flat surface and a thread that screws onto the headstock mandril. Small faceplates have holes for screws. Larger faceplates also have slots (Fig. 8-4K). If turning is done at both ends of the headstock, the faceplates for each position will have different threads.

Several other items of equipment, such as supports and chucks, can be made by the turner. Wooden mandrels and formers to hold special parts while they are turned may be made on the lathe as needed, but a stock of these will be built up and used either unchanged or adapted for later jobs.

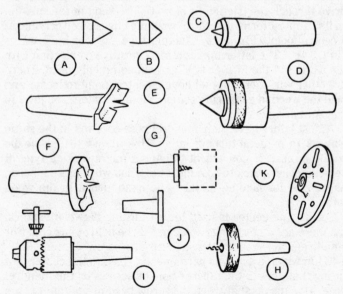

Fig. 8-4. Lathe attachments. (See text for descriptions.)

TOOLS

Nearly all turning is done with chisels and gouges. They differ from the hand tools with similar names used for other types of woodwork and are not interchangeable with them. There are several sizes of turning tools, but all are longer than those used for general woodworking and are fitted with very long handles. Because the tools do not have to withstand hitting, there is no shoulder where the tang enters the handle. The extra length is needed to provide leverage and control.

A professional uses what are often called *long and strong* gouges and chisels. The gouges have quite a thick cross section, and the bottom has metal thicker than that at the sides (Fig. 8-5A). These gouges are especially suitable for making large bowls and other heavy work. Normal gouges have a more uniform cross section (Fig. 8-5B). Try to get fairly large tools rather than using the light ones sometimes offered with small lathes. A large tool will do most of the things a small one can, and the greater size will give more freedom from vibration and chatter, along with better control.

Most turners, having their own preference for handle shapes, make their own. Some possibilities are shown in Fig. 8-5C. Homemade turning handles for lathe tools can provide interesting work on the lathe, as well as the satisfaction of having created your own patterns, patterns that would not necessarily be like anything available from a tool shop.

Turning gouges come in many widths. At one time there were several depths of curve available; those available now come in a more limited range. For most work between centers, a ½ inch gouge is the general-purpose tool. A ¼ inch gouge is needed for hollows the ½ inch one will not go into; for broad, sweeping cuts, there are advantages in having a wider one—probably ¾ inch, although something even wider may be needed later.

The gouge for between-center turning is sharpened on the outside to a rounded point (Fig. 8-5D). It is sometimes called a *spindle* gouge. For working inside a bowl, long and strong gouges sharpened straight across the end (Fig. 8-5E) are best; for a variety of work, there is an advantage in getting two gouges in each size, one with each type of end.

At first, get three chisels in the same widths as the gouges recommended. A wider one (1 to 1½ inches, or more) is easier to control for broad sweeps. Chisels are sharpened equally on both sides, the cutting edge going across the center of the thickness (Fig. 8-5F). The cut is made diagonally along the work (Fig. 8-5G); to allow the tool to be held at a convenient position, the cutting edge is diagonal (Fig. 8-5H). The angle of the cutting edge can vary according to preference. A few workers prefer an end that goes nearly square across. A diamond-pointed chisel (Fig. 8-5J) has limited uses. There is more use for a parting tool (Fig. 8-5K).

For some work, particularly for working cross-grained wood into a bowl, a whole range of scrapers is needed. Scrapers are chisels ground to a fairly obtuse cutting edge (Fig. 8-5L). In the other axis they may go straight across or be diagonal, rounded to various curves, or rounded on one side and square on the other (Fig. 8-5M). Scraper tools can take the form of ordinary chisels, or be adaptations from them; many turners grind their own from old files. Files are tempered very hard, which means they are also brittle. Because of this, it is unwise to make a turning tool from a thin file; it might snap in use. If the facilities are available, the temper might be reduced to reduce brittleness, but a turning scraper made from a heavy file with its original temper will keep its edge a long time.

The instructions given earlier for sharpening other edged tools are generally applicable to turning tools. The points to watch are mainly concerned with angles.

A gouge is ground with a rolling motion, mainly to keep wear on the stone even. (If the stone were only used for gouges, it would not matter if it became hollow.) The angle can be steeper or more obtuse than for general woodworking gouges (Fig. 8-5N). A spindle gouge with a rounded end can have a longer bevel, making it comparable with a firmer gouge (Fig. 8-5O).

A turning gouge may be sharpened on an oilstone to obtain a second sharpening bevel, but many turners prefer to let the oilstone rub at almost the same angle as the tool's original bevel, so there is no distinct sharpening bevel. Using an ordinary oilstone, rock the gouge as you move it around the surface. Because a turner's gouges need to be sharpened much more frequently than those of the general woodworker, it is worthwhile having a hollow gouge slip (Fig. 8-5P). The hollow part of the stone can be used on the outside of the gouge. The tapered form allows the matching of several gouge curves. The edges of the slip can be used inside the gouge to deburr the edge.

Chisels are best sharpened without distinct angles; the bevel on each side should curve from the flat to the bevel,

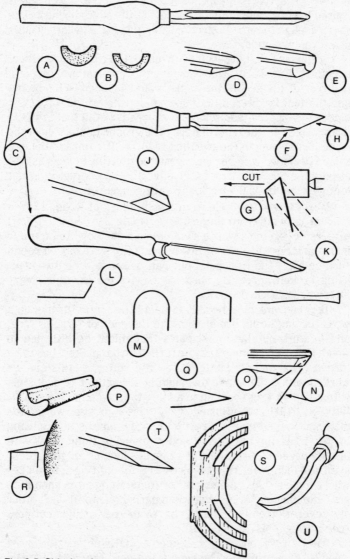

Fig. 8-5. Chisel and gouge details for wood turning. (See text for descriptions.)

continuing to the edge (Fig. 8-5Q). It would not matter if there were angles at the change in bevel, but chisels are normally supplied without them.

A parting tool is sharpened top and bottom like a chisel. It is used to cut straight into the wood, but the edge should still be sharp enough to remove shavings, not just the powdery results of a scraping action.

Scrapers are sharpened by grinding the end to an angle of about 60° (Fig. 8-5R). This is done on the grindstone against a tool rest. If the heel of the angle is first touched to the stone, and the tool is lowered until sparks appear on the top of the blade, the original angle will be reached. If the tool is made from an old file, the top will have to be ground on the side of the stone just enough to remove the file teeth. The top and the end should be honed with an oilstone, so the meeting edge is as fine as possible. The grindstone will leave a fairly coarse edge. But for all except finishing work, this may be good enough.

When a bowl is made from a solid block of wood, a large amount is taken from the inside as waste. Professional bowl turners devise tools whose shape allows one bowl to be made inside another (Fig. 8-5S). Bowls made this way have a rough surface after the first cuts, but can be worked further after being broken apart. By choosing bowl sizes carefully, very little wood is wasted.

It is convenient to be able to do a little metal turning on a wood-turning lathe, if only to make the ends of ferrules true, and to work similar metal parts that might be attached to wood. Brass and copper may be turned by hand. Steel has to be turned on a metalworking lathe. The softer metals can be worked with a tool made by grinding a length of ¼ inch steel with a square cross section to a long, tapered end (Fig. 8-5T). With a tool rest adjusted very close to the work, the diamond-shaped end can be tilted so its edge is at a cutting angle. Tools for measuring and comparing dimensions will also be needed. Besides a rule 12 inches long or longer, a 6- or even a 4-inch steel rule is necessary for getting into places where longer rules cannot go. For many things it is enough to gage dimensions by eye, but when parts have to fit each other or several identical parts have to be made *calipers* (comparing tools) are needed.

The simple engineer's caliper is satisfactory for most wood turning projects. The *outside caliper* (Fig. 8-6A) is used most; the *inside caliper* is used for gaging the insides of holes and hollows (Fig. 8-6B). Combination calipers (Fig. 8-6C) do the work of both; if the "inside" end is spread against the inside of a ferrule, the other end will be adjusted to the size of the handle to fit it.

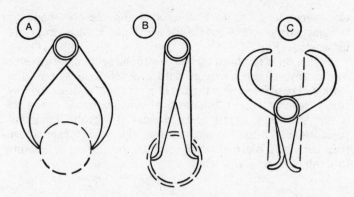

Fig. 8-6. Outside calipers (A); inside calipers (B); combination calipers (C).

Friction-joint calipers have to be set by pulling them apart and tapping them together. Because these calipers can lose their setting as they are used, it is better to get a spring-bow type with a screw adjustment (Fig. 8-7A). They are available in many configurations. *Hermaphrodite* (also *jenny,* or *odd-leg*) calipers with one point (Fig. 8-7B) are engineers' tools, but they can be used for finding the center of a piece of wood.

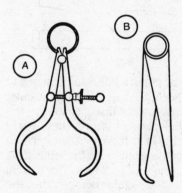

Fig. 8-7. Spring-bow calipers (A) will hold their setting. Hermaphrodite calipers (B) can be used to find the center of a piece of wood.

The end of a piece being turned to a particular size can be tested with a piece of wood with a hole that size. This is the best way to test parts that have to be assembled; the hole can be made with the same drill used on the part. The test piece can hang on the dead center, if it is at that end that the part is being made to size. For establishing and maintaining a size elsewhere along the work, a wooden gage can be made by hinging two pieces of wood drilled with holes of the appropriate dimensions (Fig. 8-8A).

When wood has been turned to a round section, lengthwise measurements can be made with a pencil held against the work and positioned with the aid of a rule held against the tool rest. If several pieces the same size have to be made, say, a set of four stool legs, a strip of wood marked with the important positions (Fig. 8-8B) can be used as a gage. Some turners drive nails through a piece of wood, using the projecting nail points to scratch the revolving work.

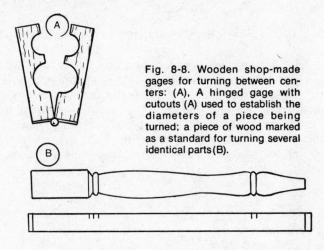

Fig. 8-8. Wooden shop-made gages for turning between centers: (A), A hinged gage with cutouts (A) used to establish the diameters of a piece being turned; a piece of wood marked as a standard for turning several identical parts (B).

A square piece of wood can be put in a lathe and reduced to a round section quite quickly with a gouge. The initial cuts, when the flat sides slap the gouge, may be disconcerting to the beginner; in the days of treadle-operated lathes, these early stages were also hard work for the foot. If desired, the corners may be planed off before the wood is mounted in the lathe. This can be done with the aid of a trough (Fig. 8-9A). There is no need for precise planing to an exact, regular octagon; but the bevel corners should be almost as wide as the surfaces between them.

It is often necessary to find the center of a piece wood before it can be turned. Two diagonals drawn between opposite corners will cross at the center (Fig. 8-9B). A marking gage or a hermaphrodite caliper, used in four positions to draw a small square, allows the center to be estimated (Fig. 8-9C). Of

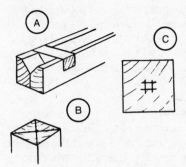

Fig. 8-9. A square piece of wood can be roughly "rounded" by planing it to an octagonal shape in a trough (A). The center of the end of a piece of wood can be found by drawing intersecting diagonals (B), or by drawing a small square (C), using hermaphrodite calipers.

course, it is fairly easy to just estimate the center, especially if there is enough wood to waste on errors in judgement. In jobs where a part has to *remain* square, such as some table legs, greater accuracy in centering is needed.

It is helpful, in making many articles, to use a center punch to make a dent at the center of the end of wood, either to locate the dead center or the spike of the driving center. To get the driving center into the wood, make a shallow, diagonal saw cut across the end of the wood. Much depends on the wood. The wood may be merely pushed onto the driving center, or it might require a light blow with a hammer or mallet. Some turners use a second, unmounted driving center, that matches the one in the lathe, as a punch to make an impression in the wood.

WOOD FOR TURNING

Fortunately, almost any wood can be turned. For most purposes, softwoods are not very satisfactory for turning, although if a turned part is needed to match some softwood part, it can be made, providing there is not too much fine detail. Of the hardwoods, those that are close-grained are more suitable for intricate turning than those that have a more open grain. However, there is a lot of turned Tudor work still in existence that shows attractive detail work in fairly coarse-grained oak.

Many types of wood unsuitable for other woodworking can be used for turning. Awkward grain that would not respond to planing or other machining may give an attractive result when turned. However, for the beginner, beech, birch, and other moderately hard woods with reasonably straight grain are best. The very hard woods should be kept for later work.

When wood is seasoned it sometimes develops shakes and cracks. Such wood is best avoided in turning. A crack could open, causing the wood to fly out of the lathe. Obviously, wood should be properly seasoned, but some turners get green wood, turn it roughly, then put it aside to season naturally for several months before turning it completely.

TURNING BETWEEN CENTERS

To mount wood between the centers of a lathe, use a center punch to make dents in each end and saw a cut at the driving end (to help locate the driving center). Bring the wood up to the driving center and give it a light tap to settle the point and knife edges in the wood. Locate the tailstock in the dent at the other end of the wood. Position the tool rest and turn the wood around by hand to make sure it does not touch the tool rest.

A plain center needs lubrication. A squeal will warn you if it is running dry. Although ordinary lubricating oil is sometimes used, any excess could fly off the lathe; it may soak into the wood and soil it. Tallow is better for lubricating a dead center. If a revolving center is used, there is no need for lubricating the point, because it does not turn in relation to the wood; but the bearings in the center may need oil or grease. Lubrication of the headstock bearings is important. The method of lubricating varies. Lubricators on the lathe should be filled and set to work.

Lathe speeds are not critical. Good work can be done at many different speeds. Individual workers have their own preferences, favoring much higher or lower speeds for the same type of wood and diameter of work. It is the speed at which the surface of the wood passes the cutting edge of the tool that counts. A point on the circumference of a large-diameter piece will revolve at a higher speed than one on a small-diameter piece, even though the lathe turns at the same speed for both. To keep surface speeds approximately the same, the lathe is adjusted to a lower speed for a large disk than it would be for a small cylinder.

A three-step cone pulley only allows a choice of three speeds. The slowest speed—the large pulley on the lathe, the small pulley on the motor—is used for bowls and other things large in diameter. For smaller work, one of the other two speeds is used. What the speeds are varies between lathes, but they will likely be between 700 and 3000 rpm. A greater range may sometimes be desirable, but in practice the three speeds will be adequate.

For turning between centers, the tools should cut rather than scrape. In nearly all turning of this type, waste wood should come away as a shaving. If the waste comes away as powder or small broken pieces, the tool angle is wrong and a scraping action is being produced.

If one side of the tool rests on the turning wood at a tangent (Fig. 8-10A), it will not cut. If the angle is reduced slightly (Fig. 8-10B), the edge will enter the wood, and the tool will cut; this relative angle of the part of the edge that is cutting produces shavings. If the angle is reduced more (Fig. 8-10C), the effect will be scraping instead of cutting. Some beginners tend to err toward scraping because of the reduced risk of digging into the wood. But good work cannot be produced this way. Proper tool control should be mastered.

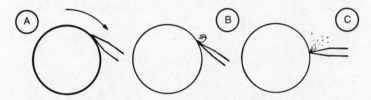

Fig. 8-10. Turning tool angles: With the bevel of the cutting edge at a tangent to the work (A) there is no cutting; a shaving is produced (B) when the angle is correct; when powdered waste is produced (C), the tool is scraping rather than cutting.

Lathe tools are held with both hands fairly wide apart. To make all the cuts required, it is often necessary to change hands. Turners, being right- or left-handed like anyone else, prefer doing things one way, but they should be able to handle a tool just as effectively with either hand. One hand bears down on the tool quite close to the tool rest. The other holds the handle near its end. Manipulation of the tool is a combination of actions by both hands; but if there is any division of responsibility, the hand at the tool rest should be mainly concerned with holding the blade in position and preventing it from jumping or vibrating, the other hand moving and turning the handle to get the desired effect at the cutting edge.

There is a difference of opinion on how to hold the hand at the tool rest. The firmest grip is obtained by having the fist clenched over the tool, either on or close to the tool rest. Although this is necessary for heavy cuts in hardwoods, the fist may obscure part of the work. For more detailed work, and for lighter cuts, it is better to hold the tool with only the thumb on top and the fingers underneath.

Whatever the work, the tool must be held firmly. This applies to even the finest, lightest work. It is not unreasonable to assume that fine work means a light touch; but in turning, tool control must be just as firm for fine cuts as it is for coarse cuts.

The tool rest should be as close to the work as possible. Usually, its top is at the same height as the lathe centers. This is not critical, but it affects the angle at which the tool is held. The tool-rest height may be adjusted to suit the height of the worker, then kept at this height for most turning. If the tool rest is low (Fig. 8-11A), the hand on the end of the tool handle must also be low. Raising the tool rest slightly can afford a considerable rise in hand position, because the distance from the cutting edge to the hand is great compared to the distance from the cutting edge to the fulcrum of the tool rest (Fig. 8-11B). A turner of average height, operating a lathe mounted at an average height, should be able to obtain a comfortable, effective stance by having the top of the tool rest at lathe-center height.

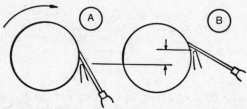

Fig. 8-11. If the tool rest is low (A), the hand holding the tool must be kept low; raising the tool rest slightly (B) affords a considerable rise in hand position.

Roughing a square or octagonal piece of wood to a cylindrical form usually requires a broad gouge with a rounded nose, but an expert may prefer to use a gouge ground straight across for the same job. The problem with using a gouge ground straight across is that its corners could dig into the wood if it is used incorrectly.

Touch the gouge to the wood with the bevel almost tangent to the circle described by the wood's turning edges (Fig. 8-12A). Slide the tool down the tool rest slightly until the edge begins to cut. Cut in further by advancing the tool. As the diameter of the work is reduced, adjust the angle of the tool slightly (Fig. 8-12B).

If a length of wood is being rounded, the initial approach can be to make individual cuts into the irregular shape; but as you gain experience, move the gouge along the tool rest, without relaxing your grip; slackening the grip may cause a kickback. Angle the gouge slightly in the direction it is moved along the wood (Fig. 8-12C). Also roll it so different parts of the edge share in cutting.

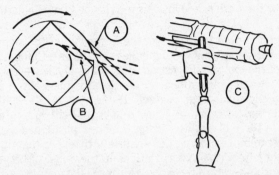

Fig. 8-12. Rounding a piece of wood with a square cross section on a lathe: Initial cuts are made with the gouge's bevel held almost tangent to the circle described by the work's revolving edges (A); the change in tool angle corresponding to the work's reduced diameter (B); angling the gouge into the direction of its movement along the tool rest (C).

Initial cuts in an irregular piece will remove small pieces, making the correct cutting angle difficult to determine; but as the wood becomes round, the waste will be in the form of small lengths of shavings—if the cut is at the best angle. Early cuts may be light and cautious, but as experience is gained, they can be quick and bold. Holding a gouge in one position will produce grooves that match the curve of the gouge; moving it along the work will produce a fairly even surface. While the wood is rotating at a fairly high speed, the quality of its surface will look deceptively good; when the machine is stopped, however, it will be rough. This does not matter, but it does demonstrate that the gouge, used in this way, is for roughing to shape—not for finishing.

Before attempting to make any particular item, turn several lengths of wood as practice pieces, without being too concerned about the shapes produced. Use your gouges to rough out the wood to the general form required, but leave a little excess thickness. When size is important, use calipers. When you have become more confident, you will be able to produce free-flowing curves by directing the tool to the shape that is most pleasing to you with a minimum of measuring. (It is only when a shape has to be duplicated that templates and calipers come into use.)

Chisels are held like gouges, but are used with a slicing action. At first, use as broad a turning chisel as can be employed. On a long, flat surface, or one that has broadly undulating curves, a broad chisel makes getting the desired curve or flat easier, and lessens the risk of a long point digging in.

When viewed from above, the lower end of the slope of a chisel with a diagonal cutting edge is on the side that cuts. The bevel of the tool should rest on the surface of the wood almost tangent to the circumference, with only the center of the cutting edge in actual contact. If the tool is tilted slightly toward the lower edge (Fig. 8-13A), it will start to cut. Advance the tool slightly, using the hand positioned over the tool rest to move it along the wood. A little experimenting will show the effect of slight variations in the angle of tilt across the blade and toward the wood. Cutting is done almost entirely along the lower half of the cutting edge. At no time must the long point enter the wood. If it does, it will dig in, marring the wood and causing the tool to kick back.

Experiment with cuts in both directions on roughly turned wood. Use the gouge to rough the end to a barrel shape, then follow this down with a chisel—always leading with the shorter side and only about half of the edge cutting. Try tilting the tool more in the direction of travel, watching constantly that the long point does not enter the wood. An angle will be found (varying slightly between woods) for the best slicing action, the smoothest removal of waste, and the best quality surface; something close to the ideal is shown in Fig. 8-13B.

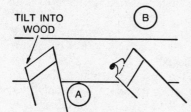

TILT INTO WOOD

Fig. 8-13. From its position at rest on the wood with only the center of its cutting edge in contact, the chisel is angled into the wood toward the lower portion of its diagonal edge to start the cut (A); the best slicing angle (B) is indicated by the smooth removal of waste in the form of a continuous shaving.

A chisel has to be used *with* the grain. An attempt to cut the other way will lift the wood fibers. Even if the cut can be completed, the surface will be rough when the lathe is stopped. If a chisel is directed at the wood with the long point downward, the tool angled directly at the wood, it will cut a line into the revolving work. This is how the rings around handles are produced. It is also the way to mark the positions of different sections of the turning. Although pencil lines may suffice for this, lines cut with a chisel will be more positive.

Usually, a cut line that marks an indentation forms the first step in working a bead or other shape. Beads occur in many turned articles (Fig. 8-14A). They are produced by chisel work, with the short side of the chisel leading into the cut. The limits of the bead are marked by cutting in with the long point of the chisel (Fig. 8-14B). A narrow chisel (¼ inch wide for small beads) is brought to the work, with the shorter side toward the cut, and turned on the tool rest to produce the curve (Fig. 8-14C). This is repeated at the other side of the cut (Fig. 8-14D) to produce the other side of the bead. If the first cuts are not deep enough, the long point can be pushed in straight a little further, the curve of the bead can be increased with the short side and lower part of the cutting edge.

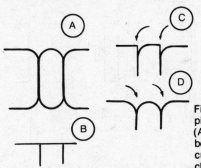

Fig. 8-14. Turning a bead on a piece of wood: the finished bead (A); chisel cuts marking the bead's outline (B); initial curves cut in one direction with the chisel (C); complementary curves cut in the opposite direction (D).

A chisel can be used for squaring an end by using a variation of the long point's straight-in cut. Instead of holding the tool straight in, the bevel is held at a right angle to the lengthwise axis of the wood, next to what will be the squared end (Fig. 8-15A).

After pressing the tool in a short distance, use the lower edge to cut away waste wood toward the cut (Fig. 8-15B), then cut the end a little further and remove more waste. If the extreme end next to the dead center has to be squared, it will be sufficient to cut in with the bevel held next to the wanted part, at a right angle to the axis; the small amount of waste will break away as the cut progresses.

A parting tool can also be used to square an end. It is used on the tool rest, pointing squarely into the wood. Its first approach should be near level, with a scraping action, but when it enters the wood, lower the handle so the edge actually cuts (Fig. 8-15C). The relief at the sides due to the hollowing of the surfaces should prevent binding, but the tool may be rocked to increase the clearance if it has to go in far. If the tool is to part off wood, the handle will get progressively higher to retain the angle of cut in relation to the diminishing circumference as the groove becomes deeper.

Fig. 8-15. To square the end of a turned piece, the bevel of the chisel is held perpendicular to the long axis of the wood (A), then the lower edge is used to remove waste toward the cut (B). A parting tool can be used for the same process (C).

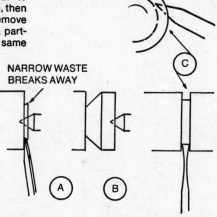

NARROW WASTE
BREAKS AWAY

A parting tool may be used first to reduce the work to size prior to other work, even if the wood will eventually be cut off completely. Care is needed not to weaken the wood too much, or the action of subsequent turning may cause the wood to bend. Even if it does not break off, the effect of vibration and bending will leave an uneven, wavy cut under the tool.

The coordination of various tool actions is probably best shown in a sample project, such as making a file handle (Fig. 8-16). The wood is cut an inch or so too long, and centered in the lathe. Then it is turned to a cylinder with a gouge (See Fig. 8-12C). Some of the waste is removed to the approximate outline by roughing out the shape with the same gouge.

Fig. 8-16. The file handle used for the sample turning project.

Cut a piece of tubing for the ferrule and remove any burrs from the inside with a round file. Hang the ferrule on the dead center (if it will fit). It is advisable to fit the ferrule next; if the wood is turned too small, there will be enough length to spare for the end to be cut off for another attempt. Use the chisel, long point down, to make a mark where the end of the ferrule will be. Allow about ⅛ inch extra length there. Cut straight in with the bevel facing toward the main part of the handle, that is, using the same positioning shown in Fig. 8-15A. Remove the waste on the ferrule side of the line. Set a pair of calipers to a little more than the inside diameter of the ferrule. If there is much wood to remove, use a narrow gouge to supplement the squaring cuts (Fig. 8-17A). Change to a chisel of a width suitable for the space. Cut from the center of the space outward. The finished ferrule end should have parallel sides (Fig. 8-17B); there can be a small bevel on the end to help it fit into the ferrule. The ferrule (on the dead center) can be used to test the diameter of the end, but calipers should also be used, because the ferrule must make a tight friction fit; it should not just slide on with little pressure.

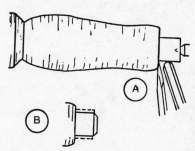

Fig. 8-17. In turning the file handle, the chisel cut should be supplemented with gouge work (A) if a lot of wood has to be removed from the ferrule end. The ferrule end may be beveled (B) to facilitate fitting it into the ferrule.

The end of the ferrule part should be square. Avoid cutting in too far with the squaring cut. Go far enough to sever fibers, but not so much that the wood is weakened. At this stage, remove the wood from the lathe and drive the ferrule on. This can be done over another piece of tubing, or with the ferrule resting on a metal vise set so the wood will pass between them while holding back the ferrule.

Although, in theory, it should be possible to remove wood from a lathe and replace it with the driving center engaged the other way, in practice there are usually slight variations; if the work is removed to fit a ferrule (or for any other purpose), it is advisable to mark the wood and the center, so they go back together the same way.

Use a broad chisel to turn down the handle toward the ferrule, with its short side leading into the cut (Fig. 8-18A). Change the direction of the chisel and turn the opposite way (Fig. 8-18B). Move the chisel to the highest point on the largest part of the handle and turn into the hollow just formed (Fig. 8-18C). At first you may have to make one or two cuts from both directions to get the hollow the way you want it.

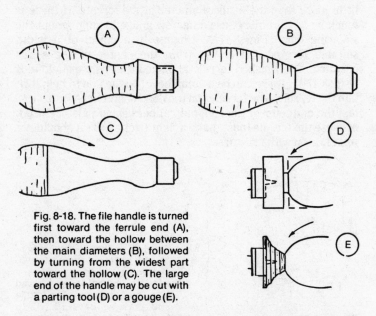

Fig. 8-18. The file handle is turned first toward the ferrule end (A), then toward the hollow between the main diameters (B), followed by turning from the widest part toward the hollow (C). The large end of the handle may be cut with a parting tool (D) or a gouge (E).

There are two ways of dealing with the headstock end of the handle. You could use a parting tool to cut in until there is just enough to still support the work (probably ⅜ inch in diameter), then shape the end toward that cut (Fig. 8-18D). Alternatively, there may be a general hollowing with the gouge, then the reduced diameter can be squared by cutting in with the long point of the chisel and removing more waste with a narrow gouge (Fig. 8-18E). Whatever method you use, be careful to leave enough thickness to support the wood until you are certain no more heavy pressure has to be applied.

At the ferrule end, cut in far enough to remove the small surplus projecting from the ferrule. The dead center should be in far enough to continue to support the wood. If your tool work has been good, you should now have an almost completed handle with a surface that is as good as if it had been planed. Finally, finish the handle by sanding it. How much you need to do depends on the quality of the tool finish.

Using too coarse an abrasive may make some rather obvious rings around the work. Moderately coarse abrasive paper may have to be used if the tool work is not as good as it should have been; otherwise, fine abrasive paper will be all that is needed. A suitable abrasive or metal polish can be used on the ferrule while it is revolving. A handful of shavings held against the revolving wood is a final treatment often used by many turners (although they may have difficulty in explaining what effect this is supposed to have).

Although the hole for the file's tang might be drilled by eye, its accuracy will be automatically insured if it is made with a drill mounted in a chuck in the tailstock. Remove the dead center and mount a chuck there with a suitable drill bit. Hold the handle until the drill has been centered in the hollow left by the dead center, then start the lathe and feed in the drill. The hole can be made to accommodate the taper of the tang by using two drill bit sizes, one about the size of the end of the tang, taken to the depth of the tang's length, and a larger one taken to a depth of about half the tang's length.

The mouth of the hole should be small enough to keep running on the dead center, which can be replaced for final handle treatment.

When the handle is finished—except for the narrow piece at the large end—rub it with polish, then cut into the narrow piece to it. The chisel may cut in to remove more waste. To get the best end, stop cutting just before the end is about to break off, remove the work from the lathe, saw off the last piece, and clean the small center with a chisel and sandpaper. The alternative is to cut in with a parting tool. Toward the end, use the tool with one hand, the other holding the revolving work loosely until the cut goes all the way through. The work will immediately cease to revolve, but the hand holding it will prevent it from dropping.

For a project like this, with not much variation in diameter, it is possible to do all the work with the tool rest set fairly close to the largest diameter, once the wood has been roughed to shape, without having to move it again. But even for a file handle, there may be some advantage in moving the tool rest. Tool control is always easier if the rest is set fairly close to the part being cut. A long tool rest can be angled so one end is close to the curve being worked; a narrow rest may be easier to position.

FACEPLATE TURNING

When a piece of wood to be turned in a lathe is longer than it is wide, it is usually supported between centers and turned in the way just described. Large-diameter work must often be turned at its face as well as its circumference; the presence of the tailstock and its center, in this case, is not wanted. This type of work entails making such things as bowls, trays, pedestal bases, and cups.

Such work is normally only supported at the headstock end of the lathe, although sometimes the tailstock is used for additional support during initial turning, then withdrawn when the tool has to be used near the center of the wood. An eggcup, for example, would be supported and driven by a screw center, the dead center providing extra support while rough cuts are made.

Screws can be driven through the holes and slots in the faceplate directly into the piece being turned (Fig. 8-19A), if there is a broad, flat surface and the diameter of the wood against the faceplate will remain larger than the faceplate. If the finished diameter is less than that of the faceplate, there is the danger of the tool contacting the faceplate. In this case, it is better to place some wood between the work and the faceplate. This could be a piece of plywood, turned in position to a little more than the faceplate's diameter and fastened with screws going through it and into the work (Fig. 8-19B).

Usually, the surface of the work that is against the faceplate is the base of the article, so the screw holes do not show. For a base, a piece of cloth or nonslip plastic may be glued on to provide more friction between the base and the surface upon which it rests and to disguise the screw holes (which may also be plugged).

It is sometimes possible for the wood being turned to be thicker than the final thickness needed, so the part with the screw holes can be cut off after the turning is completed. But because this is wasteful, it is more usual to glue on a temporary piece, which is screwed to the faceplate. A piece of paper is included in the joint (Fig. 8-19C) so the two parts can be separated later. When the time comes to remove the temporary piece, a knife or chisel is inserted into the joint to sever the paper fibers, then the wood is scraped or planed smooth. If a nonwaterproof glue is used, the surface can be wiped clean with warm water.

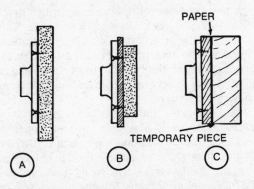

Fig. 8-19. If the finished diameter of the work will be greater than that of the faceplate, it can be screwed directly to the faceplate (A); otherwise, an intermediate piece should be placed between the work and the faceplate (B). To avoid having to use an excessively thick piece of wood (to allow the part with screw holes to be cut off), a temporary piece is glued to the work and screwed to the faceplate (C).

It is advisable to fix the assembly to the bench, as it will act like a flywheel and be eccentric until the work is turned true; this will put considerable strain on the screws. If the work moves during turning, it will be very difficult to relocate correctly. Consequently, it is important that the screws be as secure as possible. Use screws as thick as possible and make sure they have a good hold on the wood. Screws near the rim of the faceplate will resist movement better than those near the center. A screw put through a countersunk hole with a washer will not permit much movement. A screw driven through a slot has a better resistance to movement, if it is against the end of the slot.

The action of turning, particularly of a large-diameter piece, will tighten the faceplate on the mandrel nose. Some lathes have a means of locking the spindle. If this can be done, it is usually fairly easy to pull the rim of the faceplate to loosen it. Without the locking arrangement, the drive pulley must be held while the faceplate is pulled loose. Removal may be made easier by putting a leather or plywood washer over the mandrel behind the faceplate. However, it should not be very thick. If the faceplate and mandrel nose are examined, it will usually be found that, besides the thread, there is a short unthreaded section on each that must be mated accurately for the true running of the faceplate; the washer must not be thick enough to prevent this.

A large piece of wood with a diameter much greater than its thickness will have its grain going crosswise. This means that as it rotates, the grain exposed at its circumference will be presented to the tool in every direction, from directly against the cut, to with the cut, and back again to against the cut. This gives rise to several considerations not encountered in turning between centers.

The best woods for faceplate turning are the closer-grained hardwoods. They must be free from shakes and other flaws. The multidirectional approach of the tool to the grain will almost certainly cause the wood to break out if there are any such weaknesses. Softwoods are, in the main, unsuitable for faceplate turning; the more open, soft, and loose grain tends to break out. Hardwoods with a more complex grain structure—the sort that will not plane properly in any direction—often lend themselves particularly well to faceplate turning. The absence of a positive grain direction may help tool work. The result can actually look much more attractive than a piece with reasonably straight grain.

With modern glues—that give a joint at least as strong as the wood—it is possible to laminate (build up layers) thick enough for turning. As far as tool technique is concerned, it allows grain to be arranged so the worst aspects of cutting against the grain are avoided.

The wood to be turned should be cut as close to round as possible before it is mounted on the lathe. This usually means drawing a circle and cutting with a bandsaw. Other machine tools can be used, but if the wood has to be shaped by hand, its corners can be sawed off by hand, then pared further with a chisel to a reasonably accurate circle. Perfection is unnecessary, but the more accurate the outline is before turning, the less risk there will be of the grain breaking out or a tool digging in during the early stages of turning.

The first stage in faceplate turning is done with a gouge, preferably a long and strong one with its end sharpened straight across to a fairly obtuse angle. Set the tool rest fairly close to the work and hold the gouge firmly, with your fingers on top of the blade and your other hand well down the handle. The bevel of the gouge should come against the circumference of the wood, then lowered slightly until the edge begins to cut. You can expect the tool to be jerked by any unevenness on the circumference of the work, as well as the periodic passing of against-the-grain parts.

Some turners slide the gouge along the tool rest, but a gouge sharpened straight across can be rolled on the tool rest to widen the cut, then moved to a new position. When looked at from above, the tool should be pointing straight into the work—not angled in the direction of the cut, as is sometimes done in spindle turning.

Turning a large-diameter piece can put considerable strain on the tool. The part of the hand positioned over the tool rest should bear on the tool to prevent it from moving. Do not hold the gouge with only the thumb on top; this is a spindle turning technique that is inappropriate to faceplate turning with a gouge.

With a gouge sharpened straight across, the direction of roll should lift one corner clear while the other is angled in the direction of the cut. To maintain the same cutting angle, lift the end of the handle slightly as the roll approaches its limit. When the wood is cut deeply enough for shavings to come away from all parts, adjust the angle so they stay uniform in thickness as the gouge is turned to make the side of the cut.

Many cautious beginners direct the gouge almost straight into the work, resulting in a scraping cut. This minimizes the risk of the tool digging in, but the force needed to make it remove wood will blunt its edge almost immediately. A gouge is not a scraping tool—it should be *angled* so the edge cuts.

Once the outside has been turned to a true curve, external shaping can be started. If it is a bowl, the shape will be reduced toward the faceplate (Fig. 8-20). As in turning

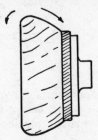

Fig. 8-20. As in turning between centers, faceplate turning entails cutting from a high point to a low one; the main shape of a bowl is reduced toward the faceplate.

between centers, always work from a high point to a low one. Rough the outside to shape. The rolling-gouge method should leave a reasonably smooth surface. Even more so than in spindle-turning, changing hands is vital. For a cut to the right, the right hand should be over the tool rest; the left hand, at the handle end. Change over to cut to the left.

HOLLOWING

Hollowing a bowl or something similar calls for special methods. Preliminary work is done with the same gouge used on the outside. Some turners start near the center; others work inward from near the rim. In this regard, the technique used does not matter. Set the tool rest across the surface, parallel to it. Any unevenness may be turned level, but because most of the wood will be removed, this is not important—except perhaps near the rim. Do some practice hollowing before attempting to make anything.

With the leading corner of its edge downward, tilt the tool enough to keep the other corner clear of the work (Fig. 8-21A). As you start the cut, lower the handle for more of a cutting action (Fig. 8-21B). Do not try to take off too much with each cut. Although your handhold will become increasingly important, lowering the angle of the tool to the wood (Fig. 8-21C) toward the center will reduce the risk of digging in.

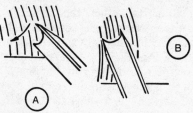

Fig. 8-21. Gouge-handling technique for faceplate hollowing: The leading corner of the gouge's edge is tilted to clear the other corner (A); as the cut is started, the handle is lowered to deepen the cut (B); the tool's angle is lowered to the wood, toward the center, to prevent it from digging in (C).

Bring the inside of the bowl to the approximate shape with the gouge. If it can be left for several weeks before further working, it is likely to finish with a better shape, particularly if the wood is not completely seasoned. Turning the wood roughly to shape will alter internal stresses in it, promoting warping. This can be turned out later, if there is time and enough extra thickness to spare before finishing.

The surface is finished by scraping, using various scraping tools (the shapes of which are depicted in Fig. 8-5L & M). Use the scraper pointing straight in toward the center of the work (Fig. 8-22) or very slightly downward. The best angle will soon be found by experiment. If the edge is very sharp, shavings rather than dust will be produced.

Fig. 8-22. The faceplate turning is finished with a scraper pointing straight in toward the center of the work, or very slightly downward.

A scraper does not have to be used with the pressure required for a gouge. It can be held with the thumb on top of the part that is over the tool rest if preferred. For the inside of a hollow, a short tool rest that can go inside is helpful. Keep the overhang of the tool to a minimum wherever it is used. A scraper can be moved to follow a shape. A straight-edged one can arc around the outside of a bowl. One with a curve less severe than that of the inside of a bowl can pivot on the tool rest to follow the shape. A curved scraper can work the flat bottom inside, but a flat-ended scraper that is wider than the bottom's radius will produce a truer surface.

Because of the cross grain, some fibers will be lifted by the scraper, while others may be bent over instead of being cut off. If the lathe can be reversed, the tools can be used the other way, with light cuts to make fibers even. Of course, this might unscrew the faceplate, unless there is a washer behind it. If it did unscrew completely, it would only drop off the lathe. However, it would likely damage the work by allowing it to strike the tool rest, so it is better to keep the faceplate tight by scraping lightly.

If the work has been left after rough turning and has warped, use a gouge or scraper to obtain a true edge on the rim, then work from the edge with more shaping.

For the best finish (on most woods) get as close to the required shape as possible with gouges. Leave the finishing for scrapers. A gouge cuts through wood fibers. A scraper does some cutting, but is more likely to turn over fiber ends. This will be quite minimal, but enough to mar the finish. The best result comes when only a thin layer has to be scraped.

Nearly all faceplate turning is done with gouges and scrapers. A broad shallow piece, like a table top, is turned the same way as a bowl. Decorating an edge may call for some work with other tools. The only time a skew chisel (one with a slanted cutting edge) might be used is for cutting a line (used point downward). A recess can be cut with a parting tool, if it is rocked a little from side to side as it enters the wood to make a cut wider than the tool; otherwise, the varying directions of grain in relation to the cut might cause the tool to catch, breaking out some of the wood.

A gouge in unskilled hands can catch and dig into wood. Practice will soon show how to prevent this. Unfortunately, if a gouge digs in, the tool is liable to catch on the damaged part on the next cut, causing it to dig in again. Until you have mastered the gouge, use a scraper to get through a damaged part before resuming work with the gouge.

When turning a broad flat surface, work with a broad flat scraper. Adjust the tool rest a little higher than the center, so the scraper can be tilted down slightly to get the best cutting angle—exactly at center height (Fig. 8-23). Then allow the tool to overlap the center slightly, and draw it slowly outward from the center to the rim. If the scraper is cutting perpendicular to the work at the center, and is kept at this angle, the surface should finish flat. Test the surface with a rule and remove high spots, but try to give a finishing cut with one smooth sweep from the center to the rim.

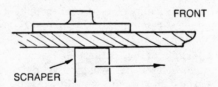

Fig. 8-23. When turning a broad, flat surface, the tool rest is adjusted so the scraper can be tilted at exactly center height.

Sanding faceplate work can be done the same way as for work between centers, preferably by reversing the machine during the process, if possible, to remove minute fiber ends that may have been bent instead of being rubbed off. Be careful not to use excessively high speeds. The rim will be traveling at a considerably higher speed than parts near the center. While a reasonably high speed is advantageous in sanding, too high a speed combined with heavy pressure can cause the wood to become discolored and charred, since so much heat is generated. Nothing can be done about this, except removing the charred part through further turning.

Your pressure on the abrasive paper should be regulated according to the surface speed of the work. Use fairly heavy pressure near the center, reducing it progressively toward the outside. Stop the lathe occasionally and examine the surface to determine how to best regulate the pressure on the abrasive paper. For a flat surface, use a block behind the paper; elsewhere, hand pressure may be needed. Parts with sharp angles suffer most from overheating.

The various methods of polishing work in the lathe are subject to the same precautions applicable to sanding, because of the vast differences in speeds on the same surface. If uniform polishing seems impossible to obtain on a rotating item large in diameter, find out which part is polishing best; then vary the speed of the lathe to give about the same surface speed elsewhere, slowing it if the periphery will not polish like the center, or speeding it if the center does not come up to as good a finish as the outside.

TURNING TECHNIQUES

There are many ways the lathe can be used to produce special effects, and there are many things the turner can do to make his machine produce better work or cope with awkward or unusual turning. Much of the enjoyment of lathe work comes from improvising and adapting techniques to produce results different from straightforward turning—not that straightforward turning ever seems to lose its fascination, but these other methods widen that interest.

It is possible to get a special woodcutting screw tap for some lathes that will cut a thread in the work to match that of the mandrel nose, allowing you to make special wooden chucks that can, for example, provide a friction drive for a small decorative final (Fig. 8-24A). The same idea can be used for turning small chess men. The tapered end is cut off after the main turning is completed. If such a chuck cannot be screwed on the mandrel nose, one can be made to mount on a screw center.

A variation of this type of chuck is the wooden *split chuck* (Fig. 8-24B), which can be adjusted over a small range. Its back is turned first, so it can be mounted on the lathe, then the rest of it is turned in position. The central hole is drilled parallel, then two saw cuts are made across it (Fig. 8-24C). Its grip is tightened by sliding a ring on the tapered outside. The ring could be metal, but it is an interesting test of turning skill to make a wooden one.

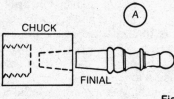

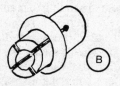

Fig. 8-24. Shop-made wooden chucks for special wood-turning projects: a threaded chuck with a tapered hole (A) to hold decoratives turnings, such as finials; a split chuck (B), adjusted by sliding a ring on its circumference.

Rings and Balls

Wooden rings, circular picture frames, and other items with holes present special problems. The wood has to be turned on both sides, so it has to be mounted on a faceplate or screw center smaller in diameter than the part to be worked (Fig. 8-25A).

The wood, sawed to a circle, should be a little thicker than its finished size. Turn the outside to the correct diameter, and true the two sides to the right thickness for a little more than the final depth (Fig. 8-25B). Round the outside to a semicircular section (Fig. 8-25C), if it is a round-sectioned ring that is being made. If an exact section is required, use a cardboard or metal template to test the curve. A wooden template can be made by drilling a hole of the right size through a piece of thin wood, then cutting it in half.

At a distance from the outside equal to the thickness of the ring, cut into the wood and round the ring using the template (Fig. 8-25C). A narrow, pointed scraper may have to be specially ground for this. Continue the cut until it gets fairly close to the back, then part off the waste by careful cutting from the back. Be ready to catch the ring as it comes away. In some cases, it may be possible to round the piece from the back and front, then part it at the point where the curves meet near the center of the thickness. But if the inside of the ring has to be smooth and true, it is better to cut through to the back and deal with the final quarter-circle of section with the ring supported on a special block.

Turn a recess in a block of wood (mounted on the faceplate) that the ring can be pressed into and held by friction (Fig. 8-25D). Turn the final quarter of the section. (Having the ring in a recess helps it resist bursting strains.) For some work there may be a choice of support on the inside or outside, but outside support is always better for slim sections.

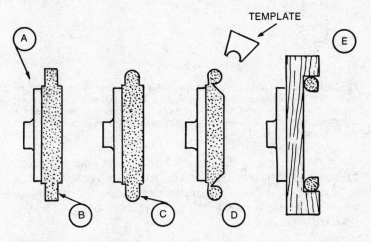

Fig. 8-25. Turning a ring with a round cross section on the faceplate. (See text for the procedure.)

An inside support for an article with a recess can be a simple block with a hublike extension (Fig. 8-26A). The recess is turned first and pressed onto the support block for turning the other side. There is a similar problem in turning a round frame for a picture or mirror. The first steps are similar to those for turning a ring. The wood is mounted on the faceplate. It could be screwed to a backing piece, which will be turned to hold it again at a later stage (Fig. 8-26B). Turn the recess, then continue right through to remove the center (Fig. 8-26C). Turn the backing piece to fit the recess and hold the wood while the molding is turned (Fig. 8-26D).

If a hole is to be drilled in the work from the tailstock end, and the final piece will have fairly thin walls, drill while the wood is thick and turn the outside afterward. A drill creates a bursting action when it works into wood. If the drill is taken into turned wood that has only a thin wall, it will probably split.

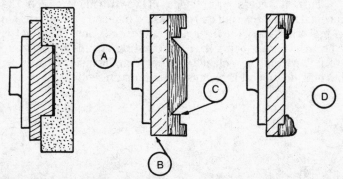

Fig. 8-26. A piece with a recess can be supported on the inside by a block with a hublike extension (A). A round frame is turned from a piece of wood mounted on a backing piece (B) screwed to the faceplate; after the recess is turned, the center is cut out (C) and the backing peice is turned to hold the frame for finishing (D).

If drilling is done first, it will be difficult to hold the wood for subsequent turning. This can be overcome by mounting the work on a plug turned with parallel sides for most of its length, and terminating in a slightly flared end that can be put on the dead center (Fig. 8-27).

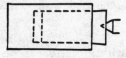

Fig. 8-27. A wooden plug with a slightly flared end mounted on the dead center to support a piece with a hole.

If wheels have to be turned, make a set of four together to insure uniform sizes. If they are not very large in relation to their thickness, their outsides can be shaped between centers, then a parting tool can be taken a short distance in between them, followed by the drilling of the axle hole (Fig. 8-28A); then they can be parted off completely, one at a time.

For much larger wheels, glue disks together with paper between them, and mount them on the faceplate. Use the dead center to provide additional support. Turn all four wheels to size, then drill the axle hole.

Turn the outer wheel to its profile on the rim and do any surface turning required. Split off the outer wheel by inserting a knife or chisel into the paper joint (Fig. 8-28B), and repeat the process for the other wheels.

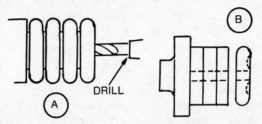

Fig. 8-28. Sets of small wheels should be turned together and drilled for axles before they are separated with a parting tool (A). Larger wheels are turned from disks glued together with paper between them, then drilled and separated (B).

Turning a really true sphere is a test of a turner's skill and his capacity for careful work. While the best finish is obtained by turning with a chisel, it is useful to grind a scraper into a profile tool (Fig. 8-29A). A ball can be turned between centers by eye, using a template as well as the profile tool. This will give a ball that is geometrically accurate, depending, of course, on the degree of skill used; but there will be small pieces at the ends (Fig. 8-29B) that will have to be worked by hand after the ball is removed from the lathe.

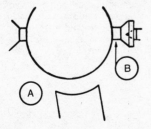

Fig. 8-29. A ball can be worked on the lathe with a profile tool (A) made by grinding a scraper; the small pieces left at the ends (B) are worked by hand after the ball is removed from the lathe.

Making a ball to finer limits is more involved. Two holding devices are needed. One is a *cup chuck*: a piece of hardwood turned to fit the taper of the mandrel nose (Fig. 8-30A) or a screw center. It has a hollowed end with slightly less of a curve than the ball is to have. Its overall diameter need not be very big; 1 inch will be about right. The other side of the ball is supported by a block smaller in diameter than the cup chuck, which will take the dead center and has a hollow that rests against the ball.

To start the ball, turn a cylinder of the diameter the ball is to be. Several balls may be made from one piece. Remove some of the waste by roughing to shape oversize, going down at the ends as far as possible, but not so far as to weaken the wood. Turn the center portion as accurately as possible to the final shape. The width of the center portion should be the same as the outside diameter of the cup chuck (Fig. 8-30B). Use a template, calipers, and profile tool. Hold a pencil against the work to mark a line around the center. Turn the other part so it is only a little oversize, and go down as far as possible each way. To avoid tearing into the grain, remove the wood from the lathe and saw off the ends, instead of parting them off while the wood is revolving.

Mount the ball so the penciled circle is lengthwise, and support it by the cup chuck and block on the (well-lubricated) dead center (Fig. 8-30C). Maintain on the work by tightening the tailstock as necessary and keep the cuts light. Use the

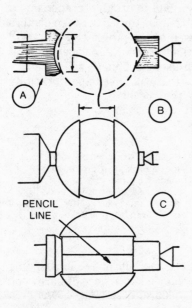

PENCIL
LINE

Fig. 8-30. Turning a sphere: a cut chuck (A) holds the work at the mandrel; the first turning makes a center portion equal in width to the diameter of the chuck (B); the portion worked first is located lengthwise within the lathe for the final turning (C).

penciled line, a true circle, as a guide to turn away the waste. If this is done just down to the line, the result will be true; the ball was circular in the direction now lengthwise, and the pencil line insures accuracy the other way.

For final cleaning, sand the ball, altering its position several times to achieve a true, smooth result.

Unequal Turning

Interesting effects can be obtained by changing the positions of centers. If a piece of wood is turned round, and the positions of both centers are moved slightly and the wood turned again, the result will be an approximately elliptical section.

A furniture leg may be made ornamental by changing the position of the dead center. The normal position is used to turn the leg initially (Fig. 8-31A). If the leg is to have a square top section, the dead center is moved diagonally in relation to it (Fig. 8-31B) for the next step. Using the new center, the tapered part of the leg is turned (Fig. 8-31C). There will have to be some handwork to make the parts blend after turning. The amount the center is moved controls the thickness of the leg. The further it is moved from the original position, the more slender the leg will be. Quite a small amount of movement will give enough taper without weakening the leg. A movement of a ¼ inch, or a little more, is enough for legs 1½ to 2½ inches square. For the reproduction of antique furniture, turning may be followed by carving (usually) a claw and ball for the foot.

Fig. 8-31. A furniture leg with a square upper section (A) can be made ornamental by repositioning the dead center (B) for another turning (C).

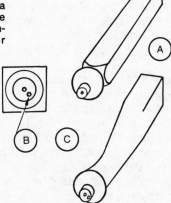

Sometimes a turning is thicker at the center than at the ends. Some furniture legs have balls at the center that are quite large compared to the square ends (Fig. 8-32A). A thick piece of wood could be prepared by sawing the ends to the reduced size before turning (Fig. 8-32B). A more economical alternative is to build up the center by gluing pieces onto a piece of wood of the section required at the ends (Fig. 8-32C). Doing it this way also makes shaping the ends true easier.

Fig. 8-32. A furniture leg with a ball at its center (A) could be turned from a thick piece of wood reduced to a rough shape (B), but it would be more economical to build up the center of the piece with wood (C).

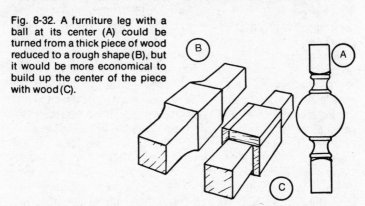

Turned shapes are sometimes used as moldings. A turned piece can be sawed down the middle to produce two moldings (Fig. 8-33A). It might be simpler to glue two pieces together with paper between them to make up a square for turning and split them apart afterward. A cup center used at the tailstock end will be less likely to cause a premature split than a plain center. The same idea can be used by cutting a turning into four sections to produce quarter-moldings (Fig. 8-33B).

Another type of molding can be made by gluing wood (over paper) around a square core, and turning it down to the corners of the square to produce flatter turned moldings (Fig. 8-33C).

For such things as lamp standards, there has to be a hole through the turning that might be too long to be drilled by any means available. One way of dealing with this is to make up the part to be turned from two pieces, which are grooved before they are joined. If the grain must match, a solid piece may be sawed in half lengthwise, grooved, and glued together again. If the piece will be fairly slender, there will be less risk of it warping or distorting later if its parts are reversed when they are glued together.

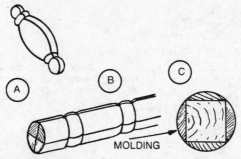

Fig. 8-33. Moldings made from turnings: a turned piece sawed in half (A) for half-moldings; a turning cut into four sections (B) for quarter-moldings; four very thin, rounded moldings (C) turned from pieces of wood glued to one with a square cross section.

When turning a slender piece, there is a risk of the wood bending under the cut, causing unequal turning and leaving tool marks on the surface that may be difficult to remove. To prevent this, always turn thick parts before thin parts to maintain rigidity as long as possible. The strain is less when turning thin parts than when turning thick parts. If the work is planned with this in mind, the risk of bending will be reduced. Jobs that are slender throughout need support, however.

Although a skilled turner may support thin work by holding his hand loosely over it, while supporting the tool with finger and thumb, this is something of a compromise that does not always work. For some lathes, it is possible to buy a *steady* that mounts on the lathe bed and stands behind the work. There are adjustments that allow it to be brought up to the back of the turning to support it against the pressure of the tool. Steadies come in several forms. The type that holds two wheels against the work (Fig. 8-34A) works very well.

It is possible to improvise a satisfactory steady by using a piece of wood that can be wedged between the ways (guiding surfaces) of the lathe bed or held in some other way (Fig. 8-34B). A steady tends to mark the wood bearing against it; the affected part should be left for light, final turning after the other parts are finished.

A special effect can be obtained on light-colored wood by burning a fine groove into it. A skew chisel is used point-down to cut the grooves, then a piece of fine wire is pulled against each groove as the piece is turned again. This soon generates enough heat to char the wood and darken the groove, making it much more obvious.

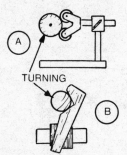

TURNING

Fig. 8-34. Steadies, used to support the work against the pressure of the tool, can be bought (A) or made from a piece of wood (B).

Laminating

The building up of wood to be turned from several pieces (laminating) has been practiced for many centuries, but early examples suffered because some of the glues used were not durable; others lost their grip in damp conditions. Modern glues hold more positively; many of them are completely waterproof. These glues not only guarantee success in built-up turning, but they insure that finer parts can be relied upon to remain glued.

Laminating is done either for decoration or to impart strength. When strength is the main consideration, a strong piece of wood is sandwiched between two less strong pieces. This results in something quite light in weight, compared to something made of heavy wood throughout. The same principle used in making plywood can be employed; that is, several pieces can be glued together with their grain crossing. If a bowl is built up in several layers, alternating the grain direction of each (Fig. 8-35A), the tendency of one piece to warp will be resisted by the others. For a bowl, the center of each layer may be cut out before the parts are glued together.

For a large wheel rim, the laminated parts need not be continuous. Each layer can be built up as long as the joints are

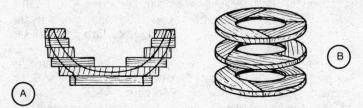

Fig. 8-35. If the grain of the layers used to laminate a bowl goes in alternating directions (A), they will have less of a tendency to warp; if the layers are built up from pieces, the joints should be staggered (B).

staggered (Fig. 8-35B). This allows a large article to be made of small pieces. The grains can more closely follow the circumference, giving greater strength and exposing less end grain, thereby reducing the risk of the wood breaking out against the tool.

Parts may be built up purely for decoration. Woods of contrasting colors, glued together and turned, can give many pleasing effects. Odd pieces of random thickness and shape glued together and turned can give interesting ellipses and other shapes where the turned surfaces break through the different layers. Experiment with some scrap pieces of different colors. Make the parts diagonal to the lengthwise axis for ellipses (Fig. 8-36).

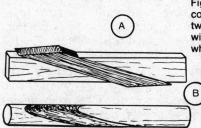

Fig. 8-36. A piece of wood of one color placed diagonally between two lengths of another color (A), will give an elleptical design (B) when turned.

Most laminated and checkered turning is done with an even, geometrically arranged plan of parts. The woods need not be of great contrast, although the greater the contrast, the more obvious the effect. Pleasing designs can be obtained with pieces of the same wood, the differences in grain giving a less blatent built-up appearance. In general, the better designs come from using no more than two different woods, although some very attractive articles have been produced with many different woods. This technique is a better way of displaying a collection of woods than merely having rectangular specimens.

If a bowl is to be built up of several layers, each assembled from contrasting segments, some geometry is required to lay out the shapes. Their thicknesses have to be carefully controlled. Machine planing should be followed by hand planing or light sanding to give a good surface for the glue. Divide a circle into the required number of segments and use it as a guide for cutting the segments (Fig. 8-37). Although straight-sided pieces could be glued together and cut to shape afterward, there would be some difficulty in clamping them. It

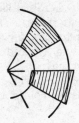

Fig. 8-37. Divide a circle into the required number of segments as a guide for making a bowl with checkered laminations.

is better to saw inside and outside curves approximately to shape, then pull the parts together with a *circular clamp* (a band that goes around the parts and is tightened with a screw).

Joints should be made carefully to provide a close fit. The grain of the glued parts in each layer will be end-to-end—not the best arrangement for gluing. If gaps fill with glue, there will not be much strength in the joint. A poor fit in the joint may also show as a flaw in the finished bowl. Fortunately, the staggering of joints as layers are built up (bringing side grain to side grain for stronger glued joints) will give strength to the whole assembly.

Sawing jigs and power saws that can be set to exact angles allow the accurate cutting of segments, but a careful worker can cut by hand after marking the work with an adjustable bevel and correcting any discrepancies in sawing with a block plane.

Checkered segments seem to be used more for bowls than other things. Although the laminated assembly will resist the tendency of any part to warp, the base may be a comparatively large piece, and the warping stresses on it could be enough to distort or crack the bowl—particularly if the shape has a fairly thin cross section. Because of this, there is some advantage in making the base plywood and the built-up wall section no less than ⅜ inch thick. If the plywood base is set back during assembly (Fig. 8-38A), its edges can be

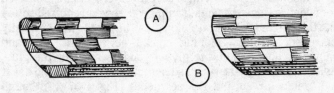

Fig. 8-38. The plywood base for a bowl could be set back from the bowl's lower edge (A), or turned as an integral part of the bowl's profile (B).

concealed by the laminations of the bowl; but turning it as part of the bowl's profile looks quite good (Fig. 8-38B).

It is best to turn a bowl built up from many small pieces by scraping, without using a gouge at any stage. The many grain directions could be troublesome if a gouge were used. However, there is no exposed end grain to be picked up by the scraper, so a good surface should result from scraping only.

Avoiding the use of a gouge is also a safety precaution. There should be no danger with a perfectly glued bowl, but if there is a weak joint, a gouge would be more likely to break it open. Stop the machine after preliminary turning to examine the state of the joints. For safety, wear a face shield or protective goggles.

DESIGNS

Ideas for things to make may be found by examining articles, looking at photographs, visiting museums, and by thinking about how something turned could be better than an item made some other way. Many articles are plastic instead of turned wood only because of economy in production.

Although you may turn many items in one piece for a period, to gain proficiency, you will reach a stage when you will want built-up assemblies. A tall lamp standard is a simple example. The stem will have its grain going lengthwise; the base will have it going across. A dowel, turned as part of the stem, fits into a hole in the base (Fig. 8-39A). The base may be lifted on three feet, either glued or located by dowels (Fig. 8-39B). Raising the base gives clearance for a wire, if the project is a table lamp. It is always better to have three feet rather than four or more. Three feet will stand firmly, even if the surface is uneven; four or more might wobble. Dowels make the best joints for parts that have to be assembled concentrically.

Another example is a bowl with a stem and base. The stem has dowels turned at both ends to fit into holes in the other parts (Fig. 8-39C). A tray can be incorporated in a joint in a pedestal between the upper and lower parts (Fig. 8-39D).

Dowels should have slight bevels turned on their ends so they can enter their mating holes easily. Blind holes should always be a little deeper than the length of the dowel, to reduce bursting stresses as the joint is assembled. A groove sawed into the dowel's length will allow air and excess glue to escape. Many doweled joints can be merely assembled with glue, but where extra security is needed, a wedge can be driven into a saw cut in the end of the dowel that goes into a blind hole before the joint is assembled (Fig. 8-39E). The wedge should go across the grain of the piece with the hole, so the dowel end is spread toward the end grain; otherwise, it could cause a split.

Long spindles can be built up by doweling them together in sections. This allows slender pieces to be made that are longer than the capacity of the lathe, and a section that would be too flexible to turn as one piece (even if short enough to go in the lathe). These assemblies can usually be identified by the decorative turning used to disguise the joints (Fig. 8-39F). If a column has to accommodate a wire, it may be made of drilled shorter sections, when otherwise it would be impossible to make a hole through the whole length.

Legs for chairs, stools, and tables are common turning projects. In many cases, there is a square top and another square part connected to a rail. Except for careful centering, there is no difficulty in working parts with squares. If many identical legs have to be made, an alternative to the ordinary driving center is used. A block with a slightly tapered square hole at its center is mounted on the faceplate (Fig. 8-39G). The legs are inserted into the hole for a positive, nonslip drive.

Traditional furniture legs have many beads and small, angular shoulders between curved parts (Fig. 8-39H). Sweeping, freehand curves are those the turner usually finds most pleasing, rather than following any accepted pattern. The angular shoulders give prominence to the curves. Turning a piece without them produces a less attractive result. They also provide a division between the different tool actions in turning.

The main problem with legs is that they have to match. After making one leg, mark a thin strip of wood with the main divisions. Mark the diameters derived from testing them with calipers at several points (Fig. 8-39I). With practice, much can be done by having the first leg just behind the one being turned, so it can be used for comparison as the various cuts are made. The bottom of the leg should be turned slightly hollow. If there is to be a caster or other fitting at the end, let the dead center mark remain as an indication of the end's center for the possible location of a drill or screw.

Rails usually go into holes in legs. Because there can be considerable strain on the joints in a chair that is rocked, take the rail ends as deep as possible. If there are rails going in two directions from the leg, they can go deeper if they are at two

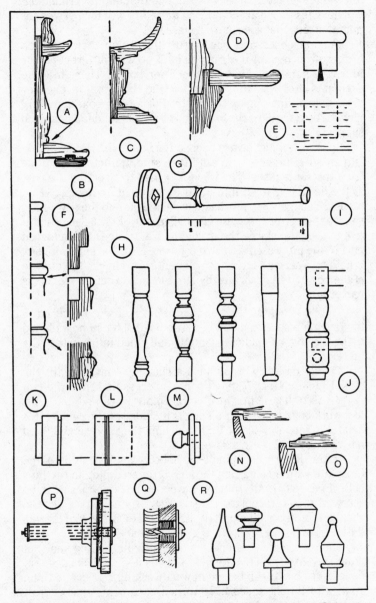

Fig. 8-39. Design details for items made from separate turnings. (See text for descriptions.)

different levels (Fig. 8-39J). A rail end that enters a round leg will have less wood around it, and therefore will form a weaker joint than one that goes into a square leg.

Making boxes and bowls with lids is another common branch of turning. A box may be built up with different woods in a way similar to that described for bowls. There may be segments for the full depth of the box, or a checker arrangement making up the depth. For a deep box, there will have to be a temporary scrap-wood end for the dead center to support.

Special techniques are needed for fitting lids. An example is a small round box with a lid the same diameter and made from the same piece. The wood is turned to size, and the part of the lid that is to fit into the box is turned on the end (Fig. 8-39K). Enough wood for the lid is parted off and the new end is squared. Most of the waste is drilled out (Fig. 8-39L), and a tool is used to enlarge the inside to size, while the shouldered part of the lid is used as a size reference. At this stage the box is held by a screw center or a self-centering chuck. The outside of the box can be decorated by rings or beads before the box is parted off.

The lid is held in the recess of a piece of wood secured to the faceplate so its top can be turned. A knob can be included in the turning, or made separately, and glued into a hole in the lid (Fig. 8-39M).

The lid on a bowl may have a shoulder that overlaps the rim (Fig. 8-39N), or it may fit into a recess turned in the rim (Fig. 8-39O). These lids involve faceplate work and, perhaps, tool work on both sides. If a knob is included at the center, it is helpful in mounting if the lid for turning the knob can be fixed into a central hole with a dowel.

If the headstock spindle is hollow, hold the lid to the faceplate with a bolt going through a tapered plug in the lid's hole (Fig. 8-39P). Alternately, a wooden backing piece can be screwed to the faceplate (Fig. 8-39Q). If there is a recess, shoulder, or decorative part at the rim that can be used to keep the lid true, it may fit into a recess in the backing piece.

The turner can exercise his ingenuity in making knobs of many designs, from traditional to modern—and in shapes that have never been seen before in woodworking. The same thing applies to finials, those little turned ornaments that project from the ends of supporting columns (Fig. 8-39R).

9

Carving

The phrase *wood carving* often conjures up visions of elaborately worked panels in intricate designs, depicting stylized foliage or figures sculptured in infinite detail. These examples of carving, some of which can be found in ancient cathedrals, represent years of work by devoted, skilled craftsmen. But the term covers many other, usually less complicated, wood-decorating activities as well.

Man has used carving to form and decorate wood since ancient times. He probably used his primitive axe and knife to embellish a piece of wood whose original shape suggested some design to him. Primitive man everywhere has carved idols and decorated wood for his ceremonies. Examples can still be found among people today who are little touched by civilization. Tourists to these hinterlands often buy examples of native craftsmanship produced by quite primitive means.

Wood carving in its more elaborate sense involves the use of a large range of tools. From medieval days onward, skilled wood carvers used their tools to make elaborate designs, the man having artistic ability producing sculptured scenes, and the carver with tool-handling skill—but less esthetic appreciation—covering wood with formal, stylized forms dictated by cultural standards.

Although much of this carving may evidence the skill involved in executing it, by modern standards it is far too elaborate; the sheer quantity of it, confusing. The eye is easily drawn away from skilled work that should be appreciated. There was a stage in the art's history where every visible piece of wood in a work (and much that was not normally seen) had to be carved. This need was felt for the woodwork in churches for several centuries. This and the nonecclesial use of carving reached a peak toward the end of the 19th century.

Perhaps, at the zenith in the development of that style, the designers and the public they were supposed to be serving became satiated with elaborate carving; whatever its cause, some sort of artistic revolution lead to the contemporary view of wood carving. Today carving is used by the artist/craftsman as a means of expression. Modern carving, for the most part, does not have the elaborate and intricate detail produced in earlier days. Effects are obtained with sweeping curves and forms not necessarily intended to depict, in wood, the exact shape of animals, humans, or scenes. Carving of the more formal, traditional type is used for panels set off by plainer surrounds. Carving is a comparatively small feature of today's furniture; no longer is it used over most of the exterior. Carving is used now as a focal point in the overall design of a piece. Any woodworker who can carve can give anything he makes an individuality that sets it apart from more routine pieces.

Carving is actually too broad a term for all decorative wood cutting. Not all who do such work regard themselves as carvers. Shaping wood with just a knife is called *whittling*. Using variations on the knife to make geometric patterns is called *chip carving*. Then there is *incised* decoration, and *pokerwork*, in which a design is burned into the surface of wood.

Pokerwork got its name from the use of a hot poker, but now it is done with an electrically heated point. Maybe it cannot really be called a craft, but burned designs (often on plywood) sell quite well in souvenir shops. If it can be regarded as a member of the family of woodworking skills, its closest relative is wood carving.

WHITTLING

Whittling is carving with a knife; usually no other tool is used. Historically, the knife was used for work that might have been done better by another tool, had one been available. Circumstances often dictated the restriction of using just the one tool—patience had to make up for the lack of others. Whittling was used by seamen in days past, to pass the time when the lack of wind meant sagging sails and long periods with little to do. A scrap of wood that took a long time to fashion with a knife was welcomed. The long time involved was an important antidote to boredom.

Whittling was also practiced by settlers and pioneers seeking an activity needing little equipment and only requiring materials at hand. Although whittling is usually thought of as something done to wood, whalebone, hard gum, meerschaum, and other materials that can be cut have all come under the knife for similar treatment.

Its use as a diversion in the past made whittling the source of items of no real value, in both the decorative and ultilitarian senses—balls in cages, wooden chains, ships in bottles. These cannot be regarded as anything except a demonstration of the craftsman's skill and patience; they are curiosities and little else. Whittling as an end in itself is still often an antidote to boredom, but the technique can be used to produce useful, attractive things. Today it is probably better to regard whittling as incidental to something made with other tools.

If all of the work is to be done with a handheld knife, the wood must be amenable to cutting. In general, soft woods are preferable, but a very soft wood will not accept a lot of detail. It should have a fairly straight grain, without interlocking fibers. Resin in wood usually means hard patches. Knots should be avoided, unless they can be incorporated into the design.

Wood, being a natural material, is a variable. It may be necessary to reject some to obtain others that are workable. In general, these are examples of some woods suitable for whittling: alder, ash, butternut, cedar, sugar pine, white and yellow pine, poplar, redwood, some oaks, and some fruit woods; some woods difficult to whittle: buckthorn, hornbeam, Western chinquapin, lignum vitae, obeche, and yew.

Most whittlers in the past have used whatever knife was available. Fortunately, the common penknife blade is good for whittling. A larger blade is needed for more robust work. Sharpness is very important. Apart from giving a clean cut, a sharp knife is safer to use than a blunt one; a blunt blade that resists cutting calls for extra and unusual leverage and handling that can lead to an accident.

Wood being whittled is often held in one hand and cut with a knife held in the other. It is always better to rest the wood on something solid than to merely hold it freely. Of course, it is obviously dangerous to rest it against the thigh. It is better to fix the work in a vise or clamp; then both hands can be used on the knife for better control and more safety. Wherever possible, the hand holding the knife should be behind it. Similarly, it is safer if all cuts are made away from the body, if possible.

The common penknife blade (Fig. 9-1A) has a shape convenient for general cutting, and is regarded as common for whittling. Sometimes there is an advantage in having a straight blade with a point (Fig. 9-1B). This is found in some seamen's knives. The point of this knife will get into hollows and corners better than the other one. Another type of pointed knife has a *clipe blade*, which has a cutting edge like a penknife, but its back is hollowed to a fine point (Fig. 9-1C). It can be dug-in and twisted to make hollows or holes.

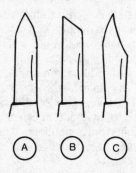

Fig. 9-1. Knife blades for whittling: penknife blade (A); straight blade (B); clip blade (C).

A larger knife, in which the blade folds into the handle (like a penknife), is often called a jackknife. It may have any of the blade shapes of the penknife; but being larger, it is more suitable for heavier projects. Hunting knives with very thick blades may not take a fine enough edge.

It is sometimes useful to have a blade that cuts with its end, like a chisel or gouge—a sharpened, broken knife blade, for example. The variety of knife blades available seems infinite. It is better to start whittling with whatever is available and look for other knives later, as your experience makes you feel the need for them.

The way to learn whittling is to whittle—there is not much that can be learned from a book. Practice will soon show what can be done. Even if a whittler claims to have little or no artistic ability, some area of specialization will emerge that will produce worthwhile results.

The basic method of cutting, known to everyone who has shaved a stick, is to hold the wood in one hand, grip the knife handle with the whole fist, and slice away from you (Fig.

9-2A). This is certainly the way to remove as much wood as possible, but it affords little control of the cut. You sever the wood unintentionally, going below the line, or further than you want to, right through the wood.

More positive control can be obtained by putting your thumb behind the blade and pushing rather than slicing with the knife (Fig. 9-2B). In both cases, the blade will cut fairly straight through the wood, acting as a wedge to spring fibers apart. If the blade is used for more of a slicing cut (Fig. 9-2C), the fibers will be severed more cleanly, less pressure will be needed, and the final surface will look better.

Sometimes a better cut can be made with a pulling action, with the holding hand at the far end of the work, behind the cut (Fig. 9-2D). This sort of cut should only be used when it is necessary to complete a part with the grain; it should be avoided whenever possible, particularly if the cut is toward your body.

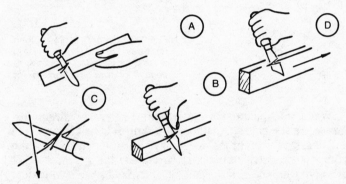

Fig. 9-2. Elementary whittling techniques: basic method (A); pushing with the thumb behind the blade for more positive control (B); the slicing cut (C); the pulling cut (D).

If a cut has to end before the end of the piece, cut in a V-shaped nick first (Fig. 9-3). If the cut has to be very long, make a few intermediate cuts across the grain as well, to break up the shaving being removed, and to prevent a split

Fig. 9-3. If a long cut will stop before the end is reached, cut a nick at its end first, and slice the waste part into several pieces.

from going too far. Cuts for a hollow have to be made from both ends if the grain is parallel with a side.

Initial cuts should always be made across the grain before any are made with the grain. This will reduce the risk of splitting. Support the blade along its back with a finger and use the point to make an incision across the grain (Fig. 9-4A). To cut a straight line, run the knife along the edge of a rule. If the outline of a shape has to be followed, use the thumb of the other hand to bear against the side of the blade to assist in guiding it.

Cutting a curve, as when rounding the entrance to a hole, is done with the grain. For a complete circle, cuts have to be made in four directions (Fig. 9-4B); if a sweep is taken too far, the blade will go against the grain and lift it. If a knife has to be used to make a hole, turn it a few times on its point, then pare out some of the waste before going deeper.

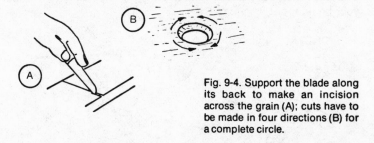

Fig. 9-4. Support the blade along its back to make an incision across the grain (A); cuts have to be made in four directions (B) for a complete circle.

When manipulating a clasp knife in several directions, beware of its closing. Although a knife is not a saw, in whittling it is sometimes necessary to use it with a sawlike action, as when easing pieces apart along the grain; a short sawing movement with the pointed end may be the only way of making a final, separating break through something like a ball in a cage or the links of a chain—but without actually removing wood. When cutting directly across the grain, sawing with a rocking motion will sever fibers reluctant to be cut.

Much of the technique of whittling evolves from an appreciation of grain and what is likely to happen when you cut into it. This has already been covered in the instructions for general woodworking, but the important thing to remember is that if the cutting action is used to "stroke" a lot of loose fibers smooth, the cut should be satisfactory. If you cut the other way, you can expect the fibers to lift and the wood to split. (At best you will get a ragged surface.)

As suggested for other types of woodworking, practice on a few pieces before attempting serious whittling. Try whittling a round stick square, working by eye. Try making a square piece into a circular section, by whittling away corners until you have fairly regular octagon; then carefully shave enough from the eight corners so the result is fairly close to round. Let the light come across the wood as you turn it slowly, to see any particularly high ridges that need careful shaving. Try rounding an end, by first shaving off a little at a time, creating rings of facets (Fig. 9-5A) that slope more acutely as they approach the center of the end, while rotating the piece slowly against the light to highlight high spots that need lowering.

Try cutting beads around a stick. You will not get the perfection of lathe work, but some of the beauty of whittling is producing something like a toasting fork handle decorated with knife cuts. For this effect, roll the stick under the knife blade, cutting two rings around it (Fig. 9-5B). Having incised these, work around the piece, chipping toward the rings a little at a time to form the bead (Fig. 9-5C). You will probably have to go around again to make the central rings deeper, then cut more into them.

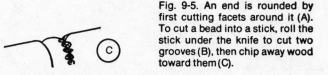

Fig. 9-5. An end is rounded by first cutting facets around it (A). To cut a bead into a stick, roll the stick under the knife to cut two grooves (B), then chip away wood toward them (C).

It is interesting to make twists (Fig. 9-6A) using the technique for beads. Mark the circumference into four sections at one bead. Hold the knife at an angle and, by rocking the knife as you rotate the stick on a bench, cut a helical line around the stick. Do this at each of the four positions, then go around, chipping away to each side of the twisting lines, deepening the cuts further if necessary.

If you want to whittle two prongs for a toasting fork, use a stick with a knuckle near one end (Fig. 9-6B); it will serve to keep a split from developing. The end of a suitably bent piece of wood could be made into a back scratcher.

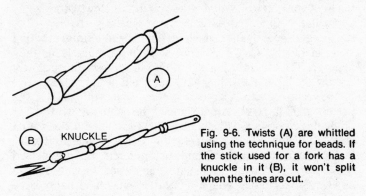

Fig. 9-6. Twists (A) are whittled using the technique for beads. If the stick used for a fork has a knuckle in it (B), it won't split when the tines are cut.

Most whittling is done with natural pieces of wood rather than pieces from a lumberyard, their shapes often suggestive of things to make. A spoon may come from the natural crook between a tree limb and a branch (Fig. 9-7A). A piece of wood may have an outline that would not take much conversion to make it into an animal. Whistles can be made from hollow pieces (Fig. 9-7B) or the bark of some trees. If you are uncertain of your ability to whittle an animal or person in the round, start by whittling a silhouette. For starting a fire it is helpful to make "fuzz sticks." These are pieces whittled to shavings all around, but the cuts are stopped short of severing them. This is good practice in restraining cuts as well as producing something useful for getting the camp fire going.

Fig. 9-7. Products of natural wood formations: the outline of a spoon that could be cut from the crook of a tree (A); a whistle that could be whittled from a hollow piece, or from the bark of a twig (B).

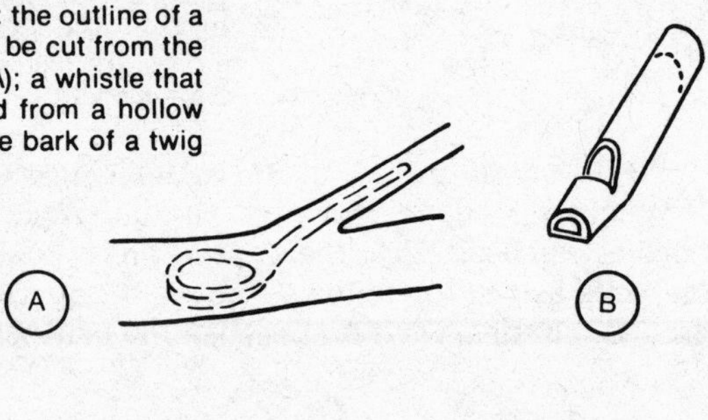

WHITTLING TECHNIQUES

Most whittling is just the fashioning of figures according to the carver's own ideas. If you have doubts about your artistic ability, aim at fanciful caricatures rather than true representations of people or animals. For instance, it would not matter much if a dog intended to be rather grotesque were cut out of proportion and did not come out quite as you visualized it. But if you were trying to get a true representation of a particular breed and you made the same mistake, it would be so obvious that the job would have to be scrapped.

When you begin, whittle in a size that can be handled easily, yet take fairly bold cuts. If you try to make miniature carvings before your knife control is really developed, slices may go astray or something may be cut off unintentionally. At the other extreme, the piece may be too big for simple knife work. But, then again, with experience, totem poles and other more massive carvings can be made with saws and axes as supplements to knives. Some whittlers get a lot of satisfaction out of producing very tiny objects, even to the extent of fashioning figures from matchsticks.

The safest way to get the shape you want in a whittled figure is to get the outline correct in two perpendicular planes. Start with a piece of wood having a square cross section. Draw one view of the figure on one surface and cut around the outline right through the wood's thickness. Then draw the figure, as viewed from a position 90° to the first view, on one of the cut surfaces and whittle that outline right through. From this stage, round the wood by taking off the corners. Knowing that in two directions the shapes are right, you can modify the section without disturbing the main shape.

This method of working is particularly important to getting an acceptable final shape for a four-legged animal. Cut the outline as viewed from the side first, making allowance for differences in leg positions if the animal is shown as if moving.

A lot of traditional whittling consists of tricks and special effects that allow the ingenuity of the whittler to mystify anyone examining his work. Wooden chains, balls and other objects in cages, joints that move, ships and other things in bottles, fans, and parts that interlock are examples.

Chains

A wooden chain can be made from any easily whittled wood, but because part of each link is cross-grained, a wood too soft and weak might break as it is worked. As with other whittling, it is advisable to make the first attempt a moderate size; start with wood about 1½ inches square. The overall width of each link will be the thickness of the original piece of wood. Any length will do.

First cut the wood to a cross-shaped section (Fig. 9-8A); the thickness of the arms of the cross will be the thickness of each link. If a table saw or a rebate plane of some type is available, the section can be produced with precision, but the whittler—with only his knives—can slice the recesses lengthwise, removing a small square from a corner first, then progressively going deeper. This may be done one link at a time. It is helpful to have soft, straight-grained wood.

Mark the lengths of the links, allowing a little space for waste between each pair in a line, and allowing enough clearance where the links will fit into each other. Draw the outline of each link, using a cardboard template to insure uniformity (Fig. 9-8B). Make one link at a time, going from one end toward the other. This allows the remaining stiff piece to be held, either in the hand or in a vise. Notice that the links in one plane come midway between those in the other. The end link may have a shape different from the others. It may be round, or it may be part of a carved hook.

The outline of the end link can be whittled. The easiest way to cut the inside of each link is to drill a hole to start a fretsaw

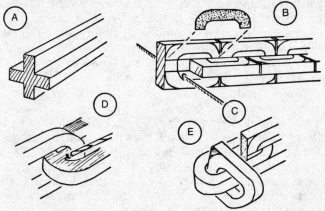

Fig. 9-8. A chain with seamless links begins as a piece of wood cut to a cross-shaped section (A), onto which the outline of each link is drawn with the aid of a cardboard template (B), and cut out inside with a fretsaw blade (C). The links are separated by drilling (D), then turned so their outline can be completed (E).

blade (Fig. 9-8C) and cut around the exposed profile. Alternatively, you could use a finely pointed knife to remove waste a sliver at a time; but always make sure to cut through the cross-grained part of the outline before splitting out waste along the grain.

Reaching as much of their outline as you can, separate the links by drilling holes diagonally through the waste between them (Fig. 9-8D), or by cutting V-shaped nicks in all four directions until the wood is cut through. Once a link is freed from its neighbor, turn it to expose its ends and complete the true outline (Fig. 9-8E). When a whole link is the right shape (but still square in section), whittle away around the angular edges to reduce the wood to a reasonably regular octagonal section. Be careful to keep the cuts with the grain (Fig. 9-9A). Cutting the wrong way on a thin section might break the link.

Leave the final shaping and smoothing of each link until all are at the same stage. When the first link is the right shape, but still shows tool marks, move on to the second and so forth, progressing along the wood. The links could be scraped smooth with a knife edge, but for a final smoothing, sand carefully, followed by polish or varnish. Apart from what this can do for appearance, it will reduce the shrinking and swelling of the wood in different states of humidity, thus helping to prevent cracks in the short grain.

A chain alone may have little use, except as evidence of the whittler's skill. It could be used to hold back drapes, but even for this, it might be better to have a carved hook or long loop at the end. Of course, addition to the chain has to be carved from the same piece of wood, if glued joints are to be avoided. It was the custom in many parts of Wales, until quite recent times, for a suitor to present his girl with a whittled spoon as a token of affection. If she accepted it, they were engaged.

These spoons often had a few links of chain, or there might have been two spoons joined by chain. The spoon has a shape that can be included in the overall section at the beginning of the chain. Its end is treated like the first link. A spoon outline is easy to whittle, but its bowl presents a special problem. It has to be hollowed out, working from the middle outward, using the curved cutting edge near the point of the penknife with the grain, and getting a hollow cut along the grain before working in from the sides (Fig. 9-9B). If a gouge is available, hollowing is a simple matter if you cut in all around a little at a time. In both cases, it is better to work the hollow before doing the

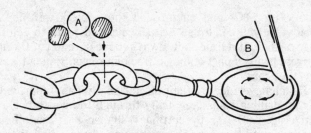

Fig. 9-9. After the chain links have been separated, they are whittled, with the grain (A), to octagonal shapes; a spoon (B) might be included as an integral part of the chain.

outside curve. This leaves solid wood for support and allows for variations in the depth of the hollow.

Ball in Cage

Although the basic idea in this project is to carve a ball inside something from which it cannot be removed, there are many variations. Instead of a ball, for example, the thing imprisoned could be a bird or other animal, or it could be a geometric solid other than a sphere. There could be several balls in the same cage or one ball inside another, the inner ball visible through holes or decorative openwork on the outer ball. However, wood does not allow carrying this progression much further in small sizes like those many balls inside each other found in ivory carvings—a technique at which the Chinese seem to be particularly proficient. This sort of thing is for the skilled, patient worker with plenty of time to spare. The principle, though, can be learned by carving one ball in a simple cage.

For your first experiment, start with an easy-to-whittle piece of wood about 5 inches long and 1½ inches square. The diameter of the ball will be only a little less than the distance across the flats of the wood. The size can be seen by drawing a section, allowing ¼ inch square sections for the corners of the cage (Fig. 9-10A). Mark out the wood on all the long faces and, near the center of each, mark a length equal to the diameter of the ball (Fig. 9-10B); if a drawing has not been made, this will be the length of a diagonal drawn between the corners of an end, within the outline the cage's thickness (Fig. 9-10C).

Remove the waste between the block that will be the ball and the top and bottom of the cage (Fig. 9-10D). Drilling out some of the wood will help, but it can all be done with a knife if you make sure that deep cuts are made across the grain before splitting out pieces. Do not make the corner pieces narrower than marked, otherwise the ball will fall out. Make *V*-shaped cuts at the lines separating the inner block from the rest of the cage (Fig. 9-10E). Do this progressively, until the cuts at each corner meet and the block can slide freely. Square and smooth all the cut parts of the cage—but do not round the inner corners of the side pieces (bars).

Slice away excess wood from the ball-to-be with a pointed knife. This has to be done mainly to eye, but the diameter may be checked with calipers in all directions as you work. Round the ball at the gaps between the cage sides and ball first; revolved the wood and cut the angles off the end grain, and reduce the whole thing gradually to a ball that will turn around in all directions in the cage (Fig. 9-10F). Be careful not to take off too much anywhere, or part of the ball may become small enough to stick out of the cage.

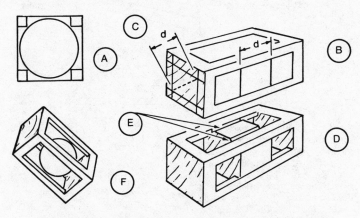

Fig. 9-10. Carving a ball within a cage. (See text for procedure.)

Pivot Joints

Pliers, pincers, scissors, and other similar things made of wood in two parts that pivot on a pin (Fig. 9-11A) may seem mysterious, since three thicknesses can be seen at the joint. The basic form is rather like blacksmith's tongs. From that shape, the outlines of other gripping tools can be fashioned by pure cutting, that is, without shavings being produced. If you want to try it, begin with a piece of wood 4 inches by ⅝ inch by ⅜ inch and mark out the outlines as shown in Fig. 9-11B).

Referring to Fig. 9-11C, slice the diagonals on each side, followed by rocking cuts to the depth indicated on the edges. Split the ends toward the cuts (Fig. 9-11D), but don't go too far. If you are unlucky and the wood splits despite all your care, you can at least be consoled in not having done much work that has to be scrapped. It might help in this respect to soak the wood for a day in cold water, or about a half-hour in hot water. This will soften the wood and make it easier to cut, besides making it less liable to split in an uncontrolled manner.

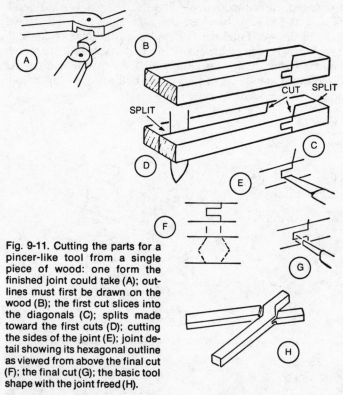

Fig. 9-11. Cutting the parts for a pincer-like tool from a single piece of wood: one form the finished joint could take (A); outlines must first be drawn on the wood (B); the first cut slices into the diagonals (C); splits made toward the first cuts (D); cutting the sides of the joint (E); joint detail showing its hexagonal outline as viewed from above the final cut (F); the final cut (G); the basic tool shape with the joint freed (H).

Push and rock a very thin, sharp blade through both lines forming the sides of the joint (Fig. 9-11E), working in from both sides of the wood. Rocking is necessary because the outline of the joint does not have parallel sides, but is a hexagon (Fig. 9-11F); all of this area has to be severed to the lines. The final stage is cutting the narrow thickness of the inner part of the joint (Fig. 9-11G) straight across the grain with the end of a chisel-shaped knife blade. A piece of a razor blade sharpened on its end could also be used.

When all of the cuts meet, the joint should open (Fig. 9-11H). If it doesn't, go over all the cuts again until it does. Shape the other parts to complete the article. Even though there is no pivot pin, the hexagonal shape of the joint will make the two arms retain their position as the joint is opened.

Fans

Fans can be made from a single piece of wood. Besides fans, the same method can be used to represent the feathers in the tail of a peacock or the headdress of an Indian, or—well, just let me leave the possibilities to your imagination. Whatever its application, the basic form is the same.

Use a straight-grained softwood. The overall width of the wood will govern the number of blades in the fan, but it should be no more than the length of your knife blade. For an experimental fan, use a piece about 1 inch by ½ inch in section; its length can be up to 6 inches. The fan will have a base that will remain uncut; you can make the blades above it any shape you fancy. Mark the blade shape on the narrow edge (Fig. 9-12A) and cut out its outline across the wood.

Soak the wood in cold water for a day, or in hot water for half an hour, to make it easier to split where you want it to. Use a knife to split the blades (Fig. 9-12B). If the grain is reasonably straight, the direction of the cut can be regulated by twisting the knife as it is pressed down. How thick each slice should be depends on the wood, but try to make them less than $1/16$ inch. Try to cut right to the base without going into it.

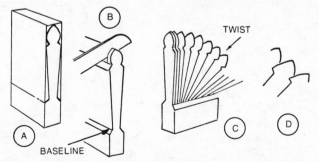

Fig. 9-12. Making a fan from one piece of wood, using a knife: the shape of the blades is marked on the side of wood (A); the blades are split apart to the baseline (B); each blade is twisted to open the fan (C); notches in the blades allow them to be interlocked to maintain the fan's shape (D).

Hold the base firmly and give each blade a twist to open the fan (Fig. 9-12C). If the top of each blade has a notch in its pattern (Fig. 9-12D), each blade can be twisted to engage the next, thus holding the fan's shape. If there are no notches, the blades can be held open by intertwining cord or thread around the blades and removing it when they have dried out. This will be necessary with feather shapes and flower petals. Fans can be made with enough blades to form a complete circle. After a flat fan has been made and allowed to dry, it can be formed, after a further soaking, to make cup-shaped petals or the parts of a billowing skirt.

Ships in Bottles

A ship or other article in a bottle calls for considerable care and patience rather than a high degree of skill. No part must be too big to go through the neck of the bottle. The whole thing has to be built outside, then reassembled inside. A ship is the usual thing, but the bottled subject could be anything.

A ship makes an undeniably attractive subject. The bottle chosen has to be supported, normally on its side (Fig. 9-13A). It is advisable to make the stand first and fix it to the bottle, so you have a firm foundation to work on, one that won't move while glue is setting or a delicate piece of work is in progress. At one time, the bottle would have been lashed to its stand; now, the bottle may be fixed to the stand with epoxy glue.

The hull of the boat, the largest thing that must go through the bottle neck, governs the overall size of the ship. A larger hull could be made in parts and assembled inside, but most

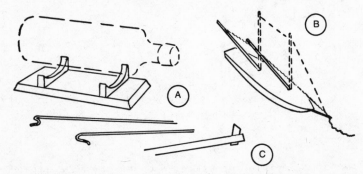

Fig. 9-13. Bottles containing ships are usually supported on their side (A); threads are pulled to raise the masts in the bottle (B); further work is done inside with improvised tools (C).

models have solid, one-piece hulls. The hull is cut off at the "waterline" and set in a putty sea.

The ship's masts are mounted on hinges on the hull. The hinges may be little staples or pieces of adhesive tape. The boat is entered stern first. The bowsprit—the large spar that projects forward from the ship's stem—should be thick enough to take some small holes for thread rigging. The hull, with masts attached, is inserted in the bottle, then threads are pulled to raise the masts (Fig. 9-13B). This operation should be done outside the bottle first, for practice, then repeated inside.

Paper sails, other spurs, and thread for other parts of the rigging, are all attached to the masts and folded down. With the ship in position and the masts raised, the thread is glued at the holes in the bowsprit. After the glue sets, surplus thread is cut off.

It is advisable to paint the inside of the bottle to disguise the putty, or use colored putty. Painting is done with a small brush on a long handle. Other tools have to be improvised: pieces of wire to push or pull parts; a piece of razor blade with a handle to cut inside the bottle.

Scenery may be built into the putty—a length of shoreline, a lighthouse, a small boat beside the main one. Have your parts ready before you put in the putty. Roll the putty into long pieces, to go through the bottle neck, and insert enough that can be pressed into position with a flattened stick (spatula). Work the surface into waves. The hull may have a few tacks in its bottom to grip the putty.

Blue and green paint on the putty can be augmented with white to simulate whitecaps. Almost certainly there will have to be some touching up of paint inside the bottle, but the less there is to do then, the better. The boat has to be put in the bottle while the putty is soft; after that, wait a day or so for the putty to harden before hoisting the masts and doing further work on the model.

Leave the bottle open in a warm, dry place for several days, so everything inside becomes absolutely dry. If the bottle is corked too early, condensation inside may make the glass misty. When everything is satisfactory, seal the bottle.

CHIP CARVING

Chip carving, one of the oldest forms of decorative carving, is a system of cutting triangular recesses that are built up into geometric or symbolic patterns. Because of its limitations, it is not considered comparable to normal carving, but examples of the art can be found on many old pieces of woodwork. For present-day decoration, it has the advantage of requiring very few tools, none of them specialized.

Some older pieces of furniture are chip-carved all over. Following the esthetic philosophy regarding general carving, today it is better to be more restrained, having patterns surrounded by uncarved surfaces. Properly used, chip carving can be very effective.

Most of the work is done with a knife. Aside from a penknife, one with a slanted cutting end is also needed (Fig. 9-14A). Ordinary woodworking chisels are also useful. Most of the work, being fairly light, can be done with paring chisels. Some specially shaped chip-carving knives are made, but ordinary tools can be made to suffice.

Although, by definition of the techniques, the patterns have to be based on triangles, their outlines need not be straight. There can be any number of curved sides, producing long, leaf-like forms, or more geometrically correct triangles with equal sides. The basic triangular recess is shown in Fig. 9-14B.

To apply this technique, begin by drawing a triangle. Cut in two sides (Fig. 9-14C), going deep at one apex and tapering the depth toward its base. If you want the sides of the triangle to be straight, draw the knife along a steel rule. Most workers favor cutting from the surface towards the deep part, using several slices to get the cut deep enough. Use a knife or a chisel to cut away waste wood in a series of shavings or chips to make a smooth, tapered slope to the apex of the triangle (Fig. 9-14D).

A series of these cut triangles could be used to decorate an edge (Fig. 9-14E). It is more usual to have a pattern of three adjoining triangles, producing an effect that looks as though a pyramid had been pressed into the wood (Fig. 9-14F). This is done by drawing a pyramid as viewed from above, and cutting the lines so the center is deepest. Pare from the outline to the center (Fig. 9-14G) on all three sides (Fig. 9-14H).

Two sides of the triangle can be blended into a curve; a pair of these shapes could form part of a leaf or petal pattern. For this effect, draw a centerline (which need not be straight) and curves to each side of it. Cut along the centerline (Fig. 9-14I), going deepest near its middle and sloping up to its ends. Pare the curved sweep on each side down to the centerline (Fig. 9-14J). In any pattern with a curved outline, the pared surface of the depression will also have to be curved. If the

Fig. 9-14. The tools, technique, and refinements of **chip carving**, a system of decorative carving based on an incised triangle.

outline is straight, the sloping triangle will be flat; flat and curved surfaces have to be blended into each other at the cut lines of the depression.

Many chip-carving patterns are based on radiating triangles, like a compass star. These are effective as central motifs, or as part of a corner (Fig. 9-14K). Outlines can vary; the lines need not always be straight. Curving the radiating lines gives a windmill effect. The pattern can be adapted to suit a lid with a knob at the center.

Chip carving can be used to make border patterns—an effective way to make an otherwise fairly plain piece of furniture more attractive. Triangles, squares, or curves may be used together (Fig. 9-14L) for an almost limitless variety of patterns.

Because chip carving is geometric, it has to be laid out fairly accurately. Small errors may not matter, but great variations in the size of elements in a pattern, or changes in proportion, will be more noticeable than similar variations in more freely executed, carved patterns. Some designs may be worked out with rule, compass, and pencil, directly on the wood, but it is better to draw the design on paper and transfer it to the wood—with carbon paper, for example. When the carving has been completed, sand the uncut surface lightly to remove any marks.

Polish is inappropriate to chip carving, but if the wood really needs protection from dirt, a coat or two of wax may be brushed on and rubbed with a cloth; but watch out for wax buildup in the bottoms of the recesses.

Success in chip carving depends on the tool being able to make smooth cuts without meeting uneven opposition. Resinous wood or wood with a pronounced grain can be difficult to work with. Most traditional chip carving was done in European oak, which has a pronounced grain. Maybe it was the only wood available. It should certainly be avoided for your first efforts. A soft wood with little obvious grain is more suitable.

EDGE DECORATION

It used to be that wood was decorated by carpenters, cabinetmakers, and wheelwrights, people whose occupation it was to produce utilitarian articles. Although they did not consider themselves wood carvers, they added decoration to their work, sometimes as relief from the heavy labor associated with their main occupation, when there were no power tools to help.

Not all of this decoration can be regarded as carving, but it was certainly allied to it. Chip-carved edge decorations are an example of this type work, done with tools intended for ordinary woodwork.

The wheelwright, who made all the parts of carts and wagons, worked with very strong, heavy sections of wood. He was adept at shaping the compound curves of many wagons, with an adz and drawknife. As a cart or wagon neared completion, he decorated it by working its angles into patterns with his drawknife; the patterns are now usually called *wagon beveling*. Although wheelwright work is no longer needed, its method of decoration is used now to give a pleasing effect on furniture legs and rails. The wheelwright's drawknife is also gone, the work today being done with chisels.

The basic wagon bevel is a *stopped chamfer* (Fig. 9-15A). After it is marked out in pencil, the ends are cut in, and the bevel is pared to suit the grain. Another version has a step at the end (Fig. 9-15B). Less common is the hollowed chamfer, which is worked with a gouge (Fig. 9-15C). The chamfer (beveled edge) may be broken up on a long edge, with intermediate nicks (Fig. 9-15D). The wheelwright favored curves, which can be made using a chisel bevel-downward to sweep in from the ends (Fig. 9-15E). A spokeshave will also make this shape. The curves can be combined into a surface pattern (Fig. 9-15F). A point to watch is the possible weakness of a sharp point between two parts of the beveling. There should be a short length of unbeveled edge between cuts (Fig. 9-15G) to avoid this.

Although this type of decoration was traditionally done by hand, long bevels could be made accurately with a spindle having a suitable head, either as a special machine or as an attachment to a drill.

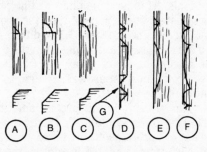

Fig. 9-15. **Wagon beveling**, a form of edge decoration traditionally practiced by the wheelwright.

Another form of decoration uses a firmer gouge sharpened on the outside. The basic action is a cut made straight in, followed by a slice toward the cut, either at a constant depth to give a parallel-sided hollow (Fig. 9-16A) or at an increasing depth to give a taper (Fig. 9-16B). A simple pattern can be made with a series of these cuts Fig. 9-16C). A line of cuts going in the opposite direction, made next to the first, makes the pattern slightly more involved. Two cuts facing each other will result in a round center (Fig. 9-16D). Turning a gouge completely cuts out a cup-shaped circle. Many variations are possible with one gouge (Fig. 9-16E).

TOOLS

Typically, carving tools are made in different grades. Some manufacturers describe their better tools as *workmen's*

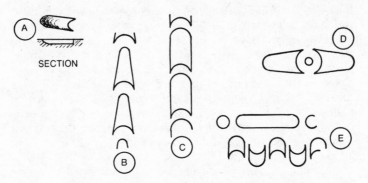

SECTION

Fig. 9-16. Decorating an edge with a gouge.

or *craftsmen's* carving tools, and their series of lighter types, as *amateur's* tools. This is a peculiar distinction—the wood carved by the amateur is the same cut by the professional. So why shouldn't the tools be the same? The difference probably comes from a form of prejudice dating from the days when the amateur was assumed to only "play" at carving with light, superficial work; the craftsman was the one to tackle work involving heavy cuts.

Carving tools should be of professional quality. The number of different tools available in the days when carving played a much more prominent part in woodworking ran into the hundreds, each type available in widths from $^1/_{32}$ inch in small steps up to as wide as 1½ inches. One manufacturer in Sheffield, England still supplies sets with as many as 120 different tools.

What tools you will need first will depend on the type of carving you want to do, but assuming a total of 12 for a basic carver's tool kit, a reasonable selection will include a ½ inch straight chisel, a ⅜ inch skew chisel, a ¼ inch shallow-curved gouge, a $^5/_{16}$ inch gouge with a slightly deeper curve, ⅜- and ½-inch gouges with fairly deep sections, two ¼ inch or ⅜ inch gouges with moderate curves, a deep ⅛ inch gouge and one narrower, plus a parting tool about ¼ inch wide. As you can see from this list of tools, most of the work is done with gouges. Outlines and things like veins in leaves require narrow, deep ones; for backgrounds, curved ones; and for general shaping, wider ones. (Chisels do not get as much use.)

Straight gouges will do most work, but a few curved ones may be added for working into hollows. Spoon-bit gouges and bent-back tools are rarely needed, but they may be the only tools that can make certain cuts for intricate carving. What tools you add to these depends on the type of carving being done. Master the use of the basic tools, learn to keep them in good condition, discover what can be done with them—then add other tools when you really need them. Carving tools have to be sharpened frequently. This can be time-comsuming if there are many, so it is better to keep their numbers down. Use each to its full extent before expanding your collection.

Mallets will be needed. The round type, favored by carvers, is the best initial investment. Measuring tools are essential to many projects. For some work, dividers and calipers are used for comparing measurements. For larger wood sculpture, it may be necessary to make wooden calipers in the form of simple metal calipers (on a grander scale, with plywood arms possibly 2 feet long) held together with a bolt and washers. A leather washer between the arms will provide friction to keep them in any position.

For some modern carving—with symbolic shapes and sweeping curves instead of detailed cuts—shaping can be done with saw, plane, and spokeshave; but other tools like those that use a series of teeth for a filing action are also useful for this. Rifflers, files with two cutting parts at opposite ends of a smooth center, are used to get into hollows that are difficult to work with edged tools.

HOLDING DEVICES

Many kinds of carving keep both hands occupied, both on the tool, or one holding the tool, the other wielding a mallet. In these circumstances, the work has to be held down, except, of course, items heavy enough to resist movement under the tool. Sometimes it is convenient to be able to move things being carved easily to expose a different face, or tackle a cut from another direction. Because of this, it is helpful to have quick-release arrangements.

Engineer's vises are usually at a more convenient height for carving than bench vises. They can be mounted on a block fitted into a woodworking vise. Unless a scrap piece of wood can be put in the vise along with the work to protect it, sheet-metal vise clamps that wrap over the jaws and are faced with wood should be used (Fig. 9-17A).

Flat work may be held on the bench with a holdfast. It is also possible to hold the work within a framework of wood pieces screwed to the bench, and secure it with folding wedges (Fig. 9-17B) or a cam (Fig. 9-17C).

For reasonably bulky pieces of wood that have to be turned to be carved on all sides, the professional carver uses a large screw, driven from under the bench into the bottom of the work, like the screw center of a lathe; a large wing nut and washer holds the work steady (Fig. 9-17D). A similar device can be improvised by bolting a piece of wood to the bench, to which the work is screwed (Fig. 9-17E).

When screw holes would not be acceptable in the finished piece, the wood may be glued down with paper in the joint, which can be split open with a knife or chisel later.

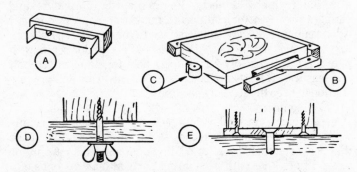

Fig. 9-17. Wood to be carved can be kept from getting marred by vise jaws if they are covered with sheet-metal vise clamps faced with wood (A). Flat work can be held within a frame of wood pieces screwed to the bench, and secured with folding wedges (B) or a cam (C). The professional method of holding large pieces: screwing the work to the bench (D); the work screwed to a piece of wood bolted to the bench (E).

INCISED CARVING

Wood can be decorated with cuts that form patterns. The patterns can be made more elaborate by punching designs in parts of them. Parts of the design can also be colored. Most of this sort of work can be done with a knife. For straight lines, any knife with a sharp point can be drawn along a steel rule. A linoleum-cutting knife (the kind with a hooked end) is especially suitable for following curves (Fig. 9-18A), as is a deep, narrow gouge, sometimes called a veining tool (Fig. 9-18B). A parting tool with a fairly steep angle (Fig. 9-18C), can also be used.

If you use a knife for this technique, aim to make two cuts that will remove a small sliver of wood between them (Fig. 9-18D). A simple cut will not show enough contrast under sidelighting to emphasize the design. A veiner or *V*-sectioned tool will not follow a line easily, but cutting in on the line with a single knife cut first will help in controlling its direction. Grooves cut by these tools will give a more prominent line particularly appropriate for larger patterns. Many straight-line patterns are possible (Fig. 9-18E); curves can make stylized flowers (Fig. 9-18F).

Patterns may be drawn directly on the wood or transferred from drawings on paper. Sanding out marks on the surface afterward will give emphasis to the patterns; the cuts should be blown out of the cuts after sanding. Another way of emphasizing the pattern is to paint within the cuts. Providing the wood does not allow paint to flow along the grain by capillary action, it will not matter if some of the paint goes over the edge of a cut, onto the surface. When it has hardened, clean it off, and sand the surface to remove any excess paint. This method can be used for making a family name plaque for your house. For outdoor use, protect the wood with varnish.

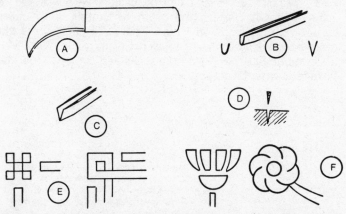

Fig. 9-18. A linoleum-cutting knife (A), a deep, narrow gouge (B), or a parting tool (C) are good for incising curves. If a knife is used to incise straight lines, make two cuts that will remove a small sliver (D); the patterns that can be produced this way are many (E). Curves can make stylized flowers (F).

More pronounced incised lettering can make a very attractive, more formal "shingle." Cut the letters boldly, close to the depth achieved by chip carving. The simplicity of this technique calls for the choice of the right alphabet—and flawless workmanship. A Roman alphabet lends itself well to this project (see Fig. 9-19A); choose one with moderate serifs (the "feet" at the ends of the letters' "legs"). The spacing of the letters is an important consideration. Some of the letters are open at the side, like C, E, L, etc; others are not: H, N, M, and so forth. Because of this, spacing all letters equally could actually create an illusion of *unequal* spacing.

Also a letter with a sloping side—V, for example— has to be closer to one that is round or has vertical sides than regular spacing would dictate.

With this in mind, make an experimental layout on paper. It may be worthwhile to cut the letters you need out of paper or cardboard to try out the spacing. Make sure the outlines are clear on the wood, if necessary, going over the transferred lines with a pencil and rule.

Start by cutting along the centers of the letters with a knife. For large work, cut into the lines with a chisel, paring away some of the waste (Fig. 9-19B). At first, get rid of the bulk of the waste, so final shaping can be done with fairly light paring. A gouge may be used in some places, but a chisel will sweep around curves and can be used bevel-downward in hollowed curves. Adjust the depth by cutting the centers deeper with the knife, where necessary. Try to get straight parts even in depth, and blend the curves into them. Work with the grain at all times. Blend the serifs and corners, from the surface down to the deepest cut.

Fig. 9-19. Letters of the Roman alphabet (A) are ideal for incised name plaques. If the letters are large, the waste wood should be pared away with a chisel after work with the knife (B).

At first, remove the waste in little bits. The smoothest sides, however, will be obtained by confident cutting. Be careful of the tool jumping across and damaging an opposite slope. Cut the centers deep enough so the wood pared from one side breaks off without tearing up the other side. To get the smoothest surface where the grain is diagonal to the cut, slice with the chisel. Cut the main parts of letters first, then blend the serifs and other small parts into the cuts.

Incised lettering should have a clean, tooled appearance. Do not sand depressions. The lettering can be made more prominent with paint. Dark lettering on a nicely grained piece of wood can be very effective. This method of incising can be used for other things beside lettering, but except for borders, it is seldom seen elsewhere.

Incised designs can be used to outline a pattern or make a picture. If the surface can be altered as a background for the pattern, a different effect can be achieved. One way of doing this is with a punch (Fig. 9-20A). A punch with a patterned end can be made by filing grooves across the end of a steel rod (Fig. 9-20B). After incising the outline, stamp the background all over by hitting the punch with a hammer, using even blows. Turn the punch so the background pattern is random. Punches with different patterns can be used where parts of the design have to be made distinct from each other.

Fig. 9-20. An incised design can be given a punched background (A) with a steel rod having a pattern of grooves cut in its end (B).

If a punched design is stained, the punched part will absorb more stain and become darker, emphasizing the design even more. An alternative to punching is to use a veiner or V-sectioned tool to make closely spaced, shallow cuts across the background. Making the cuts cross will produce a pattern of small dots.

A punched background can leave the design in the form of a silhouette. (Name plaques can be made this way.)

A traditional form of decorating with incised patterns—called *intarsia* or *tarso work*—has color between the cut lines. The effect is something like the use of veneer or marquetry, but instead of the pattern being built of different pieces of wood, one piece is colored to produce a similar effect.

Use bold outlines in a simple pictorial form that does not need shading, other than tonal changes to distinguish the shapes. After the whole pattern is incised, color it and sand the surface. Use stains or dyes rather than paints; spirit and aniline dyes are suitable. Water-soluble stains are less likely to creep along the grain than oil stains. Do not use anything so dense as to be opaque. Let the grain show through. The color in each section of the design should be even; do not attempt to graduate the color for shading. A wax polish or furniture cream may be applied when the stain is dry. Be careful to avoid anything that might dissolve the coloring.

A variation can be introduced by filling the grooves. Apply the filling so it stands above the surface. After it sets, sand it level. The grooves if filled with a colored material, can be combined with colored panels or used with an uncolored, incised pattern (Fig. 9-21).

Fig. 9-21. An incised design can be emphasized by cutting through, and removing, part of it.

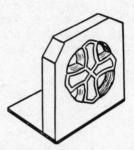

Many specimens of traditional carving is pierced, producing those patterns of leaves in some old church windows, for example. Besides being carved on the surface, the designs are outlined by cuts going right through the wood. This style of decoration can be applied to most types of carving, but it is particularly striking as emphasis for an incised pattern. The open work can be created with a fretsaw or jigsaw, either by hand or with a power tool.

LOW-RELIEF CARVING

The methods of carving described so far are little more than two-dimensional—they have very little depth. The full beauty of carving comes in its three-dimensional effects. But this is a goal that has to be worked up to. Low-relief carving provides an intermediate step in attaining that goal. In this form of carving, backgrounds are cut away to give prominence to a design, which may also have some tool work on it.

Patterns similar to those described for incised carving can be worked in low relief. Instead of punching a background, the wood is cut away to a greater depth than the punch can compress it. For simple, fairly shallow work, outline the pattern with a V-sectioned tool, then cut away the background with a gouge. For work around an edge, use a straight gouge (Fig. 9-22A); for a hollow between the parts of the pattern, a curved gouge (Fig. 9-22B).

Background cuts could be made with the grain, but it is more usual to cut diagonally to the grain. Always keep the corners of the gouge's cutting edge above the surface of the wood. Use a gouge with a more shallow curve to make light, finishing cuts. Its flatter curve will reduce prominent tool marks, making the surface generally flat.

Most of the waste can be removed with cuts of any convenient length and depth, but trimming to the final depth should be done with a series of comparatively small scooping cuts (Fig. 9-22C). This will give a uniform pattern over the background. Try to get the background reasonably uniform in depth. Machine-like perfection is unnecessary, but excessive variations should be avoided.

It is possible to do very similar work with a motorized router. An enthusiastic carver may not approve of this method—it is not, after all, real carving—but it can be very effective for formal signs and name plaques. If you want the lettering (or other pattern) to remain high, use the router to follow the outside of the profile and remove the background to a uniform depth. A rounded cutter that will blend the letters' edges into the background is better than one that makes more abrupt edges that could be weak at some parts of the grain.

Another alternative is to use a router cutter to serve the same purpose as the tools used in incising a pattern. A cutter with a rounded or conical end will follow the pattern and leave the surrounding wood level. This gives a clean-cut groove, which may be prominent enough without further treatment; but paint or stain in the groove will give further emphasis. A good way of making outdoor signs, name plaques, and direction signs is to use colored, recessed lettering against natural wood, protected with varnish.

For a shallow recess, just cutting to the outline is satisfactory. For larger or deeper work, cut a preliminary outline a short distance from the final line (Fig. 9-22D), then remove most of the waste and cut back to the final line with chisels and gouges (Fig. 9-22E). For most parts, the sides of the cuts should slope slightly (Fig. 9-22F). Undercutting (Fig. 9-22G) should be avoided, unless it is needed for emphasis, as at the side of a leaf.

If the background is cut away, and nothing is done to the pattern remaining, it will be just a silhouette. This is quite

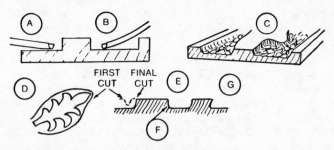

Fig. 9-22. Low-relief carving: a straight gouge is used for work around an edge (A); a curved gouge is used to work in a hollow (B); waste is scooped out for final trimming (C); a preliminary outline is cut for deeper work done with a router (D); the cut made to the final line within the preliminary outline (E); the very slight slope necessary in the sides of the cut (F); the undercut used for design emphasis (G).

effective for some things, but usually some surface carving is needed to improve the work, like simple incised work, for example.

A lot of relief carving is based on leaves. The carved leaf form, however, can be stylized so much that it may be hard to recognize as any leaf found in nature. Oak and maple leaves are shapes frequently used (Fig. 9-23A). There is no rigid form; leaves in nature differ quite a bit from each other. Carved leaves may vary, but they should at least have a family likeness in their proportions, number of points, and other individual peculiarities.

Use a piece of easy-to-cut wood, but not one too small. Sketch in the outline of a leaf, about 4 inches across. Outline the leaf with straight or curved cuts (Fig. 9-23B). Do not cut the leaf's outline at this stage. To have a natural form the leaf will have a slightly wavy surface, so its eventual outline will be broadly rippled in relation to the background. (A close cut to the outline now would only suit a flat leaf.) Cut down that part of the background outside the grooves to allow room for the tool to move as you work on the leaf; it need not be a finished surface yet. The background may be within a raised border, or it can be taken right to the edge of the wood. Do not go too deep. The surface carving on the leaf should be comparatively shallow. It would not look right if the background was cut very deeply; about ¼ inch is about right.

The surface of the leaf can be given a wavy appearance by cutting curved grooves with a gouge. A compass can be used as a guide, but the grooves should not be too geometrically

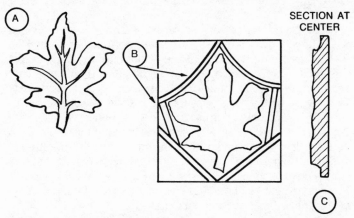

SECTION AT
CENTER

Fig. 9-23. The maple leaf (A) is a common motif in relief carving; after it is drawn on wood, it is outlined with straight and curved cuts (B), and worked into a wavy surface (C).

accurate; a leaf is not like that. Rounding the raised parts will make the grooved sections undulate from the center outward (Fig. 9-23C).

Cut in the outline of the leaf, preferably by cutting downward with chisels and gouges, or with a parting tool where applicable. Starting with the deepest indentations, cut away the remaining background to the same depth as that outside the outline. Level it with a gouge to give a pattern of small, scooped out indentations.

The main lobes of the leaf should be given veins. Draw them in, making them wide toward the leaf's center and tapering to points, but following easy curves. Cut the outlines with a veiner or other V-sectioned tool, keeping the depth slight and tapering out to the surface at the end of each vein. There should be no obvious flat part of the original surface remaining in the finished leaf.

The repetition of motifs, or of panels matching in overall size and general appearance, but different in detail, was common in the carving of yesteryear. The overall effect is uniformity, but closer inspection reveals individuality of detail. The patterns in a series of squares may be geometric, or stylized leaves or flowers. Quite often the design is symmetrical around a center. When such a design is marked out, only half or a quarter of the design need be drawn on paper; it can be rotated a quarter- or half-turn when the design

305

is transferred to the wood. These panels make good practice pieces.

The geometric pattern shown in Fig. 9-24A was devised with the use of a compass; the cross-sectional view in Fig. 9-24B shows the final form. None of the cuts for designs like this need by very deep, but they should allow the light to cast shadows, to give prominence to the design. The hollow parts are worked with a gouge, as already described, but in circular work it is particularly important to go around removing the central waste with a deep gouge first, then deal with the sides of the hollow by working back to the outlines in the direction of the grain. Where the curved, carved bands meet, the hollows should be even in depth and meet with a neat miter. The other hollows are cut out by methods similar to chip carving. The central part should be left high (Fig. 9-24C).

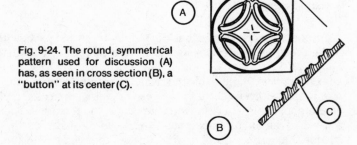

Fig. 9-24. The round, symmetrical pattern used for discussion (A) has, as seen in cross section (B), a "button" at its center (C).

A floral pattern can be marked out with a drawing of only half or a quarter of the design (Fig. 9-25A). The hollow border is worked the way for a geometric design, and the flower is carved in a way very similar to that described for a leaf.

Outline the flower with chisels and gouges. Work the background with shallow cuts. In these comparatively narrow spaces, it is important to make cuts across the grain *before* making those *with* the grain; otherwise, the wood may break.

Outline the central "button" with a gouge. In preparing these designs, have all the tools you intend to use at hand, so the parts can be drawn to suit the tools. In this case, the work can be simplified if the button is made by standing one of the gouges on the wood and turning it around. Cut in the shape of each petal by paring toward the central button (Fig. 9-25B). The cross-sectional view in Fig. 9-25 shows how the work should appear after being tooled all over.

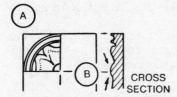

Fig. 9-25. A drawing of a quarter of a floral design (A) can be rotated to produce the final symmetrical pattern, which is carved toward the center (B).

CROSS SECTION

In the past, simple shallow relief work was used on many articles for the home. Lords had even more elaborate carving in their castles. Churches and cathedrals contained much more advanced carving; some of the less wealthy churches, only low-relief carving.

The agricultural worker had little furniture to carve. The more prosperous farmer had chests, tables, and benches or stools. These were products of local carpenters, none of whom specialized in embellishing their work. The wood used, of fairly hefty proportions, was stronger than necessary, so it could be carved without weakening it.

This sort of furniture was decorated with low-relief carving done by craftsmen whose main activity was constructional rather than decorative woodworking. Many old chests and other pieces of household furniture are still around; if they can't be seen "in the wood," at least they can be appreciated by looking at photographs. These can be studied for patterns that can be used today, either in making reproductions of antique furniture or as decoration for modern pieces.

Low-relief carving is a good way to learn how to handle carving tools. Often it is the only sort of carving needed on modern pieces of furniture. Carving in high relief is not only inappropriate to the severe lines of modern furniture, it is a dust collector. However, three-dimensional carving, or high-relief carving that simulates it, has more appeal to the artist/craftsman who wants to carry on a tradition that might otherwise die out.

CONVENTIONAL RELIEF CARVING

While low-relief carving has many uses, it is through deeper relief carving that the carver can let his artistic flare develop. This does not exclusively apply to the artist, however. Where the artist may depend mainly on his esthetic judgement to make large, sweeping cuts, the less artistic carver can get equally satisfying results using suggested guidelines and more

307

conventional patterns. The artist is concerned with design; the craftsman, with execution.

Although the artist may prefer to execute original scenes and figures, and the craftsman, work of a more stylized character, certain conventions accumulated over centuries can provide a basis that anyone who claims to be a carver should understand. Many of these praxes go back to the heyday of ancient Greek and Roman cultures, when they were used to decorate wood and stone. Although most of the wood has disappeared, examples in stone may still be found, examples that the modern carver can use with a feeling for the very long tradition behind them.

Even though relief carving of this sort is deeper than low-relief carving, it is often not as deep as it appears. The skill is in giving an effect of perspective that leads the observer to think that the whole thing is much deeper than it actually is. Examine a carved piece in a museum and see how the work from the front seems to have considerable depth compared to its relatively (and surprisingly) thin edge.

Be prepared to work deeper to get away from the overall flatness of low-relief carving. In most finished pieces, the carved area will not show any of the original flat surface. Every bit of wood in the design is tooled, quite often with cuts not parallel to the original surface. Also, most of this carving has very few straight lines and flat surfaces. This is one reason why chisels are used much less than gouges.

Leaves, prominent motifs in conventional relief carving, may have a natural form or be extremely conventionalized. The natural leaf form for conventional relief carving is given a more wavy appearance than the one for low-relief carving, creating the appearance of being wafted in the breeze.

A solitary leaf (Fig. 9-26) is a good example for an initial project. Begin by drawing an outline. Cut the background deep enough to be below the lowest point in the leaf's eventually wavy surface. Although the surface of the leaf will have different levels, sink the ground to a uniform depth.

Because the veins of a leaf are stiffer than the parts surrounding them, in a breeze, twists and turns in a leaf occur between the veins rather than across them. Make bold gouge cuts, radiating from near the stem, to make the leaf "flutter." Alter the surfaces so they are not at the same level. A part of the leaf may dip toward a point or dip in the body, swinging up again to a point. The whole leaf may be at an angle to the background. Any treatment that makes the surface depart

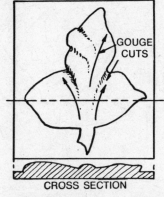

Fig. 9-26. A relief-carved leaf can be given a "fluttering" look with gouge cuts.

CROSS SECTION

from flatness will help. Next go over the surface with gouges having flatter curves to produce the cross section shown in the illustration.

For the sake of perspective, the parts of this sort of carving have to appear to be at different levels—although in fact the differences may be very slight. An example is the small shield (which could have a design or monogram) with leaves spreading out behind it in Fig. 9-27A. The shield may be at the same level as the surface. The leaves have to be lower. They are deeper where they meet the shield, but the tips of some of them may be close to surface level.

Draw the pattern, cut in the outline, and sink the background. The surfaces are at three levels. Leave the shield level with the original surface, but cut down the levels of the leaves, two coming a little way down (at least where they meet the shield), and the others, below that (Fig. 9-27B). Cut the centers of the leaves with a V-sectioned gouge, then taper the surfaces into the grooves. Make the surfaces appear to curve from the center in their length. Overlapping parts may be undercut slightly, but be careful of weak grain; an angle slightly less than a right angle (Fig. 9-27C) is enough to make one part stand out above another.

The form of the acanthus leaf may have, at one time, been one of nature's, but the form used by carvers is, quite unnaturally, a symmetrical, conventional shape. Found on the capitals (crowns) of the Corinthian columns in Greek architecture, it is characterized by its bold treatment and the distinctive "eyes" between its main parts.

An acanthus leaf is easier to work if it is not too small. A piece of wood about 6 by 8 inches is suitable; it should be at

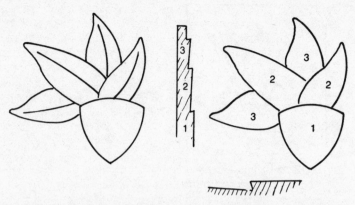

Fig. 9-27. The parts of the shield-and-leaves design (A) are cut to three levels above the background (B); the distance between levels can be accentuated by undercutting (C).

least 1 inch thick. Draw the design on paper (Fig. 9-28A); half a drawing can be turned over for the complete design. The part of the leaf on either side of the central stem is divided into three lobes, separated by a curled-over fold ending in an "eye." The top of the stem leads into another part that curls over. In cross section, the stem reaches the original surface and the other parts fall back, the tips of the lobes almost reaching the background (Fig. 9-28B).

Mark a centerline on the wood, but do not transfer all of the design yet; if you did, many of the lines would be cut off before they could be used. Draw the main outline and cut the background down to ⅝ inch. Do not cut on the outline of the leaf at this stage. Go around it with a deep gouge a short distance from the outline; ignore smaller inlets. Then cut in the general outline (without details) with gouges and chisels (Fig. 9-28C). Do not finish the background until the carving is almost completed; at this stage, just remove enough waste to give room to work. Leaving it unfinished will allow you to remove any tool marks later.

The next step is the general shaping of the surface to get parts into the right plane before detail carving. The two "eyes" will remain near the original surface. The folds leading to them should not recede much. The parts of the leaf on either side of the stem should sweep down to within ¼ inch of the background. Make the stem taper from near surface level (at its base) to about half the depth of its meeting point with the turned-over part at the top; use a fairly flat gouge to get the general shape, after marking key lines in pencil (Fig. 9-28D).

The central stem can now be cut to its final shape. Outline the folds with a veiner. Cut the surfaces to almost the final shape with free-flowing curves. Cut away the bulk of the waste everywhere else. At this stage, get rid of unwanted bulk, without reaching the final surface at every point. By removing the thicker waste, the remaining work can be done more delicately. Some of the work done in the beginning may necessitate using a mallet. A skilled worker may be able to do finished work with a mallet, but while you are learning, make the initial cuts light enough to allow handwork at the end.

Draw in the exact outline and cut into it nearly vertically with gouges and chisels. A skew chisel may be used (carefully) in the acute angles between petals; the cut need not be vertical. Providing the outline has been cut sharply at the surface, the edges close to the angles may slope into the background. Slight undercutting at the top will emphasize the rolled effect. Undercutting may also be used at the edges of parts that appear to overlap to increase the effect.

Draw the lines dividing the surfaces of the lobes (Fig. 9-28E). Outer lobes should appear to overlap inner ones. Undercut the inner edges of the lobes slightly (Fig. 9-28F) and hollow their surfaces with shallow gouges up to the lines. The curves should be smooth, easy sweeps, preferably done without hesitation. The resulting curve, even if it does not go exactly as intended, will look better than one with kinks produced by using the gouge in stages, or altering the cut part of the way along a sweep.

Round the outside of the central stem and the folds. The "eyes" should be cut deeply enough to cast prominent shadows. They should appear to have been formed by the rolled edge of the lobe (Fig. 9-28G). Cut vertically around the inner edges with a small gouge. Gouge a deep hollow in the bottom.

Cut vertically around the outline at the top, toward the other part of the leaf (Fig. 9-28H); shape the surface to a strong curve toward this edge, leaving a little thickness to allow slight undercutting to make the edge more prominent (Fig. 9-28I). Shape the end of the stem so it can go into the undercut edge.

All of this work should be done with the wood secured to the top of the bench. Carving depends on the effect created by light shining across it, highlighting surfaces and casting

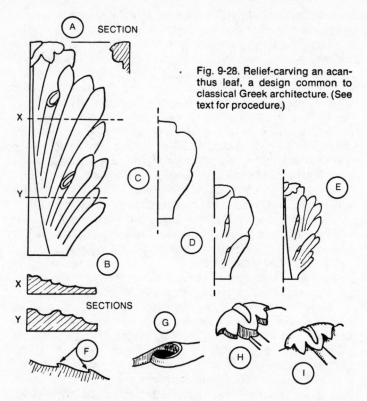

Fig. 9-28. Relief-carving an acanthus leaf, a design common to classical Greek architecture. (See text for procedure.)

shadows around edges. Flaws may show up at some angles and not others. The acanthus leaf may look perfect while it is lying flat, but hold it at an angle to reveal blemishes. Hold the carving vertical; try it with the light coming from either side. If you know where you want it to be viewed, try it there. Apart from showing you what corrections may be necessary, viewing it like this will also show you dust, odd fibers clinging in recesses, or other parts not properly cleared of waste.

The steps in carving the acanthus leaf exemplify the usual procedure for carving other leaves, coats of arms, and other decorative panels that need a semblance of perspective. General outlines are drawn, backgrounds are lowered, and surfaces are shaped approximately. There may be a little outlining of the main parts to indicate their positions, but at this stage the important thing is to remove unwanted wood without attempting to reach the finished surface. This is followed by more careful outlining and some detail work, usually starting with high parts. From here, special points—like the "eyes" of the acanthus leaf—are cut. The whole surface is finished with careful tool work. The background can be leveled and given final treatment at any stage following the heavier carving.

LINEN-FOLD DESIGNS

Another form of conventional relief carving, which was developed in Tudor days (but used frequently since), is the linen-fold design (Fig. 9-29). It is used on panels, either as part of the paneling in a room, or as part of a chest or other piece of furniture. The pattern imitates the way Tudor altar cloth was folded. The wood is carved to a conventionalized form to give the effect of cloth folded back on itself at several places, with the grain running the length of the folds. In most traditional constructions, the carved panel is mounted in a frame, nearly always with the folds vertical.

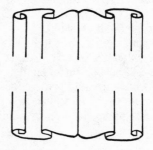

Fig. 9-29. The linen-fold design used to imitate the folds in Tudor altar cloth.

There are carvings in existence with many intricate folds. There is no standard arrangement; some designs were devised by carvers as examples of their skill. Normally, the design's symmetry is established by letting the cloth rise to a ridge at the center. For a first attempt, use a simple example with only a few folds.

This type of carving really only calls for work with carving tools at the ends; most of the rest of the shaping can be done with planes or by machining. The first step is to lower the background all around. The wood for a linen-fold panel should be no less than ¾ inch thick. The background thickness should be about one third of the total thickness and can be cut down with any tool that will work a rebate (Fig. 9-30A). A quarter of a drawing can be made and rotated about the centerline on the wood to get the outline of the lengthwise profile first (Fig. 9-30B).

How the folds are made depends on the tools available. Cut grooves to remove the bulk of the waste in the hollows (Fig. 9-30C). Then plane off high spots. Much of this can be done with a plane having its blade the full width of the sole. Whatever cuts you make, go through the entire length each time to keep the section uniform. Traditionally, hollow rounds and other molding planes were used. If they are available, they will help in shaping the surface, but a lot can be done with sandpaper wrapped around pieces of wood shaped like the curves. If the shaping is done with a flatbased plane, sanding will remove the slight angular marks left by the plane. Complete all lengthwise work before carving the ends.

Mark out the ends of the design from the drawing. Do the same stage of carving at both sides and both ends at the same time to insure uniformity. If several panels are being made for a piece of furniture, do the same to each in assembly line fashion, so the result is uniformity between panels.

Cut around the outline, down to the background, with gouges and chisels (Fig. 9-30D). Cut down the profile of the second fold to about half the thickness of the wood; use a penciled line to indicate the curves at the end (Fig. 9-30E). The lowest part of the fold underneath should be high enough above the background for the edge to show. The edge of the "linen" should be an unbroken line, which may be ⅛ inch wide on a large panel, less on a small one. Cut in under the edge to

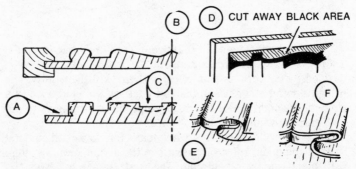

Fig. 9-30. The linen-fold design is first roughly cut with a rebate tool (A); work on its lengthwise cross section (B) is begun by removing most of the waste from the hollows (C). Then the top and bottom are cut down to the background (D), followed by work on the second fold (E); cut in under the edge to emphasize the line (F).

emphasize the line (Fig. 9-30F). Gouge out the curves to a reasonable depth and, where the "cloth" folds over the lowest part, blend the edge into the underside of the curve.

A little experimentation will show the amount of undercutting necessary to provide the right effect. This will be influenced by the final position of the carving. An end near eye level requires strong undercutting to be effective, while at floor level or far above eye level it needs very little undercutting.

The fascination of linen-fold panels can be appreciated by examining specimens in churches or by looking at antique furniture. Photographs are valuable for study, but they do not always have sufficient detail to indicate how the effect is achieved. Many experimental variations can be prepared by rolling and folding cloth.

CARVING FIGURES IN RELIEF

The carving of animals, birds, and similar figures in relief, calls for artistic skill—if anything—but for our purposes, basic designs can be used.

An appreciation of lines and curves is an important requisite for this kind of work. Some knowledge of anatomy is helpful for the execution of some designs. A preliminary drawing is necessary—but a flat drawing cannot indicate all the details and depth of cut at various points. Only shading can give a clue to the shapes.

The easiest thing to carve is a simple figure without much detail, both in line and texture. Fur or feathers only add complications. A short-haired dog (Fig. 9-31A) would be suitable for a first attempt. It is helpful to make a frame-like border around this sort of work. It will draw attention away from imperfect tool work. Viewed at a low level, it will emphasize the apparent thickness and solidity of the carving (Fig. 9-31B).

The thicker the wood, the more latitude you will have in shaping the figure. Cut down the frame to half the thickness of the wood; the background to one-quarter the thickness. Transfer the outline to the wood and cut down the background, getting rid of the bulk of the waste before cutting close to the line. Curve the background up to the border by working around its edge with a deep gouge.

At this stage the outline of the animal is a silhouette. It has to be rounded to meet the background, but not by simple, uniform rounding. It has to be done with an appreciation of the

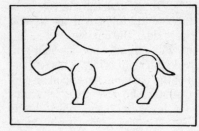

Fig. 9-31. The dog design in this relief-carving(A) is surrounded by a frame-like border (B) to accentuate its thickness and solidity.

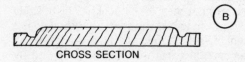

CROSS SECTION

animal's form. Remove some of the larger pieces of waste with fairly vigorous slices. Blend the legs into the background. If you want the dog's legs positioned to simulate walking, they will have to be carved in different levels.

Once the outer curves are about right, work the curves on the surface. No part of the animal should be flat. There should be curves rising over the rump and leg joints, and hollows toward the waist and neck. Cut in carefully around the ears. Positioning the eye exactly is more important than shaping it carefully.

The final piece should have cleanly tooled surfaces. Do not use sandpaper on the carving. As was suggested for other carvings, move it around and look at it with the light coming from various directions, then make any necessary corrections and remove any stray fibers still clinging to the wood.

Some carvers find it helpful to model a figure in clay before carving it. Dimensions can be taken from the model with dividers or calipers and transferred to the carving.

SMOOTH CARVING

A modern trend in figure carving is the smooth figure with a flat back, which may be either mounted directly on a wall or a panel. One of the simplest examples is a fish (Fig. 9-32). To make it, cut its outline with a band saw (or hacksaw) and mount the work temporarily on a block that can be gripped in a vise, so some of the shaping can be done with a plane; a lot of it can be done with a surface-forming tool. Fins (and generally any pieces that extends from figures like these) can be made separately and glued on. It may help the effect to use

316

contrasting woods for these things. A white tusk would enhance an elephant with a dark body, for example.

Most of the external curves can be made with a flat tool, used with a sweeping motion. Hollows are made with a half-round blade. Alternatively, coarse files or rasps could be used. Make recesses and grooves between legs or at joints with the edge of a triangular file, perhaps augmented by a V-section gouge or veiner.

The coarse finish left by tools may represent the skin texture of some animals, but most carvings of this sort have a smooth finish. Work surfaces to a fine finish with successively finer grades of sandpaper. Parts to be glued should be finished before they are attached; make sure that adjoining surfaces are flat and free from abrasive dust or grease before gluing. A small glass eye can be glued in a hole in the carving or a hole can be filled with sealing wax to represent an eye.

Fig. 9-32. This fish illustrates the technique for smooth carving.

WOOD SCULPTURE

When carving becomes fully three-dimensional, it makes the transition from craft to art. While the tool-handling techniques already described are important, this work requires more of an appreciation of form from an artistic viewpoint—something not everyone possesses.

Relief carving uses a third dimension to a limited extent, through the various devices used to give an effect of depth—but it is just an effect. In wood sculpture the third dimension is in equal proportion to the other measurements. When the carving stands alone without a background, it should look right when viewed from any angle. This makes thinking in terms of the pictorial representations used to lay out flatter carvings obsolete; instead, you must think "in the round." Now, this is easier for some than it is for others. But those without this ability may get enough satisfaction from carving more orthodox work, concentrating more on craftsmanship than artistic ability. Those who aspire to sculpting in wood often have little need for written instructions once they have mastered the technique, depending on their artistic sense rather than relying on conventional designs.

It may be possible to work from sketches—but no flat drawing can give all the vital dimensional information. However, a drawing showing more than one view (Fig. 9-33A) will provide a start. It might be useful to include one or more sections (Fig. 9-33B). Using two main views could easily result in a carving that is too square, unless they are supplemented with a drawing of sections or other views to indicate where rounding is needed and how much.

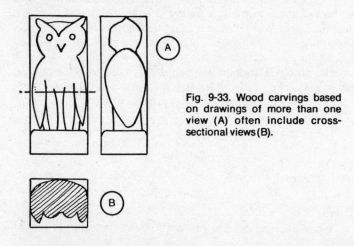

Fig. 9-33. Wood carvings based on drawings of more than one view (A) often include cross-sectional views (B).

What may look thin on a flat drawing may seem thicker when carved. Instead of a drawing, or more to supplement it, the design may also be modeled in clay. The clay model need not be very detailed, but it should be accurate enough to verify the general proportions as drawn or visualized. The clay can be altered to allow the design to be modified accordingly. Some carvers whittle a block of soap with a knife to provide a first model, instead of using clay.

Even more important than in carving panels is having the wood supported firmly and securely, preferably where you can walk all around it, or on something that can be turned easily. It is helpful to have a fairly large, flat base that can be screwed down or held in a vise, even if at a later stage most of it is carved away. Plan to include a broad base as a part of the design.

Some carvers find their most satisfying artistic outlet in carving very small wood sculptures. Others favor more massive pieces. A large block of wood that is suitable for carving can be quite expensive. If the carver of large figures isn't sure he can sell what he produces, he must be prepared to support a fairly costly hobby. Smaller pieces of wood without flaws are much easier to obtain, and their price is better than proportionately less than that of large pieces. Your first figure should not be too small. A block of wood 4 inches square and 6 inches high will afford satisfying work with average-size tools. (The effect of grain is the same in any size piece of wood.) Skill is needed in working small pieces with narrower tools, to keep the grain from "taking charge" and causing cuts to diverge in different directions uncontrollably. When working larger pieces with larger tools, the grain form is less of a consideration.

The wood used need not be square at the start. For some figure carving it is interesting to take a piece of twisted log and carve it according to whatever its form suggests. However, at first start with wood that has flat surfaces and square corners.

Transfer the outlines from the two-directional drawing to one surface of the wood *only*. If this was done on a second face, the lines would be cut off in the first shaping. It would be helpful to make a mirror copy of the first outline on the far side as well. Cut the outline with the greatest amount of detail first. A band saw will do the cleanest and easiest job. If the outline has to be chopped out, make a number of saw cuts almost to the outline and remove the waste between them (Fig. 9-34A). This will reduce the risk of splits developing and going into the carving.

When the profile is cut to shape on one side of the wood, mark the outline of the other view to one side of the first. Because the second side to be marked is no longer flat (Fig. 9-34B), most of the marking may have to be done freehand, using measurements from the drawing. Cut to the second outline.

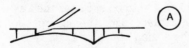
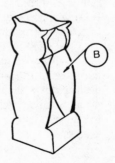

Fig. 9-34. Making saw cuts to the first outline and removing the waste between them (A) will reduce the risk of the wood splitting; the outline of the second view will have to be drawn on a surface that is no longer flat (B).

At this stage the outline is correct in only two directions. If you have made a drawing of the view in a third direction (say, from the top) sketch in its shape and cut away to its outline. For many figures it is difficult—sometimes impossible—to make a satisfactory drawing of a view in the third direction.

The next step is to remove the bulk of the waste wood until the general shape is right, without reducing it to its finished size, and without including the finer details. This is done mostly with a fairly wide, deep gouge and mallet; other tools will be needed for special shapes later. From this point, your drawings will be of little use. But a clay model will help to indicate where to remove excess wood.

Although it is natural to proceed cautiously, don't be too timid. Decide on a cut and make it—rather than nibble away small amounts. Keep the points of the gouge above the surface and make most of the cuts to remove waste across or diagonal to the grain. Initial shaping leaves the wood with a square cross section. By the time you remove enough waste to get the general shape, there should be very little squareness left. There should be little evidence of the cuts made straight across, although some of the original cuts may be left at key points, if the original outline is needed for guidance.

Drill out most of the waste between legs and other parts that have to be separated. It may be possible to use a power saw on a large carving, but for most carving it is better to rely on a keyhole saw. Follow with chisels and gouges to separate legs, make spaces under bodies, or to get through places between other carved parts. Be careful of the grain direction inside openings when using edged tools. A fine knife may be better than a carving tool for removing waste from narrow places, such as where legs meet.

When the figure has the general shape of the overall design, look at it from every angle. If any excess wood remains, remove it before doing any finishing elsewhere. However, some extra wood may have to be left near the base to provide strength for work at a later stage. Although most of the final shaping of a figure can usually be done by paring, a mallet may be needed for some parts, depending on the hardness of the wood. Beginners will find it is easier to get a desired cut without using a mallet. There is less control of the direction and depth of a cut when the tool is hit with a mallet. Facial details can be difficult, and may have to be left until greater skill is acquired.

The finish given to the surface is a matter of choice. Wood sculpture is art, the expression of the carver—not a slavish copy of some standard design. Consequently, the final surface treatment is the individual's choice.

While figure carving based on traditional lines will never (hopefully) lose its appeal, there is a faction among carvers that uses smooth, symbolic outlines as indications of natural forms, without attempting any detail. Some of the carvings are purely abstract, their appreciation depending on how "sophisticated" or esthetically aware the viewer is. The technique used is rather different from any discussed up to this point in that little use is made of normal carving tools. The method is an extension of that described for carving a fish in relief. Drawings of views in two planes may be used as a guide, but most of the shaping is done with a saw, a plane, and surface-forming tools, according to the dictates of the carver's imagination.

CARVING AND TURNING

The craftsman who can combine carving and turning in his work will produce very individual pieces of furniture. Parts of the same piece may be turned and carved, but it is turned and carved wood that provides scope for the exercise and expression of individual skill. The traditional woodwork of more leisurely times included turned and carved legs, pedestals, and other parts.

Normally, all the turning is done before the work is removed from the lathe and carved. If the lathe has a dividing attachment, it can be used to space points around the work's circumference equally—an essential step in marking out the many parts of a turned-wood carving.

Another way to divide the circumference is to wrap a strip of paper around the wood and prick a hole through its overlapping ends (Fig. 9-35A), then unfurl it and divide the space between the holes into the required number of divisions.

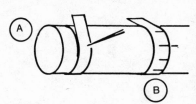

Fig. 9-35. The circumference of a turned piece to be carved can be equally segmented. Wrap a strip of paper around the wood and punch a hole through the overlapping ends (A). Then, after marking the strip with the required number of divisions, replace it over the wood and transfer the marks.

The paper is put back in place, and the marks are transferred to the wood (Fig. 9-35B). For some work it may be necessary to do this at several different diameters. It may be possible to draw lines lengthwise between the points with a pencil held against the lathe's tool.

Precautions have to be taken to avoid damaging a round part with a holding device. If the wood is supported between lathe centers, something has to be done to prevent it from turning. Some lathes have a locking headstock spindle. If yours is not one of these, it may be possible to prevent rotation by putting a strap over the wood and holding it down with a foot put through a loop in its end. If the turning has to be removed from the lathe, it might rest in a trough held by a similar strap (Fig. 9-36).

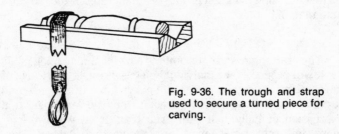

Fig. 9-36. The trough and strap used to secure a turned piece for carving.

Legs with straight flutes around them (Fig. 9-37), found on many pieces of antique furniture, may have to be made for the

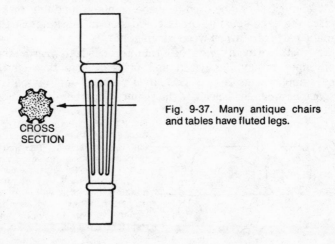

CROSS
SECTION

Fig. 9-37. Many antique chairs and tables have fluted legs.

repair or reproduction of such pieces. Careful marking out is important. Cut the end of a flute by pressing a gouge straight in, then lowering its angle to scoop out wood. Pencil lines determine the width of the flute; the curve of the gouge determines its depth. Work from both ends. If there is only a moderate taper to the flute, one gouge can be used throughout its length. As the flute narrows, the gouge does not cut as deeply. If there is very much of a taper, it may be necessary to change gouges, using a narrower one to regulate the tapered depth.

If a flute is very long, it may be easier to gouge only the ends and remove the part between them with a hollow plane. Flutes should be fairly deep to benefit from the effect of lighting. Instead of flutes there may be beads, rounded at the top with grooves between them.

Another variation of this sort of linear decoration is the twisted flute or bead (Fig. 9-38A). Although this may seem more difficult than straight fluting or beading, there is the advantage of slight flaws or inaccurate cuts being less obvious in the finished work. The two ends of the carved part are divided into the same number of sections. There is no rule about the amount of twist.

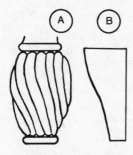

Fig. 9-38. All the twisted flutes or beads (A) for a piece can be produced from a template with the desired curve (B).

Experiment with a string stretched between pins at each end of the work to see the effect of various amounts of slope. Too much twist should be avoided. A slope of no more than 30° to the carving's central axis should be about right. Mark in a suitable curve, either along the string or freehand. Although using string as a guide may be satisfactory, the curve will look more graceful if it straightens toward the ends. Make a cardboard template with the outline of the curve you want (Fig. 9-38B) and use it to mark all the other lines. Except for the need to watch changes in grain direction, carving a twist is little different from carving the same type of cut lengthwise.

Of course, many turned things can be carved in various forms of relief. A bowl, for example, could have a pattern of leaves around it, either all over or just as a border. Or it could have a chip-carved pattern. Incised carving, and other simple carving, is sometimes more effective on a curved surface than on a flat one.

A ball-and-claw foot (Fig. 9-39A) is a design feature seen on the legs of many Queen Anne chairs and tables. The turned foot has to be made large enough to allow for the carving of the claws.

Although the ball has to be round, the lathe cannot do much in shaping it because of the claws. However, if the recesses between claws that form the ball are kept the same depth before carving the claws, the ball should qualify as spherical. As a guide, holes can be made with a drill without a spur and fitted with a depth stop (Fig. 9-39B). Then, the waste can be cut out almost to the full depth. This clears the surrounding wood for carving the claws, then the ball can be cut to size, using a cardboard template as a guide (Fig. 9-39C).

Making chessmen is a popular turning exercise. The greater part of all of them can be turned, but several parts need a little carving; the horse's head of the knight calls for skill. Of course, there is no need to follow conventional (Staunton) designs exactly. Sets of chessmen with very different designs give more scope for carving, but at first, keep to the usual design.

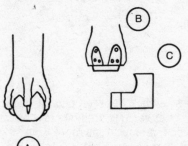

Fig. 9-39. The ball in a ball-and-claw foot for a furniture leg (A) is carved by first drilling holes between the claws (B) to a uniform depth, then using a template (C) to get the shape.

The best chessmen are made from very hard wood, such as box (genus *Buxus*) and ebony. The carving has to be done with very sharp tools, following the removal of waste with a saw or file. Start with pieces of a reasonable size, say, for a set with a 4 inch king (Fig. 9-40). Most of the handwork is simple notchings. The horse's (knight's) head may be given a nearly conventional form with a few cuts, or you could attempt to make it more lifelike in appearance.

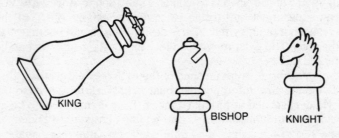

Fig. 9-40. The king for a chess set can be simply turned and notched; the knight requires skillful freehand work.

In carving any number of turned parts, it is always advisable to work in assembly line fashion on parts that should match. If a carving is to be asymetrical, it is usual to make matching complementary pairs. For example, if the design is leaves entwining around a post, their direction will be opposite between a pair of bulbous legs. They should go in opposite directions between adjoining legs. In a set of four, of course, two will have the twist one way; the other two, the other way.

TWIST TURNING

An intriguing combination of turning and carving is seen in so-called twist turning. There are machines that can produce the twists, but machine-made twist turnings cannot equal the variety of handmade ones. The twist can be likened to the thread of the "screw nail" (shown in Fig. 6-1H). The twist is also like that of a screw in that it has a *pitch*: distance between the top of one thread and the top of the next.

When planning a twist turning, the important considerations are the number of parts, the pitch, and the depth of the twist. Because wood is stronger with the grain than across it, you have to consider strength. A twist with a short pitch—the twist is fairly "tight"—will have a lot of short grain that is liable to crack under a load. At the other extreme, a very long pitch will give strength, but may not be very attractive. The depth of the hollows must also be considered. A good depth improves appearance; but in a leg that has to support much weight, very deep grooves could seriously weaken the wood.

A twist of moderate pitch and depth will suit most purposes. A single twist with a pitch about equal to the diameter of the wood is a good configuration to start with. You can experiment by turning twisted candlesticks. Lay out the twists on a plain cylinder; any design chosen can be turned at the ends. The twist may blend into the ends, or hollows can be turned there (Fig. 9-41A).

Draw lines, from one end of the cylinder to the other, that divide the circumference into quarters. Mark lines around the cylinder, spaced at pitch distances. They do not have to be as wide apart as the diameter, but can be arranged to give even spacing in the length available. However, make the spacing more than the diameter, rather than less, for the specimen carving. The lines may be drawn with a pencil held against the tool rest of the lathe as the wood is turned around. If the circles have to be marked without the aid of a lathe, draw them along the straight edge of a piece of cardboard wrapped around the cylinder.

There are several ways of marking the twist. The first line should mark the apex of the twist (Fig. 9-41B), and may be sketched freehand. Starting at the end of one straight line, the twist has to make a complete turn before it touches the same line at a "pitch circle." It therefore crosses the longitudinal lines at one-quarter, one-half, and three-quarters of the pitch. After these points are marked, join them with freehand pencil lines (Fig. 9-41C) going from pitch line to pitch line, to the other end of the twist.

One way to get a more accurate line is to pin down a thread that goes through the marks (Fig. 9-41D). But a strip of cardboard would afford a firmer edge to hold a pencil against (Fig. 9-41E); it will not lie flat in its helical path around the wood, but its edge, at least, can be kept in contact with the work. Another cardboard guide—which will lie flat—is a truncated triangle with edges equal to the pitch and circumference (Fig. 9-41F); it can be wrapped around the wood so the twist can be marked between the sections outlined by pitch circles.

Two other lines have to be marked, one on each side of the first line drawn to establish the width of the twist for the initial shaping. They are spaced a quarter of the circumference to each side of the first line. The part to be hollowed out will be between these lines, which should be labeled to avoid confusion later. This completes the marking out.

The lathe can be used to support the work while the twist is cut. Support the wood firmly by tightening the centers, and get the tool rest out of the way. An alternative to this, one particularly successful if the work has a square section, is to hold it in a vise; if a round part has to be held, pad it well. (A trough and strap could also be used.) For the first step, sawing, hold the wood against a bench hook with one hand.

How waste wood is first removed depends on the size of the job. A V-shaped groove has to be cut around the cylinder. For moderate-sized work, this is done by cutting alternate sides of the groove at an angle with a fine backsaw (Fig. 9-41G). This has to be done in stages as the work is turned around for each cut and small V-shaped pieces are removed. The cuts should not be deeper than the hollow will be. For a small twist the waste could be removed with a V-sectioned tool; it has to be used in stages and kept sharp, because one side will be working against the grain. Once a light, preliminary cut has been made, cut one side of the groove with the grain, then reverse the tool and cut the other side.

The twist has now been roughly cut to shape. Further steps are aimed at getting the final shape. This involves two stages: hollowing the groove evenly; and rounding the top of the twist. Round the bottom of the groove with a gouge that has a curve deep enough to keep its corners clear of the wood. Ideally, the gouge's curve should approximate the final hollow, and be almost as wide, so the last shaping stage can be done with a single sweep.

If the grain seems liable to tear up if cut the wrong way, use a gouge narrow enough to work one side of the hollow with the grain, reversing it to do the other side. It may be possible to use a round rasp or file, if it has the right cross section, to follow or take the place of the gouge. During the final shaping, the tool can be used in one hand while the wood is moved around with the other.

The top of the twist can be rounded with a gouge or chisel (Fig. 9-41H)—or even a small block plane—followed by filing and sanding. Follow the line going around from the apex of the twist to keep the work even; do not sand away this line until everything else is satisfactory. Keep the cut even and not too deep. (It is easy to go deeper at one point than another.) A cardboard template (Fig. 9-41I) can be used at several points to check the accuracy of depths and shapes.

Double or triple twists are worked the same way, but they are marked out differently. The pitch may be the same, but

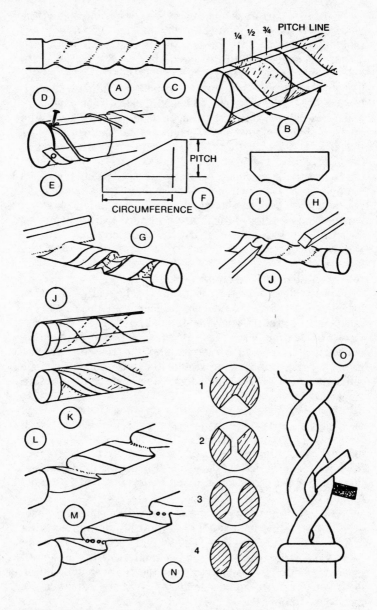

Fig. 9-41. The methods for producing open and closed twist-turnings. (See text for procedures.)

each entwining section travels double or triple this distance in a complete turn. This has the effect of making each twist steeper; the pitch can be reduced, if desired. The depths of the hollows are relatively less with double and triple twists.

To mark a double twist, start with the four lengthwise lines and pitch circles used for a single twist—but also make intermediate marks at eight equidistant positions around the circumference. Draw two helical (spiraling) lines, using any of the methods already described, starting at opposite sides, and each making a complete circuit at double-pitch intervals (Fig. 9-41J).

From each of the eight points around the circumference (which should now be on either side of the lines) draw more helical lines; these will indicate the first width of the entwining sections. Mark the two waste parts as indicated by the unshaded parts of Fig. 9-41K.

From this point the work is like that for a single twist, except waste has to be removed from two hollows. A double twist has a more delicate appearance than a single twist but is just as strong, because the entwining parts are narrower. A triple twist is dealt with similarly, except the main, longitudinal lines divide the circumference into sixths (with 12 intermediate lines). There is no reason why any number of twists couldn't be worked, but it is unusual to have more than three. Only when the wood is very thick, relative to the size of the entwining parts, is a larger number worth considering.

Can this technique be further embellished? Yes, by separating the entwining parts. Although this is usually done with a double twist, it is not impossible with a triple twist; but it calls for greater ingenuity. Of course, separating the entwining parts removes much of the turning's strength, making the method inapplicable for legs and other things that have to take much of a load. It is best to use this method for light constructions whose appearance is more important than strength.

An open double twist is started like an "ordinary" double twist. The bulk of the waste between the outlines of the entwining parts is removed with a saw or V-sectioned tool taken deeper than necessary for a closed twist (Fig. 9-41L). Outside shaping should be left until the hollows are formed and the parts are separated; otherwise, the surface could be damaged by tools while work is done on the inside.

The entwining parts are separated by drilling, followed by carving, or by carving exclusively. Drill a large number of small holes along the center of a groove (Fig. 9-41M), directing the drill toward the center of the other groove. If you want to do this by carving, use a veiner, progressively deepening the center of each groove until the two meet. A combination of the two methods allows the amount of any waste remaining to be seen through the holes. The holes also reduce the risk of splitting that might be caused by the veiner cutting against the grain.

The first opening will be rough, but it can be cleaned with a gouge and chisel; a sharp, fine-bladed knife can be used to shave the insides of the entwining parts. When enough of a gap has been made, work a thin, half-round file diagonally up and down on the insides of the entwining parts to remove inequalities. When the inside has been shaped, work on the outside with a chisel and gouge, as you would a closed twist. Although the parts should be round in cross section when viewed at a right angle to their twist, their section straight across is elliptical; this is shown as the last of a series of steps in Fig. 9-41N. The two twists combine at the ends, just before they go into the now relatively plain remaining parts of the column.

Finally, smooth and round the work with sandpaper. Pull a strip back and forth against the inside surfaces (Fig. 9-41O); but finish all of the wood by sanding lengthwise to remove the marks of previous sanding, as well as any tool marks.

In making a three-part open twist there is the complication of not being able to drill straight through between the sections. The drill has to be directed toward the center. The carving requires patience; you have to avoid cutting into an opposing entwining part when removing wood at the center. A four-part open twist is actually less troublesome: the hollows are opposing pairs, making it possible to drill or carve between them.

The carved parts of a twist-turned piece, whether closed or open, need not be parallel. If the piece to be carved tapers, the whole design will also taper. A twist turning that has an irregular lengthwise section is not usually very attractive. An exception might be a bulbous turning with entwining parts that taper from a thick center toward the ends.

10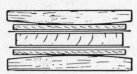

Veneer
and Inlaying

The word *veneering* is applied to the process of gluing thin pieces of wood to thicker, more solid pieces, sometimes to plywood. The method varies according to whether the veneer has been cut thin with a knife, or is the thicker, sawed type. Veneering can give the appearance of expensive decorative wood. In this case, economy is a consideration. Sometimes, veneering may be the only way to use woods that are unsuitable for construction.

Veneer is available in single rectangular panels or, more usually, in pieces with bordered geometric patterns or designs that enhance the beauty of grain when seen at different angles (called *patterned* veneers). The process of using veneers to build up a picture, the grain and color of each contributing to an artistic effect, is called *marquetry* (pronounced *mar*-keh-tree). The term *parquetry* is often applied to similar but boldly geometric patterns on floors built up with wood about ¼ inch thick. It has been applied to Louis XV and XVI furniture as well, in which geometric patterns were built up from the same kind of wood inlaid at different angles.

Veneering with knife-cut veneers can be tackled in the home shop. The use of sawed veneers is limited to small items, because they can only be affixed satisfactorily with the rather large equipment used by industrial furniture makers.

Inlaying differs from veneering in that the wood used to form a pattern is set into the solid wood of the item being decorated, allowing the grain of surrounding wood to show around the inlaid part. The inlaid wood may be only as thick as a veneer, or it can be thicker; but for most purposes there is nothing to be gained by using pieces thicker than ⅛ inch—the greater the thickness, the more labor involved in cutting the recess for it.

KNIFE-CUT VENEERS

Knife-cut veneers can be very thin; some can be stacked 100 to an inch. Very thin veneers allow the average woodworker to use pieces of rare (expensive) wood with attractive grain, but extremely thin veneers may present problems in their application; it is better to work with thicker veneers (no more than $1/32$ inch thick, for example).

Traditionally, veneering was done with natural glues that had to be heated before they could be used—and they were not waterproof. One advantage of these glues, however, was that any surplus could be removed with hot water; also the veneers could be adjusted before the glue set, or removed later by heating the glue. Heated presses were used in commercial veneering to soften the glue, thus allowing the veneer to be bedded down close to the surface being covered. Modern glues for constructional woodwork can also be used for veneering. They should flow smoothly so they can be spread evenly without lumps. They should not get tacky too soon after being applied, so the veneer can be moved as the joint is made.

Veneer can be adversely affected by the expansion and contraction of the base wood. It is best to use a stable hardwood, that is, one inclined to warp and shrink less than a softwood. Yellow pine, a softwood, is an exception that makes a stable base for veneering. Plain Honduras mahogany was chosen in the past because it warps and shrinks very little and, therefore, makes a good base for veneers. Today more use is made of plywood and other manufactured boards, which are even more stable.

Resinous woods should be avoided. And it is best to avoid putting very hard veneers on softwoods; softwoods have a tendency to absorb more than their share of glue. Glues that dry dark will show through very light colored veneers. Often the base wood pulls toward its veneered side as the glue sets, making the finished surface convex. To a certain extent, this can be counteracted by veneering the heart side (i.e., the darker, denser side) of the wood, taking advantage of its tendency to warp the other way; the pull of the glued veneer is counteracted by a natural force.

If the several boards to be glued together to make a wide base have their grain going in alternate directions, any overall tendency to warp will be minimized. Even plywood may pull, particularly if it is comparatively thin and not retained by a frame or molding. This can be counteracted by veneering the back as well. (It does not have to be the same veneer used on the front.) Most of the pull comes from the drying glue and is not as great after the glue has set. If the other side of the base wood is not veneered, it may be enough to dampen it. The moisture, drying out at the same rate as the glue, will produce an opposing force—maybe strong enough to prevent warping.

The background surface should be as flat as possible and free from blemishes that might show through the veneer. Sometimes this happens a long time after the work is done. Small holes can be filled with a mixture of a stopper or filler, glue, and sawdust, or with plaster of Paris. Larger flaws are better dealt with by setting in a piece of similar wood and working it flush with the surrounding surface.

It used to be necessary to roughen the background surface after it was planed and sanded, to provide a foothold for the glue. It still wouldn't hurt to do this, but it is not as important with modern glues because of their greater adhesion. The tool used for roughing the surface is called a toothing plane (Fig. 10-1A), a small plane with a single, nearly upright blade grooved on the face, giving the effect of sawlike teeth. Burrs are left on the edge, when it is sharpened, to help it cut a pattern of close scratches. This is done in crossing directions to give an overall roughness. In traditional veneer laying, thin glue (sizing to fill pores) was spread on the wood and allowed to dry; then more glue was used to hold the veneer. A similar treatment may be needed—particularly on softwoods used in conjunction with modern synthetic glues—to prevent the background wood from absorbing glue excessively.

If a toothing plane is unavailable, a similar effect may be obtained by dragging a backsaw across the wood. A piece of a hacksaw blade may be put in a slot in the end of a strip of wood and used the same way.

Knife-cut veneers are laid with the aid of a veneering hammer (Fig. 10-1B), a tool that can be made easily. Its handle is glued into a part that holds a brass or steel blade about ⅛ inch thick. The edge of the blade is rounded, and the corners are slightly curved to prevent accidental cuts. In spite of its name, the "hammer" is pressed, not swung.

To begin laying on veneer, spread glue quickly and evenly on the base wood with a large brush, then place the veneer in position and stroke it down flat, using the side of your hand.

Dampen the surface with hot water. Hold the hammer by the handle with one hand while pressing against the back of its blade with the other.

Work from the center of the piece outward with a zigzag motion (Fig. 10-1C). Work in several directions. The object here is to press the veneer into good contact with the background surface, squeezing out air bubbles and surplus glue at the same time. Tap the veneer lightly with the hammer handle; a hollow sound means there are blisters or pockets of air below the veneer. Sometimes an air pocket near the middle of a piece cannot be worked out toward the edge. If you are plagued with this predicament, prick the spot with a needle to let the air out, then press down the veneer. With fast-setting, permanent synthetic glues it is necessary to rely on careful workmanship from the beginning; corrections later are impossible.

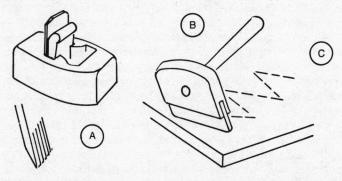

Fig. 10-1. A toothing plane (A) is used to roughen the background surface for veneers; the veneers, specifically thin ones cut with a knife, are pressed into place with a veneering hammer (B) used with a zigzag motion (C).

Let the glue dry fully before going on to anything else. If necessary, weigh down the work or use clamps to prevent warping.

If you are working with thin veneers that have warped, dampen and press them before cutting them to shape. But don't use scissors; they will distort the grain and may cause splits. Thicker veneers may be sawed. A fine backsaw may be satisfactory, but veneer saws (with very fine teeth) work better. One type has a straight blade with a handle curved to the side (Fig. 10-2A); another has a blade with teeth on two sides, held in the middle by a straight handle (Fig. 10-2B). Either of these will make a cut that will need little further treatment to produce a good edge.

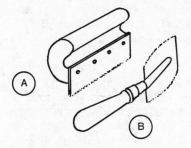

Fig. 10-2. Two types of saws are made for cutting thicker veneers.

SAWED VENEERS

Saw-cut veneers cannot be laid with a hammer, unless they are narrow strips. Instead, they have to be pressed with wood (mahogany, pine, or plywood) or metal pads tightened by clamps (Fig. 10-3) or a special press. For work of moderate size, the pads are flat. For larger work, their faces are rounded, so that as pressure is applied at the sides, the tendency of the wood to flatten will maintain pressure at the center.

Fig. 10-3. Commercially sawed veneers must be pressed into place between wood or metal pads.

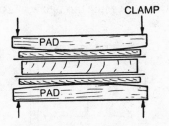

Prepare the veneer and its background in the same way for knife-cut veneers. Apply the glue and locate the veneer. Because any movement of the veneer cannot be seen in the press, hold the parts with pins driven into waste (or inconspicuous) parts. Cover the pads with paper to prevent glue from adhering to them. Soaping the pads will also reduce the risk of glue sticking where it shouldn't. If there are any irregularities in the surfaces, use several layers of paper, or place a piece of cloth behind the paper; these meausres should take care of any unevenness.

As when laying knife-cut veneers, pressure should be spread from the center outward. There is a similar risk of air bubbles being trapped, but (stiffer) sawed veneers are less susceptible to this problem. If you are using several clamps, tighten those near the center before tightening those at the rim.

Metal-strip clamps can be wrapped around curved rims, such as the underside of a round table top, and tightened somewhat like pipe clips. They will pull veneer around many shaped parts. Pads have to be made for complex curves, often one for each side of the job. Veneer can be worked to a moderate compound curve, but this involves careful work on the base wood. The veneer can be dampened to make it flexible, then pressed with a wood pad clamped over a bag of sand molded to fit the desired curve. After a trial assembly, put register marks on the parts so the veneer can be replaced in the same way; then apply glue and clamp the parts together.

PATTERNED VENEERING

Much of the beauty of veneering comes from building up patterns, either of one wood or with a mixture of contrasting colors or grains. Quarter-veneered panels are very popular (Fig. 10-4). They are made of four veneers fastened together with pins going through waste parts.

Fig. 10-4. A quarter-veneered panel with a cross-grained border; the quarter-panels could also be arranged for a radiating-grain effect.

BORDER

To achieve this effect, begin by making a cardboard template of one panel and transfer its dimensions to the top piece of a stack of four veneers; cut through them with a fine saw, leaving a little excess at the edges. Plane the meeting surfaces for an accurate fit. Turn two of the veneers over to get the diamond pattern shown. (They could also be turned to get a radiating-grain pattern.) Butt the panels together and tack strips of paper over the joints with glue, or use adhesive paper; a strip of transparent adhesive plastic will keep the joint visible. Apply glue to the background and fix the assembly, using the hammer as you would for a single sheet. After the glue sets, peel off the (temporary) strips at the joints. Trim the edges. The veneers can be planed with a finely set, low-angle steel plane on a shooting board; hold down the veneers with a strip of wood when you do this.

The completed panel may be given a border of veneer cut across the grain (shown in the illustration). Several pieces may have to be mitered at the corners and butted together along a side. A space can be cleared on the background wood for the border by cutting away strips of veneer with a knife held against a steel rule, then peeling off the waste veneer and scraping away glue.

If you want to make a more complicated pattern, draw the pattern on paper and fit the parts to it, and to each other, by carefully cutting, filing, and sanding their edges. One piece of veneer can be duplicated by cutting it on top of another with a fine fretsaw; the thickness of the kerf will be too slight to affect the appearance of the final joint. Building up the design on paper first is particularly appropriate if there are curved lines involved.

INLAYING

Much use has been made in the past of inlaid bands, both in veneered work and in solid wood. An inlaid band is constructed of many pieces of veneer that form a pattern. In production work they used to be formed by gluing many long strips of wood edge-to-edge and cutting across them perpendicularly. Today more variations are available (Fig. 10-5A).

A simple herringbone pattern (Fig. 10-5B) is made by cutting diagonally across the grain of a sheet of veneer, then turning every other piece around and joining them.

Although an inlaid band could be included in a pattern made by other means, it can also be set into the surface of veneer or solid wood. The sides of the groove needed to accommodate the band are cut with a knife and steel rule, or a

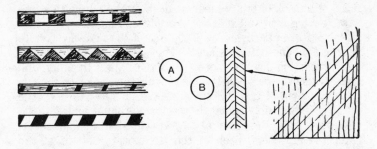

Fig. 10-5. Commercially produced inlaid bands are available in several patterns (A); the herringbone pattern is made by joining several pieces (C) cut diagonally across the grain of one piece (B).

cutting gage (Fig. 10-6A) if the band is to be parallel to an edge. The waste within the groove has to be cleared out to the depth of the band. If the surface has been veneered with a glue that will soften when heated, a hot iron may be drawn along the surface to soften the glue, allowing the waste strip to be lifted. Alternatively, the waste can be removed from both veneer and solid wood with a *scratch stock*: a scraper so mounted that its distance from an edge can be controlled. It can be used in place of the point of a marking gage (Fig. 10-6B), and consists of a piece of tool steel having a ground end (in various widths) that is sharpened to a burr for a scraping action. Tilting the gage allows fine adjustment of the required depth.

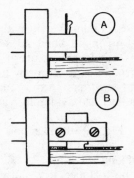

Fig. 10-6. The groove for an inlaid band may be cut parallel to an edge with a standard cutting gage (A) or one fitted with a scratch stock (B).

Another form of inlay that can be built up is a pattern of alternate squares of different colors. A chess board can be made by first gluing nine strips of alternating colors side by side. Nine may sound like a strange number for a chess board—being far from the square root of sixty-four—but nine strips are needed so they can be staggered (Fig. 10-7A).

This method is suitable for making patterns of veneer on plywood (or other background), or it can be applied to patterns made of thicker wood.

This is a good opportunity to use odd scraps of veneer. Use the pattern you have chosen to mark the size of the pieces of veneer; their grain can be arranged to complement the radiating pattern of flower petals, the textured appearance of leaves, and so forth. Most of the outlines of the recesses will probably have to be cut with gouges and chisels. A knife—held against a rule—can be used on long, straight lines. Remove the waste to the required depth by carefully working with chisels, used (mostly) bevel-downward. For knife-cut veneers, the recesses will be quite shallow. For sawed veneers, it will not be necessary to go the full depth of the veneer. A little can be left projecting to be sanded off after gluing.

The pieces for the inlay may be cut from knife-cut veneers with a knife, or a number of similar ones may be cut together with a fretsaw. Sawed veneers may be sawed to shape, followed by planing, filing, and sanding their edges to fit the recesses.

Besides veneers, thin pieces of other kinds of wood may be inlaid. Some woodworkers find these alternatives to veneer easier to shape and handle. If the edge of a piece is given a bevel that slopes outward from its underside, and the size of recess is derived from the bottom of the bevel, the inlay will tighten in its recess as it is pressed in (Fig. 10-7B). Of course,

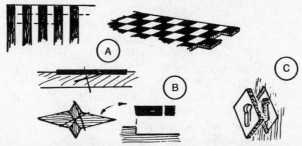

Fig. 10-7. A chess board is made by joining staggered patterned bands whose squares have been cut from nine strips (of veneer, e.g.) of two colors (A). Beveling the edge of an inlay will make it fit tightly (B). The escutcheon for a keyhole could be an inlay of a material other than wood (C).

the joints between adjacent inlays should be upright. Leave a little to sand level afterward.

It is possible to inlay other things into wood besides wood. Mother-of-pearl inlays were used in some antique furniture. Various metals have also been used. Another method uses semiliquid inlays. Colored sealing waxes, for example, can be heated and poured into shallow drilled holes, then sanded level and polished along with the surrounding wood after it hardens. Plastic sheeting can be used like mother-of-pearl. Plain or patterned hard plastic sheeting can be inlaid at a point to prevent wear, or it can be shaped for purely decorative purposes. The escutcheon (plate) surrounding a keyhole could be an inlay (Fig. 10-7C).

MARQUETRY

Building up pictures in wood requires a large range of veneers. A variety of colors and markings can be used to emphasize individual features. Although veneers are sometimes dyed or their edges charred for special effects, a marquetry enthusiast usually tries to get most of his effects with natural wood only. Suppliers specializing in marquetry veneers offer a very large range of woods in standard' thicknesses and stock sizes.

If natural woods are used exclusively, the craftsman's palette will necessarily be limited—blue-green, or violet woods just do not occur naturally. So the picture has to be planned with this limitation in mind. Surprisingly, there are some rarer woods available as veneers that have quite bright, naturally red or yellow colors. Some woods are nearly black; others, nearly white. The clever use of very light and dark woods can make the other woods in the picture more effective.

The usual base for a marquetry picture is a sheet of plywood. A thin piece should be prevented from distorting by veneering its back with material as thick as the pieces used for the picture. There are several ways of forming the picture. Pieces of veneer can be cut and fitted to a design drawn on the background, and to each other, progressively glued down individually as the work proceeds. Tube glue is convenient for marquetry, because only a comparatively small area has to be glued at a time. Make sure the glue is intended for wood, however.

Make two copies of the design. Trace one onto the backing board, and use the other to mark the shapes of the veneers. Cut the veneers with a knife and trim them to shape with a fine file or sandpaper. Cut and fit the larger parts first (say, the sky and mountains in a scene). That way, if the smaller parts don't fit. not much wood will be wasted. Trial and error may have to be the method used to get the desired grain effect.

Instead of sticking each piece to the background as it is cut, the whole picture may be built up first, then glued down as one assembly. This allows more scope for artistic expression; the overall effect can be examined before it is made permanent. If the first assembly seems to need a different veneer somewhere, another one can be easily substituted. Masking tape, or any tape that can be peeled off without leaving a residue, is used to hold the parts together. This has to be done on what will be the front, so the picture has to be examined for the effect on what will be the back.

A knife tends to "squeeze out" the surface where it enters (Fig. 10-8A). This means that the best side of the cut for marquetry is on the other side, that is, opposite the knife's point of entry. For the most precise edges it is better to cut from what will be the back of the picture. To do this, mark out the picture on the back of the veneer, using a reverse copy of the design. Cut the parts for the picture and mount them on pieces of masking tape (Fig. 10-8B). The result, a mirror image of the final picture, allows design details to be checked and corrected if required. When everything is satisfactory, turn the completed picture over on the glue-covered background and fit it in place like a complete veneer.

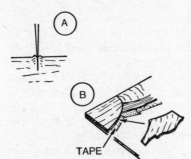

Fig. 10-8. Because a knife tends to squeeze out the surface around the cut (A), it is best to cut pieces for marquetry from the back; for preassembled work, they are mounted face-down on masking tape (B) before being transferred face-up to the background.

TAPE

Veneers can be cut with a fretsaw machine to produce matching bevels that will fit together perfectly. Extremely fine blades—those really intended for cutting metal—are needed for thin veneers; sawed veneers should be cut with thicker blades to reduce the risk of breaking the surface. The sawing table is set so the veneers are cut at a slight angle (Fig. 10-9A); how much of an angle depends on the thickness of the blade. An experiment with two thicknesses of scrap veneer will show what angle is needed. When two (or more) pieces of veneer are sandwiched together and cut to a shape, the lower piece should fit flush next to the top one, resulting in a completely closed joint (Fig. 10-9B).

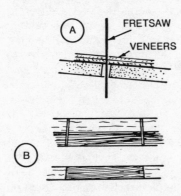

Fig. 10-9. The edges of two or more veneers can be beveled with the fretsaw's cutting table set at a slight angle (A), resulting in a very accurate fit when they are butted together (B).

Few pictures look their best unframed. A framed effect can be obtained for marquetry by laying down strips of veneer on the picture's background. A frame made of strips cut across the grain (Fig. 10-10A) will more strongly direct the eye toward the picture than one made of strips having grain going lengthwise. It is important that the grain be even around the border. If the grains do not make a reasonable match, the picture will seem distorted. The corners of the frame can be mitered by cutting one strip of veneer on top of another as they are held to a right angle (Fig. 10-10B). Another way to arrange the grain in the border is to make it appear to radiate from the picture. This is done by cutting four right-angled pieces diagonally to the grain and butting them together, forming joints halfway along each side of the picture (Fig. 10-10C). Yet another way to frame the picture is to create the illusion that it has been set into a solid piece of wood. How? By cutting a hole in a large veneer to fit the picture (Fig. 10-10D). Another way to get the same effect is to cut pieces with lengthwise grain for the sides of the picture, matching cross-grained pieces for the top and bottom, then assembling them around the picture. If the panel is to be free-standing, the back and edges could be veneered with the same type of wood. Some pictures may have a border that touches the pictorial part, but often a more striking effect can be obtained by putting a light or dark strip (depending on the artwork) around the picture before framing it (Fig. 10-10E).

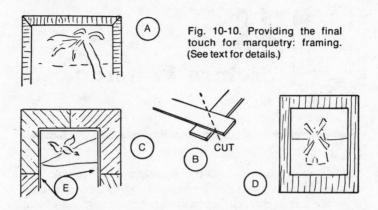

Fig. 10-10. Providing the final touch for marquetry: framing. (See text for details.)

Marquetry has to be sanded to a level surface. Thin veneers dictate very light sanding. It is obviously impossible to sand every piece with the grain, but sanding by hand with a circular motion, and finishing with a very fine grit, should leave no scratches large enough to be visible at normal viewing distances. Although polishing is definitely called for, a high gloss is inappropriate to most marquetry. Instead, it should be waxed to a light sheen, both for appearance and to keep out dirt. The completed marquetry may be mounted in a regular picture frame, but it is best not to use glass.

11

Picture Framing

Making picture frames with molding seems, offhand, to be a simple matter of cutting miters and fitting them together. In principle this is correct, but skill is required to make a neat job. And there are some secondary considerations not immediately obvious. Some craftsmen call themselves picture framers—and claim nothing more than that. So there is obviously more craftsmanship involved in picture framing than the beginner might suspect.

MOLDING

Most pictures are framed with manufactured moldings, of which there is a great variety. A visit to an art gallery will evidence the ornate types favored in the past. We may have little use for them in the home today, but similar types are still being manufactured. Finished moldings—that is, stained and polished—require care to avoid damaging the surface in making the frame.

The important part of a picture-frame molding is the rebate. It is easier to make strong corner joints if the wood outside the rebate is broad than if it is narrow or has been cut away too much to make a pattern (Fig. 11-1A). The rebate need not be very wide, but it should be deep enough to take the glass, picture, backboard, and, possibly, a mount between the picture and glass (Fig. 11-1B). The backboard should be set deep enough into the rebate to provide space for nailing and for a paper covering to keep out dust.

The alternative to buying molding is to make it. While it is better to buy the more elaborate patterns, simple designs can

344

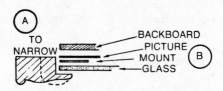

Fig. 11-1. The corner joints of a picture frame can only be strong if the area outside the rebate in its molding is wide enough (A); the rebate has to be wide enough to take the sandwich of parts it must hold (B).

be made that will give individuality to a frame. The rebate should be made first. If the rebate is worked on the edge of a piece of wood wider than necessary, the work can be gripped in a vise for hand planing—or to keep fingers away from a power cutter. Then it can be cut to the size required.

Although the vital measurement is the size of the picture that will be inside the rebate, molding made in a single piece should be a little longer than the total outside size; making molding in sections (Fig. 11-2A) may result in slight discrepancies at the joints.

For things like certificates and small photographs, a plain, narrow molding is appropriate (Fig. 11-2B). Except for careful surface finishing, there is little special work required in producing moldings for this type of frame. Slightly more advanced than this is a flat molding with a bevel sloping toward the picture (Fig. 11-2C); the thinnest part of the edge that touches the glass should be at least $^1/_{16}$ inch. A further step is to work a bead around the outside (Fig. 11-2D).

Spindle cutters or planes can be used for a more elaborate molding. But the molding should be designed with these tools in mind, rather than devising a design first—only to find later that you don't have the tools to execute it. Nearly all picture molding is thicker at the outside than it is next to the picture (Fig. 11-2E). This has the effect of leading the eye into the picture. For certain pictures, however, and for a modern appearance, the opposite effect may be desirable (Fig. 11-2F). Some moldings are deeper than they are wide (Fig. 11-2G), but it is usually better to keep the molding as shallow as the thickness required for the rebate, within the limitations of the design.

Besides stock picture moldings, those sold by specialist suppliers, pine molding sold by lumberyards for trim (around doors, etc.) can also be used. These flat moldings can be

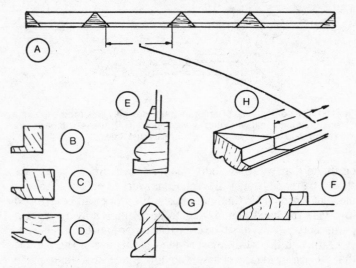

Fig. 11-2. Various ways moldings can be treated for picture frames: a molding made into sections for a frame (A); the cross section of molding commonly used to frame certificates, and a beveled variation (C); a molding with a bead (D); a molding used to make a frame slant toward the picture (E), and one that slants away (F); molding that is deeper than it is wide (G); key measurements marked along the rebate (G).

backed with a piece into which a rebate can be cut. Some can be combined to give interesting shapes.

The size of a molding has to be related to the associated picture. Although it is fairly safe to assume that wider moldings are suitable for bigger pictures, there are exceptions. Quite often a small picture has a wide mount and a wide molding. Usually, if a picture has no mount or has only a narrow one, its molding is narrow. A narrow frame over a wide mount does not usually look right, regardless of the size of the picture.

The vital size is that of the recess produced when the frame is assembled. It should provide an easy fit for the glass, the picture, and the mount—but not so easy that they move around (making your work look sloppy). A margin of about $^1/_{16}$ inch oversize should do, or just a little more for a really large frame. The key measurements are marked along the rebate (Fig. 11-2H). Mark out opposing moldings at the same time. A frame that is out of true by only a small amount, because opposite sides are not an exact match, can be all too obvious to the viewer.

346

JOINTS

The miter has to be a 45° angle if the joint is to be tight—no more, no less. It could be marked with a miter square and cut with a backsaw without a special guide, but even the most skilled worker may wander slightly from the line. Most picture frame miters are cut with something to control the saw. The simplest are the miter block and miter box.

The miter box gives better control than the block because of the widely spaced guides that hold the saw at the correct angle. A miter box made entirely of wood will have a reasonably long life, depending on how much it is used. Always back the molding being cut with a piece of scrap wood to keep the saw teeth from damaging the bottom of the miter box. There is bound to be some wear on the slots, which will lead to inaccuracy. Some miter boxes have adjustable metal guides that keep the saw teeth only in contact with wood (Fig. 11-3A). Other versions have roller guides. Some are adjustable to allow other angles to be cut, making them suitable for octagonal and hexagonal frames.

The basic miter-sawing guide relies on the molding being held either by hand or by a separate clamp. There is an obvious advantage in having a built-in clamp to prevent the wood being cut from moving. Some sawing guides have a dual-purpose clamp. The molding is held by one part of the clamp for sawing; the corner joint can be held by both parts of the clamp (Fig. 11-3B) during the frame's assembly. It is better to cut from the front so you can keep an eye on surface to make sure it is not damaged as the saw breaks through; however, cutting the other way makes it easier to watch the cut in relation to the length marked inside the rebate.

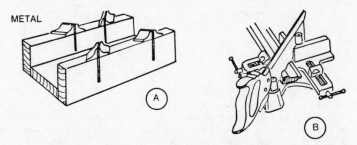

METAL

Fig. 11-3. Mitering guides: a miter box with metal saw guides (A); a guide with a clamp to hold the work being mitered (B) and later to hold the resulting joint.

With a fine-toothed backsaw it is often satisfactory to leave the end as sawed, assuming it is accurate and the face of the cut is clean. When the joint is glued, the slightly rough surface left by the saw will provide a good bond. With larger molding, or when the saw cut is behind the final line, it is necessary to plane or chisel the miter. Using a chisel without a guide can lead to unevenness. It is better to use a plane on a shooting board. There are shooting boards for miters that have a swinging knife controlled by a long handle, giving the effect of a controlled chisel cut.

Check the size of the sides in relation to the glass, mount, and backboard. Check opposite sides of the frame against each other to insure uniformity. Make a trial assembly as a check for appearance. Do not rush into the final assembly until you are certain the joints will make a close fit.

CLAMPING

The joint for a small frame is usually made with glue and one or more fine nails crossing each other at the corner (Fig. 11-4A). The nails should be the type with a minimal head. For the best finish, punch the nails below the surface and cover their heads with stopping. With lighter moldings, or for nails that will be near the outside apex of the joint, drill slightly undersize holes first, to reduce the risk of splitting during nailing. Another way to strengthen the joint is to put pieces of veneer into saw cuts across the miter (Fig. 11-4B).

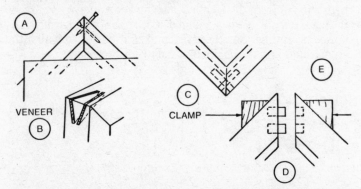

Fig. 11-4. The parts for small frames are usually joined with glue and nails (A); the joint can be strengthened with strips of veneer fitted into slots in the corners (B). Very large frames might be assembled with dowels, either staggered and crossing at the joints (C), or parallel, at a right angle to the joint (D); in this case, triangular pieces are glued to the corners so they can be clamped (E).

Very large frames with thick moldings may be assembled with dowels. The dowels can be staggered in both directions (Fig. 11-4C), or they can be at a right angle to the joint cut (Fig. 11-4D). This is a good way to make a very strong joint without marring the surface, but clamping it is a problem. The only way to draw this type of joint closed is to glue on triangular pieces to take C clamps (Fig. 11-4E).

Corrugated fasteners that are driven into the back of a mitered joint grip well and, in effect, pull the edges together. Even those not considered cabinetmaking devices will work well in these circumstances.

The two adjoining sides of a frame can be merely held in a vise while the glued surfaces are nailed together, but this leaves too much to the skill of the craftsman and does not afford very precise control. The members of a frame can be clamped together without store-bought equipment. Four strips of wood, somewhat shorter than the sides of the frame, can be nailed or screwed to the bench (or a strong board) to surround the frame an inch or so from it. The frame is put inside with the backboard, to help hold its shape, and tightened within the strips with folding wedges (Fig. 11-5A) until the glue has set. Put paper under each corner to prevent excess glue from gripping the baseboard.

Instead of using wedges, the work can be held by eccentric cams (Fig. 11-5B). If a lot of picture framing is anticipated, the baseboard can have a series of holes so the dowels (axles) for the cams can be positioned according to the size of the frame being clamped.

Another rather basic way of pulling a frame together is to tie a cord around it, preferably with wood blocks at the corners (Fig. 11-5C). The cord may be tightened by twisting a Spanish windlass, or wedges can be forced under it. The blocks that enclose the corners can have large holes to allow nails to be inserted and punched in.

Several clamping devices are closely related to the cord-and-blocks arrangement. Most are metal corner pieces used with a strap (flat or round, and made of metal or plastic) held with a tensioning device. One has a screw at one corner (Fig. 11-5D); others use a ratchet on one side (Fig. 11-5E).

There are a variety of corner clamps for individual situations, some of which include a saw guide. Some have screws on the outside (Fig. 11-5G), providing good clearance for driving nails, but they don't push joints together; the parts

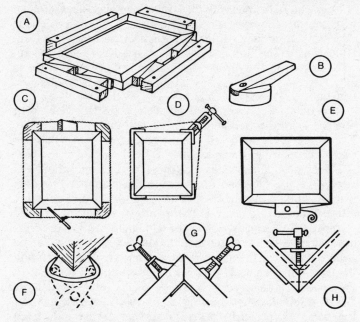

Fig. 11-5. Various ways a frame can be clamped for assembly and gluing.

have to be pushed together by hand before the screws can be tightened. But in practice this works satisfactorily.

If a corner clamp is to pull the parts of one corner together, the force needed should be applied from inside the corner. This has been done in a number of ways, but most clamps press against the rebate when a screw (diagonal to the corner) is tightened; this is a good arrangement (Fig. 11-5H), because any marks left will be on the rebate where they can't be seen.

Nearly all picture frames have simple miters, but for exceptionally heavy construction, it is best to use stronger joints. Actually, there is no other choice if a miter is to look neat from the front. The corner can be mitered for a *halving* joint (Fig. 11-6A), but this is slightly complicated because of the rebate needed. The overlapping piece at the back gives a broad surface for glue and screws.

A better alternative is a variation of the mortise-and-tenon or bridle joint (Fig. 11-6B), which is even better for gluing. Screws may be driven in from the back to produce a joint that will keep the frame from twisting better than any other.

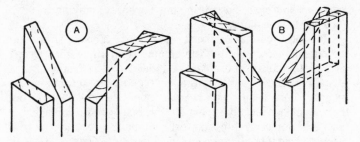

Fig. 11-6. Preparing the corners for mitered **halving** joint (A) is better for heavy frame construction than a simple miter; preparing the parts for a bridle joint (B) is more complicated, but results in an even stronger assembly.

MOUNTING

In Victorian days, Oxford picture frames (Fig. 11-7A) were fashionable. They may not seem very appropriate in a modern setting, but they go well with some antique furniture. This type of construction is a real test of skill; part of the rebates end in the halving joints (Fig. 11-7B), so they cannot be made in a continuous cut like those in ordinary picture molding. For a smaller frame, the rebate must be made carefully by hand. For a larger frame, the ends of each rebate are cut by hand, but the remainder can be planed or worked by machine.

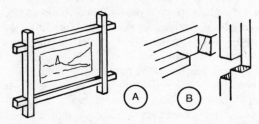

Fig. 11-7. An Oxford frame (A) has parts that fit together in halving joints made between the ends of the molding (B).

Although some photographs or pictures look better when they fill a frame completely, it is more usual to surround them with a border in the form of a mount. It may be cut as an open rectangle from cardboard or stiff paper, or cardboard can be cut to extend beyond the boundaries of the photograph to form a border. A mount may also be cut from veneer, an idea the enthusiastic woodworker may feel more appropriate for his work. In any case, cut the mount carefully, leaving a clean edge around the picture.

It is best to mark on the reverse side of the veneer and cut the outside before cutting the center. If anything goes wrong on the outside, the flaw can be hidden by the frame. But a mistake made in cutting the center means scrapping the mount. There used to be special mount-cutters' knives, but they have been largely superseded by holders with replaceable blades. If you cut against a steel rule, put it over the part that is wanted, so if the blade wanders it goes into waste wood. Cut on a level piece of plywood, across its grain, or diagonally to it; that way, the grain won't grab the knife and direct it away from the cut. Cut the veneer across the grain before cutting it with the grain. When cutting within the frame's opening, cut from the corners. If you are working with thin veneer, try to cut it in one slice. When working along the grain, keep the knife close to the rule, so it is not diverted by the grain.

A frame made from prepared molding that is already polished will need little done to it before putting in the picture. If there is any sign of cut fibers showing against the stained surface of a joint, a little stain dabbed on with a cloth should fix it. If the frame has yet to be stained and polished, there is a choice of doing it before or after assembly. If you do it before assembly, avoid getting polish on surfaces that will still have to be glued. In any case, the stain and polish should be dry and hard before the picture and glass are fitted.

Clean the glass, paying particular attention to getting the inside surface as perfect as possible. Work in a warm, dry atmosphere. Moisture in the wood or in the paper could condense and affect the inside of the glass. Check for dust inside the frame and on all the parts going into it.

Before the days of plywood, picture frames had backboards made of thin pieces of wood, often in several layers with paper glued between the joints to make a greater width. Today it is better to use plywood. Although light, thin plywood may seem attractive, it is better to use something stiff enough to hold an unmounted picture flat. The top grain of the (plywood) backboard should run lengthwise rather than across the width, for greatest stiffness. Also in this vein, make the backboard fit fairly closely in the frame. Clean its edges, so sawdust or chips cannot find their way to the front of the picture.

Place the frame on a flat surface and put a supporting piece against the outside of the frame, facing you. Press the other parts into the frame. Hammer small headless nails (or cut the points off other nails, if necessary) into the frame, toward the supporting strip. Keep the parts pressed down with one hand while sliding the hammer along the backboard to drive the nails (Fig. 11-8A). Do not lift the hammer—it may crack the glass. Drive a nail close to each corner, then turn the frame over to make sure everything looks right from the front.

Use enough nails to press everything flat. Depending on the stiffness of the backboard and other parts, a nail spacing of about 3 inches will probably be right. If you are using light molding, check each side for straightness after it is nailed, and push it back if it has bowed.

The last step is covering the gap between the frame and backboard to keep out dust. Gummed paper tape or adhesive plastic tape can be used. See that its edges bed down close to the frame and board (but don't press on the nails, or they'll break through the tape). If the backboard is a single piece of plywood, of course, there is no need to put paper all over it.

Usually pictures are hung by a wire or cord strung between two screw eyes in the frame. Braided wire is probably best. Once a picture is in position, it doesn't often get moved, so the first evidence of a rotted cord may be a falling picture. The wire should be short enough to not be seen above the frame. The position of the screw eyes will affect the angle at which the picture will hang. Adjust the angle to suit the height of the picture. A high picture should slope more downward than one hung at eye level. At eye level, the screw eyes can be near the top of the sides; lowering them allows the picture to tilt out more. However, do not put them so low that the picture becomes unstable—no lower from the top than one-third the depth of the frame.

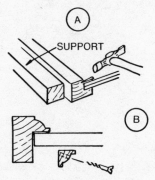

Fig. 11-8. When securing the sandwich of parts in a frame with nails, slide the hammer along the backboard (A), rather than lifting it and risk breaking the glass. To display a coin collection from two sides, a double-sided frame can be made. using a filler piece (B) to make the main molding symmetrical in cross section.

A double-sided frame can be made to display coins or medals to their best advantage. This method involves fitting the coins or medals into cutouts in wood or cardboard of the same thickness. The wood is then stained or painted, according to whatever is suitable to the display. Then the whole thing is sandwiched in glass. It is best if the frame looks the same from both sides. This is easier to achieve if the molding is fairly simple. (In any case, such a display does not usually require an elaborate surround.) One way to do this is to use a main molding with a deep rebate to take a filler piece that, when installed, makes the two look like one (Fig. 11-8B), producing a matching appearance in front and behind. Since the frame may have to be opened occasionally, it should be assembled with thin screws.

12 Finishing Wood

Most wood constructions are treated on the surface, either for protection or to improve appearance, or both. A few woods have natural properties that give them sufficient protection without additional treatment; two are Western red cedar and teak. But most woods suffer if left untreated. They deteriorate at varying speeds, depending on their type and application. Some rot quite rapidly through exposure to weather. Some used indoors may not suffer in strength or durability, but their pores become clogged with dirt, making them unattractive.

There are innumerable treatments. New synthetic materials, being introduced almost daily, make it difficult to keep pace with them. However, most are treatments for reviving existing finishes, rather than applications for bare wood. Advertisements and instructions have to be read carefully to differentiate between maintenance treatments and surface coatings for just-completed work.

Because of this, it is advisable to become familiar with both traditional and modern finishes. A craftsman concerned with repairing antique furniture or producing reproductions should know about traditional finishes and how to use them. Traditional treatments, having stood the test of time, are still the best finishes for the craftsman who wants to stamp his work with individuality, marking it as an obviously handcrafted product—not like something that could have been made in a factory.

Wood should be planed and sanded to a smooth surface before any finishing material is applied. A painted finish may not require quite such a good underlying surface, but no polish (all of which are transparent or translucent) should be applied to a surface that isn't smooth and even in color. Stoppings or fillings should be as inconspicuous as possible. Make sure that final sanding is with the grain and that no scratches remain on the surface that go across the grain; sometimes, stain or polish will emphasize scratches, making them visible as slightly dark lines.

For the finest surface, it may be necessary to wipe some woods with a damp cloth and let them dry after the first sanding. This will lift any bent fibers, which can be rubbed off by a light, second sanding.

BLEACHING

Bleaching can be the remedy for uneven color, or it may be used to make a piece look better by making it lighter. Wood can be bleached with commercial solutions intended for clothing, but the solution should be much more concentrated. How much should be used will have to be determined experimentally. Single-application bleaches are applied in one coat that must be given a period to dry completely, during which the bleaching takes place. Residual moisture could affect subsequent treatment. Bleaches can be sprayed or applied with a rubber sponge or fiber brush. If they are sprayed, they should be rubbed down with a sponge. Because the action of some bleaches is affected by metal, avoid using metal containers, or brushes with metal parts. Glass or plastic containers are better for bleach. And because bleaches can be rendered virtually useless by sunlight, always store them in the shade or in brown-glass bottles.

Most commercial bleaches have a caustic effect on the skin, so wear rubber gloves and protect your clothing with an apron. If *any* bleach touches your skin, flush it off with plenty of water and apply boric acid to neutralize it. Read the instructions carefully.

The manufacturer may advise that the bleach be neutralized after it has dried. If a neutralizer is not provided for this purpose, one can be made by disolving an ounce of borax in a quart of hot water and allowing the solution to cool. The (alkaline) solution will remove any trace of acid remaining in the wood after the bleach has dried.

Bleaching with homemade preparations can be just as effective as using commercial products. One method involves the use of two solutions. The first, made by dissolving 3 ounces of oxalic acid in a quart of water, requires extreme care in its use. The acid can cause severe skin damage, and its fumes can irritate the throat. It is applied first, followed by an accelerator, the second solution: 3 ounces of sodium hyposulphite dissolved in a quart of water. Sodium hyposulphite, ordinary photographic *hypo*, is not dangerous.

Apply the oxalic acid solution with a rubber sponge or fiber brush. When it has partially dried, apply the hypo the same way. Let the wood dry completely. (If the color is uneven, more bleach can be applied.) Use the borax solution to neutralize the bleach, then wash the surface with clean water and let it dry completely.

Of course, not all wood needs bleaching. In many shops the treatment is rare. Apart from its use in correcting uneven color, bleach is used to enhance certain woods by producing special effects like "amber walnut" and "honey maple."

STAINING

Many woods are improved by staining. The beauty of the grain can be enhanced and the general appearance given a richness greater than that of the natural color. Although, in general, stain is used to deepen the color of wood, there are exceptions. A light-colored wood may be blackened to look like ebony, a useful technique for making chessmen, for example. But care is needed not to stain a wood the color of another when its grain is wrong for the transformation. Stains do not obscure grain; they only change the color of wood at its surface—they do not cover like paint.

Broadly speaking, stains are supplied as ready-to-apply liquids, or as powders (sometimes crystals) to be dissolved in a solvent. The most common and cheapest stains are water-soluble aniline types that give even, clear tones. Vegetable stains can be used, but they are less reliable. The powdered stains are dissolved in hot water and used cold. Once mixed with water, most stains will keep indefinitely. They are available in all the shades and colors likely to be needed, and can be applied with a brush or sprayed, although some craftsmen prefer to soak a cloth in stain and wipe it on. Small items may be soaked in stain. If more than one coat is desired, the first should be allowed to dry completely before the second is applied; otherwise, the result may be patchy.

Water-soluble stain may raise very prominent grain, making it necessary to sand again after staining; but this in itself could affect the wood's appearance—calling for further staining. Although slight, there is a risk of a nonwaterproof glue becoming softened by stain.

Penetrating-oil stains (wood dyes) are made of powders dissolved in light oils, which penetrate wood more than water and dry quicker. Some of the solvents used are gasoline, benzine, and naptha. Most of these stains are sold in liquid form under proprietary names. Their resistance to fading is not quite as good as the water-soluble stains; but, on the other hand, they don't raise grain. To reduce the risk of a polish partially dissolving a stain, a sealant can be applied before the polish.

Penetrating-oil stains give an even result; adjoining areas will not show overlaps. One advantage of these stains is that a little can be wiped off while it is still damp, if the color is too dark.

Concentrated wiping stains are used to get shaded effects. The stain is applied, then wiped from the highlights. Shading stains made with a binder and solvent (so they dry quickly) can be used for special effects or to touch up the uneven color of sapwood.

In spirit stains the colored powder is dissolved in a blended solvent (mainly alcohol). They dry very quickly and work best when sprayed on. The solvent takes the color into the wood, but not so deeply as to be fade-resistant in strong sunlight. Since the drying time may only be 10 minutes, further treatment has to follow quickly. The stain may bleed into polish; but with care, this will not be a serious problem.

Most stains are only satisfactory for new, untreated wood, but it is possible to use spirit stains on wood that has been previously finished in some way. The solvent will penetrate old varnish or polish left in the pores. This means spirit stains may be the only satisfactory choice for repairs and refinishing.

Varnish stains (varnishes to which stain has been added) are also available. The object is to provide stain and varnish in one coat, instead of having to use two or more. There are snags involved, problems that account for so many skilled craftsman refusing to use varnish stains. The stain in the varnish does not penetrate the wood, so there is not the same rich effect of stained and polished wood. And the type of varnish used does not give the gloss of a polished surface.

The only condition under which a varnish stain might be worthwhile is for something made from cheap softwood that is streaked, marked, and uneven in grain; where ordinary stain would produce a very patchy appearance as it soaks unevenly into the wood, the color in varnish stain stays away from the wood, creating an even appearance.

FILLING AND SEALING

If varnish or polish is used directly on wood, early coats will soak in, and there will have to be several rubbing down stages between coats. If the wood is open-grained, it is probable that even after several coats, there will be hollows in the surface over the more open parts of the grain. Filling and sealing prevents all this.

Fillers come in paste or liquid form, the former being available in colors to match woods. Some thinning is usually necessary to make fillers workable. Oil stain can be added to paste filler to alter its color.

Paste fillers are intended for open-grained woods. Birch, maple, and other close-grained woods should be treated with a liquid filler. White shellac is a liquid filler used for light woods; common orange shellac, for darker woods.

The object of applying a filler is to fill the grain. This is done by applying plenty of paste filler with a stiff brush to open-grained wood, first along the grain and then across it. It is left for a few minutes to dry slightly, then rubbed across the grain; a piece of canvas or burlap is used, so the paste won't be lifted from the spaces. This removes surplus filler and presses the remainder into the grain. Final wiping is done in the direction of the grain with a cloth that will not leave lint.

This is easy on plain surfaces, but care is needed in treating moldings, carvings, or other intricate surfaces. There must be no excess paste left. For these surfaces it may be better to use a liquid filler, even if it is open-grained wood. Although some paste fillers *appear* to dry in a short time, they must be left until absolutely dry before subsequent treatment. This can take as long as 2 days. Because liquid fillers are used on woods that don't have pronounced gaps in their grain, there is no need to press them into the pores; brushing is all that is needed.

The filled wood will need light hand sanding with fine sandpaper. (Power sanding would be too violent.) The sanding should be no more than is needed to remove slight imperfections. (There is no point in applying filler, then sanding it all away.)

The filler may be followed by a sealer—good practice, in any case. The advantages are the prevention of further treatment from lifting, dissolving, or bleeding into what has already been applied, and the saving of effort and materials in excessive polishing or varnishing if some of it soaks into the wood. Shellac dissolved in alcohol is often used as a sealant. If shellac has been used as a filler, another coat will insure good protection, particularly if most of the first coat has been rubbed down.

Not all name-brand sealants are intended to be used before a polish or varnish. Some, meant mainly for floors, penetrate the wood and impart a luster to it, making further treatment unnecessary. They are described as sealants, but they are really complete finishes. Special sealants are needed for soft woods, such as fir, if they are to be varnished instead of painted.

VARNISH

Varnishes are transparent (or nearly transparent) finishes that may be sprayed or brushed on, and dry to various degrees of gloss. Varnish is used extensively for boats, garden furniture, exterior woodwork in general, paneling, and constructional work—but rarely on indoor furniture. Cabinetmakers prefer polish to varnish for good furniture.

Varnish can be thought of as paint without pigment. It is not exactly the same, but for all practical purposes it is very like paint in its application and in the protection it affords.

The varnishes used throughout history were made of various gums and lac (a resin secreted by an insect) dissolved in oils. Varnishes were compounded to suit particular purposes. For a long time it was thought that there was no universal varnish. Although modern synthetic gums and lacs have made a variety of varnishes possible, each has an almost universal application.

Most varnishes can be used directly from the can. Those that produce a very hard, waterproof surface come in two parts that have to be mixed just before use. If varnish is used on wood that has had no preparation other than sanding, the first coat should be thinned in the proportions instructed by the makers. Today it is advisable to use only the varnish and paint of one maker together, as these products are not always compatible between brands. Most of the first coat, acting like a sealer or undercoat, soaks in. But if the wood has been filled and sealed first, this won't happen. If the wood is open-grained, varnishing it directly is likely to produce hollows over slits in the grain that will remain even after many coats: filling is advisable for the best finish.

Modern synthetic varnishes have many advantages over natural varnishes, but there are a few disadvantages.

Synthetic finishes are normally tougher and harder; in particular, two-part varnishes have a longer life in exposed situations, such as on a boat, and are much more waterproof. A synthetic varnish may be expected to retain its gloss longer than a natural one.

A drawback with traditional varnishes was their fairly lengthy setting time, during which they could attract dust and insects. It's still important to protect a freshly varnished surface from these contaminants, but many varnishes become dust-free in a couple of hours. They may take longer than that to dry completely, however. Ideally, varnish should be applied in a well-ventilated, dust-free environment at about 70°F; below this temperature it is helpful to stand the can in hot water. Ventilation is important, because drying varnish takes oxygen from the air; drying will be slowed if the depleted air is not replaced.

Anyone experienced with traditional varnishes might be tempted to brush on synthetics in several layers with crossing brushstrokes, but this should not be done. Most synthetic varnishes will drag on the brush, and will be lifted by it as it is taken from the surface, leaving a rough coating. The only way that this could be done successfully is to let each coat dry and sand it down before applying the next.

Brush just enough to spread the varnish, avoiding runs and curtains on a vertical surface. Use a minimum of strokes, and take the last ones back toward previously varnished areas in the direction of the grain (or the long way for a panel). The brush marks should dry out. If they don't, at least those going lengthwise to the grain will be less obvious. Conditions permitting, vertical or sloping surfaces should be coated from the top downward, with each brushful of paint laid below the previous one; only the final strokes should be taken upward. This way, there is little risk of joints showing or runs occurring.

How many coats are needed depends on the desired finish, but on bare wood there should be a minimum of three, the first one thinned. For filled wood the minimum is two. Rub each coat lightly with sandpaper before applying the next. Because varnish begins to dry quite quickly, it is important to plan the work so new varnish can always be brushed back toward some that is still wet. On a large area this means working fairly quickly.

The number of coats required for a really high-class job depends on how patient you are and on how much time you have. A flawless, mirror-like gloss results from maybe 15 coats, each rubbed smooth before the next is applied.

SHELLAC

Shellac has already been mentioned for filling and sealing, but can also provide a final finish. From medieval days, at least, it has been the finish used for good-quality furniture. Used as a polish, it gives one of the most beautiful finishes. It is still a finish favored for its appearance, but because it can be marked by heat and liquids, it is not really good for table tops.

Shellac is a hard gum obtainable in solid or granular form to be dissolved in alcohol. The orange type used on darker woods is partially refined. White or bleached shellac has a pale color, while dewaxed shellac is clear. Various concentrations are available. It is best to buy a thick solution and thin it as its need arises. Shellac stored for more than a year will be unusable. To prevent the solvent from evaporating too rapidly, and to keep out dust, always leave containers of shellac closed.

The first coat (on bare wood) should be thinned, so it can fill the grain. Shellac is more fluid than varnish and dries quicker. Work quickly, using long, flowing strokes, without going back over an area more often than necessary. Allow a coat to harden, then sand it and apply the next.

If it is the right consistency, shellac can be sprayed. Avoid excessive pressure that might cause ripples. Don't try to spray too much at one time. It is better to apply several thin coats than one thick one.

French polishing is used on fine-quality antique furniture. This method is an art that has to be acquired through practice. Although the technique may appear simple, skill (in its execution) can only come with experience.

French polishing is done on close-grained woods, like walnut, for example. It is ineffective for open-grained woods (e.g., oak).

Begin by filling the surface (and for best results, sealing it as well), then rub it smooth. The polishing is done with a special pad: a piece of cotton batting in a soft piece of linen (don't use a synthetic material). The pad is saturated by removing the cloth and soaking the cotton in shellac polish. Use enough to thoroughly wet the cotton and the cloth around it, but not enough to drip out without applying pressure. Twist the cloth cover above the cotton to stretch the bottom smooth and to have something to grip.

The first step in French polishing is called *fading in.* Stroke the "charged" pad back and forth with the grain, working with long sweeps to deposit a coat of shellac; the friction of rubbing will cause the solvent to evaporate almost immediately. If the pad sticks to the surface, it is becoming exhausted and should be recharged. If it starts to stick right away, the polish should be diluted a little. Let the wood dry and store the pad in a tightly closed container.

The next step is bodying. Use the same pad, but in a second, finer cloth. Charge the pad and use it in small, overlapping circles. If the pad drags before its polish is exhausted, lubricate it with a very small amount of raw linseed oil—a little on the end of a finger is enough. Again, the friction of rubbing will make the polish harden. For the best finish, five or six daily bodying sessions are necessary.

When a sufficient body of polish has been built up, the final treatment, *spiriting off,* is in order. Put some pure alcohol on a cloth that is wrapped in another. The amount of moisture oozing out should be absolutely minimal. Wipe the work with the grain until the whole area is bright and clear.

LACQUER

Traditional Oriental lacquering is a very long process, involving techniques that might be described as "trade secrets." Modern lacquers are mostly synthetic solutions, either clear or colored, that have the virtue of drying very quickly.

Lacquer is used by following a sequence similar to that for varnishing. If you want to brush it on, use a large brush and load it well with lacquer. Apply the lacquer rapidly in one direction, overlapping previous strokes slightly and lifting the brush at the end of the stroke.

It is better to spray lacquer than brush it on. When you thin it for spraying, make several test mixes and try them on scrap materials, until the right consistency is obtained.

Several synthetic finishes are more closely related to lacquers than anything else. Several of them are anything-proof. Most are only suitable for spraying, but some can be brushed on. The toughest and hardest synthetics come in two parts, a catalyst being one of them. They can be used on the top of a table or bar with the certainty that no common liquid can mark it, nor hot utensil affect it.

If a synthetic lacquer has to be thinned, it is very important to use the thinner supplied with it, or one recommended by the maker. Synthetic finishes that have to be oven-cured are not suitable for use in the home shop.

WAX AND OIL

Where French polishing was the favorite finish for high-class furniture made of close-grained woods. European furniture made of oak and elm was given a wax or oil finish.

The trouble with oil-polishing is the time it takes. The attractive gloss seen on the enormous old tables in some baronial halls is the result of years of use and polishing. Linseed oil, rubbed in with sufficient vigor, can eventually be built up into that kind of finish, but it could take as many as 50 rubbings to do it—a very long program, to say the least. (The rubbing of clothing and other things against the surface serves to increase the shine.)

If an oil finish appeals to you, a suitable mixture for today's needs is two parts of linseed oil to one part of turpentine. Before applying it, warm the solution by standing its container in hot water. (Heating it directly over a flame could burn the oil.)A little coloring may be added to the oil if desired. Use a soft cloth with plenty of oil on it. After rubbing the wood. wipe off the surplus oil. Make sure no oil is left on any angular parts, or it will become sticky. When all the surplus oil is gone, rub the surface with a fairly coarse piece of cloth. The coarseness will help to generate heat by friction, thereby setting the surface. For flat surfaces, it may help to wrap the cloth around a brick.

This procedure has to be repeated as many as a dozen times, at 2 day intervals at first, then less frequently. This should result in the typical oil-polish luster—but all is not done. The process must be repeated monthly for a year; after that, annually.

The process can be accelerated by mixing as much as an equal quantity of varnish with the oil/turpentine mixture. The first few applications of this mixture will fill the pores quickly. Later coats are applied without varnish.

Polishing with wax is probably as old as polishing with oil. Several paste polishes, sold to be used on household furniture, are, basically, wax. The usual solvent for wax is turpentine. Paraffin, although too soft for polishing, may be used to fill grain. Beeswax, whether white or yellow, is a good general-purpose wax.

Carnauba wax is the one most used for polishing. A product of a Brazilian palm, this pale yellow wax is one of the hardest known. Cadelilla, similar to beeswax, comes from a Mexican shrub. Ceresine, a wax derived from a hydrocarbon, is often mixed with carnauba wax.

Polishing bare wood with wax could involve a process as time-consuming as oil-polishing. An equally good result can be obtained by filling and, possibly, sealing the wood, followed by a coat of shellac or varnish rubbed down to a mat base for the wax.

Use paste wax between several layers of wide-mesh cloth. Rub the wood and wait at least 10 minutes for the wax to start drying. Then rub the wax with a soft cloth, in circles first, and finally lengthwise. After at least an hour, apply a second coat. Further coats can be applied to build up the polish. The harder waxes produce a better shine, but they require more effort. A stiff scrub brush can be used on the surface before being rubbed with a cloth. This method is similar to oil-polishing in that friction is needed to heat and harden the wax. A polishing buff mounted in an electric drill will lessen the amount of physical effort.

Wax can follow other polishes. It is best to take the gloss off varnish before waxing. Pumice stone or some other fine abrasive powder can be used as an alternative to abrasive paper. Wax can be used to revive the finish on furniture, even if the existing polish is something other than wax. There are many brand-name polishes claimed to be capable of reviving polished surfaces. They should not be used in place of waxes to build up a new polish. Other polishes, sometimes described as waxes, may be adequate for floors, but not all can be used on furniture. Spray types and other liquid or semiliquid forms are mostly for finishing, not for building up the body of the polish in the first instance.

PAINTING

Of the many methods of finishing, painting is the only one that obscures the grain. Usually, exterior work and inferior wood that would be unsuitable for grain-exposed finish is painted. If a really good finish is to be expected, proper preparation should be made first. Softwoods need special attention, because they are very often resinous and have knots on the surface. Cracks or open joints should be stopped, as long as the stopping used is compatible with the paint. Knots are liable to ooze resin that will go through the paint and spoil the finish. This can be prevented by coating the knots with what is usually called *knotting* (often only shellac).

Fillers can be painted or troweled on if a fine finish is needed. The success of a paint finish is dependent on what work has been done underneath. A troweled filler can be used on a poor surface to form a base for a smooth coat of paint. Obviously, it is better to start with a good surface, but if you are prepared to spend time on a bad one, there are now fillers to help you.

There have been many changes in the makeup of paints—and there will probably be many more. At one time, when paints were compounded mainly of natural materials, there was little choice between brands; it was fairly safe to assume that one brand of paint could be used with another. In some cases this may still be so, but it is always better to use one manufacturer's complete paint system for a particular job. Most paint manufacturers provide adequate instructions, booklets, and charts to help you select a suitable system.

Traditionally, the first coat for bare wood was a primer, usually followed by another coat. This may still be necessary, but with some paint systems, the surface can be primed with the same paint used for other coats. The primer bonds to the wood. It penetrates the fibers of the wood, gripping it, as it were, providing a layer upon which other coats can be built up. Priming paints need considerable stirring before use.

The next layer, an undercoat, should be a color that complements the top coat, but it need not be a perfect match. Actually, there is an advantage in having it a different shade: the coverage of top coat can be easily seen. It is the undercoat that builds up the body of the paint skin. It should be thick enough to dry with an opaque finish, yet fluid enough to dry without brush marks. A second undercoat may be desirable.

Painting conditions are not quite as critical as those for varnishing. Dust or insects on a tacky first undercoat may not be too serious, but successive coats should be rubbed down and cleaned of dust. The quality of the undercoats determines the quality of the top coat. Normally, there is only one top coat, so it is unwise to rely on it to hide or correct any imperfections. If it is necessary to make good any flaws with a stopping or filling compound at this stage, there should be another undercoat. Of course, how much care you will want to take with all the stages involved will depend on what use the surface will get and where it will be seen.

The top coat is nearly always glossy. This means that, in effect, it is a pigmented varnish requiring the same treatment given to any modern synthetic varnish. The paint should be at room temperature (slightly on the warm side); the shop should be ventilated and as free from dust as possible. Apply the paint with a minimum of brushwork. Make the final strokes in the lengthwise direction of the part, and lift the brush at the end of the stroke as it reaches a previously painted part. Cover the whole area quickly, so no part of the painted surface dries so much that it bonds with new paint when they meet. If the painting conditions have remained good for 2 hours or more, the work can be left for a day to dry (properly), resulting in a good finish.

If anything goes wrong, the paint must be left long enough to get really hard before the, gloss can be sanded off and another coat applied.

PRESERVATIVES

The majority of woods will rot if exposed to damp conditions. More durable woods should be chosen for exposed places, but there are treatments that will prevent, or at least delay, the onset of rot in more vulnerable woods. Various methods have been tried. The ends of fence posts have been charred before being driven into the ground. This provided protection to a limited extent.

The preservatives used today offer protection against fungi, worms, and other forms of attack, besides the effects of dampness. Usually, preservatives are liquid, either clear or colored. The best way to apply them is to soak the article needing protection. Where this is not practical, the liquid must be brushed on thoroughly, preferably several times. Because the liquid will penetrate best along the grain, soaking the end of a piece of wood will insure deepest penetration.

Liquid preservatives are particularly suitable for outdoor woodwork. They impregnate the wood, and thus are functional rather than decorative, although the color of some may be regarded as attractive. Because they are liable to fade, it is inadvisable to expect much decorative value from them. Many preservatives may be painted over, so exterior work can be protected during construction.

Boats and other underwater woodwork often suffer from attack by marine borers (worms). They enter through comparatively small holes, but then move around within the wood, almost completely destroying it. Fortunately, they are only found in certain waters. Elsewhere, marine growths attach themselves to wood and attack it. The worst marine borers can only be held back by completely sheathing the wood in copper. Less zealous borers can be discouraged by *antifouling* paints; but because not all of them are suitable for every condition, it is advisable to get advice about local conditions before buying one.

The more potent antifouling paints never dry completely; they give off chemicals continuously to discourage attack. This means their life may not be very long and they will have to be revived every few months. In fresh water, where the problem is not as acute, more permanent antifouling and preservative treatments can be used; but even here it is still advisable to find out what local problems have to be faced.

Rot in woodwork, both afloat and ashore, occurs "between wind and tide"—on a post, where it enters the ground; on a boat, at the waterline. Ashore, the problem is taken care of by continuing an underground preservative above ground.

While penetrating preservatives are valuable, underground protection entails sealing the surface of the wood to make it waterproof. If water cannot enter, the wood cannot rot. Tar is a common treatment. It is heated and applied with a long-handled brush. Bitumastic treatments (mixtures of asphalt and a filler) have a similar waterproofing effect, if the coating is thick enough and covers completely.

Creosote, a byproduct of coal, is another preservative for outdoor woodwork. It can be used on woodwork above ground to provide protection against insects, worms, and plant life. It does not seal the wood, but it provides some resistance in inhibiting the start of rot.

The term *rot* is used to indicate attack by any of numerous kinds of fungus. Besides treating the wood, providing ventilation is vital. Attack starts where air is stagnant. There is no way of reversing the effects of an attack. Rot cannot be cured. There are treatments that prevent it from spreading, but the only way to deal with rotten wood is to remove it. To play it safe, also remove any surrounding wood suspected of being even slightly affected. The protection of wood susceptible to rot, or in conditions where it might be expected, is always worthwhile.

13

Outdoor Woodwork

Woodwork for use outdoors, whether a yard, garden, patio, or deck, can vary in quality and detail from crude hammer-and-nail carpentry to carefully fitted cabinetry. There is a tendency toward robust sizes and the use of rough-cut wood that might not be good enough for better quality work. Outdoor construction, of course, does not ordinarily justify an interior-quality finish or the use of carefully cut joints. But the enthusiastic woodworker will not want to take *too* casual an approach to craftsmanship.

Exterior woodwork should be weather-resistant, whether natural (as with redwood) or artificial (treated with preservative or paint).

FENCES

There are various ways of erecting field fences, either with wire or wood rails. Posts for small fences may be pointed for ease in driving (where no postholes are needed), but too fine a point may cause weakness or even the further sinking of the post after it is in use.

A great deal depends on the type of soil. Where postholes are required, it is better to make the hole the full depth, and not attempt to drive the post at all.

When "planting" a series of posts, it is advisable to have them slightly long; then mark them all to the required height—probably by stretching a string along them. Once they're set, trim them all with a top that will shed water. (If water settles into a hollow at the top of a post, it could cause warping or premature rotting of the wood.) The simplest top is a single slope; but a taper all around may look better in some situations. Figure 13-1 shows several satisfactory techniques, progressing from the bias cut to a separately constructed cap

Fig. 13-1. Methods of finishing fence posts to insure adequate water runoff.

If the rails are flat they can be nailed directly to the posts, with butt joints where necessary (Fig. 13-2). If the rails are to be carried over more than two posts, the joints should be staggered. But a simple fence like this would have to rely on the strength of the nails to sustain a load from the back of a

Fig. 13-2. Fence rail butting.

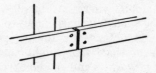

rail. It is better to mortise the rails into the posts. Usually the mortise (the slot) is the same size as the end of the rail, unlike the practice for furniture construction. The rails are cut at an angle, the rise of which matches the thickness of the post at the joint (Fig. 13-3A). Nails are driven through the posts to hold the rails. In better work, hardwood pegs are used, instead of nails (Fig. 13-3B). They could be prepared dowels, but it is

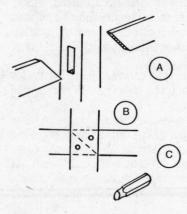

Fig. 13-3. The joint of mortised rails is angled (A); the rails are secured within the mortise with nails, or with pegs (B) that are only roughly rounded (C).

traditional to use hardwood pegs, tapered to allow entry, with only the main part of the peg approximately round (Fig. 13-3C); its rough shape grips better in a round hole than would a peg that is absolutely round.

Attractive rails may be made economically by cutting a square section of wood diagonally to make *arris rails* (Fig. 13-4A). They can be nailed into posts that are notched on the surface (Fig. 13-4B), or fitted into mortises, with meeting ends cut to overlap (Fig. 13-4C).

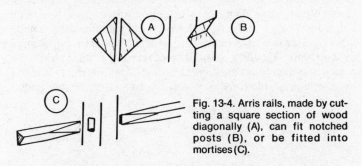

Fig. 13-4. Arris rails, made by cutting a square section of wood diagonally (A), can fit notched posts (B), or be fitted into mortises (C).

Fences are often made to provide privacy. A semiprivate type may have horizontal rails staggered on opposite sides of posts (Fig. 13-5A). A point to consider in a very windy situation is the large, closely boarded exposed area that may be unable to stand the strain of wind that cannot get through. Boards on alternate sides of posts allow wind to pass through.

For close boarding, upright pales (stakes) tapering into rebates in their neighbors can be used (Fig. 13-5B). In better fencing the pales are tongued and grooved (Fig. 13-5C). This type of construction, however, is more suitable for a patio than a garden or yard. For a simple construction up to about 4 feet

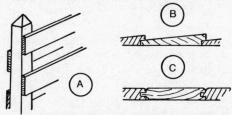

Fig. 13-5. In very windy conditions, a semiprivate fence with rails staggered on either side of the posts is best (A). For close boarding, tapered pales that fit into rebates can be used (B), but tongue-and-groove joints are better (C).

high, two main rails and a lighter counterrail at the top are required; for a taller fence, there should be three main rails (Fig. 13-6). The pales are nailed to the rails between the posts. It may be necessary to have one narrow pale, but this can be avoided by carefully spacing the posts, and making the joints in the pales allow for a little adjustment (widening or narrowing the spacing progressively along the fence). Nails should be galvanized or otherwise weather-resistant. As the bottom of the fence may rest on uneven ground; it is advisable to let the tops of the pales extend above the counterrail during construction. Saw them level after a complete set has been fitted between a pair of posts. Although the top need not be worked after this, it is much better to install a *capping*, shaped to shed water (see Fig. 13-6). The posts may extend above the capping with shaped tops, or each post may be cut off level at the counterrail, making it invisible from the front of the fence.

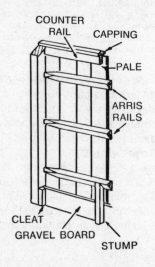

COUNTER
RAIL

CAPPING

PALE

ARRIS
RAILS

CLEAT

GRAVEL BOARD

STUMP

Fig. 13-6. For privacy-fences over 4 feet high, the construction illustrated is preferred. The capping at the top provides protection by shedding water, while the gravel board prevents wear at the bottom.

It is usually the bottoms of fence pales that show the first signs of wear. A gravel board at the bottom will forestall this. It is fixed by cleats to the posts so the front is level with the pales; there may be a central stump to support it, usually going up to the first arris rail. Another way of building a new fence, that is, besides building it piece by piece, is to make up each bay (section of pales, between posts) as a panel in the shop; they can be made as halved frames to be joined at the

372

site (Fig. 13-7A), or constructed to be tenonned together (Fig. 13-7B).

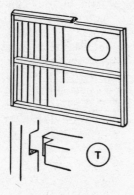

Fig. 13-7.Prefabricated fence bays can be assembled at the site as framed panels (A), or as parts that can be tenonned together (B).

The problem then is the exact alignment of posts. It is best to mount a permanent post for one end of a bay, and a temporary one for the other end, and stretch a string between them as a reference line. Then the end of a panel is nailed to the first post, the next post is positioned against it, in line with the string, and so on.

Another type of fencing that is particularly appropriate to a rural setting uses waney-edged boards, boards that have edges as they came from the tree; but bark should be removed, together with any soft wood at the edges, to discourage boring insects and rot. If possible, each board should taper in thickness toward the top edge of the fence (Fig. 13-8A). The boards must be supported by upright pieces behind them. Although they could be fixed to the horizontal rails of an existing fence, it is better to use panels faced with waney-edged boards (made like vertical pale panels), but supported by uprights instead of horizontal members.

A light, attractive fence can be made of panels covered with slats about 3 inches wide and ¼ inch thick, interlaced horizontally with similar vertical slats spaced at about 1 foot intervals (Fig. 13-8B). The interlaced slats are mounted in framed panels that have light strips over the ends and another at the center, forming a bay 5 feet long, or longer.

A field fence can be made more animal-proof or more attractive for a yard by converting it to a *palisade*. In its simplest form, the pales are nailed to the rails with spaces about the same width as the rails. The tops may be pointed or decorated in some way (Fig. 13-8C), or they could be cut straight across and fitted with a capping. The next decorative step might be to have alternate pales at different heights (Fig. 13-8D).

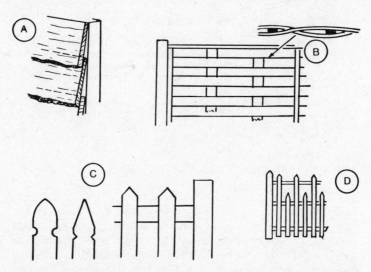

Fig. 13-8. Fences for rural settings: detail of a fence made of waney-edged (natural) boards (A); interlaced-slat construction (B); pales (pickets) made decorative with specially shaped ends, and staggered heights (C & D).

GATES

A fence nearly always needs a gate, one that matches the fence. A gate, being suspended by hinges, puts considerable strain on the width of the assembly, often making the side furthest from the hinges sag. A door with solid panels is not subject to this problem. Some entrance gates may be so built-up that they are almost completely paneled. But in most cases it is important to include at least one brace to prevent the gate from sagging. In smaller picket gates the brace can act as a strut to take compressive loads by sloping up from near the bottom of the hung side (Fig. 13-9A). Larger gates may have a similar brace, supplemented by a second in tension the other way; or there may only be a long one in tension taken from a higher, specially made anchoring stile, which could also act as a decorative feature (Fig. 13-9B).

In the simplest paled gate, rails or ledges are fixed across the pales, either with screws or clenched nails. The brace, cut

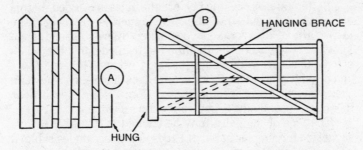

Fig. 13-9. Small picket gates may get enough support against loads with a simple diagonal brace (A); the brace for a large gate may have to be anchored to a special stile (B).

to fit between the ledges, is nailed to the pales (Fig. 13-10A). Before construction goes too far, it should be checked for squareness by comparing diagonals (Fig. 13-10B). After a few nails are driven through the ledges and outer pales, the brace can be fixed to "lock" the gate's shape before the other pales are driven. Personal touches can be added to the top. It can be straight, curve up or down, form a point, or be round (Fig. 13-10C).

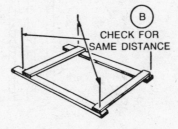

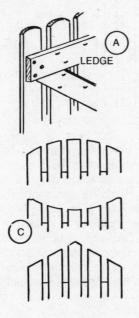

Fig. 13-10. Simple paled-gate construction: the ledges that bracket the brace (A); check for squareness prior to the main construction (B); some of the shapes that might be given to the gate's top (C).

Better gates are framed before the pales are added. In this construction the sides are thicker, and therefore stronger; the main parts of the frame are connected by mortise-and-tenon joints. A brace is cut to fit within the framed part. The joints are made secure with waterproof glue, wedges (Fig. 13-11A), and pegs. It is usual to slope the top edges of ledges so they can shed water, thus preventing water from being trapped near the joints—usually the first place to start rotting.

The tops of the pales may be treated in any of the ways suggested for simpler gates. If exposed tops are undesirable, a capping piece could be put across the top of the whole gate, or the pales could end at the top ledge (Fig. 13-11B), nailed to a strip of wood below it, or tenonned into the ledge (a better construction).

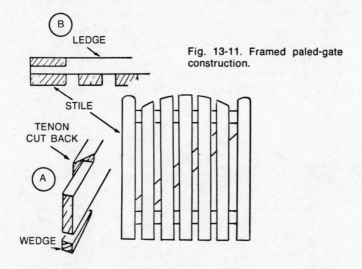

Fig. 13-11. Framed paled-gate construction.

Field gates can be made in a generally similar way, but a substantial upright is needed on the hinge side. Bars and rails should be tenonned into the uprights, then wedged, glued, and pegged. Where other members cross, bolts are used rather than screws or nails. A hanging brace, or two crossing braces, are best to keep a wide gate in shape (refer to Fig. 13-9B).

A framed and boarded gate is more suitable for the entrance to a yard or garden. If there are to be a pair of gates, it might be worthwhile to make one wider than the other, the narrow one opened for pedestrians, both opened for vehicular traffic.

This type of gate is best treated as an exemplary specimen of joinery: the structure should be properly framed and jointed, rather than using simple hammer-and-nail joints. The horizontal members must all be tenonned through the upright members. The boarding, tongued and grooved, is rebated into the lower parts of the uprights. The thickness and location of the tenon for the bottom rail should suit the thickness of the boards. A pair of gates at an entrance should meet in interlocking recesses. If it seems likely that the gates will settle, however, it may be better to leave their meeting edges unmodified and rely on a latch to hold them in place. Figure 13-12 shows the main features of the construction.

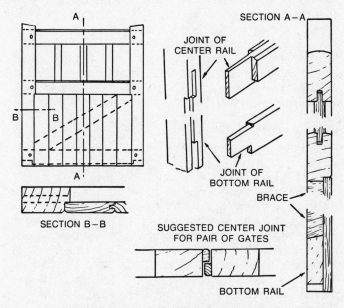

Fig. 13-12. Constructional details for gates in pairs.

It is important to build this type of gate so the top sheds water. The rails may be beveled or rounded. The boarding should extend a short distance past the edge of the bottom rail, to help the water run off and to reduce the amount of water that seeps up into the boards. Gates of this type should be treated with a preservative before being painted.

Gates should be hung on strong hinges. For a picket gate and other light types, a surface-mounted *T* hinge is a good choice. (Two are normally used.) If more than two are needed (for a high gate, for example) the knuckles must align to take the strain of the gate's swing. A larger hinge should extend well onto a heavy gate (particularly in simple hammer-and-nail construction) to provide a broad anchoring surface for bolts; in this kind of structure, as many bolts as possible should contact as many parts as possible.

Heavier gates, particularly of the field type (much wider than high), need hinges with long metal strips, preferably spanning both sides of the gate, and a socket that drops over a pin that is part of the gate post's hinge.

Any of several catches and latches can be used to hold a gate shut. A gate should close against a stop of some sort, rather than rely on a fastener to stop it. The type of latch that automatically engages is best. In this case, one of a pair of gates closes against a stop on the ground, and has a bolt that drops into a socket, either in the stop or in the ground; the other gate closes against the first, latching to it. Plan the installation of latches with the height of the gate and what you can reach over in mind.

RUSTIC WOODWORK

In laying out a garden there is often a need for "scenic" structures: something for climbing shrubs and plants to cling to, lawn furnishings, etc. They can also be used to divide a garden or act as natural screens. To look "right," it is best to use natural, round poles rather than sawed, square wood. For a woodsy touch, the bark can be left on; but first make sure you aren't dealing with a wood whose bark will become loose and fall off as the wood dries. Another thing to look for is bark that harbors insects that may bore into the wood, and bark that could trap moisture, promoting rot. If the bark has been removed, and the sap has dried out of the wood, roughly clean off the surface and treat it with linseed oil or varnish.

Most rustic construction is merely nailed together, although there are places were a simple, halved-joint is useful (Fig. 13-13). Nails used for these constructions should be weatherproof and driven into holes drilled for them, particularly near ends. The hole in a top piece should only be slightly undersize, to grip the nail as it is driven. The hole in the lower part (also undersize) should be just short of being as deep as the nail will go; unfortunately, most wood used for rustic woodwork tends to shrink in time, and may split, even if no splits were seen at first.

Fig. 13-13. A simple halved-joint is particularly suitable for rustic outdoor furnishings.

As much as possible, a free-standing screen or arch should be triangulated structurally, that is, the distortionless property of the triangle should be taken advantage of. A simple screen may have parts crossed by other members, with diagonal struts in corners (Fig. 13-14A). Besides providing decoration and something for plants to climb, they hold the assembly in shape, even with a solitary nail in each joint.

It is a good idea to prefabricate assemblies. The top of an arch, for example, should include some crossmembers (Fig. 13-14B) made up as framed units. If rustic woodwork is expected to last long, precautions similar to those suggested for fences should be observed. Parts that enter the ground should be protected with tar or some other waterproof coating. End grain exposed above ground should be cut at an angle to shed water. A climbing plant may take many years to grow all over a rustic frame. It would be a pity if the frame rotted because of negligence before the plant could naturally terminate its journey.

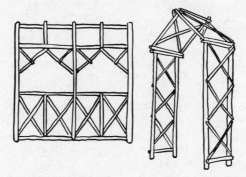

Fig. 13-14. A screen or an arch may be prefabricated as panels to be erected or assembled in the yard.

Trelliswork, although not exactly within the topic of rustic woodwork, should be discussed here. In a typical construction, a large number of laths, about one inch wide and ¼ inch thick, cross each other. Every crossing is secured with a central, clenched nail.

A piece of trelliswork can be used for two purposes: to fill a gap above a wall; to provide something for a flower to climb. Green seems to be a popular color for this sort of thing. Since the wood has to be treated with a preservative, a green one could be used; or the wood can be painted (green or a color to blend into the background), following a plain preservative.

A piece of trellis can be quite versatile: It can be used temporarily, then folded until required again. It can be nailed to a framework to form a screen. Sections can be nailed to uprights to form the sides of an arch. It can even be incorporated into a boarded fence or gate as a top layer.

Rustic boxes for plants or flowers can be made from the waste cut from the outsides of logs. Although not very durable (it will be sapwood), such a box (Fig. 13-15) can be easily replaced. Holes in the bottom for drainage can be made more effective by keeping the box clear of the ground with crosspieces. Design in this construction will have to be adapted to suit the materials available.

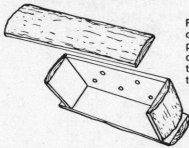

Fig. 13-15. The waste cut from the outside of logs could become the parts of a rustic planter; the drainage holes work most effectively when the box is raised off the ground.

Cut sections without trimmed edges can also make outdoor stools and benches. A finished central rail connecting the rougher ends will keep the assembly rigid (Fig. 13-16A). The parts may be simply nailed together, but it is better to put a groove in the top for the legs to fit into.

Another version has round legs, possibly pieces of natural pole (log). The top of each piece is pared down so it can be driven into holes in the top. The legs should slope outward slightly for stability (Fig. 13-16B). They can be secured with waterproof glue and wedges (put in saw cuts made across the

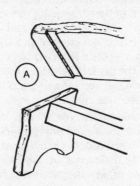

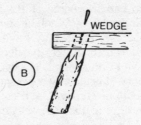

WEDGE

Fig. 13-16. Rough-hewn benches: end-slab supported (A); round-legged version (B).

grain of the top). It is advisable to leave the legs overlong when they are made, so they can be trimmed to length after assembly; otherwise, it might be difficult to make a bench, or other object, stand on unlevel ground. If a stool or bench is expected to stand on uneven ground, three legs (triangulation) will be better than four; they will stand on any surface without rocking. I hope you have guessed by now why old-fashioned milking stools always had three legs.

DECKS

A deck used for family cookouts, as a children's play area, or merely as a place to relax, must be made of fairly substantial sections of wood for rigidity; otherwise, there can be a disconcerting flexing, making its users fear its collapse. If the lumber used is not rot-resistant, it should be treated with a preservative. It is best to support a deck on concrete in a way that provides ventilation from below. (Putting it directly on the ground results in untimely decay.)

Basically, a deck is a simple rectangle, framed for structural integrity, and covered with boards. During initial assembly, compare diagonals to insure that the corners form right angles. Check in every direction with a level before securing the framework and boarding it over. In some situations, a slight slope may be worthwhile in keeping rainwater off. The most important thing to guard against is a twist. A twist will be immediately obvious if you sight across the deck at a distance from it.

The method of construction depends on the material and the situation as well as your skill, but much of it can be satisfactorily nailed together. If you don't want to cut joints, you can use some of the metal hangers available that suit standard 2- by 6-inch lumber, which can then be used as joists, (beams). Posts may have to be used at the corners and in between, to make the deck level if it is on uneven ground. (Even if the deck is not raised, corner posts will provide good joints. It is usually best to assemble the deck in position; but if it is to be removable, it could be made in sections to simplify storage; in this case, they can be made in the shop.

The recommended sizes of redwood parts for a deck are given in Fig. 13-17. The important constructional parts are the 2- by 6-inch joists and 2- by 4-inch ledgers (horizontal members), all of which should have their tops at the same height. Use aluminum, galvanized, or otherwise weatherproof

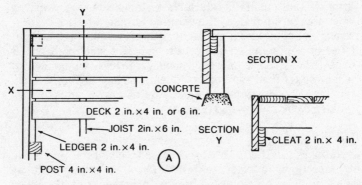

Fig. 13-17. Recommended sizes for redwood decking components.

nails. Drill holes for them near board ends. The posts may be left uncut and the other parts nailed on, or the ledgers and skirt boards can be notched together (Fig. 13-18A). After the posts have been assembled with the ledgers, make sure opposite sides match. Mark out the positions of the joists, they should be evenly spaced, with no more than 2 feet between centers. Cut the joists and fit them with metal hangers. If hangers are not used, nail the ends of the joists, also putting cleats below them to take the thrust. Instead of cleats, there may be a continuous piece of lumber (Fig. 13-18B) that has been checked for straightness across the ledgers, so the top surface of each joist is level as it is fitted (Fig. 13-18C).

The 2 inch thick decking could be made of boards 4 or 6 inches wide. There should be gaps between the boards for drainage; they need not be much more than ⅛ inch. A piece of

⅛ inch plywood could be used as a gage for the gap while each piece of decking is nailed in place. If the end grain of a decking board curves, lay the board so the outside of the curve faces up (Fig. 13-18D); this way, the surface is less likely to splinter. Putting two nails in the outside edges of the boards will make them resist any tendency to warp. Annual rings tend to straighten when warping takes place, making the board curl upward at the edges.

Leave a gap at the skirt board and lay the deck boards (at the correct spacing) across it. Use one or two nails at each joist. Leave a little excess length overlapping the ledgers; it will be trimmed later. It is important that the layout be planned and measured beforehand, so the spaces between deck boards are even. It may be necessary to modify the spacing slightly while the deck is being laid. Spaces tend to grow rather than shrink. It is also necessary to keep the deck boards parallel. Mark the ledgers at key points at each side, as references for periodic checks.

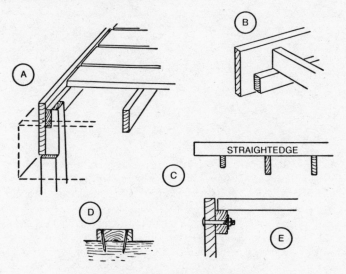

Fig. 13-18. Decking construction details.

An alternate way to put down decking so you won't finish with uneven spacing at one side is to lay the first board centrally, then halve the distance between the central board and the skirt with a second board, and so forth. Mark these positions and nail the boards in turn from the center outward.

When the decking has been laid, trim off surplus at the ends and install the remaining skirt boards. Nailing the skirt boards to the posts and ledgers may be enough, but it would be wise to bolt these parts together at intervals as well (Fig. 13-18E). The uppermost edges of the skirt boards should be below the top surface of the decking. Rounding the outer edges will reduce any risk of shoes catching on them. Any joints used in the deck boards should butt together on a joist. It is best to avoid joints around the sides, but if there must be joints in ledger or skirt boards, make them over a notched post.

14

Woodwork in the Home

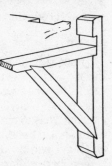

A considerable amount of woodwork can be done to improve the home, add to its comfort, make it better suit the needs of its occupants—and make it more valuable. The work can range from putting a shelf in an alcove to doubling the size of the house. Of course, not every alteration to a building is done best with wood. Even though wood can be the most convenient material for a project, the construction of the original structure and its situation must be taken into account. If wood was not used originally, there may be a good reason for it—climate or vulnerability to insect attack, for instance.

Even if wood is inappropriate for the main part of a job, there is usually plenty of scope for supplementary woodworking. Wood has a quality that makes it more pleasant and attractive than many other materials, even if the amount is not much more than just the trim on another material. The hobbyist with the right facilities can maintain and improve his home by doing the work himself, at a great savings over employing someone else to do it.

For many things that you may want to undertake in your home, there is no need to consult anyone but your family. If you are hurting for space and want to build a closet, it is your concern. But if you are renting, you must make sure the owner knows about the modifications you plan, and that your lease allows them. If you intend to make a major alter-ation—building an extra room or adding a porch—then local building regulations become your concern. You may have to submit plans for approval; there may be regulations specifying the types of materials for the kind of construction you have in mind. Even if these preliminaries seem troublesome, they are for the benefit of the community, and for your protection.

BUILT-IN FURNISHINGS

Free-standing furniture has the advantage of portability. But it doesn't make much sense to have a chest moved into a recess between walls, with only inches to spare all around, spaces not fully used, and where things can fall. The alternative is to build something to do the same job, something that can use the three sides of the recess as some of its parts, and make use of wasted space. This can be very important in a home where children's toys call for plenty of closable storage space.

The easiest thing to build into a recess is a shelf. Although, in theory, all floors are horizontal and all walls vertical, meeting in 90° corners, it is usually wise to assume that none of these assumptions is correct. Some or all may be correct, but don't bet your work on it; test existing surfaces before you begin to work. This calls for the frequent use of a spirit level, preferably the largest that will fit the space. Generally, plastered walls are pretty close to being level, so testing them for only a short distance may not be all that informative; it is better to make several checks over a greater distance and average your findings. Panels covering studding can be expected to be flatter, but uneven studs may distort a panel in places. If several shelves are being built in, make the first as accurately as possible and use it as a standard for making the rest.

For a simple, single shelf, mark the position of one end on the back wall of the recess. Extend a line from that mark onto a side wall, using the level (Fig. 14-1A). Make a brace to support the shelf near its end; if it will be exposed, bevel its front and chamfer its edges. Butt the end of one brace against the back wall and screw or nail it to the side wall (Fig. 14-1B).

Some walls will not take screws or nails directly (brick, for example), requiring that plugs be installed to take the fasteners. If this is the case, drill holes for screws or nails in one brace and use it as a template to locate the holes for the plugs. If a wood wall is solid enough, it can be drilled anywhere, but thin paneling concealing studs has to be treated differently. Studs can be located by looking for telltale nail heads, or by tapping the paneling with a piece of wood while listening for a change in the sound. Screws going into studs will be the most secure; otherwise, use expanding bolts to fasten braces to paneling.

Lay the level on a straight piece of wood and place one end of it on the first brace to find the height of the second (Fig. 14-1C). After both braces have been fixed in place, see if the corners of the recess are square. If they are, take the shelf's dimensions from those of the recess, but allow a little extra depth to project over the braces. If the corners are not true, measure the back and front positions and use an adjustable bevel to get the correct angles.

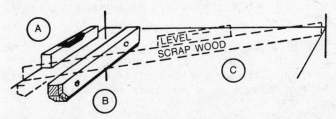

Fig. 14-1. Preliminary work on an alcove shelf installation: extending a line on a side wall from a mark on the back wall with the aid of a level (A); the first brace, located by the line on the side wall (B); spirit level resting on a piece of wood pivoted on the first brace to locate the position of the second (C).

In an awkward place it may be better to transfer measurements, using a cardboard template that has been cut to the right dimensions through several experimental fittings in the recess. It may be enough to make templates of only the ends, and space them by measurement. It is usual to screw shelves to braces without using glue, so they can be easily dismantled.

A shelf should be reasonably strong. A light piece of wood will gradually sag under the load of something like a row of books, a development that may not be apparent for some time. The shelf can be plywood edged with strips of wood underneath, as long as the strips extend over the braces, or rest on shoulders cut in them (Fig. 14-2A).

It is poor construction practice to rely only on plywood resting on braces for strength. A shelf can be further stiffened by covering the front with a strip of wood wide enough to hide the ends of the ledges (Fig. 14-2B). A plywood edge can be hidden with molding (Fig. 14-2C).

If a shelf fits into a corner with one end free, it can be supported on a metal bracket. If a wooden bracket is made, its

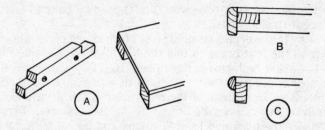

Fig. 14-2. If the alcove shelf is plywood, it should be edged with strips that rest on shoulders cut in the braces (A). The braces can be hidden by a strip going across the front (B); exposed plywood edges can be disguised with molding (C).

back should be slightly higher than the shelf; then an additonal diagonal brace can be notched into the other parts (Fig. 14-3). It may be advisable to make the front of the shelf very slightly higher than the back, if you anticipate that it will settle under its load.

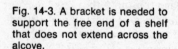

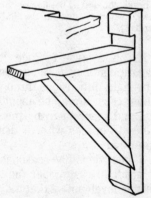

Fig. 14-3. A bracket is needed to support the free end of a shelf that does not extend across the alcove.

The back of such a bracket may be a longer piece to take several shelves. Shelves may be hidden by a curtain hung from a rail extending between pieces of wood attached to another overhanging the front edge of the top shelf (Fig. 14-4A). Usually, it is enough to have separate ledges for each shelf, but in some circumstances it may be better to have notched vertical pieces on the side walls, like the backs of the brackets, for the shelves to slide into.

A door can be fitted to an alcove by screwing a strip of wood to the wall and anchoring the jamb to it (Fig. 14-4B). Usually it is better not to have anything going across the recess at floor level. It would prevent the bottom from being cleaned out easily, and would make it necessary to lift out heavy items that would otherwise slide out. The sides of the door frame should be vertical, even if the wall is not. The door itself must have square corners and be upright, even if this means cutting the wood to a taper or an irregular outline.

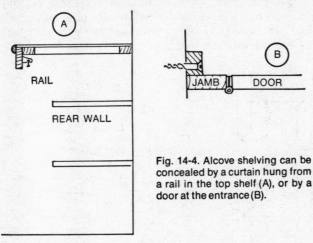

Fig. 14-4. Alcove shelving can be concealed by a curtain hung from a rail in the top shelf (A), or by a door at the entrance (B).

DOORS

Doors need to be substantial enough to withstand rough treatment. An exterior door needs to be weatherproof. The wood and finish have to stand up to rain and cold; this entails construction with waterproof glues to prevent water from getting into the wood.

One of the simplest doors is made very much like a gate with tongue-and-groove boarding. This may not be acceptable for a modern house, but it would suit a colonial home, and is certainly a good choice for a shed or anywhere an expensive door would not be justified. Because the door relies on the boarding to keep its shape, it should not be too thin—1 inch is a good choice for an outside door. The ledgers and braces should be the same thickness or slightly more. In the usual construction there are three ledgers connected by two braces sloping up from the hinge side (Fig. 14-5A). In the simplest construction, the braces butt against the ledgers and all parts are nailed. In a better door, screws are used and the braces are notched into the ledgers (Fig. 14-5B). Do not use glue; the wood should be able to expand and contract without restriction.

If the door opens inward, the ledgers should be as long as the door is wide for maximum strength. If the door opens outward, there will be stops inside, so the ledgers will have to be cut back. There may be T hinges on an inward-opening door. Use butt hinges for one that opens outward, unless the T hinges are fixed with bolts (instead of wood screws) and the inner ends of the bolts are burred over to prevent them from being unscrewed. Wood screws on the outside could be removed, allowing the door to be opened in that direction.

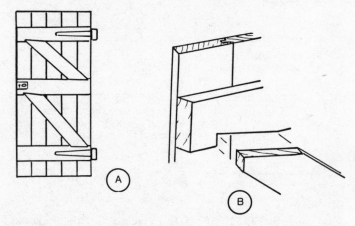

Fig. 14-5. A simple door can be made very much like a gate (A), but for utmost strength, the braces are notched into the ledgers (B) rather than being simply nailed.

Most doors in homes are framed and paneled (Fig. 14-6A) with haunched mortise-and-tenon joints. Plywood panels are included during construction. If there is to be a glass panel, the molding on one side should be removable (Fig. 14-6B). The door relies on the wood and its construction for stiffness. A door that is fragile and becomes distorted in use is a nuisance. Although light doors have been successful, a thickness of 1½ inches is regarded as the minimum; something closer to 2 inches is better for a normal room door (about 6½ by 2½-feet).

Some provision has to be made for a lock. A surface-mounted lock merely requires enough area to support

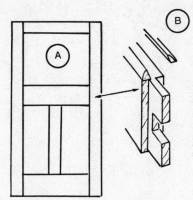

Fig. 14-6. A glass pane in a framed and paneled door (A) should be retained by a removable molding (B).

its base, screws, and a keyhole. If a mortise lock (one set into the wood) is used, enough wood should be left around it for adequate strength.

In the right situation, this "traditional" type of door has a beauty unsurpassed by any other. But it would look as out of place in an ultramodern setting as a flush-finished door would in traditional surroundings. A modern door, one made as a single flat panel, is really a product of modern materials: it depends on manufactured boards and the latest glues for strength.

Typically, a door to a room is a plywood panel the size of the doorway, framed with solid wood without joints. Other pieces support the panels and give solidity to key points: where the lock is installed, where fittings are mounted, etc. The plywood panel, and the other members attached to it, are covered by forming a sandwich, so to speak. The corners are often mitered, particularly if they are visible, but they need not be at the bottom.

Such doors are mass-produced without nails or other fasteners, instead being glued and held in presses while the glue sets. In the home shop it is advisable to use small-headed nails to supplement the glue. They can be punched below the surface and covered with stopping later. For an average room door, use ¼ inch plywood spacers 1¼ inches thick. Some doors are made with the plywood left exposed at the edges, but for a better appearance, cover the edges with thin pieces of wood (Fig. 14-7A); if the plywood has a surface veneer and the door will be given a clear finish, use strips that match, if possible.

The edges of double doors can be rebated to interlock (Fig. 14-7B). Rounding the outer edges slightly will minimize the risk of their chipping or splintering. If the bottom of the door has to swing back against a stop, or if you suspect it will be subjected to frequent kicking, make the inside spacer at the bottom wide enough to back up the plywood.

Similar doors can be covered with hardboard. With adequate reinforcement inside, even ⅛ inch material will be strong enough. Untreated hardboard is inadvisable for outside use or in areas of high humidity, but oil-tempered types have a good resistance to dampness. Hardboard can be used as door panels instead of plywood. Pieces with a smooth surface on both sides can be used singly; but if one side is rough, it is better to glue two pieces together so their smooth sides are outward.

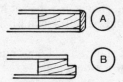

Fig. 14-7. Door-edge treatment: wood strip concealing exposed plywood (A); rebate for a pair of swinging doors to make them interlock (B).

If a glass panel is to be fitted into a flush-surfaced door, the hole should be framed during construction. For an accurate fit, it is better to leave some plywood to remove after assembly, then get the framing accurate and fit the plywood to it (Fig. 14-8A). If one side is to be exposed to the weather, glue the framing to seal the plywood edges; if the design allows it, make the framing project, with a groove under the edge to break the flow of water on the underside (Fig. 14-8B).

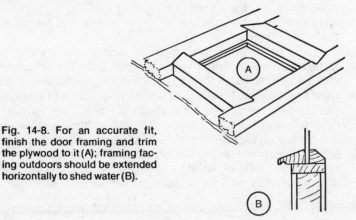

Fig. 14-8. For an accurate fit, finish the door framing and trim the plywood to it (A); framing facing outdoors should be extended horizontally to shed water (B).

One problem with an exterior door is water running down and finding its way back underneath. This can be alleviated with drip molding across the bottom that sticks out far enough to shed the water over the step (or at least far enough to be effective). It could be solid wood (Fig. 14-9A) or a board supported on triangular fillets (Fig. 14-9B). It is important to seal the joint on top so water doesn't get behind it. If the door is flat, the joint may be made with glue; otherwise, it is better to screw the wood against a jointing compound. (The groove under the solid piece prevents water from creeping back underneath.)

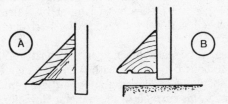

Fig. 14-9. Rainwater can be kept from entering a door with solid drip-molding (A) or a skirt on a triangular fillet (B).

PANELING

Plywood and hardboard can be used to panel an existing surface, or they can be used in new construction. The numerous decorative surfaces and prefinishes available will suit almost any room decor. Paneling is usually supplied in 8-by 4-foot pieces, with any special pattern going lengthwise. (Simulated joints come this way.) Quantities can be worked out by measuring the room and marking 4 foot distances around a plan (making allowances for doors and windows). By careful estimation you can arrange for the waste cut at a window to fit over a door. Although all prominent panels should not have joints in their length, it may be possible to economize by joining two or more pieces in an obscure place.

Some paneling is so designed that when edges of two panels are butted together, they look like similar parts repeated across the panels. This could be a dark line or a shallow groove intended to look like a joint between boards of random width. For that sort of "joint" there is no need to make any special provision; one panel is merely brought up to the previous one and nailed. Elsewhere, you have to decide whether to hide the joint or make a feature of it. Getting a perfectly butted joint over the length of a sheet (8 feet) of plywood is very difficult. But there could be pieces covering the joints, or a bead could be put between the two adjoining panels. When laying out the work, allow for as many 4 foot widths as possible, to avoid the unnecessary cutting of panels; there may have to be some allowance for trimming at the corners of walls that are not absolutely vertical.

In old construction, arrange vertical furring strips (1- by 3-inch boards) at 4 foot centers. The horizontal members may be set at 16 inch centers (see Fig. 14-10A), which divides into the 8 foot length of the panel evenly. Panels that are ¼ inch thick should be rigid enough, but anything less than this may need bracing; short pieces of furring strips (also on 16 inch centers) placed vertically between the horizontal members should do.

The size of the studs depends on the construction, but they are likely to be two-by-fours (with the narrow face outward). The studs should be good enough in quality to remain straight and present a flat surface to the panels. How the paneling is assembled depends on how enthusiastic and skillful you are. Merely nailing the joint can be effective (Fig. 14-10B), providing the parts fit closely and are not allowed to move during their installation. It is better to have the bottom of the uprights fit into a notch (Fig. 14-10C), and the horizontal ones tapered into notches in the uprights (Fig. 14-10D). Nails provide strength, while the notches insure accurate location. This is important because the wood being nailed may not be

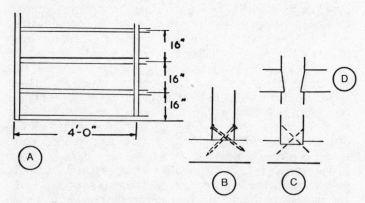

Fig. 14-10. Studs to take paneling should be arranged according to the standard 4-by 8-foot pieces available. They can be merely nailed at the bottom (B), but it is better to notch all the members together (C & D).

visible, making it necessary to rely on your measurements. (If they are all the same, there is less chance of error.)

If you are installing panels against an existing wall, check them with a level. If the studs or furring strips are not truly vertical but lean left or right, the first panel will have to be trimmed and put up in a corner so its other end can be adjusted. Cut the panel to the final width plus as much extra as the stud is off vertical. Put the panel in position against the corner and position the outer edge vertically with the aid of a level. Secure the panel temporarily with a few thin nails. Use a small piece of wood, as wide as the greatest amount of error, as a guide to marking a vertical line on the corner edge. Butt against the corner. Now the corner edge can be trimmed and the panel permanently mounted against the corner.

Large pieces of paneling should be sawed on a firm support to prevent flexing, and thereby causing the saw to wander and the wood to split or crack. Lay several parallel boards across a pair of sawhorses for adequate support. A portable saw is easier to control, when cutting a large sheet, than a table saw. Finish the edge with a block plane.

Position the first (corner) panel experimentally and make a mark where its edge contacts the stud. It is best to secure a panel with a combination of adhesive and nails. The adhesive may be any of the glues for plywood, but for hardboard it may be better to use a contact cement (which is also suitable for plywood). The nails may be 1 inch finishing types, but experimentation may show that they will have to be longer or shorter. The adhesive will take most of the load; the nails are primarily for locating surfaces and bringing them into contact. Punch the nails below the surface and cover them with stopping that matches the wood.

Apply adhesive to the stud and the edges of a panel. Position the panel and nail the top to position and support it. If contact cement is used, pull the bottom of the panel out until the surfaces are tacky, then drive in the rest of the nails. The spacing between nails depends on the panel material. With plywood, 10 or 12 inches around the edges, and about twice that for horizontal members, is about right. Drive the nails where they will be camouflaged by the pattern (in the grooves, for example).

Plywood panels should be brought close together, even if the joint will be covered. Some hardboard makers recommend that a narrow gap be left between (their) panels. The gap can be made parallel throughout its length by partially driving a few nails into the stud against a panel's edge, butting the next panel against the nails, and withdrawing the nails.

The nails in hardboard may have to be spaced closer than in plywood. In both cases, there is an advantage to driving nails at alternate angles (in opposite directions) for a dovetail effect.

If panels are to be fixed to a flat wall, little preparation is needed, particularly if it will take nails. Even then it is best to bed the panels in adhesive; otherwise, pockets could form between the two surfaces, which could lead to bulges or bubbles on the outside. Contact adhesive or one of the compounds sold for putting down linoleum can be used.

Adhesive and nails could be used directly on a plaster wall that is true; but when tested with a long straightedge and a level, most plaster walls will be found to be too far off for satisfactory direct paneling. This also applies to walls of stone, brick, or other blocks. The wall has to be covered with *furring* pieces.

Furring pieces are used to make a surface level for paneling. A section of pine 1 by 3 inches is suitable. The first strips go around the top and bottom edges of the room. Make sure they are true with each other by checking them with a straightedge and level. Put up upright studs and horizontal furring with partially driven nails. Use a long straight piece of wood as a straightedge to compare diagonals as well as to test vertical and horizontal spacing across the assembly. Drive nails in completely where a part is level. Elsewhere it may be necessary to pack something behind a panel, such as wood, linoleum, or folded plastic sheeting to get the surface level before driving a nail. If there are high spots caused by bumps in the plaster, it may be necessary to remove the wood and cut some of it away.

Once the furring is true, the paneling can be installed as it would be in studs. If it is an outside wall, plastic sheeting behind the panels will act as a vapor barrier (this may be a requirement of a building regulation); heat insulation can be used in the space as well.

Paneling usually only forms part of a new decorative scheme. If it is on furring pieces, and therefore stands out from the wall, the molding around windows and doors may have to be thickened. Electrical outlets may have to be moved forward. And although the paneling itself may be beautiful, its appearance will be enhanced by the addition of complementary moldings, moldings that can also be used to finish modified windows or doors.

Some paneling manufacturers offer a range of moldings that match the surfaces of their panels. But stock moldings can be used effectively, too. Rather than staining them to match the panels, it may be easier—and more effective—to make them contrast.

Dark moldings over light paneling is particularly attractive. The overall effect depends on the circumstances. A dark wall covering makes a room look smaller than one covered with a lighter material.

There should be molding at floor level to protect the walls against being kicked or knocked by furniture. This could be a standard base, possibly faced by a *shoe* molding (Fig. 14-11A). At ceiling level there can be a *crown* or *cove* molding (Fig. 14-11B). If a corner joint between panels is not as good as it should be, an inside corner or cove molding (Fig. 14-11C) may be used to match the larger crown molding. An outside corner ought to be protected by an outside corner molding (Fig. 14-11D).

Several kinds of moldings can be fitted around door and window frames. Lumberyards sell them as *casing* moldings (Fig. 14-11E). In general, it is a good idea to cover all panel edges so a casing molding can be put under window sills. For some rooms it is effective to have panels going only part way up a wall; the wall above them can be plain, papered, or used for a mural. In this case, it is necessary to cover the top of the panels with special *ply cap* moldings (Fig. 14-11F).

Many panels come prefinished, and so require no special treatment after they have been put up, except possibly for touching up cut edges and finishing molding or cover strips. However, if prefinished panels are used, apply the desired finish to anything put over the panels before installation, so there is no risk of marking the surfaces with stain or polish. The stopping for nail holes can be a problem in matching some finishes. The stick type that is wiped over a nail hole is convenient, providing the color is a match. If no standard stopping is exactly the right color, it may be possible to mix a batch with some stain. Dry, colors are not always the same as when wet, so there will have to be some experimenting.

Paneling is not just a matter of covering walls. A door could be made with the same paneling material. After paneling a room, remnants of various sizes will be left. These can be used to make furniture or small items to match the paneling. A bar or counter top could be built up in the same way suggested for a flush door, with ordinary plywood

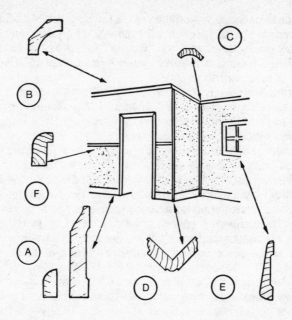

Fig. 14-11. Shown in cross section, the various moldings needed to finish a paneled room.

underneath. This is important; a panel framed without a compensating material on the other side may distort.

Furniture made with paneling material should include some contrasting color. This may be in the form of a different wood, a plastic-coated material, or metal legs or fittings. Having too much of one finish in a room could destroy some of the effect it was intended to create.

SEATS

Seating may be built into recesses, under windows, or anywhere indoors or outdoors—providing the wall at that point is strong enough. Built-in seats that fold down can be made with a minimum of materials, and will occupy a minimum of space. Boxed seats can be used for storage space.

For a seat to fold down, it has to be hinged far enough from the wall to allow the supports to fold back when the seat drops. The height determines the maximum depth of the seat. If the ground or floor below is unstable for a leg, the supports can be made like shelf brackets (Fig. 14-12A), but this puts considerable strain on the hinges, and even more so on a wider seat, so this type of support is best for narrow rests rather than full sheets.

It is better to arrange the supports like legs (Fig. 14-11B); then the extremity of the seat is supported from the ground, putting less of a load on the hinges. The top hinge must be far enough from the wall to allow the seat to hang vertically when the support is folded back. It is helpful to make a full-scale layout of the assembly before making any parts.

The seat may be a piece of strong plywood or particle board that will take screws long enough to provide strength at the hinges. Broad hinges or T hinges on the underside are better than narrow hinges between the edges.

In a small, light seat it may be possible to use T hinges connected directly to the support rails, without having an upright in the framing, but it is usually better to include one. Joints may be halved, but it is better to use mortise-and-tenon joints or dowels. A diagonal brace or angle bracket will keep the support frame in shape (Fig. 14-12C). The legs should open against a stop on the seat.

Similar construction can be used for a table. A table top should be about 30 inches above the ground. If a table (or seat) is very broad or must support much of a load, a block on the bracket will provide the needed support near the hinge line; but having the whole top of the support close to the table top can lead to difficulties if a part warps.

A box seat may be against a flat wall, in a corner, or built into a recess. A seat built as a box in an alcove is attractive.

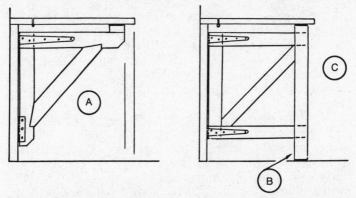

Fig. 14-12. Folding-seat supports made like shelf brackets (A) will not take the load as well as ones built more like legs (B); a diagonal brace (C) will keep the frame from distorting.

There can be doors in front and a fixed top, giving access to the inside without disturbing seating. The most common alternative is to have a fixed front and a movable top. This means removing cushions to get at the storage space, then it is easier to see inside, which is convenient if the seat is used to store blankets and other things that get almost daily use.

Flush panels can be made like doors, with plywood on both sides of the framing. A more traditional approach is to use hardwood assembled with mortise-and-tenon joints, with veneered plywood panels (Fig. 14-13A). A front made this way creates the effect of a medieval chest. Carried to its logical conclusion, the panels could be carved with family initials or a coat of arms. If the seat has one end exposed, it should be made the same way. Where the seat contacts the sides of a recess, frame the top and front supports (Fig. 14-13B). (This is all the assembly needed for an end.) At the back, another piece goes between the end assemblies, then all the parts are screwed to the wall.

Fig. 14-13. A hardwood box seat for an alcove.

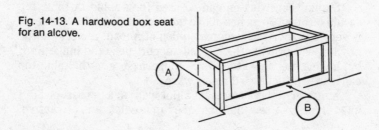

It is possible to make the top from one piece of plywood—³⁄₈ inch thick for a small seat, up to twice that to seat three or more people. This would be cut away for a lid. It is better to frame the top (Fig. 14-14A), particularly if the front is a good hardwood that must match the seat edge. If the sides are not restricted by walls, the top can open completely as one piece.

The lid inside the framing may be hinged at the back, and close either on a full-length front stop (Fig. 14-14B) or on stops that go across the corners. An alternative to a hinged lid is one that lifts off. In its simplest form, the opening is framed and the lid drops into place. A finger hole in each end can provide a means of lifting the lid, or there can be two handles that are flush-fitting or fold-down types. Another type of top has supports under the ends and pieces across the top that project

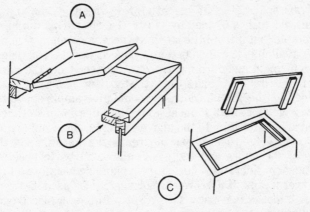

Fig. 14-14. Lid detail for box seats: a framed seat top with a hinged lid (A); the stop for a hinged lid (B); a lift-off lid with runners that engage the framing at the back (C).

under the framing in back (Fig. 14-14C). A broad seat would have to be supported at least part way along the front as well.

A large box seat can have one or more divisions for storage, with a matching divided lid. Such a seat can usually be made comfortable with cushions around the walls, as well as on the seat top. It can be made more comfortable by building in a sloping backrest. The distance it will be from the wall will limit the width of the opening, however.

STAIRS AND STEPS

Arranging a means of getting from one floor to another requires some planning. The method of construction has to allow for the total horizontal distance available (run).

Anyone climbing steps should be able to lift his feet the same distance all the way. Variations could cause an accident; you can't make up for them—the plan has to be accurate from the start. Ideally, this should apply even if the climb is broken by landings or other changes. Where the stairs turn a corner, the landing should be as high as a stair tread.

It is the surface-to-surface distance that counts. The number of treads required can be estimate through interpolation. A reasonable height (determined by the *risers*) between treads for a stair tread is between 7 and 8 inches. Suppose the distance between floors is 9 feet. That's 108 inches; dividing 7 into that, you get 15.43. Ignoring the decimals and dividing 15 into 108 inches results in 7.2 inches, the stair spacing (riser height) for 15 treads. Then try 14 treads; 108 inches divided by 14 is 7.71 inches. This might be acceptable, but it is a little steep. If there is ample horizontal space available, it will be better to have 15 treads. The height has to be maintained from surface to surface: from the lower floor to the first tread and so on to the top floor.

Ideally, the depth of a tread should give ample space for an average foot (12 to 15 inches). Usually there is insufficient run available for this. In the above example, this would come out to over 14 feet. The deeper the treads, the more shallow the angle of the stairs and the easier they will be to use, but practical considerations during their planning usually call for narrower treads. If narrower treads have to be used, between 9 and 10 inches is usually satisfactory. Fifteen 9 inch treads would require 11 feet, 3 inches of run. If this horizontal space isn't available, the stairs will have to break at a landing, and either continue at a right angle (Fig. 14-15A) or double back overhead (Fig. 14-15B).

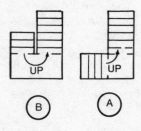

Fig. 14-15. With insufficient available run, stairs have to turn (A) or double back (B) at a landing.

A handrail should be provided at one or both sides, 30 to 34 inches above the treads. When climbing stairs, you reach ahead of vertical. But on a landing, where you use the handrail alongside you, it should be slightly higher. As with risers, try to keep handrail heights the same for stairs that continue for several flights. Planning is very important. Be sure of the number of treads and how they will have to be arranged in the space available before starting on detail work. It is too easy to make sketches of attractive staircases and find, when measurements are taken, they will have impossibly narrow treads or excessively high risers.

The width of a staircase must also be considered. Although not as critical as other criteria, for the average home the width should not be less than 30 inches; 36 inches is probably best, if there is enough space. A single flight will probably be workable with any width selected, but if the stairs take a turn or double back from a landing, extra inches may be more than can be allowed, and the width will have to be reduced slightly.

Akin to stairs are steps. Steps form a more upright angle than stairs, and tread depths have to be ignored. The treads are made as deep as reasonably possible. Typically, steps go from a floor to a raised deck. The spacing from one level to the next should be even all the way. The total height may be divided by any convenient number of steps. Steps may be spaced slightly wider than stairs, but 9 inches is regarded as optimum.

Almost vertical steps are awkward to climb, but in a confined space they have to accepted. It is better to have them at a moderate angle. At too great an angle, however, the steps become stairs and have to be treated as such. (A slope of about 15° off vertical is reasonable.)

To begin the layout of steps, first decide on the run. Then divide the distance into equal spaces according to the number of treads (Fig. 14-16A). This may be done with a rule, but not many rules are marked to the several decimal places that are often needed. It is better to use a pair of dividers to step off the spacing (Fig. 14-16B), experimenting with the setting until it is right.

Treads must be horizontal; use an adjustable bevel to mark the top of each (Fig. 14-16C). Draw another line for the tread thickness. It is usual for a tread to span the width of the

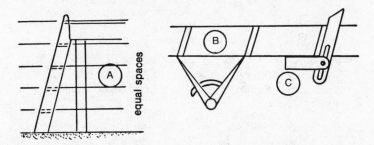

Fig. 14-16. Marking out steps: the run divided by the number of treads for equal spacing (A); caliper-derived spacing (B); an adjustable bevel (C), used to maintain the step's attitude (horizontal).

stringer (side support) and project forward a short distance, where its front edge is rounded (Fig. 14-17A). The stringer should be thick enough to allow the removal of wood so the tread can be fitted. Treads set ½ inch into 1⅜ inch wood will do.

If there are only a few treads and the stringers will be permanently anchored at the top and bottom, glue, and screws entering the joints from below, may be all that is needed (Fig. 14-17B). But if the steps are part of a ladder, or are more than a few treads long, at least some of the joints should be stronger. To that end, a fillet glued under the joints (Fig. 14-17C) or a rod screwed under the top and bottom treads (Fig. 14-17D) will help. End treads and a few in between can have tenons going through the stringers, which are secured with

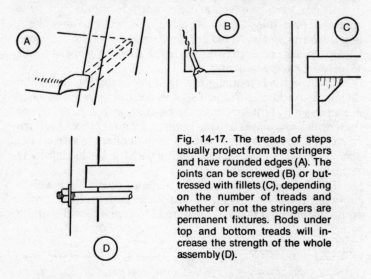

Fig. 14-17. The treads of steps usually project from the stringers and have rounded edges (A). The joints can be screwed (B) or buttressed with fillets (C), depending on the number of treads and whether or not the stringers are permanent fixtures. Rods under top and bottom treads will increase the strength of the whole assembly (D).

wedges and glue (Fig. 14-18A). Steps can be made to look very attractive by strengthening every third tread with a slotted tenon taken far enough through the stringer to be fastened with a peg (Fig. 14-18B).

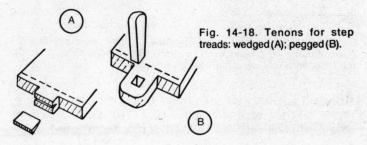

Fig. 14-18. Tenons for step treads: wedged (A); pegged (B).

The stringers for steps with a moderate slope provide something to grip, making handrails unnecessary. This means the stringers should be rounded for comfort. For steps at a more acute angle, a separate rail can be connected to the stringer with spacers (Fig. 14-19A). The bottom of a flight of steps should be attached to the ground or floor. The top is best secured by being notched into the deck. To maintain an even ascent all the way, make the edge of the deck project as if it were another tread (Fig. 14-19B).

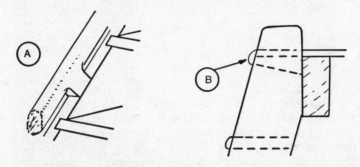

Fig. 14-19. Convenience/safety features for steps: handrail supported on spacers connected to stringers (A); extended deck at the top of the run to allow uninterrupted stride (B).

Although the stringers provide something to hold, the last few steps at the top have to be negotiated with hands above deck level. Handrailing around the deck should provide support at the steps when hands are above deck level, going up or down. Normally, steps are at too steep an angle for anyone to descend facing outward; the climber faces inward going up or down (the same way as on a ladder).

Stairs differ in detail according to their situation and size, but the stringers always need to be substantial enough to take climbing without vibrating or bending. Obviously, sound and good-quality wood is required. The treads can be open, making the stairs similar in construction to steps. This makes for a simple design that can be effective in some situations. It is more usual to have closed risers, however. This gives rigidity. If risers and treads are screwed together, each strengthening the other, the wood need not be as thick. Gluing blocks behind the joint of tread and riser will provide more strength (Fig. 14-20A). Normally, stairs in a home get considerable use, most of the load being applied centrally. This means an open-tread

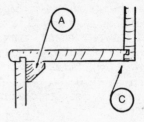

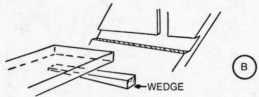

Fig. 14-20. Blocks glued behind tread-and-riser joints help to strengthen stairs (A); some professionals wedge the treads into dadoes (B). Best woodworking practice calls for tongue-and-groove joints between treads and risers (C).

WEDGE

staircase may eventually develop sags. If this varies between treads, it could be dangerous as well as unattractive.

Stair treads fit into dadoes in stringers. It is important that they look like a close fit, and are tight for utmost strength. Some carpenters make stairs using a system of wedges pushed in below the treads into dadoes in the risers (Fig. 14-20B). After glue is applied, a wedge is driven in tightly and cut off to make space for one inserted the other way. Sometimes the wedges are thicker than the depth of the dado, giving extra surface for more glue. Or they may be as thick as the dado is wide; then, glue blocks are placed over the wedges.

It is good woodworking practice to use tongue-and-groove joints between risers and treads (Fig. 14-20C). Where the outsides of the stringers will not be visible, screws can be used in the ends of the treads for extra strength.

Appendix A

Details of Common Nails

PENNY SIZE	LENGTH (INCHES)	GAGE	NUMBER PER POUND
2	1	15	840
3	1¼	14	540
4	1½	12½	300
6	2	11½	160
8	2½	10¼	100
10	3	9	65
12	3¼	9	65
16	3½	8	45
20	4	6	30
30	4½	5	20
40	5	4	17
50	5¼	3	14
60	6	2	11

Appendix B
Wood Screw Holes

GAGE	SHANK DIAMETER (INCHES)	PILOT HOLE DIAMETER HARDWOODS	(INCHES) SOFTWOODS
2	0.086	3/64	–
3	0.099	1/16	–
4	0.112	1/16	–
5	0.125 (⅛)	5/64	1/16
6	0.138	5/64	1/16
7	0.151	3/32	1/16
8	0.164	3/32	5/64
10	0.177	7/64	3/32
12	0.216	1/8	7/64
14	0.242	9/64	7/64
16	0.268	5/32	9/64
18	0.294	3/16	9/64
20	0.320	13/64	11/64
24	0.372	7/32	3/16

Index

Index